The Edge of the Abyss

The Recapitulation Diaries

Volume Two

July-December 2002

J. E. Ketchel

Riverwalker Press

Cover art by J. E. Ketchel: *Blue* 2003

Cover design by Nick Reilingh

Riverwalker Press
PO Box 101
Red Hook, NY 12571
www.riverwalkerpress.com

ISBN: 978-0-9800506-5-3

MEDICAL DISCLAIMER: The information in this book is intended for informational purposes only. It is not meant to diagnose or treat any mental health disorder whatsoever, nor is it intended to replace treatment with a competent mental healthcare provider. Please seek appropriate support and put the book aside if it proves to be too disruptive. Any application of the material presented in this book is at the reader's discretion and is his or her sole responsibility. The author and publisher are in no way responsible or liable for misuse of this information.

Table of Contents

Prologue

The Bite of the Ostrich

As the story goes, I was about a year old when my parents pushed my stroller up to the ostrich exhibit at the Bronx Zoo. Without warning or provocation, an ostrich poked its head through the bars of the cage and bit me on the arm, only releasing me after being whacked repeatedly over the head. Other than a nasty pinch, little damage was done. This curious tale was often told during my childhood, though the retelling was always brief, the details left to the imagination.

"An ostrich bit you!" my parents would say in a dumbfounded tone, as if a dragon had bitten me.

"But why?" I'd ask. "What does it mean?"

"An ostrich bit you!" they'd simply say.

By the time I was twelve this story no longer intrigued me, in fact, I was rather bored and embarrassed by it. I'd often wish it had been some other bird or noble creature that had bitten me, or that it had happened to some other girl. Why didn't a handsome peacock or beautiful swan attack me, why the ugly ostrich? And why did this have to be the only story my parents ever told about me as a baby, and why did they have to tell it so often? I was never satisfied by their presumption that it was just a plain and simple fact of my life; I knew there had to be more to it. Now, after all these years, the possible significance of that bite emerges. Both an omen and a warning, I believe the ostrich was marking me for the journey ahead, for shortly thereafter, by the time I was two, my trials began. Perhaps, with that nip on the arm, the ostrich was saying: *this child will be challenged, but this child will also find the means to transcend the ugliness of those challenges.* Perhaps the mark of the ostrich signified strength and groundedness in this world, but the severing of all ties to this world as well, for only in having experiences of transcending this world would the innate abilities of the spirit self find reason to emerge. I believe the bite of the ostrich was preparing me for what was to come, predicting encounters with a sexual predator and the lessons I would learn during my life.

And so began my solo journey, ritually initiated by the ostrich at the zoo. I was stamped by the keeper at the gate, so that I would be recognized in the dark and dreary world I was soon to enter. For I believe I *was* guided as I left the world of protected infancy and ventured into the unknown, as I innocently meandered down a path that led into the shadows of a forest filled with dangers far more fantastical and abhorrent than that meager nip on the arm.

Within a few months of that ostrich bite, a new baby brother took my place on the lap of our distant mother, ending my brief year of maternal tenderness. I was sent out into the world to play, to explore, to gain sure-footedness, to become self-sufficient and strong, worthy of the bite that had been placed on my arm by that ostrich at the zoo. The mother with the new baby on her lap receded from view. She was rarely turned to, as each year a new baby replaced the last and as I stepped, unknowingly, into the sexual predator's world; a world full of ritual and dark secrets, bound by a pact that I would not break for nearly fifty years. That dark world had no parents or siblings. No words were spoken there to explain, illustrate, or connect it to the familiar. I entered a completely unknown world, a world composed of new laws, strange constructs, and bizarre conduct where nothing was quite what it seemed. I had to learn the rules of this new world, so that I could navigate it without physical, mental, and spiritual annihilation, so that I could survive and return to the world of the familiar.

My first book, *The Man in the Woods,* recounts the beginning of my quest for reconnection with my lost self through the life-changing process of *recapitulation*, an ancient shamanic practice that offers valuable and practical tools for total healing from Post-traumatic Stress Disorder (PTSD). In recapitulation, a deep inner journey is undertaken; a most valuable process whether one has suffered from trauma or not. During recapitulation, accumulated personal inventory—in the form of experiences, attachments, beliefs, habits, and feelings—is offered up for sorting, review, and disposal, as one takes forward into new life only that which has real meaning and value. Having shed the protective casings that once defended a deeply wounded, vulnerable self, a new self is free to emerge. And just who that new self may be constantly changes as the journey unfolds.

In my case, recapitulation meant stepping into a past so deeply hidden that I had no idea of its existence until I was back in it, reliving it. As I relived memory upon memory, in great detail, I learned exactly what happened to my child self each time I entered my abuser's world. I discovered that I became an amnesiac each time I took his hand and stepped through the cold misty curtain that separated one world from the other. As the known world quite literally disappeared, I transmogrified into a little girl of darkness. This process was repeated in reverse when I left his world and returned to the everyday world. The abuse, the encounters with the predator suffered but moments before, erased from conscious memory as the curtain reopened and I stepped back into the warm light of day and became a child of ordinary reality once again.

This forgetting process was repeated hundreds of times. It was what kept me sane. However, for a great deal of my childhood, and in the years immediately following, I existed in a hazy netherworld. I was caught in the cold misty curtain that separated the two worlds of my childhood. This strange in-between world became my everyday reality. In this world, my wholeness—shattered by the experiences I'd endured—lay in fragments, lost behind me in the darkness of the predator's world, while my innocent self remained equally distant and inaccessible. Though I did not perceive of my life as being sad or unbearable, I had to deal with this dissociated, fragmented self every day. Suffice it to say; I adjusted. And even though the world of the sexual predator haunted every moment of my existence in some way—constantly begging me to *remember, remember, remember*—I could no more remember than I could get myself out of that veiled world. In spite of these limitations, I found the means to survive and thrive. I took my frightened self seriously. I honed skills of invisibility, disappearing into the background whenever possible, never being noticed if I could help it. I found expression and solace in creativity, in shyness and solitude that suited my intense introversion and my need to find safety and comfort in a world that I knew lacked both of those things. I became an artist, a writer, a poet and, for the most part, I kept to myself, both as a child and as an adult.

The abuse happened outside, out in the world, never at home. Unlike children abused in their own homes and own beds, my bedroom and my bed were safe. I was untouchable there. I could sing and dance and laugh and feel good about myself there. I could be smart and witty and advanced in everything while there, but when I stepped outside of my safe home environment—where the rules where perfectly clear and the day-to-day process blandly mundane—everything changed. Each day, as I left the house, I put on the armor that I wore out into the world. I left the real girl safely shut away in my room and let the half-robotic stick figure girl go out into the world to face the challenges that lurked at every step.

This wearing of protective armor persisted into adulthood. However, despite the limitations of fear, I was capable of traveling alone, often navigating life with great success and daring. As a teenager, my experiences were limited by how much I could trust and how far I could venture before the inevitable feelings of numbing dissociation and exhaustion would necessitate a return to my home sanctuary. Back home, I would rejuvenate, recharge with enough energy to venture out again. I remember looking at myself in the mirror once when I was a college student, alone in my dorm room at the end of the day. I watched my face relax and lose its pale, strained, and haunted look, warming up right before my eyes—a pretty girl, with bright dark eyes, thick brown hair and beautiful skin, flushed and alive. But that girl only came alive when she felt totally safe, when she was alone. Otherwise, the hunched and fearful girl wandered the streets, ever watchful and alert.

I dealt with feelings of dissociation and detachment on a daily basis, so familiar that they became my normal states and yet, by my intentions alone, I could transcend them. I learned to *stalk*, as the shamans of Carlos Castaneda's lineage call it. I learned how to be present, in whatever way was appropriate for a situation, though I could never stalk anything that required physical grace or adeptness. I was far better at being mentally alert and energetically present. I could be in the world quite successfully, working, teaching, meeting people, pursuing a career as an illustrator and writer. If I had to go to an art opening, I could dress and act the part, engage others and talk about the exhibit, appear to have my act together. To sustain this practice of stalking for more than a few hours at a time, however, took considerable effort and energy. The familiar self always beckoned me, most enticingly, back into the safety of solitude.

It's only now that I can say that I also learned valuable lessons during my early experiences in the sexual predator's world. In fact,

I am proposing that all sexually abused children be viewed and treated as empowered beings. As a sexually abused child, I was forced to grapple with some of the most difficult situations in life. I had powerful out-of-body experiences and gained access to innate abilities while in heightened states of awareness. In the process, mature skills of detachment were honed. In the end, I not only survived the abuse, but also grew into a highly functioning adult—alert, intelligent, and creative. Although my ability to be fully present in the world was compromised, my spirit remained intact, my zest for life bubbled inside me, and my desire for adventure remained unbroken. As a result, I do not bemoan my past. I do not pity my child self. If at any time I did feel self-pity, it was fleeting, because I was taught to leave feelings for the self far behind on a shelf in the dimness of other realities, for they had no use in the worlds I entered. I was not a broken child, but I was a child who was challenged, as many are, from the very beginning of life to learn how to survive in the most dire of circumstances.

The skills of dissociation and detachment did not come easily, nor did I grasp at them with joy, for they were hard earned, though extremely necessary for survival. And so I can say that I learned them well, at a very early age, and I did not hesitate to use them. From my perspective now, I understand that I learned in the shamanic tradition. In those early years of my life, the shaman's world became very familiar to me, though I had no inkling of such a world—I simply lived in it, as many do. Sent on an initiation journey by that ostrich at the zoo, I went out into the world at a very young age. I encountered life-threatening circumstances in the form of an evil sexual predator and, yet, I did not succumb. Such are the parameters of a shamanic journey.

The ultimate challenge of a shamanic journey is to not only return physically intact, but to return *transformed*. A shamanic recapitulation affords the opportunity to complete unfinished business; that is, to retake the shamanic journey of the traumatized self in *full awareness* this time. In full awareness, experiences are understood within the context of a journey of transformation, and all the fragmented parts that have been left behind in those experiences are finally able to come home. A fully integrated self emerges upon completion—wholeness is achieved. I use the terms *shaman* and *shamanic* with the utmost respect. I am not a shaman. I do not purport to be anything other than a human being on her own journey, but I cannot dismiss the fact that I have transformed as a result of what I learned through the use of the ancient shamanic practice of recapitulation, as made available to the world through the works of Carlos Castaneda.

Whether our journeys are initiated by the bite of an ostrich, or at the hands of a kind and loving guide, I believe that at some point in our lives we will all be challenged to recapitulate, to pull together the fragmented truths of who we truly are. In the process, we will discover the meaning of our personal journeys; access the potential that we all, as human beings, hold within; and experience reality from many different and honest perspectives.

Sexually abused children do not become prey by accident, rarely by happenstance, but most certainly by being chosen, by being groomed to do as the predator desires. Obviously, I am not speaking of random acts of violence and murder against children, but I am speaking of the child who is slowly groomed by the sexual predator, first through gaining trust, perhaps even love, before the relationship begins to proceed in another direction. The predator selects its prey based on opportunity and availability, marking its territory with stealth, conniving, trickery, manipulation, and domination. The predator is the stronger of the two, dominating the weaker, taking advantage of the trusting innocence of the child prey, though the child is by no means less intelligent, or less instinctually attuned than the predator.

Children who become prey are presented with the basest and crudest of life's challenges. Often groomed from early childhood, even infancy, to trust their abuser, they are carefully and patiently led down the path that leads to the curtained world where all their skills of survival are accessed and tested. They quickly become adept at survivalist skills paralleling military training. They learn the same techniques that have kept many a soldier, mountaineer, or Arctic explorer alive when faced with the inevitable fury of war or nature, of accidental misstep or unforeseen trauma, faced with being alone in the wilderness with only their wits to keep them alive. These skills, learned so early in life, become constant companions, enabling the abused child to take on the challenges of life with a stoic, goal-oriented focus at a very tender age. The goal, even if unconsciously adopted, is always the same: *to survive.*

In order to understand how children survive abuse, it's necessary to understand how different worlds, different realities are generated by sudden jolts to the psyche. Brutal trauma fragments the psyche, as it catapults it out of ordinary reality. Some parts of the psyche stay present during trauma, others are inwardly stored, and still others may dissociate and completely leave the body. When a young child is raped, fragmentation offers a safe place to encapsulate what is unbearably painful and impossible to fathom. Both physical and psychological traumas are compartmentalized, so that disintegration and annihilation do not occur. Fragmentation is a highly protective measure on the part of the psyche.

In the world of my sexual abuser nothing was quite what it seemed, nothing was certain, nothing was known. It was a strange and frightening world where what was considered normal and safe lost all meaning. The other world, everyday reality, was fairly predictable, the rules known, expectations clear. I had chores and homework; everything was pretty cut and dried. These two distinctly different worlds were totally hidden from each other. They did not exist simultaneously in reality, nor was there memory of one when in the other.

My abuser lived nearby. I played with his daughter, quite readily slept overnight, ate meals at their house. I hiked the rural mountains, walked and biked the dirt roads, often with friends but often alone, not it loneliness but savoring the solitude and resonance I felt with the beauty of the landscape, the quiet of the countryside. My abuser did not exist outside the world he had created, so I was safe, memory blocked, until I met up with him again. But the grooming process, methodically and patiently undertaken in cases of long-term sexual abuse, explains only part of the power the abuser has over a victim. The grooming process accounts for the victim's growing susceptibility, but it does not answer the victim's own questions—Why did I let myself get caught again? Why didn't I run? Why didn't I get away when I had a chance?—and the questions of others regarding the decisions apparently made by the victim—Why did you let him touch you? Why didn't you scream? Why didn't you tell someone?

I can attest that it was impossible to run, talk, or scream. My physical body could not react. Like a deer in the headlights, I was paralyzed from the moment my abuser laid eyes on me. Sometimes, even before I saw him, I felt his energy honing in on me and I was mesmerized into paralytic inaction. I could no more have picked up my feet and jumped out of the way of a speeding car than I could have run from or dodged my abuser. One minute I was happily playing, carefree and independent, and the next minute, immediately upon seeing him, the world around me dissolved as if made out of nothing, a mere figment of my imagination. A dark tunnel formed and I stood at one end and he stood at the other. No sounds penetrated the walls of that tunnel of doom. There were no escape routes. Internally, I went into a heightened state of awareness where the only thoughts were: "Does he see me? Is he coming this way or is he going somewhere else? Is it my turn?" My focus narrowed and fixated on his every move. There was only him and me. Ordinary reality ceased to exist.

Caught in frozen immobility whenever I encountered my abuser, I became zombie girl. As if I had suddenly had a stroke, my brain did not send signals in the normal way to any body parts. In essence, I was already beginning to shut down, preparing to cope with the inevitable. I was no longer a normal little girl in a normal world. The curtain had already ripped open and I was already teetering on the edge of the abyss. His shadow falling over my happy, sunny world immediately triggered a fear that hinted at a far greater unknown: *death*. However, my spirit somehow chose life every time, automatically shutting down one world and preparing to go to battle in another.

In such situations, the outer physical body is merely a carcass, its normal abilities and functions cut off by a far more urgent need. In choosing survival, whether consciously or unconsciously, an alarm sounds. A switch is flipped, and all conscious mental and physical activities cease. Energy, redirected from its normal channels, goes coursing through the body and lands in the depths of the psyche, awakening ancient knowledge of survival. When encountering my abuser, it was paramount that I shut down all normal bodily activity and take quick action to preserve what awareness and inner fortitude remained by honing my energy to a tiny flame. I did this automatically, without forethought, a natural instinct immediately awakened.

I did not retain memory of the abuse from one incident to another. It automatically shed as I left my abuser's world, as I reentered the world of family and friends, of school and society. It was impossible to carry the experiences forward into my other life, so they stayed buried deep in the woods, in his world. However, at the point of seeing him again, I instinctively, intuitively regained access to knowledge of the normally blocked abuse. As it reentered my awareness, all mental and physical reaction reverted to the processes that had previously saved me. Like a well-trained soldier, I catapulted to heightened states of awareness and dissociation, my trusty tools of survival.

I learned these things, and more, about my child self, as I recapitulated and relived hundreds of episodes of abuse. As my recapitulation unfolded, I began to study in greater depth what had been happening in my body, mind, and psyche during the abuse. I studied what my abuser had been doing to me, as well as took in the details of the environments he had taken me into. I became a multilayered observer. As if I were a movie camera, I panned out and zoomed in, recording the details of both inner and outer scenes from the past. I brought these recordings back to my adult self for deeper perusal and reflection.

I cannot stress enough that the child who lives in two such dissonant worlds cannot tolerate them becoming known to each other. The moment of impact when those two worlds collide is indescribably, painfully obliterating, fraught with the threat of psychotic disintegration. One fragment of the self carries the memory of the abuse somewhere, nestled in the vagueness of dissociation. When meeting the predator, that fragmented self recognizes, remembers, and acknowledges the pacts made in previous encounters, though they may remain disturbingly unclear. When silently gestured into my abuser's world, I had no recourse but to follow, for that was the pact. My groomed self walked into my abuser's world and did what was commanded, for it was well trained. The groomed self's response was always based on knowing that if it didn't follow instructions it might never leave that world again. I learned pretty quickly that words had no impact or meaning there. No one could hear me. No one paid attention behind the curtains of the predator's world. It's a different world altogether, where a child's scant knowledge of how the world works is no match for the conniving, wily predator.

In the spring of 2001, sparked by restlessness and frustration, I began to make some challenging, life-changing decisions. The first decision was a tiny promise to myself that I would follow where my spirit was leading me. This promise was tossed from my inner world to my outer world like a tiny pebble tossed into a small pond. As the rings of disturbance created by that tiny pebble rippled across the waters of my life, my children and my husband would suffer, my family and my extended family would suffer. People would be confronted and confused by this decision on my part to dive through the rippling surface and into the muck at the bottom of that pond, and yet I had to take the journey that beckoned. I was desperate. It was a matter of life and death, nothing less.

My recapitulation process reintroduced me to my child self, whose life in the world of the predator may have begun with an ostrich bite at the zoo, but whose horror finally ended when I rediscovered my innocence and retrieved it from the dark woods of the predator's world. As I reentered my past, I learned so much about myself as well. I began taking my life back by dissecting it, looking for the meaning of every single instance of abuse, turning it on its ear and integrating it into my being.

This book, *The Edge of the Abyss*, describes the first half of the second year of the healing recapitulation journey that I embarked on. It's predecessor, *The Man in the Woods*, intentionally contains vivid descriptions of sexual abuse perpetrated upon my child self. I felt, and still strongly feel, how extremely important it is that I be explicit. The aberrant behavior of the pedophile must be fully exposed, understood, and acknowledged for what it truly is. There is no point in shying away from exact descriptions or in suggesting that sexual abuse is too graphic to witness, because witnessed it must be—in its totality—for full disclosure, and for full mastery and reclamation of self to occur. In addition, I would fail the many others who have been abused and are unable to speak for themselves by glossing over the brutal truths of rape, sodomy, and other crimes of a sexual nature against children. And so this book also contains vivid descriptions of sexual abuse, as it was actually inflicted. I make no apologies, but I do forewarn that *this is an adult book*. Keep in mind, as well, that my story is not unusual. There are stories worse than mine.

In addition, I will not smooth over the gritty truth of how the recapitulation process itself works, how it unfolds in explicit, vivid detail. It is a viscerally raw and gripping operation, as one hacks into the bedrock of one's life and carves out all that does not belong, all that is not healthy or spiritually resonant. In the second year of my recapitulation, however, the process rapidly evolved along different lines as well. I often did feel as if I were on *the edge of an abyss* for days on end, but this feeling gradually gave way to a new sense of stability and balance, as the plunges into my inner darkness began to be mirrored by greater heights of awakening and longer periods of light and hope. Life blossomed a little bit more each day, and so did I. And so, what began as a painful and frightening journey gradually evolved into a fascinating and beautiful adventure. Feelings, emotions, and sensations that had been as blocked as the memories of the sexual abuse began to awaken and become acceptable as I took ownership of them. Some memories that first appeared in *The Man in the Woods* returned for fuller recapitulation during this second year, as I dove deeper into their dark shadows and retrieved the jewels of self buried in them. Magical experiences and a deepening connection with a spirit guide who supported me throughout the process began to occur more frequently. Dreams, visions, and out-of-body experiences offered me the means to transcend my own mundane story, guiding me to a deeper understanding of our untapped human potential.

When I first met Chuck Ketchel, LCSW-R, EMDR Therapist, and shamanic practitioner, and heard the term Post-traumatic Stress Disorder applied to my condition, I was flabbergasted and greatly relieved at the same time. After so many years of not feeling like I belonged in the world, suddenly there was a slot where I fit. Such a diagnosis offered only momentary respite, however, for the traumas of my childhood pressed on me with ever-increasing intensity, begging to be explored. That was when the recapitulation journey began in earnest. As Chuck introduced me to the world of the Shamans of Ancient Mexico, a world I knew very little about, I soon found complete validity in what it offered. At the same time that I was introduced to terminologies and processes that offered concrete definitions for what I had experienced in the confusion of childhood, I was also reintroduced to my own innate abilities, the things that had once helped me transcend the most debilitating of experiences. And so, the validity of undertaking a shamanic recapitulation as the ticket to fully healing was strikingly clear. In breaking free of the binding clutches of PTSD and successfully reintegrating the fragmented parts of the self, one emerges whole, ready to live a happy life of meaning and total fulfillment.

The Edge of the Abyss begins where *The Man in the Woods* left off, in July of 2002. At the time, I was still sharing a house with my soon-to-be ex-husband. Divorce proceedings were underway and I was in the process of looking for a place to live. I worked out of my art studio. I had a business painting murals, faux finishes, and furniture. I also did freelance writing and illustrating to make a living. I went to yoga and meditation classes and attended sessions with Chuck on a regular basis while mothering my two children, ages eleven and thirteen at the time.

I remained intent on following the path that unfolded before me, and so I repeatedly faced my abuser in recapitulation, but I also faced myself. In so doing, I came to understand that I would not be able to fully grasp the deeper meaning of the shamanic practice of recapitulation that Carlos Castaneda introduced to the world, or any other ancient knowledge, until I had completed my own recapitulation journey. I had to follow my own path to knowledge, to remembering my own life, my own hidden and forgotten truths and realities, before I would be ready to even entertain the idea of studying the shaman's world in a deeper way. I had my own work to do and, as it turns out, it *was* shamanic work.

On a pragmatic level, once the intent to do a shamanic recapitulation is voiced, all the events of daily life become players in that shamanic journey. As the following pages elucidate, dreams, visions, physical sensations, emotions, memories, and worldly encounters converge in an unpredictable yet meaningful way to lead one deeper into the unknown truths of the self.

And so, the journey continues...

Chapter 1

The Great Rescue

July 1, 2002

The memories come like bombs, fast and furious, explosions taking place in my own private war zone. As the bombing missions fly overhead I crouch down and hide, shielding myself from their impact, but in so doing I know I'm refusing to connect with what's being triggered at a deeper level. I catch a glimpse of something new as each memory bomb explodes, but I still refuse to fully accept what was truly happening to my child self. Jolted, the frightened self turns away, though it's practically impossible to do so, for the pains are almost constant now, present throughout the day; my hands numb, my shoulders tense, my genitals sore and painful. I don't have a choice in how this recapitulation process is unfolding—just as I never had a choice when I was a child—it's just happening. I know what a frightened little bunny feels like; heart beating so hard you'd think it might burst.

I admit that I'm avoiding the stark truth that my abuser was having *sex*, in one form or another, with a very small child, and that child was *me*. It's been the hardest part of this recapitulation to accept. Even while excavating all the pieces of the puzzle of the unknown self over the past year, discovering the mysterious, hidden world of my childhood in the process, I wasn't always able to face what my abuser was actually doing to me. Now, as new memories torpedo into awareness, the truth presents itself all over again, but each time I admit that he was indeed having sex with my tiny child self, overwhelming feelings of guilt and shame come tumbling out of the depths of me. At the same time, I know I won't be able to refuse the blatant truth. I must fully accept what was truly happening so long ago, and my body insists, not letting me rest until I do. As soon as I lie down in bed at night and curl up to go to sleep, it all hits me again. Fear, pain, and the desperation of my child self come crashing out of nowhere, searing through my body like shrapnel. Much as I'd like to, I can't really avoid the bombs. Even if I sit down on the couch for a few minutes of respite during a busy day, it's the same thing: BOOM! BOOM! BOOM! The memory bombs go off and all I want to do is run, to look for safe places to hide, to keep moving, ducking and dodging the incessant attacks, but I know it's not productive, nor is it really possible.

I actually had a great weekend with the kids. We had fun. We saw a silly movie and laughed a lot. Everything was quite peaceful and restful during the days, but when the nights arrived the bombs started dropping again.

July 2, 2002

It's my birthday. I turn fifty today. My sweet daughter draws me a cheerful picture of flowers, hearts, and fairies and slides it under my bedroom door. I find it there when I wake up.

July 4, 2002

I awaken early. Still half-dreaming, I recapitulate the series of springs that ran in a line down the mountainside above and below my abuser's house. As if I'm flying, I observe the lay of the land. I see the fields and woods clearly defined, the long road winding to the top of the mountain, the stone bridge to their property, and my own house on the other side of the steep mountain road. My abuser's family got their water from a big open spring high up in the woods behind their house. I remember a thick black hose snaking down the mountainside, across the wide, neatly mown lawn to the back patio and into the house. Smaller springs bubbled up out of the ground down the whole mountainside and you had to be careful where you stepped. Far below the house there was a beautiful little spring in an idyllic spot underneath a knotty old apple tree that bore sour fruit. I sometimes played there with my abuser's daughter, but more often than not I was alone, drawn by the pastoral scene. As I hone in on this fairytale setting, I am there once again. In vivid recall, I touch the bright green grass and moss, the scent of apple blossoms in the air. Clear spring water gently bubbles up from the moist earth, forming a miniature pond in the sunny meadow. Building stick houses in the moss beneath the apple tree and floating leaf boats on the water, I imagine living here forever, in this Utopia of my own creation, as tiny as Thumbelina. Happily at peace, lost in dreamy play, I'm startled out of my reverie. *He* is walking up the field towards me, my abuser, interrupting my perfect fairytale world. Dread and fear inhabit my Utopia now, cracking the shell of blissful harmony, sending me spinning into fragments. I whirl out of the recapitulation and land with a crash back in my bedroom. No longer a little girl of six, I am fifty years old now.

Does he just walk past? I don't remember.

I take my children, my little guardians, to a Fourth of July gathering at the old family estate. They keep me grounded, safe in this world so I don't do anything stupid, so I don't drive up to his house and pull down the long driveway and just sit there staring, wondering if he's still alive.

I watch my two-year old niece play under the sprinkler I've set up for the kids. Naked, she runs in and out of the cold spray of water, her cute little body so safe, so uncompromisingly free in the heat of the day. I recognize that freedom. It's the same free little spirit that I've been able to achieve lately, but only in my imagination and only in my dreams. I realize that I'm being treated to a glimpse of untampered innocence. As I watch my niece, I am gifted with a clear vision of just what innocence truly is. Safe in my thoughts—not triggered by anything, just softly gazing, taking in what I'm being shown—I watch this little sprite innocently at play while I ponder my own lost innocence. I'm doing fine with this moment of light recapitulation until everyone starts talking about how she has my body structure; her tiny bones, petite stature and perfectly proportioned body so like mine, they say. Then it hits me: *I was her age when he started. How could he! How could he invade the body of such a beautiful, tiny baby!*

It brings the truth home to me and yet, once again, I cannot fully acknowledge it. I find myself steeped in denial again, unable to fully believe what I've learned about my childhood. At the same time, I know I must keep confronting the disgusting truth—*for the truth will set you free*, as someone once said—but still, I just can't believe it! I remind myself, however, that my body and my memories repeatedly tell me how true it all is.

Back home at night, everyone exhausted from the day's activities, I lie in bed and discover that a part of me staunchly refuses to believe. Some part of me still wants to maintain the status quo, still wants to keep the old protection of denial in place. Even the other day, when I met with Chuck and told him the awful truth that, yes, my abuser did have sex with me, I felt like I was just reciting by rote, saying something I'd been memorizing. "My abuser had sex with me, a tiny child," I said out loud, but for the life of me I couldn't attach any deeper emotions to the words. They came out in a hollow tone, echoing from the empty hollow tunnel of self. In a deadpan monotone, I recited the phrase, not letting it get to me, not letting the truth touch me: "He had sex with me."

July 5, 2002

Yesterday, I was finally able to fully comprehend just what it meant that my abuser had stolen my innocence. As that innocence fully expressed itself in my tiny niece, I knew that I'd once been that young and innocent, if only very briefly. I was old from the moment he first put his hands on me, by the age of two struggling with confusing thoughts, more complicated than I could have articulated. Constantly on my guard, I was forever judging and assessing if I was safe in the situations I found myself in. I never ran naked. By the time I was two, I already knew that taking my clothes off was dangerous, already aware that I lived on the edge of a frightening abyss.

Why is the fact of my own sexual abuse so hard for me to fully comprehend and believe, especially when I feel such deep compassion for others who have suffered, fully aware that it happens all too often? Something takes over each time I ponder what happened in my own case and before I know it I'm tumbling into the numbing tunnel of darkness where I find escape from the brutal truths of my own history. However, I've discovered that by going into that numbing tunnel so often I gain more than just distance from the truth, I gain freedom from it as well. As I continue recapitulating my past as a sexually abused child, I must also face the fact that every time I retreat into that tunnel I'm returning to the old numbness of denial. As an adult, clearly aware that we live in a predatory world, I must crawl out of that tunnel of denial and face what hurts, as bravely as that little girl self once faced her abuser and did what she had to do to survive. I feel the pain in my body every day now, telling me to believe *for that little girl*. It happened, the pain very clearly states. Without a doubt, it happened.

July 6, 2002

I awaken, still half-dreaming, locked in battle with the old self. I tug at her to come out of the tunnel of denial, so I can access the pure emotions that lie stuffed far down inside that silent tunnel. I can't really blame her, since I've been unwilling to go near them myself, though this dreaming self seeks a peek. A quick glance reveals a bloody raw mess of emotions, though I can't bear to lift the old rags that cover them. The thought of touching them sends shivers down my spine, jolting me awake. I bolt up in bed, gripping the sheets, staring into blackness. My heart pounding, I realize I've been dreaming. My fear of going nuts, of spinning right off the edge of the abyss at the sight of what lies beneath those dirty rags, is only a dream. Nonetheless, I'm shaken and exhausted, ready to shout out that I don't want to do this recapitulation anymore. And yet, I hold my tongue, for I know I can't stop; I have to keep going.

I'll never get anywhere if I stop now. Chuck will tell me that too, that even if I want to, *it* won't stop, the bombardments won't stop, the emotions pushing for escape from the dark tunnel won't stop. The dreams won't stop. The truths won't stop coming to greet me no matter how hard I attempt to hold them back. At some point I'll have to give in, but I'm just not ready for the full impact yet. And in spite of the fact that I know I must see this recapitulation through to the end—just a few more years to go, as Jeanne Ketchel, my spiritual guide and Chuck's dead wife, foretold—I need to go at a pace I can handle. Even if I'm tired of it, even if I'm sick of being back in the painful past, I must push onward, one step at a time. If I don't, I know that I'll just remain blocked, emotions boiling inside me, and then I really will go nuts.

July 7, 2002

I am fixated on the thought that I must do violence to myself. This thought rages out of the depths of me, fueled by anger and frustration, but also the awareness that only in feeling physical pain will I explode the impenetrable walls of that dark tunnel where everything is stored. Memories of sexual violence perpetrated on my teenage self incite these feelings, telling me that I must sexually violate myself, do damage and inflict pain to ease the memories caught in my body. I masturbate to release the tension of these thoughts, orgasm offering some relief, and yet I still feel that I must hurt myself. As thoughts of violence attempt to take root, a despicably loathsome scent from the past comes wafting up out of the depths of the tunnel. The smell and taste of self-hatred and disgust overwhelm me as my teenage self reminds me how she faced the truth of what happened to her. She tells me that the sexual abuse was violent, painful, and disgusting.

"It made me hate myself," she tells me, Slave Girl resurfacing, speaking the truth.

"Sex shouldn't be that way," I tell her. "I know that now. It should be fun and enjoyable. It should make me feel happy and loved."

"Well, that's not what happened," she tells me. "It only led to pain and more pain, outer pain and even greater inner pain."

Once again, full of the self-loathing of Slave Girl, I face the memories of painful sexual encounters with my abuser. I fight the urge to enact violence upon myself, even though the voice of Slave Girl pushes me to go to extremes. I know it's not a good state to be in, even if I'm learning something vitally important. Afraid of getting caught, I fling myself out of bed, away from the tunnel and its violent memories. Its rotting stench wafts after me, as I quickly dress, pull on my running shoes and head out the door, intent on running from it as fast as I can.

July 8, 2002

I keep busy, working, hanging out with the kids, keeping the painful past at bay, but as soon as I take a minute, even a second, for myself, it comes roaring back. The trick is to stay very busy, to maintain control and keep everything contained, but fully acknowledge that I'll deal with it at some point. I know I can't avoid it forever.

In spite of everything that I now know, denial still poses itself as the immediate means of escape. In denial I remain safe, ignorantly protected, and yet I know it isn't productive or really safe either. It's where I've been for the past fifty years and I know the allure of that denial and self-loathing so well, their putrid scents not so bad once I'm surrounded by them. Once they permeate my being I smell only of normalcy. It's only now that I've had a taste of the good fresh air of truth—a hint of what it might feel like to actually heal and breathe the sweet scent of life—that I notice the odor of decay I've been steeped in my entire life. The truth is that the old numbness is still extremely powerful and no matter how often I talk about the abuse, it still doesn't sink in that it *actually* happened, which is pretty strange considering the amount of pain I've been in for the past year, directly related to recapitulating my abusive past. But there's still a part of me that wants to think, maybe, *just maybe* it didn't happen. But how can that be when I'm so utterly affected and devastated by it? Why don't I want to believe it? Can't I believe that people do such terrible things to children, or is it because the truth is still too painful to bear?

July 11, 2002

Cleaning out the house, as well as my soul, I prepare for moving on after the divorce. I find pictures from when the kids were little. I don't even recognize myself. Who was I? I don't even recognize the clothes I wore, clothes I got at yard sales, other people's clothing made to fit other people's bodies. Nothing looked right; nothing fit right. I was someone's wife and someone's mother, but the real me was hiding beneath those shapeless garments. Somewhere deep inside that thin figure in the photos my own spirit called out, though I could barely hear it. I wasn't *me* back then, though I constantly reminded myself that I needed to get back to me. I would often write that in letters to friends and in my journals: *I need to get back to me*...but I realize I've been saying that for as long as I can remember. Now I'm happy to report that after all these years I've started the search for just who *me* might be, but I find that I don't even know who I'm looking for. I don't even know if I'm going back to the me who once was, or if I'm discovering a totally new me.

As I sort through what we've accumulated during our marriage, separating out what belongs to me alone, I realize that I'm sorting through more that just shared belongings. I'm actually sifting through all that has been suffocating me for ages, as the entire world that once stood so solidly is crumbling now. As I dismantle what has been my world for sixteen years, I free my inner self, giving her permission to break more than just marriage vows. I elect to disobey all the old rules now in order to save my soul, to split off from all the pacts made in ancient times, relieving myself of rigid duty to society, to expectations of family. My spirit self has been hanging on for just this moment. Supremely tested in the past, it had the wherewithal to know that it just had to wait, that the moment would arrive and we'd find each other again. I too have always been aware that one day we would reunite; I just never knew that it would be such a painful process. And so, I take this strange recapitulation journey not gladly but with a new sense of duty now, duty to self and my emerging spirit. I dare myself to stay the path, to follow it far back into those other realities and explore where I've been. It's a frightening undertaking, but I know I have to relive the past in order to retrieve what lies in the past, in order to gather up that little girl, that little bundle of innocence that got left behind, and bring her into a new world, a new reality, in order to give her new life.

July 12, 2002

Spacetime is what Richard Bach calls it in his book *Running From Safety*, those other dimensions that we go into when we relive memories and things that happened in the past. I'm doing what Richard Bach did: going back into *spacetime*, confronting my fears. The here and now, the present, ties us down and keeps us anchored, but this *now-time* can also mix things up, confusing the picture with denial and disbelief, making it hard for us to seamlessly meld the two worlds together. The present fights me and I fight back.

On the way to visit my parents I pass a man on a backhoe. He's working alongside the road in the old neighborhood, near the tired old apple orchards. "Is that him?" I wonder, peering through the windshield, curious as to what he would be doing here, so far from his own property, and yet he used to work for the landowner. "Oh, that's a stupid thought. It's just an old man, just some old guy." But then he turns his head and I see his nose and mouth more clearly defined. It's almost as if he's showing himself to me, my abuser, saying "look at me," though he doesn't look at me at all but only back at where he's digging.

"Oh God, it's him! It's him! It's him!" I say out loud, realizing that I have just entered *spacetime*.

"Just keep driving, just concentrate on driving!" I command myself, confronting my fears, intent on driving right out of *spacetime* and back into *now-time*, but I can't get his face out of my mind. I recapitulate how his masklike expression never changed in public, for he smiled constantly, looking almost as if his lips had been sewn up at the corners. A totally confusing face; you'd think he looked nice and friendly, but it was a leer and a smirk more than a smile that hid everything about him. His beady eyes never looked straight at you. They turned down and away, except when he was angry, and then they bore into you like two black shotgun barrels ready to fire at pointblank range. It's almost as if my thoughts alone had the power to conjure him up because I had been recently thinking that I needed to see him, to get a glimpse of him if he was still alive, to see if my memories were right. But then, earlier today, I'd told myself that no, I don't actually need to *see* him. It might just confuse me, throw a wall up and possibly interfere with the natural flow of my recapitulation. But maybe this *is* the natural flow of the process today.

I visit briefly with my parents and then, as I prepare to pass the same spot in the road on my way back home, I am determined to get a better look. As I get closer, I hear the grinding of the backhoe, but he's out of sight now, down in a deep gully. I see trees and brush being violently ripped and trampled, sound and stench of machine filling the air, as the beast he truly is ravages the landscape. "I hope that thing turns over on top of him and crushes him!" I immediately think, but then I question that uncensored thought. "What a horrible thought! I'm not a hater! I don't hate anyone. Why would I think like that?" It doesn't take me long to realize that I do indeed hate him. If there was anyone in the world to hate it would be him. "Yes, I hate him," I decide. "I hate him. I hate him. I hate him!"

As I drive, I more firmly commit to this recapitulation. I am no longer interested in engaging in the conflict of denial, wasting my energy there. I have more important business: *to rescue all those little girls that I once was, all sixteen of them, one for every year of the abuse.* The youngest child self is only two years old, still confused and in pain, the oldest a sad and fearful eighteen-year-old, unable to feel safe in the world, even as she dares herself to venture far from the neighborhood she grew up in, even as she dares to go have a life, in spite of everything that haunts her still.

I more clearly see my job now. I must keep going back into the past until I've rescued all those little girls from under that bridge on my abuser's property. In bulldozing his property into an unrecognizable landscape, my abuser buried alive those sixteen girls in the hollow cavern beneath the remains of the old bridge that I once played under. Last October, as I passed by his property, I was astonished to see that the entire shape of the land had been flattened, smoothed into a strange and unrecognizable landscape. The woods, the stream, the bridge, and the fields are gone. Nothing exists anymore in reality, in *now-time*, but in *spacetime*—in my memories—that bridge has become a cold tomb in which all those girl-selves are still buried alive. I need to go back there and rescue them. I can't leave them there for him to drool over for fifty more years. I must unearth them and get them out of there, pile them into my little car and drive away—just get the heck out of there with them in tow, rescuing them, and myself, in the process. I need to face the big bad wolf with his big sharp teeth and his big drooling mouth and slit his belly open wide, finally freeing them from long captivity.

I'm doing what Richard Bach describes in his book, *reading the signs as they arise, learning to not only note them, but also to act on them.* I see how things get thrown down in front of me so that I'm forced to confront them. I see how my intent sets everything up for me too. I don't believe that coincidences are just that, mere coincidences. I prefer to call them *synchronicities*, as Carl Jung called them, because I know that everything is meaningful. I see how this time my abuser was thrown in front of me, set up for me to encounter, showing me where to go next in my recapitulation: *leading me to take back my fragmented child selves, all the parts of myself, waiting all these years for me to rescue them.*

"Here he is. This is the guy; this is the evil bastard that has been following you around your whole life. This is the beast that wouldn't leave you alone," my recapitulation process says.

"But he's just a little old man!" I say.

"No, he's not! He was a young man when he did all that stuff to you and look at the way he handles that backhoe now. He's not old feeble and sick. In spite of what you've heard, he's still as strong as an ox!"

"Even if it isn't him, it doesn't matter," I conclude, as I drive onward, aware that in *that moment* it was him. "It's a useful encounter nonetheless. What matters is that I do what I have to do to heal, and right now that means taking back what belongs to me, even metaphorically speaking. It's the only thing to do at this point. I must follow the guidance I receive."

I had indeed heard that my abuser was sick, near death, but if that was really him, he seems fit as a fiddle, working that huge backhoe like it was nothing, killing trees and shrubs with that evil grin on his face the same way he killed everything inside me. By the time he was done with me all that was left was a mere shell of a girl, though a tiny little flame burned always somewhere deep inside, hidden far away where he couldn't extinguish it. I'm lucky for that—lucky I could keep my spirit alive. That spirit has been smoldering all these years and now it's flaring up again, giving me new energy, giving me the energy to seek the truth of who I really am. I can't let an image or thought of him put that flame out. Even the sight of him in the flesh must not be allowed to extinguish it.

"I think it's good that you saw him," Chuck says. "It'll be interesting to see what comes next. It breaks everything wide open; all the barriers are down. Go with the flow and let's see what happens."

July 13, 2002

I hate my abuser, the fire of hatred rising up out of the depths of me. I would like to see him dead. I would like that backhoe to flip over in the gully and crush him to death, a slow and painful death. No one will hear him screaming and he will suffer the same kind of long and drawn out torture he put me through.

I don't have to feel threatened by him anymore, that I know. He's not interested in me; he was only interested in little girls. I'm not what he wants anymore, so I'm physically safe from him. This is comforting to keep in mind, but the shock of seeing him still so physically active, alive, and strong is too much to bear. Is he still capable of harming little girls? Does he still roam the countryside looking for prey? I can't even bear to think that he might still be hurting little girls, that there are other lost little girls out there suffering because of him. Maybe his family took care of it; maybe they did something about it, got him help or confronted him in some way. The burden of wondering about other children is too much for me; I don't want to feel guilty about that too. I have enough guilt to deal with at the moment.

I push the horrible thoughts away, hoping that he's being punished in some way, so I don't have to worry about all the other little girls in the world. But I will continue to hate him and I do think that allowing myself to express hatred for him is part of the healing process. I want him to die a grisly death, and I don't want to forgive him. I don't have to forgive him, do I? I can hate and move on—but will that hate fester and grow inside me? Do I have to forgive him in order to heal? Or can I dump all that hatred back on top of him, get rid of it by sending it all back, because I don't like the idea of carrying it around inside me, the burden of hate as big as the burden of fear, just another thing messing me up.

Allowing myself to hate him rather than fear him, however, is a new turn of events and rather empowering. If I can just get over the fact that he doesn't appear to be as sick and feeble as I had imagined, I might just be able to embrace this step in the process. But the evidence that he is still physically active, even if only temporarily so, has thrown me. His physical prowess poses a threat, not to me at the age of fifty, but certainly still threatening to all those little girls that I left behind, locked in his embrace, imaginary though they may be. I have to go back and get all those little fragments of self out of the crypt, buried all these years beneath his driveway. I can't leave them on his property where he still has energetic access to them, even if only in the far reaches of his memory.

I imagine him still abusing those girls in fantasy, still savoring the sick things he did all those years ago, keeping me a prisoner in his own memories, just as I've kept him a prisoner in mine. I've been Slave Girl, tied and shackled, locked in his mind where he's free to do as he pleases. That self-satisfied smirk, that leer tells me he still goes back there and does whatever he wants, anytime he wants. I need to rescue Slave Girl and all the rest of them. I need to get them out of there, take them from him and erase them from his memory. But how, actually, do I retrieve them from *his* memory? I can imagine taking them back for myself, retrieving my own energy, but how do I get them out of his conscious thoughts? Is it even possible? Is it possible to rescue them so totally that he can't even touch them in thought? Can I erase his memories by recapitulating my own? Those girls, those parts of myself, are not safe until he can't even remember touching them—because the way I see it, they aren't completely safe if he still has a smidgen of lurid fantasy regarding them.

If I'm thinking about the past and he's thinking about it at the same time, is it happening all over again, just as it feels like it's happening every time I recapitulate? Does he think of it too? Does he remember? Is his death the only sure way for him to stop remembering what he once did to me as a child? Does he have to be dead for me to be safe, before I feel totally free of him?

"You're taking your memories and your energy back," Chuck tells me. "Even if he goes to those memories, there's no energetic trace of you there. You are disentangling and retrieving your energy from the memories by facing them so honestly. All that's left in those memories for him to encounter is his own naked truth."

I use Richard Bach's book, *Running From Safety*, to search for answers as I work through this process. I understand why Chuck gave me it to me to read, it's the exact process that I'm doing, learning that I'm in control, that I'm not a victim. I'm a *master*, as Bach says, and I have *power tools* to make *choices* and be *aware of synchronicities*. I'm doing what Bach did. I go into those memories and make them reality so I can work through the issues at hand. I not only converse with different parts of myself, but I can also go back and change things. I can go back and fix things, just as I can fix things in my dreams and make them work for me.

Reality has shifted. *Spacetime* and those memories have become my reality now. I've been living in another world and this world, the real world—*now-time*—seems like a dream world in comparison, for I've been going into my own psyche *in reality*. My inner world is as real as this one, perhaps even more real as I go back into the past. I see how the synchronicities in my life have made it all happen, how everything is working out so I can do this process and all the other things that need doing. It's just as Jeanne Ketchel said when she appeared before me in her energy body back in March, when she spoke to me, telling me that this was my work now and that everything was set up so I could do it. She told me to let the process lead me, to let it unfold, that everything was in alignment. She said I didn't have to worry about anything, except staying focused on recapitulating. I've come so far since then in trusting the people involved and in trusting this process itself. I now know that things are proceeding as they are meant to. I know that I'll live in that little house that I've dreamed about—someday soon it will be a reality. I'll be happy. I'll continue to grow. I'll love and be loved. I am as certain of these things as I am that tomorrow will come, that the sun will rise and set, that I will live to take my next breath.

I may be in *spacetime* for now, but I won't always be here. I have power. I am powerful, and I also know that powerfully good things will come my way. I'm not going to stay stuck here on the side of the road forever, back in the past, watching that old but ferocious man drive a backhoe. He'll keel over and die one of these days, but I'll make him keel over in my memory and die long before then. He's not invited into my inner space anymore, to invade my energetic self anymore. I have the power of the intent of recapitulation behind me as I regain my personal power and learn to take control of my own destiny. I have the power to fix things, to rectify the wrongs in a new way, to change and move forward freed of the negative energy that has inhabited me my entire life. I have no need to stay attached to my abuser anymore, not in any sense, not even in memory, and that's what I'm learning the most about, the power of memory to keep us captive. I don't need to be owned by him, enslaved by him, or even remembered by him. He's nothing but a disgusting pile of dog shit! The shit of life! I'm working through what he once did to me, and what he once had me do as well. I'm working through the horrors of it all, and when I'm finished I'll have washed myself clean. I'll no longer have any of his shit clinging to me, nor be full of the shit of self-loathing and guilt either.

Hating him feels good. Feeling disgusted and angry is good. Hating him removes those negative feelings from myself. I do the shamanic recapitulation breath, sweeping myself free of him, giving back what belongs to him. *He* is despicable and dirty, not me. *He* is loathsome, not me. *He* is disgusting, not me. I breathe in my good self, and let the vitally fresh air of my pure self fill my lungs and clear my head. I'm in charge of my own ship. I'm the one who is in command of my life. I'm open to life, and by being open to it I'm also ready for whatever it has to offer me. "Life will happen when you are ready," Chuck suggested not long ago. *When I'm ready*. Well, okay, I'm ready. Let's do this work, let's tackle this recapitulation and see where it leads. Let's go!

As I continue doing the sweeping breath, I gain greater clarity and deeper understanding of the position my child self was once in. My abuser tried to make me believe that I was a filthy, disgusting, fucked up little girl and that I made him do the things he did, simply by being a little girl who walked onto his property. I must have been the evil one—a little girl temptress! Ha! He was the evil one, not me! He did those things to me. I didn't do them to him. His thoughts and deeds set the traps that I got caught in and I was too young and innocent to get away. I didn't even know I should try to get away. He was an adult and you did what adults told you to do. You trusted them; no questions asked, they ruled.

As I ponder all of this, the old need to curl up into a ball calls out from the depths of me, presenting itself as the only means of comfort and protection, just as it always did. I let myself lie down and feel safe again. I roll into the old silent tunnel of self where I take all the feelings, clutching them tightly so they don't overwhelm me. "What am I feeling?" I wonder, daring myself to let my feelings guide me through this recapitulation, for I know they will teach me many things. As I let myself go deeper, I acknowledge that I'm steeped in fear. Even though I know my abuser can't get me, I'm a frightened child again as the reality of what happened to me really sinks in. And, on top of it, *he's real again!* He's a real live person again, not just some figment of my imagination. He's a living, breathing being. He once did horrific things to me. As I try to grasp the reality of that, my body reacts. The old pain re-emerges as my thoughts settle on this new reality and the swollen, burning soreness between my legs immediately returns. More than just a reminder of the past, it reminds me that my body still has more to tell me.

I'm aware that I'm in that other realm, *spacetime*, back there in the past, caught in my abuser's world, but I'm also aware of being powerful enough to fix things now. I clearly see that I must rescue the girls from under the old bridge at the end of his driveway. I visualize little bodies covered in dirt as I go still deeper into my process of discovery. "They must be dead," I think. "After all, they've been there for so long. How could they survive that final indignity of being buried alive after everything else they've been through?" In my imagination, I go back to his property. I drive right up to his old driveway and park my car so I can make a quick getaway. Estimating where the entrance to the tunnel under the bridge is, I begin digging with my hands, with sticks and sharp stones that I find on the ground. Eventually, I discover that the opening has been walled up with large stones. It's impossible to get in that way. I go around to the other side.

"Whoa! A door!"

The sight of the door startles me, because it drives home my premise that he's kept the girls locked up and that he's had access to them all these years. I know it means that he's kept the adult me locked up too, my energy still feeding his nasty habits. Now, I'm furious! I refuse to be locked up anymore! I pick up a huge rock and smash the rusty lock on the thick wooden door. With heart pounding, I pull it open and peak inside. It's dark and musty, cold and damp inside, just as I'd remembered. Stale air, like an ogre's bad breath, seeps out of the darkness. I hear a trickle of stream water still running after all these years. I know the girls are inside, but I can't see them.

I step inside and wait for my eyes to adjust to the darkness. Then I see them huddled in the farthest corner, naked, clutching their ragged wisps of clothing. I see a shred of diaper, my white cardigan now frayed, the little plaid summer dress, my turquoise petal-pushers in tatters, the striped mini-dress, and that pink dress with all the pearl buttons, only a tiny bit of it left now. But I see the buttons have all been saved. They're lying in a little circle on the ground, as if they've just been played with. I see all the bits and pieces of my life, just shreds now, worn old fragments of the past. I also see that the girls are afraid of me, standing there all big-eyed and silent, holding their breath, sixteen pairs of frightened, sad eyes staring at me out of the gloom. I remember that fear. I taste it again as I take in the sight of them, standing in the darkness where they've been for decades.

"We have to leave," I tell them. "We have to get out of here before he finds us. He's still out there, and he'll come back."

They don't trust me. They don't know who I am. I'm afraid of the door closing behind me. I'm afraid of my abuser knowing I'm here, locking me in, and bolting the door shut, and then I'll never get out alive. But then I hear Chuck's voice reminding me, "*You have power!*" and I know I can take all the time in the world. This is my show now and I'm in charge.

"He did it to me too," I tell the girls calmly and gently.

"So what? Join the crowd," they say, clearly nonplussed.

"I *am* you," I say. "I am you before it started and I am you after it ended. I'm the one who got away. I came back for you because I can't leave you here any longer. I can't let him have you anymore."

They stare at me until I convince them that it's okay to leave with me, that I'm safe, that I'm the only one who knows who they are, where they've been, and what they've been through. They move as a solid unit, sixteen silent and frightened little girls. I get them out of the blocked up tunnel, out into the light of day, where they cower and squint, so unused are they to daylight. I somehow get them into my little car. I can't believe they all fit, the older ones holding the little ones, sixteen naked, wide-eyed little girls, trusting me.

And then we get out of there! I drive away like a bat out of hell, taking the longer route over the mountaintop so we don't risk seeing him. I don't want them to have to ever see him again. But where do I take them? I don't have my own place yet, no home to take them too. I ponder this as I drive. I have to take them to a safe place, to a place of healing and recovery. I decide to take them to Chuck's, and so I drive straight there and we all pile out of the car and into his little office. We sit down and wait for him to show up. It's time to ask for more help.

I come out of this very real *spacetime* scenario knowing I must keep giving myself permission to go back into the past and do this inner work. I must not only rescue those fragments of myself at different ages, but I must also prepare to integrate all those lost parts into my present adult self. I can just about hear Chuck saying delightedly, as he once did in the past: *Now the real work begins!*

Everything is telling me that the sexual abuse happened, but I seem to still be holding out, one last shred of conventional dignity refusing to fully commit to such a past. Why can't I believe it? Is it because I'm so ashamed? Is it because for forty-eight years I've had to keep it a secret, because I made a pact to not ever reveal what happened back in those woods with my abuser? Is it because I'm still afraid of him? Those girls in the tunnel under the bridge didn't believe me when I told them it happened to me too. It happened to them, not to the woman standing in front of them, a grown up. I realize they're right, that they are the tortured and abused ones. I realize I must accept *them*—they don't need to accept me. Right now, however, they don't trust me and I guess I don't blame them. I'm stumbling along as best I can, trying to figure this out, and I'm still struggling with my own resistance to fully accepting the abuse. We're in a bit of a deadlock, neither trusting of the other, but at least they're safe from him, my abuser—for the moment anyway.

I keep blaming my abuser for locking them away, but maybe I did too, leaving them there locked away with the bad memories because I couldn't deal with the pain of it all. I went on without them, leaving a big empty space in my life, a gap that nothing could fill. But I was locked up too, only in a different place, and now I need to do more than just unlock that door to the tunnel—I need to bring us back together. But how am I going to do that? I expect them to just walk out with me into the light of day and say, "Oh, hi! Nice to see you." But the truth is *they* hate me and *I* fear them. I fear the pain of having to recapitulate what they have to tell me, even though I've done most of that already, and I fear having to meet them face-to-face, all those lost little girls and the secrets they've harbored.

What do I say to them? Where do I put them? Where do they fit into my life? I've proven I can rescue them, but what do I do with them now?

July 14, 2002

The girls refuse to talk to me. They hate me. They hate me because I got away. They think I left them there on purpose. They also hate me because they think it was my fault, because they think I desired the sexual abuse and that I liked it. They suffered as a result of that supposed desire, and then they suffered again when I left them behind.

As I face those fragments of self, embodied in those sixteen girls, I discover the truth of what they're telling me. I keep pretending that the abuse didn't happen, hanging onto a small shred of dignity, but dignity has no place here. That's a figment of the old world that I'm dismantling, my mother's perfect world where no one ever speaks the truth, where presentation is everything, where everything is kept buttoned up because that's what a proper lady does, she hides everything. It's the world I'm leaving as those girls ask me to face the real truth. They're asking me to shed all pretense of dignity, that last strand of attachment to an old idea of self. And so, I unravel that last thin thread and face the truth of what I now know—that the girls are right—*I experienced sexual arousal and desire*. I plunged into deep self-loathing and self-hatred each time I experienced it. It was disgusting and I became a disgusting person as a result.

Sexual arousal brought on at the hands of an abuser isn't anything like the true desire one feels for a lover, when one innocently falls in love, bubbling in passionate romance. My abuser's brand of sickening arousal arrived with a frantic need to have something happen in a perverted, desperate, disgusting way. It meant becoming just like him, focused only on achieving the release offered by sexual climax. Entrapped by the energy of sexual deviancy, steeped in self-disgust, I experienced a desperate need for release from the whirlwind inside me, while I was simultaneously overpowered by its massive strength coming from outside of me.

I am Slave Girl once again as I recapitulate these thoughts, seeking relief in punishment. Perhaps this was the only thing my child self could come up with to counter all the confusing thoughts and feelings that found no other outlet. If my abuser hurt me then I felt punished and I could get up afterwards and go back to being in the real world. "Punish me because I'm such a fucked up, bad little girl. I have bad thoughts and I do such bad things, so punish me. Bad girls get punished, and rightfully so!"

As these thoughts course through me, I feel all those little girls run like hell, out of Chuck's office where they've been so patiently waiting for our next session. They scamper right back to the tunnel under the old bridge where they slam the door shut. They're in safe territory again, back where the enemy is so well known and entirely predictable.

July 15, 2002

Struggling to awaken, I am overtaken and dragged back into dreams. My abuser's sexual desire sneaks up on me; his evil energy overpowers me from head to toe, inside and out. I fight against him, but I'm already a player in his game, and I cannot get away. I am used and then discarded, left to wallow in my own despicable, self-imposed vile. What a disgusting, inhuman, dirty person I am! I turn to get away from both him and my own feelings of self-disgust and find myself in my bed, far from the woods of my childhood. I understand how evil took over and used me for its own purposes and then dumped me to deal with the consequences. I deserved what I got, resigned to eternity in hell because I was bad. Are those little girls right, that it's my fault? Is that my real punishment, to be totally separated and locked away from those abused parts of myself forever? How can I ever heal if I think I deserved everything I got?

I understand that I need to resolve the impression that I'm the evil one. In fact, the adult me knows that he was evil, not me. I was merely a vessel and, yes, he did just dump me, leaving me tortured and confused to deal with the consequences of his invasive actions. I accept the truth and consequences of the abuse, those facts stand, *but I was not the abuser.*

In a groggy, half-awake state, I recapitulate. I'm in the woods again. My abuser makes me rub myself against things, until I'm in a state of heightened sexual arousal. And then, when I'm totally and helplessly under the spell of it, he moves in to do his thing, carrying me to the poky tree, pushing me down on top of a hard stub, so that it goes inside. "Is it in? Is it in?" he asks, looking me straight in the eyes, his look telling me not to lie to him—don't ever lie to him. He stands up in front of me and puts his erection in my mouth, hurting me down there and choking me with his penis at the same time. I am a little girl again, no more than seven or eight. Incredible feelings of self-hatred sweep through me, feelings of dark remorse and guilt at once again getting myself into trouble. I come out of the recapitulation clearly seeing how I had been used, stimulated to arousal, painfully hurt, and then filled with hatred for myself. I ended up feeling like a bad girl because I got excited with him for a few seconds as we played our game. He set me up, but I've let the fact that I participated in his game—one of momentary sexual arousal switching to pain—torture me my entire life. I hate myself for that. They are right, the girls are right: *I am to be hated. They should hate me.*

Too young to climax, I didn't have orgasms at that time, so there was no release from the heightened state of arousal. I recapitulate by masturbating now, how it built up to an intense frenzy, the arousal sustained for a long time with no breaking relief of orgasm. He utilized that. He already knew how a little girl's body worked. Only in acquiescing to the next stage of his play—by being painfully abused—was the arousal defeated, immediately released through physical pain that plummeted into self-disgust. I must dialogue with the girls around this.

Once again, I fully understand what Richard Bach was doing and writing about in his book *Running From Safety*. I'm doing it too, finding my way back to discovering who I really am and how I got this way. I'm glad to know it's not such a bizarre process, that someone else has done something like this and even written a book about it. In assimilating all my disparate selves—those sixteen separate, fearful parts—I will become whole. In the process, I seek to eradicate my abuser from my being, every last vestige of him, leaving only room for me, for all of me.

People get stuck in thinking a certain way, in such a formulaic and conventional manner, and I have certainly been guilty of the same. It's safer knowing that things are reliably mundane, everything predictable. As Chuck told me, the shamans refer to this as the *foreign installation*, a mindset that is not truly our own but one that is predicated upon us. Basically, we live in a consensus reality based on a belief system that we've all agreed upon and are socialized into from the moment we are born. Rarely do we break away from it. More often than not we just follow blindly along, but right now I feel safer knowing that the conventional purview doesn't have the answers I seek. As I recapitulate, the world I have relied upon is no longer of much use and, in fact, I understand that it must totally disassemble for me to be able to flow with what comes to me. Each time I crack through another memory I am thrown into another world, just as I was as a kid, and nothing in this consensus reality explains that other world. Over the past year, I've been training myself to withstand those moments of shift into memory. And each time I recapitulate a traumatic event, I'm dismantling the *foreign installation* that has held me in its grip, as tightly and predatorily as my abuser once did. I know I'm the only one who can change myself and I'm electing to do it in the only way that feels right, by changing how I perceive myself and my world, the past and the one I live in every day as well. I'm challenging myself to not be so afraid of being different, to do what feels right instead of doing what's expected and acceptable. I'm giving myself permission to rebel against the status quo, learning how to question everything, seeing and experiencing the world with new eyes, changing my inner landscape as I do this deep work.

Once again I feel extremely lucky to have met Chuck. I wouldn't be doing this shamanic recapitulation otherwise, maybe not even anything close. I'd still be stuck in an old world where nothing was really clear, where nothing really made any sense because my deeper experiences and truths conflicted with it so starkly. Steeped in deep remorse long before I had any idea what it was, I was too young to understand why I always hated myself so intensely. Now I'm learning what it might mean to love myself instead, but I think I have a long way to go because I can't imagine being able to punch through that thick wall blocking me from all those little girls. Until I deal with the self-hatred and remorse, two very strong components of this whole process, we will remain separated. And the girls hate me as well, it seems, or do we all separately hate our individual selves? How am I going to get them to join me in this healing process if we all hate ourselves so much?

I go back into the woods and recapitulate those dark feelings of remorse and self-hatred. Letting them wash over me, I encounter the next truth: *my abuser turned me into his accomplice.* I became complicit in every step, from the planning to the execution, so thoroughly that my body absorbed his sexual deviancy. As I've already discovered, there was no climaxing. Possessed by sexual feelings that my child's body couldn't handle, pain was the only outlet of release. Does that mean I associate sex with pain? Does sex have to be painfully torturous?

It's clear to me now that my abuser's energy got inside me when I was a helpless child and it has stayed on, in control for all these years. I thought I had pretty much gotten rid of it, but as I find myself steeped in the old self-hatred again, I realize this is a bigger problem than at first thought. I realize the hatred should be directed only at him. As I reencounter it, however, I feel it directed toward myself alone. I feel it emerging from the darkness of my battered soul, confronting me. I know that I truly hate myself. I've always hated myself. And those little girls locked away under the bridge for all those years hate me too, and they have every right to—I am indeed a hateful being.

As I take this recapitulation journey, I notice there are days like today when I am awash in self-hatred and self-disgust. I've also noticed that on other days I feel pretty good, almost pure and light, like I'm being cleansed as I go through the memories, shedding the negative energy of them. But those good feelings don't last very long. Pretty soon the dark stuff comes rolling back in and shows me there's still more work to do.

July 16, 2002

"I DON'T WANT TO DO THIS RECAPITULATION ANYMORE!!! HOW DO I STOP IT?" I tell Chuck when we meet, yelling like a big baby. "I'm lost back in the woods wanting it to be over, over, over, over! I find it hard to focus or think about anything else."

"You're dealing with what the shaman's call a *petty tyrant* of the highest magnitude!" he says, quite delighted to share this news with me.

"What do you mean?"

"Well, a petty tyrant is an entity, human or otherwise, that comes to test you, to provoke you, to fool with you, to make you face what you need to face."

"Oh, like a trickster?"

"Yes, like a trickster, but they're present in all walks of life," he says. "They can be anyone or anything that provokes or disturbs us, or makes us face something about ourselves. Petty tyrants can be those we hate and those we confusedly love the most. Our petty tyrants show us where we still have work to do, and they are unrelenting in their presentation."

"Your abuser," he says, "is a master petty tyrant, constantly pointing out not only what happened, but also where he still has control over you. Each time you recapitulate, you dismantle some of his power and take back more of your own energy. Eventually, he'll no longer have a hold over you because all of your energy, caught in the memories of him, will be retrieved."

"Yes, we've talked about that before and I do feel my own energy returning, but then I get lost again—in his world."

"What's happening now?"

"I'm battling an intense need to cry that's extremely painful. Being exhausted hurts. Being so alone hurts. Being in the grip of memories hurts. Knowing that I'll be going into my abuser's territory again and again, as I recapitulate, hurts too. I need to move on. I have other things to do and I can't do them when I'm stuck in the past. I feel so useless and stagnant, so numb and dazed, so EXHAUSTED!!! I can't stand myself anymore either. I'm sick of *me*."

"This is a crucial point in the work," Chuck explains. "The past, where those dissociated parts of you have remained, and the future, where the adult-you went, are coming together now. They are bringing you the past and you are bringing them the future."

"Well, none of us like it," I say, "but I know I need to work through it. I can't leave those girls back in that tomb."

"Be strong for them," says Chuck. "Show them that you *can* bring them forward, that you went on, that you're strong and that you're coming back to get them, to take them with you now."

"Okay," I say, putting the EMDR headphones on. "I'll go back and see what happens. I know I won't get any relief until I do."

With Chuck as my witness, I allow myself to go into my inner world, back to the old bridge at the entrance to my abuser's property. I stand in front of the old door to the tunnel beneath the bridge, the lock now broken, hanging useless. I begin a dialogue.

"We'll all be safe now. We'll all go forward together now, no more separation," I tell those scared and angry little girls.

Keeping Chuck briefed on what's happening, I open the door and stare into the darkness of the tunnel. I don't want to scare them anymore than they already are, so I just stand at the entrance and wait.

"I don't know if they want to talk to me," I say to Chuck, feeling a little self-conscious.

"Well, just start talking and see what happens," he says, and so I close my eyes and begin talking into the pitch-blackness, hoping they're really there, hoping they're listening.

"We can be strong and deal with this together," I say. "I need to take you out of this dark tunnel so we can leave his bad world behind. It isn't our place; it's not our world. I feel your pain and I'll find a way to handle it. I need you to know that we can deal with anything. We'll be together now. We'll have a whole new life. We can get out of that tunnel forever. We'll get some new clothes, get healed and healthy, and go on with life."

"We're beautiful and good in spite of him," I continue, as much to myself as to the girls. "We always were. He was bad—*not us*—a sick coward who had to play his dirty games with little girls, the worst kind of human a child could ever meet. Why did we meet him? I don't know. Perhaps because we were strong enough, or perhaps for no reason at all. But we did survive. We all survived, on different planes perhaps, but here we are now, today, ready to merge, ready to flip him the bird and move on."

"FUCK YOU! FUCK YOU!" I shout. "FUCK YOU, YOU SICK FUCKER!"

"Come on, girls, we don't need to stay here anymore. The door is open and we can walk away. If he comes looking for us, we'll deal with him. We can chop him to bits if we want to, all of his fingers, and his tongue, and his penis and balls. We can poke a log up his ass for all I care. We can do whatever we want to him because that's what he did to us; he did anything he wanted. And remember that: it was what *he* wanted, not what we wanted."

"Okay girls, let's go, let's get into the car," I say. "We'll leave him to rot in his own dungeon, assured that he'll never bother us again. You already know you'll fit into my car, small as it is. You big girls hold the little ones, just like last time. Let's go, I'll take you to some safe place. We'll be fine. You'll be safe with me. We're all together now, and we'll be fine. Chuck will be happy to see you. He knows where we've been and what we've been through. He's the only one who knows and he's good at keeping secrets. He'll be happy to know you're safe. He'll be very happy."

As I come out of EMDR and back into the present, having corralled the girls back into my car and back into Chuck's office, I open my eyes to see Chuck sitting opposite me, smiling big, as if he's smiling at all my sixteen little girls. He tells me that what I'm doing is called *active imagination*, a term that Carl Jung applied to doing deep inner work.

"It's extremely helpful that you can do that so easily, that you just slip right into a conversation and into a scene. You can really use it as a tool to help in the recapitulation process."

"It helps me understand what's happening," I say, as I get up to leave. "It's like I'm really there, really doing it."

"Good work," he says. "Keep doing it; see where it takes you."

I return the Richard Bach book and as soon as I walk out the door I miss it. I miss opening it to any page and understanding completely what he was writing about. I miss the calmness and the sense of belonging that I gained in reading about his process. Talking to the girls is giving me some of that same sense of belonging, the same sense of calm, even though we are encountering such painful stuff. Each time I speak to them I do feel my own power returning, which means my abuser, my petty tyrant, is losing his power over me!

July 17, 2002

In a dream, my abuser wants to perform oral sex on me one last time. "I want to do that for you," he says pleadingly, almost pouting, so I let him. "Why am I doing this?" I ask myself. I don't have an answer. I simply acquiesce, numbly. Without feeling I open my legs. Suddenly, I'm plummeting down into a deep well of loneliness. Black silence envelops me. I wrap my arms around my shoulders, hugging myself against the loneliness that creeps deep into my soul. And then suddenly, I get angry. I put my feet on my abuser's face and shove him away as hard as I can. "NEVER, EVER AGAIN! GET AWAY FROM ME! NEVER, NEVER, EVER AGAIN!" I scream at him. "I HOPE I BROKE YOUR FUCKING NECK!"

As I shove his ugly face out of my bed, I wake up knowing that yesterday's active imagination worked. But, like the master petty tyrant that he is, my abuser makes one last attempt to draw me in, making me feel almost sorry for him. I acquiesced in the dream, falling right back into an old dynamic, but as soon as the anger uncoiled I immediately shifted back into my new place of power, so newly acquired. It's like Chuck said yesterday about this being a crucial time; I have to be so alert, even in my dreams, to not get pulled back. I have to be on my guard, ready to fight him off all the time now. I must do what I couldn't do as a child. It felt so good to kick him in the face and shove him away like that—the damned petty tyrant!

I wake up happy for the first time in a very long time. The dream, like a shot of adrenalin, released the pain and anxiety that have plagued me for so long. The agonizing heaviness of the recapitulation is gone too. I slept well last night, for the first time in a very long time. I wake up feeling whole, realizing I've never felt this way before in my entire life. I wake up feeling powerful! I know there's still a long way to go, but I feel safe now and I'm calmer, with a sense of wholeness that I've never experienced before. I can't help but hope that this new lighter phase will last. I never thought I'd get out of that heavy painful period of dark depression that lasted for months and months, most of the past year in fact.

As the day goes on, I'm only slightly conscious of being on the edge of my abuser's territory. At one point, I think of the bridge and I'm immediately fearful, but then I calm myself. "It's okay, the girls aren't there any longer," I say. "It's all right; we're safe." I feel detached then. I know that by recapitulating I've done what was needed. I also understand that as long as I hold onto the memories, I'm also holding onto the fear embodied in them. But by going back there again with a different mindset—by shifting slightly away from my usual thought process and associated fear regarding the bridge—I discover that the bridge no longer really holds any tension or pain, as it once did. As I realize there's nothing for me to gain by going there again, I begin to relax. I've accomplished a major step in the healing process. My energy is no longer attached to the memory of the bridge!

And where are the girls now? Well, I didn't leave them at Chuck's office. This time they're with me, right here inside me. I opened a door in my heart center and said, "Come on in," and that's where they are. I feel full with them. They're still huddled together, unused to this adult body. They're tentative and not sure of what's going to happen next, but they're feeling safe, little by little letting their guard down. They're slowly learning to trust, learning to believe again that all things are possible. They're learning to trust me too.

I've had no energy to look for a place to live, to take the next step and move out of the house I'm still sharing with my husband, but now I'm ready. Now I'm ready to find a place to make a real home for all of us, so I can finish this healing journey.

July 19, 2002

In a dream, I'm in a ghost town being pursued by some entity that I never quite see. I run through empty old barns and stone structures. I hide for a while behind a big tree alongside a highway. I finally have the opportunity to jump onto a stagecoach as it passes by. I easily leap on, open the door and take a seat inside just as the stagecoach picks up speed. As it goes flying out of town, old memories and men from the past flicker past the windows. I sit comfortably, unfazed by what I see, knowing that those memories and people are fully recapitulated, no longer attached to me in any way. Whizzing along, I know I'm escaping totally unscathed.

In another dream, I'm learning how to fly an airplane, but I'm not very good at it. First I fly straight up, nose pointed up into the heavens, soaring into the atmosphere. Then I flip the airplane around and fly nose down, zooming straight toward the ground. I'm not quite getting the hang of it, but it doesn't feel unsafe, just jerky and unprofessional. It's like I haven't really learned the finer points of flying yet, but none of that really bothers me. I'm only aware that I need to go as fast as I can, no matter what direction I'm pointing in.

In a third dream, I'm being pursued again. I want only to resort to the old method of curling up protectively into the fetal position. I look for places to hide so I can lie down and roll into a ball, but people keep asking me what's wrong. They want to know if they can help. I'm intent on keeping things to myself because I don't feel I deserve any kindness. In spite of my insistence on remaining isolated, their concern does not wane. Deeply ashamed, I feel that my issues are too ugly to be shared and that I must deal with them alone. I just cannot share my pain with anyone. It's too humiliating.

I awaken fully aware that the girls are with me now, but also that they're bringing new memories. I thought this recapitulation was winding down, that I was indeed flying out of town unscathed on the stagecoach of my dream, but I guess they need me to know *everything*. They know I'm a grown up and, as I've told them repeatedly, I can handle whatever they present me with. I've also told them that I'll find a way to bear the painful truth. I'm equally aware that I must learn everything there is to know about my past or I won't be able to fully integrate and become the person I am truly capable of being.

My dreams are a combination of all that I've been feeling lately, almost as if they're laying out the three levels of this recapitulation process. At the first level, I've completed some recapitulations, left them behind without attachment. At the second level, I'm feeling my own power as I learn how to fly, manning my own airplane, feeling what it means to be a soaring spirit. At the same time, however, I still have to face what's yet to come. And I can't just keep flying around without knowing what I'm doing either. I have to learn as I go along, and the girls are clearly telling me that there's more recapitulating to do. At the third and deepest level, I still have to face the deep, humiliating shame that lies at my core, and the self that feels unworthy of kindness and caring attention.

I've been feeling such anger lately. Long pent up, it mixes readily with deep depression. It feels old. I guess it's leading me into the next memory, though it leaves me feeling so strangely discombobulated. I've been finding it hard to focus on my mural and furniture painting business, so I'm cutting back my hours for a little while. My intention is to focus on being with the kids as much as possible through the summer months, to find a house and get through this deep depression in one piece. I have to figure out where all the feelings are leading me while trying to take care of myself too.

July 20, 2002

The girls are still there, behind the door to my heart, clustered together. When I peek in at them, I see their slightly stunned faces, but there's a definite expression of hope now too. "Do we dare hope? Do we dare hope that we're safe now?" they tentatively ask. "Do we dare hope that everything will really be fine?"

They carry unrecapitulated memories in their sad little bodies. Their faces bear the signs of woe. The old stale atmosphere of the past permeates their skin, the smells of forgotten times on their tongues. They bring old sounds and sights. The dynamics of old situations and relationships play in their eyes, the dialogues and interactions between the main players whisper from their lips. And they bring with them the horrors of those awful memories, the ones that are yet to be known and the recapitulated ones that still carry pain and fear. I need to let them cry, allow them to release the stored up torment, despair, and anger. I must listen as they tell me what they know, while I, in turn, must let them know that we're all safe now. "We got away," I tell them. "Just picture him chopped up, locked up, whatever works. He's gone and we're going to be fine. We're all together now, in a safe place. Yes, it's okay to let your guard down, it's okay to relax, it's okay to let go."

July 21, 2002

I meditate and immediately blow up into a plump woman, a familiar puffy, numbing state that happens a lot when I sit down to meditate. Pumped up like a balloon, feeling like I'm floating, I lose touch with the bed I'm sitting on. My awareness hones into a tiny speck, travels through my physical body, and lands inside my mouth. It rests awhile on my tongue before going higher into my head where it sits on a tiny balloon pillow and ponders what this state might mean and why it's happening at this moment. It's definitely a safe place. I like it.

I'm aware that this very familiar dissociative state is a throwback to my traumatized childhood and I wonder if there's another memory looming. As a child this was a place to disappear to and be safe in. From such a vantage point I once watched what happened to that other little girl who was so far away that I couldn't even identify her as myself. Now my awareness floats happily on my little balloon pillow, at a great distance from everything, but as usual I'm curious as to what's coming next. After a while, with no clarity gained as to just why I'm having this experience, I float down into my body again, which I sense as quite deflated and lifeless, though it still sits upright on my bed.

I've been visiting my parents a lot during the summer months, taking the kids on Sundays, mostly to get us out of the house, giving us all a much-needed break from the oppressive tension that hovers in the air as we wind up the final matters of the divorce agreement. My soon-to-be ex-husband and I have pretty much agreed to go about our separate lives beneath its dark overhanging presence, knowing that things are destined to change before long anyway. But even so, in spite of living totally separate lives, it's often hard to achieve any real distance. And so, I acknowledge that the trips to visit my parents are partially for reasons of escape, but I wonder if perhaps I've been going to the old neighborhood so often for other reasons as well. Something else seems to be pulling me back there, just as something once pulled me to begin this recapitulation process, and now it won't release me. I sense it asking me to keep going deeper, to keep confronting what I must. But my inner girls are not happy. I've just recently gotten them out of the old neighborhood and when I tell them we're going back again today they're furious with me.

"What if we see him again? What if something gets triggered?" they ask.

"We'll be fine," I say.

"We're not going!" they cry.

"Yes, you are. We'll be fine, it'll be okay," I say, trying to sound confident. "Look, we did it the other day and it was okay."

"We went the other day? You didn't tell us that!"

"Yes, I did, and it was fine."

"The only reason it was fine was because you didn't tell us. If you had told us, we wouldn't have gone!"

"Well, now I'm telling you, and we're going. It'll be okay," I say. "We can handle it."

"Not us, we're not going! Go away!" they say, as I hear a door slam synchronistically shut with a loud BANG!

Now they won't talk to me at all. Every time I try, I get only silence in return, so I decide to leave them alone until they're ready to communicate again.

The visit to my parents is uneventful. Nothing gets triggered, and there are no sightings of my abuser.

July 23, 2002

I meet with Chuck and in EMDR recapitulate the memory by the spring under the old apple tree that came up several weeks ago, for I am still haunted by it. The pristine beauty of the spot and the purity of my six-year-old child self are in complete alignment as I recapitulate. I am there once again. My child self, lost in play, is calmly at peace in this idyllic setting. Such feelings of contentment are rare, but wouldn't you know that my abuser interrupts even this moment of peacefulness.

As soon as I tell Chuck that I see my abuser walking up from the bottom of the field, I hear my six-year-old child self crying. I get the sense that she doesn't want me to spoil the moment for her, as if I alone have created the interruption. It's as if she's been sitting there playing, caught in the moment before he shows up, happily frozen in time, for decades. I realize that she helped me find the beginning of the memory, the good part of it, but as I go deeper and recapitulate what happens next, she gets upset.

"Now I've made her cry," I tell Chuck, "and it feels like all the other girls are mad at me too, for destroying the equilibrium. I see them gathering around her protectively, locking me out. They've been mad at me for days, ever since I went back into my abuser's territory and now they have a new reason to stay mad."

"Can you find out what happened to the six-year-old?" asks Chuck.

"They won't listen to me," I say, getting frustrated.

"So talk through the door, give them some space, but not too much," says Chuck.

So I go back. The six-year-old still doesn't want to talk to me, but the others do. As if to punish me for intruding on their fragile peace they all speak up at once, shouting out memories that are too hard and painful to listen to and which none of us are really ready to deal with. I sense our worlds crashing together, the cacophony of the impact building to a deafening and unnerving roar, and I realize that maybe I should just leave them alone for now; just let them know I'm here, that I care, and that I'm ready when they are.

I realize that while they bring me the memories they too are being forced to remember. It's hard for all of us. I'm the adult and even though I need so much myself, I know I must be the source of comfort for all of us now.

July 24, 2002

The status of the situation is immediately apparent upon awakening; *the door is still shut.* If there's one thing I've learned over the past year of doing this recapitulation, it's that talking is necessary, and so if we're to get beyond this impasse we have to communicate. The girls also have to remember that I'm the one who went back to the bridge to rescue them because I care so much about them.

"We need to keep moving forward. We're not stopping here," I tell them. "All of you need to know that it will be even better when you open the door. I intend that we will merge and become whole, but I need you—and you definitely need me—so we can continue this healing process together. I'm the guide here. I'm the one who went ahead and learned how to navigate the world, moving beyond the survival mode that you so defiantly established."

"You little ones are the strong ground that enabled me to go on into adulthood. You are so important, but now you have to trust me to carry us forward. I went back and got you. I wasn't going to leave you there. You belong with me. You are safe with me. Don't you see how much better it is here? Don't you feel my love for you? Don't you feel the warmth of my heart, my welcoming arms? Don't you know how much I care?"

"It's time to emerge from the darkness and talk," I say, feeling as if I've been talking to nothing more than a blank wooden door.

"TALK?" I hear them asking, sounding quite astonished, as if they have no intention of talking at all.

"Yes, talk. We must break the old pact we made to never speak about what happened to us. That pact kept us safe while we needed it, but we don't need it anymore. Even I find it hard to break the pact, but we have to. You have to believe me when I tell you how important it is. Talking to Chuck is just the beginning. I've been talking to him for a long time now, that's how I found you. I discovered where you were by talking to him. He stood by me while I journeyed to find you. I discovered, through talking, that you were still back there in that horrific past, waiting for me. I know you've been waiting a long time."

"Even if you open the door just a small crack today we can begin the process. Don't be afraid of me or of Chuck. Remember that I am you, and he is our guide. He's great, you'll see. He knows where we've been and what happened to us. He's as thrilled and excited by the prospect of our evolution as we are. He understands everything, no judgments, no morality, no preaching. He's just here as a receptor, as another feeling being, totally here for us."

"Are you going to open the door? Do I get to see your dear little faces again? Do I get to see that gleam of hope, that hint of a smile that says you want this too, that you know I'm doing the right thing?"

"Look, I'm scared too. If I haven't told you that, I'm sorry. *I'm very scared.* This is as hard for me as it is for you. We have to deal with the whole big mess of it and go through all the bad stuff again, but this time we'll go through it together. You bring me the memories and I, as an adult—as you girls all grown up—will help us understand. We *can* do this. No matter how painful, we can handle it. So let's get started, okay?"

July 25, 2002

"We have to conquer the fears and the first one appears to be *fear of me*," I say, as a new day dawns with no contact from my silent sixteen child selves. "I'm not someone to be afraid of! That's like being afraid of yourself, your own shadow. And I know that feeling, I know that kind of all-encompassing fear, but we have to get beyond that, we have to *trust*. We have to trust each other *in all ways.*"

"We mustn't be shy with each other or with Chuck. The shyness has to go; it only gets in our way. It was another of those protective barriers that we could always pull around us when we needed to, but now we're dismantling the barriers. We're opening the doors. There must be nothing between us and the truth."

"So, yesterday, I left you alone for most of the day, how was it?" I ask.

"Lonely."

"*Lonely*, you say?"

"Tremendously so!"

"*Tremendously so*?" I ask, incredulously, because I really don't want to hear that, but at the same time I'm thrilled to finally make contact. "Look, I don't want us to stay in this lonely spot; we've already been here too long. We need to talk and we need to get into a better place. We're strong, smart, sensitive, and we can work this out. We're not going to get hurt by our abuser anymore.

We may have to go over the memories again, and we will feel them, but they are not real. They're only memories and they can't get us. And once all the memories are fully known then they will be even less painful, in fact, they won't affect us at all."

"Come on," I say, encouragingly, "we can do this together. Don't you feel my arms around you, hugging you tight? Don't you feel my warm love filling you? Is the hurt and pain still so great that we can't feel anything else? I want us to feel love. I want us to feel safe. I know it won't just happen, that it takes time, but I have hope that the lifelong emptiness will be filled. It's part of the natural healing process. It's part of becoming whole. But I need you to open the door and come out."

"I know your feelings. I know how sore and physically hurt you are. Yes, I do. I know all the mental anguish you suffer. I know all the feelings you are holding back. I know all the words you haven't spoken and all the tears that are unshed. I know, because I was there with you."

"I went into the woods with him. I went into the barn. I sat in his truck. I felt the humming of the beehives. I walked in the orchard. I was the little girl he did all of his sick and disgusting things to. I was there. I am you. We didn't even know what he was doing. How could *we* be to blame? We knew it was bad, but *we* weren't bad. It was him all along; *he* was the bad one. We were so innocent. I too was the slave girl he tied up and stuck his tools into. I too had those raw chafed ankles, the sore vagina, the throbbing pain in the anus. That was me; all of you are me."

"I had to get away from there. That was how I survived, so I could someday go back and get you. I know it took a long time. It took forever, but that's because he did such bad things to me, horrendous things that I had to bury so deeply in order to move on into adulthood."

"You had to be so strong, but I had to be the strongest of all," I tell them, and in spite of getting no response or even a hint of acknowledgement I keep talking. "I'm sorry I had to leave you back there in those memories. It might seem heartless, but we never would have made it otherwise. But I never gave up. You know we don't give up—we never gave up—we aren't quitters, so don't quit on me now. We need to talk and work this out. You need to let me talk for all of us. Our inner dialogue needs to be spoken out loud in order for you to emerge, for us to finally become one."

"I'm going to get ready for my day now," I say. "We'll go to yoga class. We'll talk to a group of art students. Girls like we once were are coming to visit the studio. We'll work on our writing jobs and our other commissions. We can still talk. We can talk all day, but please open the door so we can talk face to face—just us for now, just you and me."

"Oh, this is good!" I say, as a light appears, as I detect the door opening a crack. "We're getting somewhere. I'm glad to know that you're all fine."

"We're off to yoga now," I say, "It'll be great, you'll like it."

And it's fine up to a certain point. We start out with a gentle caring breath, gathering and giving compassion to ourselves, hand pressed against the heart. "This is good," I think. "Perfect! Couldn't be better." A little while later, on hands and knees in table pose, I'm hit with a sudden urge to flee. I don't think I'm going to be able to get through the class. I have a sudden and desperate need to leave the class and my body too. I imagine getting up and walking out. I imagine saying, "Sorry, I can't do this today." But I tell myself to just get a grip, that it'll be all right, that I can handle it. As if I'm cracking open and breaking apart, a tremendous force rolls through my body, leaving me breathless. When I stand up to go into the next pose I realize they're gone, the door hanging wide open. No one's there! The girls are gone! "Can't be, they're just hiding," I tell myself. "Don't think about it now." But by the end of the class, I know it's true—they're gone. In a moment of panic, they skipped out. As thoughts of fleeing coursed through my body, they took their cue. Granting me my wish they ran out the door. I could just about sense them scampering across the room and swiftly disappearing down the hallway. But where did they go? Certainly not back there, never back there to the bridge! But where are they?

It feels so empty, this empty box of my heart, door wide open, dusty inside. I'm empty and lonely without my girls. Maybe it was too much all at once; maybe they just couldn't handle it. Is this going to keep happening? Am I going to lose them every time something disturbing surfaces? Where have they gone, back into the past or into the future? And I don't like the door flapping open either, the hollow box, the emptiness inside. I want them back. We need to talk about what scared us. I think the answer is pretty clear that it was the pose, that extremely vulnerable position, and one of my abuser's favorites. It has so much pain associated with it.

Warm brown wood flashes through my vision. I sense golden brown, painted or stained wood, and I wonder if the girls are signaling to me where they've gone. Surely not to the barn, they'd never go there again. Besides I'm sure they've gone to a cozy and safe place.

"So, okay girls, wherever you are, I'm sorry," I say, as I lie in bed at night, waiting for sleep and dreams to come. "I didn't realize you were so sensitive, but of course I should have realized that. I know you! But you have to remember that I'm new at this. I'm not totally sure what I'm doing. I may be a grown up, but even grown ups have a lot to learn; learning goes on all life long. So let's ease up on each other, okay? When you're ready to come back, I'll be thrilled to have you. And we'll take it slowly, one step at a time."

"I do know why you ran today. I was ready to go with you, but you left before I had a chance to tell you it would be okay. I know it's hard; it's hard for me too. But we have to confront all those scary things and we need to do it together. I need you and you need me. Wherever you are, I'm sorry. Please come back. The door is open, and I'm waiting for you."

July 26, 2002

I dream that I'm traveling along on foot, empty-handed and barefoot, with no belongings and no sense of where I'm going. I come upon a tiny old woman who needs help. She's wandering aimlessly in the road, disoriented. I get her out of the way of the traffic, and point her in the direction she seems to want to go in. Just as I finish rescuing her, however, a man comes along, sweeps her up in his arms and takes her away with him. I watch as he goes striding off with the little old woman bouncing in his arms. I walk along a little further until I come to a house. I decide to go inside and borrow some shoes. There are shoes lying everywhere, but no one will lend me a pair. Many of them are small children's shoes. I wander outside again and begin walking across the countryside, frustrated, but resolved that I will just have to go barefoot!

As soon as I wake up, my hands go to my heart and I sense its emptiness, the girls still gone, the door hanging wide open. My dream seems to indicate that I will have to go on without them, feeling disoriented and frustrated, without personal belongings, though determined nonetheless.

I must remember how severely traumatized my child self was. It's no wonder those girls are constantly on heightened alert; it's how I've lived my entire life. I can't expect to just walk in, announce that I've come to rescue them, and expect them to walk away from everything as if it never happened. I can't expect them to allow me to swoop in and carry them away like the rescuing man in my dream who just picked up the little old lady and took over. It just isn't going to be that easy. The girls bring the repercussions of the trauma with them, the symptoms of PTSD that need resolution, requiring a lot of patience on my part. These are the symptoms I've been dealing with my whole life and if anyone knows how difficult they are to live with, it's me. But the girls will just have to trust that my intentions are good and that I too feel the physical pain, the deep inner hurt, and the sadness. They have to know that we're in this together now, suffering the same remorse and disgust, as well as the same anger, defiance, and determination. I feel it all.

"I know exactly why we have those feelings," I tell them, going into active imagination. "You just have to trust me that we can work this out, but it would be easier if we were together. It would be easier if I knew where you were and if I could hold and comfort you."

"You have to understand that I need comforting too, but that doesn't mean I'm not capable of caring for you. It just means I've gotten to the point where I can acknowledge that I have needs, that I can't do it all on my own anymore, and that I need other people. Everyone needs comfort and love and caring, even adults. It's good to know that. It's not a weakness; it's a sign of growth. So don't be afraid if I seem to crumble a little bit, I'm still here for you."

"Will you come back? Will you come back and learn to trust me so we can work this out? I need you. We can't do this if you stay hiding. Well, we probably could, but it would be much harder. If you come back we can work on it together."

It appears that the girls need to stay away for longer, but the door will remain wide open. Perhaps my heart space is too tiny and cramped, too reminiscent of being trapped underneath the bridge. I just assumed it was warm and cozy and safe there, but I realize that for them no place is safe—at least not yet. Are they ashamed of me for acting all grown up and strong and then panicking at a mere yoga position? Is that a weakness they can't abide in an adult?

The memories still hurt, the triggers are still active, and I still need to roll into a ball, so maybe I'm not ready for the girls yet. Maybe I need to work on a few more things first. Maybe they left to give me some space. But no, they fled at the first sign of a memory they didn't want to have to deal with. They fled at the first sign that I still feel badly about some of the memories—they fled when I became like them again, just another little abused girl.

July 27, 2002

I dream that I'm hiking upward through a white tile tunnel that turns many corners and then begins snaking more steeply in endless switchbacks. Part of the way up, I'm stopped by officials blocking the pathway because a family up ahead had a tragedy and a little girl is dead. I plead with them, saying that I have to pass, that I have a mission. "I need to keep going," I say, "I can't stop." Eventually, I'm granted permission to proceed. I see the body of the little girl, perhaps three years old, dressed in a 1950s style dress, lying peacefully on her back. There are sticks poking out of her chest like arrows. As I pass by someone picks her up and hugs her. I feel terribly sad, but then sense that the little girl is okay. "Don't they know she's okay?" I wonder, as I continue walking up the dank, white-tiled tunnel. I come to a door, open it and step through to a large hotel lobby crowded with people eating donuts and drinking coffee, assembled for some reason. I'm shown to a room where I'll be staying. A man is there, asleep in a chair. On the floor by his feet is a messily wrapped gift, as if wrapped by a child. I know it's a birthday present for him. I go behind a desk and into a small alcove to clean up and change my clothing, and then into a bathroom where I begin brushing my teeth. The man comes stumbling into the bathroom without knocking or introducing himself. "I'm using the bathroom now!" I shout. "You have to get out!" He doesn't seem to even notice me. It's as if I don't exist. Then a little girl comes in. She's about six years old. "We're leaving now," I tell her, taking her by the hand. "It's too weird and uncomfortable here. We need to pack everything up and leave. We'll continue walking up the tunnel until we find a better place."

I wake up knowing that the girls are still gone. The thought leaves me extremely depressed. The death of the girl in my dream underscores their absence and the sadness I experience now, as I do feel as if I'm traversing through a long and winding tunnel, through a weird and uncomfortable process. Yesterday, I didn't shower, get dressed or leave the house. I spent the day writing and reading. I also baked some cookies for the kids, but I'd really love to have a fairy godmother right now. I'd love for some kind and caring angel to swoop down and take care of a few things for me, to just take over for a little while. I just want to stay in bed and do nothing. I don't want to exercise or eat or speak to anyone. I just want everything to go away for a while so I can have a little break.

My husband is gone for the weekend again. When he left last night I felt slightly liberated. And then I found out that my father, on top of his Parkinson's disease, has cancer. My mother is quite overwhelmed. I really don't have anything to offer them and although I wonder what's going to happen to them, I don't even want to think about it, it's too much for me now. I'd like everything to go away. I want to shout at the world, just like I shouted at the man in my dream. "GO AWAY! GO AWAY AND LEAVE ME ALONE!"

Okay, so the girls have been gone since Thursday morning at 9:30 and now it's Saturday night. Lickety-split they took off at the first sign that things weren't right. I'm sorry, but I can't really blame them because I've been feeling the same way. I'd like to take off too, just get the heck out of here, but I have to deal with the fact that I'm an adult with responsibilities. And I can't simply act or react instinctively either, I have to rely on reason to guide me, which reminds me all the time that the threat is only in memory, real as it may seem. I forgot that to the girls everything that happens within my psyche is still real, and I also forgot that they're still scared by things that no longer scare me. I forgot that children react first and ask questions later, if they ask at all.

As soon as I realized the girls were gone, I perceived them being in a warm brown space, and now I sense them sending me telepathic hints, wanting me to rescue them. Images flicker, but I don't recognize anything and I'm not sure if I have to go back into memory or forward into the future and, since I have to guess where they are, it might take some time.

At night I lie in bed, quite drowsy, trying to fall asleep when I'm struck by the thought that *nothing is what it seems.* Just as this insight crosses my mind, a face materializes in front of me. Rather than react in fright, I peer at it intently, trying to figure out who it is. "Is it someone familiar?" I wonder. "Oh, yes, it is! But whom?" And then, like a knock over the head, I get it: *It's me!*

This happens over and over again as I drift off to sleep and then repeatedly startle awake: *all the faces in my dreams turn into me.* Slightly unnerved, I get out of bed and walk around the house. The kids are asleep. The house is quiet. The air outside is very still. The moon is rising, full and bright. I feel like the only person on the planet.

July 28, 2002

As soon as I wake up, I fill the last few pages of my little blue diary with the agony that sweeps into me this Sunday morning. I know why the girls left: *They're just not ready yet.* They don't understand what I'm trying to do. They don't understand what's happening when I get those flashbacks or the overwhelming body memories, when I have to lie down, curl up, and wrap my arms around the pain and the old feelings. They seem to know that something bad is happening and that the thing to do is immediately escape, which is exactly what I've done my entire life. They know the feelings, but they don't understand the language I'm using as I talk us through the experience from my adult perspective. If I say, "he had sex with me," they're incredulous, because that little three-letter word, s-e-x, doesn't accurately describe what happened.

"That's not what happened! Sex? Come on!" they counter loudly from wherever they are. "He took us into a different realm. It wasn't the same world we were used to. And the words we spoke among other kids, or thought we knew the meaning of, didn't exist there. Only his words existed there."

I get it. Sex, per se, wasn't what was happening in my abuser's world and, besides, how could a six-year old equate the violence being done to her with only one little word. My abuser ruled in his realm, spoke his own language, used his own tools, played his own games, and enacted his own evil plans. No words like *sex* existed there; that's not what it was all about. That's a word from a different time, a different world, and I can't take a word from a different world and apply it to what was taking place in that evil world. Evil was taking place there, not sex! So when I use the word sex to describe what he did, it just doesn't fit. In fact, no words fit. It's all caught in the body; the body remembers. But it doesn't remember the words—it doesn't use words—it only remembers the feelings, and when those feelings return the girls can't stand it. So I think they aren't ready yet; they still feel too much. I still feel too much.

Does using that word—*sex*—make it easier for me, the adult, to speak about what happened? Is it a copout to use something so simple to describe something so complex? Am I making it easier for myself by trying to explain, without having to feel? The word *sex* means nothing in the context of that time and what was actually happening to me. It's an adult word and when I fathom it from an adult perspective it horrifies me, because he was actually having sex—vaginal and anal intercourse—with a child! But in reality, that wasn't even what was really happening because what was really happening was that he was killing me! Every time he did something to me, he was killing me, with total disregard for another living creature. HE WAS KILLING ME! And that's what those girls know! They know that he wasn't just having sex with them. They know he was brutally killing them. So I don't think they left because they aren't ready, as I've been hypothesizing. Nope, they left because *I'm not getting it yet!*

I, the adult going through this recapitulation, think he was having sex with me and I get caught in the horror that pops up, in the image my adult self imagines, but he wasn't having sex with me at all; he was shamelessly killing me. Every word he spoke to me was killing me. Every time he touched me, he was killing me. Every time he even looked at me, he was killing me. "He's killing me! Why does he want to kill me? Why is he doing this to me?" Those were the words I spoke to myself when I was a child and those are the words the girls remember. As I left the bright sunny world of childish play and entered my abuser's dark world, the only thoughts that emerged were the incessant commands, coming from somewhere deep inside me, telling me to just get through it, to live through it, *to survive the killing*. And then, like an obedient apprentice to the master, I did whatever he told me to do, in order to LIVE. I learned that fighting back could be worse that not doing anything at all, because if I fought back I knew I could die. But if I did what he wanted, I would live to walk out of there, out of the darkness of his woods, back into the light and real life. Killing and death were obviously two separate realities; even my child self was aware of this. Killing was pain and torture, but death was final.

I crack open a fat new journal, fresh white pages waiting to be stained with the bloody anguish of remembering. By the time this one is filled perhaps I'll have worked through this entire recapitulation and on the last page I'll write: *yes, finally it is done—I have evolved*. But for now I will continue this research process, plodding along from phase to phase, from one agony to another, wondering where my excavations will take me next.

By the end of the day, the girls are still gone. The door is wide open, my heart space empty and dusty, but I now know that they'll be back *when I'm ready*. Now I know they're waiting for me, waiting until I fully accept and understand, until I get over my shock.

"Don't you get it?" I hear them saying, from wherever they are in the universe. "You grew up and got away, and you conveniently forgot what happened for so long that now you have to really struggle with it. IT HAPPENED! Get that through your thick head! What else do we have to do to get you to accept that truth? You are so stubborn!"

"Yes, I'm stubborn. I wouldn't be here if I wasn't so stubborn," I reply. "So okay, back to this morning; I did acknowledge that you left because I haven't fully accepted the truth. You realized that I wasn't ready. Well, maybe I am ready after all. Maybe that last little thread of hope is thinning to nothing, my last hope that I had a perfectly normal childhood. Ha! That's a joke! I know I didn't. I know it, you know it; and I know I don't like to hear about it because my first reaction at the mere hint of a memory is to take off running. But yes, of course it happened! So don't worry, I'm getting there. I really am. I'm getting there."

July 29, 2002

Dear Little Girls,

I need you to help me remember. I get to lots of the details and I even get to some of the feelings now, but I need you to be there with me while I recapitulate, so I will eventually be able to move on. If I stay stuck here, only half-believing what happened, I'll never grow. I want to grow—I need to grow—I have a whole life ahead of me. Please be with me tomorrow when I meet with Chuck; help me talk and feel and hurt and cry. Please don't desert me now. Now is when I truly need you. Nothing new will happen if we don't connect again. I won't progress unless I can barge through this half-believing stage and fully accept what took place, and I need you in order to do that. Please don't leave me now.

You are the key to finishing this recapitulation. You are the keepers of the memories and the pain, but I'm the one holding everything back. I'm the one who pushed everything away, locked it up, which was necessary at one time, but no longer. And so, I give you permission to unlock the pain and let it release with the memories even though they still horrify me daily, gripping me and making me ill. I shudder and shake as I hold them back, even though I know it's not the way to do it anymore, that this work is all about letting them go through me, which I've been doing a really good job of, but there's so much more still to release. You girls hold those memories too. And so I ask that you be with me tomorrow, if not back in the place in my heart at least present when I meet with Chuck, so I can tap into your knowledge of the memories. Please don't leave me stranded half way to believing. We've come so far; we have to keep going. I'm not going to stop, so please don't you stop either.

Yes, I'm afraid, but I'll deal with that. I know my abuser can't get me anymore, but it's the fear that's bound up in all those memories that keeps me tied to him. His evil and my fear are so tied together I can smell them, so tightly wrapped, a huge black ball blocking everything. I have to keep tearing at it, pulling it apart bit by tiny bit, and I can only do that with you, in your presence. I can't do it alone because I don't know enough. I'll only learn the complete truth if I have you there with me. I'm only whole if I have you.

We didn't cause any of it; we have to remember that it wasn't our fault. He did what he wanted, over many years. We were so young and innocent, uninformed as to the ways of the world, making it possible for him to entice us into his dark world. We came away bruised and hurt, but we couldn't ever come away with an explanation or logical reason for what happened—it just happened. It happened because he wanted it to happen and he made it happen. We had no choice and no voice. You saw my little niece, how innocent in her naked play, too young to think or understand such evil. That was exactly when he got us, when we were too young to understand, when we were innocent. We still have so little experience of what innocence really means. We had two years of infancy before the shattering began. How could such a young child ever have been whole?

Come on, I beg you; we're almost there! We can do this! It's time to let go of the evil predator, to exorcise him so we can grow now. We can't grow if even one gripping thought of our abuser is still present. Even in memory he takes up space and energy that belongs to us. I don't want him creeping around inside me any more, in any form. I don't want to be caught in his black web any more. He's a foreign entity, an alien presence, a petty tyrant, and we must be rid of him. I now know that only by facing my own truths, with utterly focused determination to get rid of his energy, will I be released from it. And you, my dear little girls, hold the keys to unlocking the last doors and freeing us. And it needs to be now. NOW!

Some of us are meant to have traveled this path through sexual abuse; we just have to figure out why. So please be with me, my little girls, so I can figure this out. My life won't ever be my life if we don't keep doing this recapitulation. And, if you think

I can't handle this, well, think again. I intend to handle this. I intend to confront this over and over again until my abuser's energy is no longer a threat to me. I'm starting now, and tomorrow, with Chuck's guidance, I'm going full steam ahead, tackling this like never before. I only ask that you please be there with me. I admit I'm afraid, but I'm not going to let that stop me. I'm not going to let anything stop me, especially the fear, because that would mean my abuser wins, and he's not going to win. I'll win. I'm going to win. I'm going to grow and become that successful person I always knew I would be. Now is the time.

Thank you, girls, for listening.

I'm tired now, needing sleep, this being in two worlds is exhausting! I wait for tomorrow to come. Will they help me? Will the girls be there, at least in spirit?

July 30, 2002

Tuesday! I'm so glad it's finally here! No girls though, or at least I don't sense them yet, but there's still time. "Will you be there with me? I need you," I say while getting ready. "You think I should do this on my own? You're not going to help me? All right, I'll do it on my own."

"Let's do it," I say, sitting across from Chuck in his little office. "Let's get to work, but first I have to tell you about something that happened to me."

"Okay," he says.

"It was just an ordinary Saturday morning at the local recycling center," I say. "I was standing at a recycling bin putting some stuff into it when a very large greyhound dog came up to me and laid its head against me, resting it in the socket of my hip. It started communicating that it knew I had been abused, just as it had been. It was telling me how sorry it was that I had to experience such pain, that I had to suffer, and I was saying the same thing to it. We both acknowledged that it had been a part of our pasts, but that now it was over. It was telepathically spoken, sensed, communicated from this sad old dog to me, and back again. We just knew what the other was saying."

"You know what I mean?" I pointedly ask Chuck.

"Yes," he nods, "yes, yes, yes."

"I also knew that the dog was a sign that it really did happen to me, that it was telling me to accept the truth of it, to not back away from it, but to keep accepting what I was learning about my past. It was urging me to keep going and to heal, as it had done. The owner kept pulling the dog away, apologizing. 'He's never done anything like that before, how unusual,' she said. But I said, 'No, really, it's okay,' not minding at all. In fact, I just wanted to stay there like that, tenderly patting the dog's head, feeling its energy. It was really pretty cool."

Telling the story and receiving Chuck's open response to it, makes it so much easier to do what I have to do, to go back into the memories, to experience what I need to experience, and speak about the horrors I encounter there. I feel safe, as empowered by the retelling of the story of the dog as I had been by the original experience, and so, without missing a beat, I barrel ahead.

"Let's do it!" I say, just as I had told the girls I would do, and then I talk and I can't stop talking.

The energy of the old abused dog is inside me now, speaking through me, and I almost laugh when the Doggie game memory reappears. I'm able to acknowledge that it didn't happen just once. I suspect my abuser did it until he'd worn out his fascination with it. As I recapitulate it again, I see that sometimes I was the mommy dog and sometimes I was the puppy. I think it hadn't been fully recapitulated and that's why the memory of the Doggie game popped up so often.

"It's not over yet; I'm not through with it yet," I say to Chuck. "Because right now, just thinking about it makes me feel sick. I'm shaky and my teeth want to chatter and I need to make that little puppy snarl, halfway between crying and growling. I can't quite release it, but I feel it sitting there, waiting for me to let it go."

I sense that the girls are with me as I recapitulate. Chuck offers the time and the space to do this work, but the girls are with me every step of the way, making me stop and look at the details. They make me go back again if I miss something important. They make me feel myself as a child, and they make me see and feel what I've been missing.

"Why are you forcing me?" I ask them at one point.

"We're not forcing you, you are. We're not pushing, you are. We're not holding you back either, you are."

They make me see that I do have to keep going back there, to relive the memories again in order to be done with them, once and for all, in order to become whole. So I do it, I go back over and over again. All of us—Chuck on the EMDR machine, the girls inside me, and me utterly determined—are in synch, hellbent on doing this recapitulation. The girls know I can handle it, and Chuck and I know it too. We all understand that I must keep going back until I'm fully done, knowing that the fear and panic will dissipate each time I recapitulate.

The girls tell me that I knew what to do with my abuser, how to play his games, because I did them often enough, like in the bathroom with the hairbrush. When I go back into the bathroom I'm four years old again, just a robot under his control, but I know what's coming because it happens often enough. I just go and stand by the window, as I've done so many times before, my hands and knuckles turning white as I grip the empty towel rack. Once again I feel his hands on my hips, adjusting me so that my butt sticks out so he can do what he intends. Part of his fascination seems to be in watching objects going in and out, whatever he has on hand, like the hairbrush in the bathroom. He always watches closely.

The scene suddenly shifts and now I recapitulate the stick that he used in the Doggie game to give me a tail, looking like a cut-off broom handle or a wooden hammer handle. As he shoves me into the ground, I'm shocked, thrown partially out of my body by what he's doing to me. He holds me tightly while he jams the stick in, using petroleum jelly, the smell of it sickening, making me gag. Once again I hear his grunts, his strange, whimpering doggie sounds as I hang onto consciousness, staying in my body, urged to fully recapitulate this time.

I keep going back. As painful as it is, I know I have to discover every little detail, so there won't be anything left to attach to. If there's anything left, even the smallest particle, like doubt, it will continue to haunt me. I need to sweep clean those awful memories, to exorcise them from my psyche.

"I need to finish with the Doggie game memories, then the tools, and then the slave girl memories," I tell Chuck as I come out of recapitulating. "Right now it feels like I'll never be done, but if I can do what I just did then maybe I can just keep knocking down the memories, one at a time."

"Okay," Chuck says, looking at me kindly.

"My girl guides are with me," I say, sensing his nervousness about the intensity of the experience I've just had, knowing I have to get up and leave his office in a few minutes, but I'm still fueled by the same determination as when I'd started. "I see and feel their encouragement, urging me onward, encouraging me every step of the way, showing me what I've forgotten. It feels good to have such great guides. When they tell me to go back and look again because I've missed something, I know that even though it's painful it's also necessary."

"Exactly," says Chuck, looking somewhat relieved.

"It's okay, they say, we're with you. Go back and look again; you've missed something. You don't want to miss anything. It'll never leave you if you gloss over something, they say. You need to look at it as closely as he looks at you while he's doing these things. You need to look at it with such intensity that your eyes burn holes in it, so the heat of your stare burns it into oblivion."

"Yes!" Chuck says.

"They tell me I need to stare at it without a doubt in my mind, that I need to study it and then let it go. It doesn't need to stay inside me. Once I've studied it intensely, and fully understood it, I won't need it anymore. They tell me to let it go then and move on to the next memory and do the same intense scrutiny of it, understand it, and let it go. This will take some time, because sometimes the memories are too intense to comprehend at one glance, it may take several visits or numerous visits, taking in small bits at a time, until I can handle it all. We know that eventually I'll be able to handle it all."

"That's why you're still so gripped by many of those memories," Chuck says.

"Yes, they're incredibly painful, intense and intricate. And many of the games happened more than once with slight variations, so they are multilayered. My girls have become true guides through this process, telling me that it went on for a long time and that it's a painful thing I'm doing, that it's brave work, that not many people actually choose to do this so eagerly, with such determination. They tell me I'll be rewarded for all my hard work, that one day I'll be whole, free, full of light and life and love. And that's enough to keep me going for a long time."

When I leave Chuck's office, part of me stays back there, still half in the memories. Several hours later, a new lightness descends and I sense those most awful memories fading. I know that as I recapitulated today, I saw things and felt things I hadn't seen or felt previously. Perhaps I've fully recapitulated those memories now; perhaps those pictures are complete.

"Thank you for bringing me back there," I say to the girls, as I prepare for bed. "Thank you for helping me to see what I needed to see in order to finalize what happened. I already know which memory to work on next. We need to keep moving ahead, to keep chipping away, until all the doubt is gone, until all the memories are mere faded photographs, just pictures that can't touch me, can't hurt or give me pain or fear. That is the biggest project of all, to get rid of the fear."

I keep thinking that I'm almost there, almost at the end of the memories. Every stage feels like it will be the last, that the end is in sight, and then all of a sudden I'm deep in another phase with no end in sight, or at least not for a long time. But I know there will be an end, that one day the end will come. The girls keep telling me there will be great freedom when that day comes. I trust that and I'm trying not to be too impatient.

I need to take care of myself while I'm doing this recapitulation. The dog at the recycling center told me that too, that I need to still remember that I matter, even while I go back into those memories and into a time when I did not matter at all. And although anger and impatience can sometimes be a good motivator, wearing myself down won't be a good thing, the old dog told me.

Something old begins to seep into my body as I write, bogging me down again, a sign that I need to put this journal down and go to sleep. I cut my inner process short and turn out the light.

Sheer terror invades in the night. It creeps into bed with me and puts its hands around my neck. Once awoken, I am wrestled into submission, overcome by physical and emotional horror. I have no control! No visuals, no memory pictures arise—just the intensity of my abuser's barbarity slipping between the sheets—the reality of his evil intentions making me ill. Like an actor in some horror movie, I lie in bed gagging and terrorized, but beneath the surface of nausea I feel too many memories brewing, too many feelings struggling to surface all at once, telling me this is no movie script.

It's too much to handle so I get out of bed and walk through the dark house. I step out into the fresh night air of the backyard, and then sit on the stoop, just breathing and staring into the night sky until I feel sleep pulling me to return to bed. It's almost as if the work I did today has fueled my abuser's anger, but I won't be intimidated. I shake out the blanket and slap the bottom sheet hard, flicking his energy away, and then I crawl back into bed and beg for peaceful sleep.

July 31, 2002

I wake feeling somewhat better but physically tired, as if I ran too many miles, worn out after the energetic tussle in the night. I intend to take it easy today. Yesterday I felt possessed, caught in the intent of the recapitulation, and I couldn't stop it. All normal thinking was suspended while I met with Chuck. I was carried along by the intent I'd set and by the time I left his office I was in a trance. It turned out to be a good thing because I ended up much lighter and more hopeful than I've felt in a long time. But today, I feel the need for distraction.

I go for a run, take a shower, and eat breakfast, intending to spend the day with the kids. I try not to think about what happened in the night, determined to keep the panic at bay by staying fairly active. I notice that if I slow down the terror takes over again, so I keep moving, but it takes over anyway, though I constantly shift and flick it away. "Get up! Go! Move!" I command myself. "Make it go away by moving! Don't stop!" Writing in this journal helps dispel the terror. Writing helps process what was happening then and what's happening now.

Suddenly it dawns on me that the little closet in my heart where I'd put the girls, with the door that I opened and closed at will, was my invention. I'd put them there so I would know exactly where they were at all times. When they left, it was only because it wasn't the best place for them to be—for my sake—and they knew it, but I didn't. By putting them there I was restricting and controlling everything, when they're really in charge. I see that now. They had already assessed the situation and knew that I couldn't do this alone, and also that I needed them to speed things up. I'd pictured them scampering out of the yoga studio, the way I imagined myself leaving, but they never really did leave.

Yesterday, when I was doing EMDR at Chuck's, I suddenly had a very clear picture of the back of that little closet in my heart center. There's another door, a little wooden door, painted a golden brown, opening right into my deeper heart center, a warm and glowing place, and that's where they are. The whoosh of energy I'd felt rush through me in the yoga class must have been them, going deeper. They never left.

They're *in* me; they *are* me! They represent all those lost years. They're not separate or lost or gone. In fact, they guided me through the whole ordeal the other day, pushing me on, saying, "Let's do it." It was them talking from the moment I arrived at Chuck's. Spurred by the guidance from the kindly dog at the recycling center, I felt totally safe and confident.

I believe the memories are going to come directly from them now. It started already last night, memories of terror and my abuser's disgusting games. The girls are giving me those memories and feelings because they want me to believe them now. "No more disbelieving," they say. "No more doubts. This is how it feels! And this is how it feels! And *this* is how it feels!" They're deep inside me, intensely focused and determined, and careful as well. I'd asked them to stay with me and although they weren't where I'd put them they were where they needed to be. They're telling me what I need to work on, what's important, and what isn't. They're pushing me forward. "Keep going, keep going!" they say, and I see the scars on my ankles again, white and puffy, those embarrassing slave girl scars. I was a slave girl in a past life.

I am deep in the memories, but when I'm there they aren't memories at all, they're real events happening all over again. Not to some other girl or to some other person, but to *me*.

Chapter 2

Reviving Daphne

August 1, 2002

Caught in the whirlwind of a dream tornado, I awaken dizzy and nauseous. Struggling out of bed, I throw some clothes on and go to my appointment with Chuck. I have no appetite, no desires of any kind, and no energy whatsoever.

"Where do I go from here?" I weakly ask, my enthusiasm for the recapitulation process pathetically depleted.

"Well, where would you like to be?" Chuck asks.

"I want to be totally carefree, able to live without fear, without constantly being on heightened alert. I've had enough of that. I want to feel safe and happy in my own body. I don't want to be afraid all the time, like I am now. I don't want to be afraid of life."

"Hopefully," says Chuck, "you'll soon get to the point where you can go back to the memories, not because you're being pulled, but because you choose to go back. Then you can look at them without the horrid feelings. You'll be able to view them without attachment. You'll be able to view a part of your life that will no longer have a strong hold over you the way it does now. That will be freedom."

"If anything," I reply, "I'm intent on turning all of this into a creative endeavor. If anything good comes out of this, I want it to manifest in a creative outpouring."

I watch the natural path of the sunlight in Chuck's office while we talk, because the other day I'd had an experience I couldn't explain or even dare to address at the time. We were doing EMDR when an intense white light, as if the sun were staring directly into my face, appeared out of nowhere. There was no heat associated with it, however, only an inexplicable brightness. I experienced it at least twice while I was doing EMDR with my eyes closed. So bright was the light that I felt it would have blinded me had I opened my eyes. I wondered if Chuck noticed it too, but then I wondered if he was doing it, perhaps holding a flashlight as part of some new EMDR treatment technique. For some reason I couldn't find a way to ask him about it. I seriously considered that the question might be too much for him. Then I wondered if I was really only protecting myself, because I didn't really want to question it. I thought perhaps I was supposed to learn something from it, though I wasn't sure what. I definitely felt an energetic presence very close to me, but when I finally dared to open my eyes the light immediately disappeared and I saw that Chuck was sitting in his chair. He still had his clipboard in his lap and the EMDR controller in his hands, no sign of a flashlight, and no sign that he had gotten up out of his chair. I'm convinced that what I experienced was something mystical. There is no way that such an intense natural light could have been on my face anytime during the early morning session. The light in the room is very diffuse. My back is to the window, and there are no other windows or reflective surfaces to create a glare. It's equally impossible for such a bright light to have come from behind Chuck. I wonder if it was Jeanne Ketchel, come back to work with me again, for her energy has been noticeably absent for some time now.

After feeling so raw, actually ill in the morning, I'm in better spirits as the day progresses. But all day I fight the urge to crawl into bed and pull the covers over my head, the urge to sleep for hours or even days, maybe even until Tuesday when I see Chuck again. I fight the urge by keeping the memories at arm's length, letting myself ponder the mystery of the light instead, wondering if it really was Jeanne.

August 2, 2002

"No." This is the first thing I say when I wake up in the morning. I say no to my brother when he calls asking me if I can take my parents to a doctor's appointment. "No, I can't," I say. I can't, not because of the time, the distance, work, or losing the whole day, but because of everything else, because I'm only half a person right now. Because I need to preserve the other half for me, keep her to myself. I need to be free for a while, detached from family and commitments. I need to take what I'm learning about myself inwardly and study it in total solitude. I need to say no. Almost instantly I regret it. I plummet into feeling bad, guilty like a little Catholic schoolgirl. I should call him right back and offer to meet them at the appointment, say that if he can get them there I'll stay with them and take them home. But I don't, I can't.

I set the intent for stability over the weekend ahead, more determined than ever to transition through it without inner crisis. I decide that no matter what comes out of the past to haunt me, I'll handle it. The kids are spending the weekend with their dad as part of our every other weekend agreement that has been in place for the past year. Although we're all living in the same house, we've been able to establish certain boundaries as part of the separation agreement and we've been able to uphold them, for the most part, because I disappear to the studio. I have work to do, so I'll be fine. I have this journal and my own well-established coping techniques and resources that I've honed and utilized throughout this transitional period. By keeping busy and moving, I'm determined to get through the next few days in one piece.

I do some yoga and then, still lying on the floor in *shavasana* I notice how very relaxed and in control I feel. I'm positive I can handle anything. I wonder if now is a good time for a little recapitulation. "Okay," I say to the universe, "give me something! Let's see what comes up." Well, as soon as I see what comes, I know I can't handle it: an image of Slave Girl lying staked to the ground, her legs pulled wide apart. "No!" I say, immediately rejecting the memory, though I realize that in my cockiness I'd asked for it.

"What a jerk! I really can't do this now," I say. "I guess it just goes to show that I get what I ask for, but, sorry, I can't do it now. Back off!" And so I push the image away because I want to be in a happy, calm place. I decide to go to my safe place instead, established last year as I began this recapitulation, to the meadow on top of the mountain behind my grandparent's house from where I could see for five miles on a clear day. I go there in my imagination, as I once did in reality as a teenager, and immediately feel happy and good. Turning from the memory that had spontaneously appeared, I forget about the bad stuff. Instead, I lie in the golden meadow and feel beautiful and safe, the warm sun licking me clean. Even though I know what lurks in the shadows of the woods and what waits for me at every turn, right now—in this moment—I feel *incredibly safe*. Before getting up off the floor, I set the firm intent to get through the next few days without incident, to retain this feeling of safety, but as soon as I stand up I'm in a daze, already feeling some crazy pull.

Driving isn't safe, but luckily I make it to the studio in one piece. I have the place to myself, my studio partner out for the day, and so I decide I'll just camp out for as long as possible, letting the strange energy of the day rage on without me, though I wonder what's coming. I sense I'm between worlds again, in the nebulous vagueness of recapitulation, partially in my studio and partially back there, in the past, the shadow of the predator's woods reaching out to grab me.

I wonder if destiny is predetermined or if it's the end result, the place we end up after everything has fallen into place, after we've made our choices. I know that in order for meaningful things to happen we have to keep moving. If we remain stationary our chances for things to intersect our paths are miniscule. If we're constantly moving, constantly placing ourselves in the path of other constantly moving objects, the chances for interactions and synchronicities increase. If I stay in my house and never go out, nothing will ever happen to me. How could I ever reach my destiny in that case? I guess I'm answering my own questions because I know that as I step outside each day I open myself to a multitude of experiences and I already know that without experiences there is no life. Exposure to life brings experiences, which in turn brings new life. To be unafraid of life means to be unafraid of experiences, which means to be unafraid of *exposure* to life. I'm getting to that. I've opened the door and stepped out of my familiar house of self, my old self. As much as I feel the need to retreat back inside, to close the door and hide, I'm not going to do that. I'm out now, and I'm staying out. I'm living my own destiny in every choice I make, choosing it with each step I take.

Children need to be protected, diligently, for many years. They need to be respected, appreciated and tenderly taught, carefully guided and loved, but then, when the parenting job is done, it's important to let them go out into the world alone. All children have their own lives to live and their own destinies to engage. As a parent, the thought of sending my children off into the world both thrills and frightens me, and yet I know my job is to keep preparing them for their launching into adulthood, for that moment is really the beginning of their own journeys to self-discovery and maturity. Even though they must turn to me for guidance now, I have always experienced my children as individual beings, totally apart from me in many ways, holding so much promise and potential.

From my own experiences in childhood, I know that children have extremely complex thoughts going on inside their heads all the time, as they constantly struggle to figure things out, but that they are limited by a child's capacity to reason. The world they live in is limited, only so big and only encompassing so much. The larger perspective of the world and the interconnectedness of everything will come later, but as young children they live in a microcosm, largely set up by the parents they got. Something that an adult might consider as a simple fact of life often looms as a massive indecipherable confusion to a child.

In my own case, to diffuse the confusion, I elected to live in a dream world most of the time, creating a much-needed escape from what circumstances had to offer. Each time I daydreamed, I landed in a much nicer world of my own imaginings. As it turns out—I find out now—I nurtured some fabulous shamanic abilities by going into daydreams and trance, which I find out is more than just a skill to get through traumatic times. As I see it, the memories are like little tests that reawaken all the skills I'd once used, helping me brush them off and hone them to perfection again, so I'll be able to use them in the future, and perhaps learn some new techniques too.

I take a break from my work, write down these thoughts and then sit on the sofa and do the sweeping recapitulation breath, seeking to clear my head and ease the sensations of strange energy that I've been feeling all day. "Breathe in you and breathe out all the poison that's related to your abuser," I hear Chuck saying. "Do the sweeping breath when the bad memories come, breathe them out, sweeping clean and emptying out."

As I breathe, I ponder my abuser. Questions arise. What do you call someone who liked to do it in the rear end with little girls—a bastard, a devil, a sicko? Such words are too mild. Perhaps he was a son-of-a-bitch or a fucked-up-motherfucker? All too tame! There seem to be no words to describe such a barbarian, such an inhuman monster. Over and over again, as I do the sweeping breath, I feel the stick-tail of the Doggie game getting hammered into my rear end. Over and over again I see my abuser's face, so intent on the disgusting task he's given himself, to do this to a child, as if the child had no feelings whatsoever but was merely a plaything. I know why small children crawling around on the floor pretending to be doggies or kitties, woofing and meowing, used to make me cringe and gag, used to make me nauseous. "Okay, enough of that game! Play something else now," I'd snap, and at the same time I'd wonder why it bothered me so much.

I breathe the bad thoughts and nausea away. I breathe him and his dirty games away. I breathe the monster away. I breathe until I become a tiny sprite the size of a small pearl. Rising higher and higher with each breath, this delicate energy self eventually reaches the safety of my tongue. Here I sit so primly, my tiny hands touching the white enamel of my massive teeth. I am safely ensconced in the mouth of my body, a covering that means nothing at this moment, for I experience it as mere fluff, a downy cocoon sack, while I sit perched in my head, safe and warm. I can go here whenever I want to. I can go here as easily as I go to the meadow. I can remove myself from the world and my body, and place myself in another, safer, time and place, just as I used to do as a child. I've always had the ability and the control to do this, although I didn't realize what I was actually doing or that it was anything special. Even now, I don't fully understand it. I just do it, as I've always done it, out of necessity, to escape the horrific experiences that no child should have to suffer. "Someday you'll get to the point when you won't dwell on the horrors, when the horrors won't hurt you," Chuck said recently. "You'll be able to go back to that time and nothing will hurt you."

I'm still far from that time; I haven't even uncovered all the horrors. They sit just under my skin, waiting to seep out, to flow through me and into my conscious mind and become real once again before finally going permanently dormant. One day they will lie filed away like tax reports, though just like taxes they aren't something I like to think about very often, but once the taxes are paid they don't bother me. Once the memories are no longer fresh—unknown horrors pulled from their graves—they won't hurt either. But for now, I'm still in the hurting stage, feeling the tremendous pain of those childhood memories, reliving what I've spent my whole fifty years trying to banish, what I've never allowed myself to fully feel. They're bubbling up now, boiling like an awakening volcano long thought to be dead. They're hard to manage, but I'll be okay, for a few days. I'm taking it one day at a time. I'm not such a baby that I can't do that, not such a wimp that I can't hold on for a few days.

I get up off the sofa and go back to work, turning my attention to the intricate furniture painting I'm doing, a commission that must get done, but even so I continue doing the sweeping breath on and off. I return to my safe places over and over again too, breathing and focusing on getting out of the memories for now and into a safer frame of mind. I go to my mountaintop and gain brief respite. I return to my tongue, a little sprite again. And yet, in spite of my intent to achieve distance, the recapitulation is unrelenting. I feel twinges of pain, and I am helpless in the face of these truths speaking through my body. And so I acknowledge that the physical pain of the memories is most intense "down there," manifesting in a real "pain in the ass." Why was my abuser so fascinated with the anus? What was the fixation with jabbing things up a little girl's butt?

"Okay, no doubts," I said to Chuck last week. "No more holding out, hoping it didn't happen. I know it happened."

"Yes," he said. "You did seem to be holding out there for a long time. I'm not sure what it was that kept you stuck."

"I don't know either," I said, "just a hope that it wasn't true, because it's so barbaric. Why would anyone want it to be true?"

"It happened," he said softly.

"Yes, it did," I finally acknowledged after a long pause.

As I recall this conversation, I feel the presence of poor little Slave Girl, her scars showing again, and so I put down my paint brushes and turn to her instead, for I know she needs me to pay attention to her now. Sitting down once again, I do the sweeping breath with intent. As Slave Girl more fully appears, I not only see the scars but also feel them. A lump forms in my throat and I want to cry as I stroke the scars, but I hold it back because crying and tears won't help. The only thing that helps is remembering and then talking about what I remember and then believing, and then talking and believing some more. I know I must go back again and again for the details, all of them, for all the tiny painful details because they are so important, and I anticipate that life and this recapitulation will be easier once the pain is gone. Getting through the pain is the hardest part, examining it, and putting it aside, one painful thing at a time until it doesn't hurt anymore.

I become nauseous as I recapitulate, as I sweep my head from side to side and become Slave Girl once again. I'm sick as I go back into the woods, gagging on the spit collecting in my mouth, helpless because I'm tied down, unable to scream. I'm so FURIOUS! Why is he doing this to me! Why is he such a disgusting person? Why is it that everything he does makes me feel so bad? The memory rolls through me along with these thoughts and suddenly I am erupting like a volcano. In the fire and heat of my own memory, I tumble headlong back into my abuser's world, spitting, gagging, and choking. But it's too much to handle. I am no longer a tiny pearl on the tip of my tongue but a young girl lost in the confusion of a moment of agony.

I stop the sweeping breath and rush back into my cool body, back into the present adult me, far from the smells of the woods and my abuser, far from the fires of the volcano inside me. I'm just not ready yet.

August 3, 2002

In a dream, I'm riding my bicycle with the intention of delivering my daughter's artwork to her school, to someone named Rose. When I arrive at the school, I find it crammed with people. I get lost in the crowds and am unable to find Rose's office. When I ask people for directions no one seems to understand my question, they just stare at me as if I'm speaking a foreign language. "Does anyone know where Rose's office is?" I finally shout loudly and clearly. A woman points to a tiny office. I peek in the door and see Hopi *Kachina* dolls lined up on top of a desk, maybe fifteen or twenty of them in all shapes and sizes. I notice that there are no books or papers in the office, just these dolls. I put my daughter's drawing, a beautiful watercolor of a full moon, on top of the third doll from the left. When I had spoken to Rose earlier, she had specified that I should put the drawing on top of the third doll, but it wasn't clear whether she meant the third doll from the left or the third doll from the right. I leave the school building and get back on my bike. As I begin peddling I look down at my legs, surprised to see them pumping so vigorously as I ride swiftly away.

Curious to know the meaning of the dolls in the dream, I look up the word *Kachina* as soon as I wake up. Kachina literally means *life bringer*. The dolls, representing powerful spirit beings, are treated with utmost respect among the Pueblo cultures of the Southwest, foremost among the Hopi. Representing natural phenomena and spiritual beings, archetypal as well as cosmic forces, they are often used to educate children in the ways of life, in all worlds, seen and unseen. Most importantly they represent parts of the uninitiated self that if not interacted with and integrated during the course of a lifetime might lead to a failure to survive. Perhaps they represent my sixteen girl-selves, lined up waiting for me to recognize them and fully accept them. The dream is somewhat mysterious to me and the significance of putting the moon painting on top of the third doll eludes me at the moment. Yet, at the same time, the dream feels right on target with where I am right now, as I straddle two worlds, trying indeed to interact with and integrate all my fragmented parts.

Fragmentation began early. My childhood world had already split into two totally separate and distinct worlds by the time I was two years old. The one of family was fairly normal. It's the one that's talked about, stories shared about, remembered by everyone in the family, to a certain extent at least, because we were all there. The second childhood is so dark and secretive that even I didn't remember it until I was old enough to bear the truth of it and wise enough to know that it was important. So hidden and mysterious, it was a world that I entered alone, so only in my own memory is it real. Both worlds were, however, *equally* real, though they were never simultaneously real. Both shaped and influenced who I am today and who I was in the past. But those two worlds, once so separate, are like planets colliding now.

No longer parallel universes, those worlds have been revealing themselves to each other over the past year, brushing up against each other in inner-galactic collisions as I do this recapitulation. As each memory appears, those worlds crash into each other, momentarily as disoriented as I am, before they spin back out into space. Once back in their separate orbits, they wait for the next moment of collision while simultaneously reasserting the intent of this shamanic process: to fully reveal themselves. Everything is shifting and moving, forced to change because I elected to take this recapitulation journey. There's no stopping it, no putting on the brakes. This is a natural course that nothing can stop.

After collision, I hope for integration and the seamless fusion of my two worlds, but for now I must deal with the debilitating confusion, the smoke, debris, and fury of those moments of collision. When in the midst of a recapitulation experience, it's almost as if I'm inebriated or on drugs, dizzy and groggy, not fully grounded in this world, unable to see clearly. Often I'm living in those two worlds simultaneously, which creates this confusing state, or I'm split between them, part of me in one world, part in the other. So disoriented am I that it's hard to know where I am sometimes! Driving is especially challenging. Yesterday, I was in such a fog while driving to the studio that cars seemed to appear out of nowhere, objects and people suddenly materialized, as if I were driving through a misty dreamworld. Honestly, my awareness in this world is dulled while it's quite heightened in the other. I realize it's a dangerous place to be. I must constantly struggle to stay in the present as I'm pulled more fully into the past.

Part of the challenge seems to be to find a way to integrate the two, to be fully functional in both worlds. The everyday world appears so dreamy at times, but only because I'm so deeply immersed in the other. I can't close up shop and walk away from this life nor can I ignore the truths of the other; they are equally important. I must continue the merging of worlds; continue on the collision course no matter how intense it becomes. I must battle it out and fight through to the end because in the end there will be greater things to come. I have no idea how I know all this. It's as if I'm becoming clairvoyant, because I see everything so clearly spread out before me. I see the future, full of creative activity like never before, but there is also calmness and light. There is life waiting for me up ahead, and there is surely love too.

The more I ponder the light I experienced in Chuck's office the other day, the more sure I am of its realness, in an unreal sense perhaps—a light from another world. When I recall the intensity of it, I know it was no earthly light. Nothing, not even sunlight, could be that intense, that brilliant, that blinding. It was *pure* light.

I've had more mystical experiences recently than I've ever had in my life, or perhaps I'm just finally noticing them. They're as real as the hands in front of my face, yet they cease to exist as soon as I've experienced them, fading from reality, yet not from knowing. I'm discovering that experiences matter above all else, for they lead to *knowing* and that is, I have no doubt, what's important. It's becoming easier for me to admit that I am as fully capable as the next person of having truly spiritual experiences, without feeling that I'm special in any way, because there is no sense of self when in the midst of them. My ego is largely absent and I'm almost in a state of grace, without even realizing it. Until recently, I didn't understand such experiences, and often they were more frightening than informative because they were due to trauma, as I've learned. Now, as I realize that my spiritual experiences were triggered by events happening in this world, I understand that this world is, quite frankly, the launching pad to other worlds.

From a young age, I intuited that my soul belonged to me alone. I found it difficult to accept the strict laws and teachings of the Catholic Church, which I considered soul binding, offering so few possibilities, so few choices. In fact, the religion I grew up with never fed my spirit; it only fed my fear. However, in spite of the restrictions placed upon my spirit by my Catholic upbringing, I most certainly traveled in other worlds, I see that now. And maybe I *had* to go into a real hell to gain access to those transcendent experiences.

Now I'm working on freeing my mind of the ideas, rules, and expectations placed on me by that Catholic Church and the world I grew up in—a world I no longer agree with—that *foreign installation* that Chuck speaks about. How can I truly abide by the rules of that world when I know that the worlds I travel in are as real as it is? How can anyone else know what's right for me, or dare to restrict what kinds of experiences I can call real? I'm totally capable of deciding for myself the meaning of my experiences in the context of a life fully lived and fully explored. I'm more than capable of assigning them value, based on the journey I've already taken and the journey I envision for the future. I will not allow my imagination and my other-worldly experiences to be dampened or hampered any longer. Looking back, I see how restricted my life has been because of the rules of society and what was thought good for me. To be free—in body and soul—is all that I want now, to be free of the repercussions of the memories and the confines of what the Church, society, and my family taught me in my earliest days. I long to go forth into new life totally freed of guilt, cleansed and pure. And to do that I must break with what was long ago planted in me, when I had no recourse but to absorb it. Fear has continually encumbered me—fear of what others could do to me, fear of being punished for disobeying, fear of what might happen if I dared to think for myself and be different. Now, as I elect to break all the old structures I've been so confined by and all the pacts I've made, I'm giving myself permission to fully embrace all my experiences as real, as deeply and personally meaningful, without fear of judgment, ridicule, or contemptuous dismissal.

As a young child I loved being clean, fresh out of the bath, totally cleansed in body and soul, my sins sent swirling down the drain with the dirty bathwater. Dressing in a pretty dress and lovely princess shoes solidified the moment, etching it in memory. Few of such memories exist, but as I recapitulate I smell the soapy bathwater again and feel the soft tenderness of my flawless skin— surely a mark of my virginity and purity? I loved being clean and good, inside and out, as pure as I could be for as long as it lasted. And so I would be remiss if I did not acknowledge the Catholic sacrament of Penance, because if there was one ritual of the Church that I found useful it was the Act of Confession.

The telling of my sins was deeply freeing to my young child self who really only wanted to be good. I can just about recite my weekly litany of sins: I fought with my brothers; took chewing gum or change from my father's pocket without asking; had bad thoughts; didn't do my homework; ate candy (which was strictly forbidden in my family); lied to my mother, etc. Given absolution, I'd walk out of the confessional trying to remember how many Hail Mary's I was supposed to say and the other prayers of repentance I was charged with reciting. Invariably, as soon as the priest spoke the words, "I absolve you of your sins," I'd forget everything he'd just told me to do. I'd agonize on the long walk back to the pew, figuring that it might not matter if I doubled the number of Hail Mary's. Eventually, I'd feel like I had prayed enough and I'd get up and walk out of the church a cleansed soul, blessed for as long as it lasted. There was just something in the ritual itself that purified me, even if only temporarily.

The effects of such an innocence-giving ritual did not last long, nor did I avail myself of it for very many years, for it soon meant nothing to me. But, at the time, I knew that if I died at the moment of absolution I would instantly go to heaven instead of the hell that I expected to burn in for life everlasting. Everything I had done was magically washed away in the confessional and I could start over, a brand new girl. I could be the perfect child my parents and the Church thought they had in their midst, the innocent child who didn't know about male devils and their devious games. But once the light of absolution and the glow of the bath had worn off, once the crispness of the ironed dress had wilted, I was back to being a dirty, nasty, fucked up little girl again. It wasn't long before I'd be reprimanding myself, wondering why I thought I could possibly be considered even remotely clean, pretty, and sinless. Such a silly idea! Purity and good feelings never lasted. I was a sham, a shameful sham, merely tricking myself and everyone else too, though I longed for the return of such feelings, for the clean pretty lightness of no sin and no sin to come.

August 4, 2002

I'm in a public restroom in a dream. The toilets are dirty and so stopped up they can't be flushed. The doors of the stalls don't close or lock. There's no privacy whatsoever, but I have to pee and I don't care if I'm exposed. It's okay. It simply doesn't matter, I decide. A young girl standing nearby is unhappy because some other girl was obnoxious and mean to her. I calm her down, telling her that the other girl is greatly disturbed and that she has her own issues to work on. "She doesn't mean anything to you," I say. "Forget her. She has her own lessons to learn, just as you have yours."

In another dream the phone rings and when I answer it I hear a familiar voice. "Hello, it's Chuck calling." "It's you; it's you! You're back!" and I'm so happy to hear Chuck's voice that I cry.

In a third dream, I'm walking on a beach. I see a small horseshoe crab burrowing in the sand. I pick it up. Turning it over, I see my face and body delicately etched on its underside, so frail and tiny. As I stare into my face it begins crying; contorted with pain, it weeps uncontrollably. The shock of it wakes me up.

August 5, 2002

Slave Girl is most pressing today. Once again I see the ankle scars so clearly. I also notice that when the memory recedes so do the scars, but as soon as the memory surges again I am suffused in its physical symptoms and the scars pop out again. I recall having abdominal numbness and my period being late when I had recapitulated the memory of being pregnant at the age of twelve. As soon as I was able to acknowledge the truth of that early pregnancy my delayed period came, and it came as if I had indeed just given birth, in large dark clots. Now, as I feel the pressure from Slave Girl to go into her memories, the pale scars left by the ropes that tied her up are glaringly apparent. I tell my inner girls we have to wait until Tuesday to fully recapitulate this emerging memory, though I know they want to get it over with. "It's time now, it's important," they tell me.

"But I need Chuck," I tell them. "I can't do it alone, I don't want to do it alone anymore. We're strong; we can do it, we can hold on for one more day." I promise the girls that as soon as we get there, I'll let Chuck know that this memory is pressing, that it's urgent. The memory is incomplete at this point. I have only shadowy glimpses to go on right now, as no bigger picture is coming through. "Tomorrow we'll begin to piece it together," I tell the girls. "We'll look at all of it. Tomorrow."

Truthfully, I'm weak and ill just thinking about working on it. I become small and helpless again as this memory signals its approach, bringing frightening bits and pieces of my past, encased in a thick cocoon of loneliness, dusted with the ancient musty smell of my abuser. I remind myself that all the girls are with me now and that we're doing this together. We're doing this because we're hellbent on becoming the person we've never been allowed to be. That's the real reason we're doing this recapitulation, not because of the memories so much, but because of what they're blocking access to: *my wholeness and the ever-present mystery of just who I might really have the potential to become.*

Feeling lost and intensely quiet inside, I sense the need to be alone today. I work quietly at the studio, not saying much to my studio partner. Flashbacks come in tumbling confusion, as if I'm peering into a kaleidoscope, images swirling together as I work. I know I have to slow it down and look at each image separately. Only then can I make any sense out of it. Until then it's merely a jumble of sight, sound, and feeling. I'm eager for the day to end, knowing I need to allow this memory to slowly begin seeping into consciousness in preparation for my meeting with Chuck. Even though I've told the girls we have to wait until tomorrow, they can't help but tell me some of their secrets, so long have they carried them. As soon as I lie in bed at night they begin whispering to me, not in malice, but only seeking relief, the relief of knowing that soon we will talk. They know I can't do it alone, that I need to wait until I see Chuck, and so I tell them I can't listen now.

I cover my ears, pressing so hard that soon I hear only white noise, the ocean waves rolling on the shore. Pressing harder still, I push the horrors down where they came from; back down where I can control them for just another few hours. Please let tomorrow come quickly!

August 6, 2002

The day has finally come! I meet with Chuck at our usual early morning time. I notice that he looks really tired, but I immediately shift my eyes away him, telling him that I have to go right into a memory. I put the EMDR headphones on, close my eyes, and immediately drop into darkness where I see and feel my feet tied to a crowbar that's holding my legs apart. I feel the weight of it digging into my ankles. My heart dislodges as my abuser hoists me up and onto his back. The crowbar lies across his shoulders while I hang like a sack of potatoes. I hear him talking, mumbling like a crazy man, as he paces in circles, my hair dragging in the dirt. I hold in the sounds of my fear as he hangs me upside down in a tree. With dread in my heart, I watch him prepare his tools.

From my present adult perspective, I see that my abuser was very strong. I weighed very little, always small and thin, "skinny as a beanpole," my grandfather used to say. But it wouldn't have mattered how much I weighed, he would have found a way to do what he wanted to do. I hear the clanging sound of the crowbar as he throws it into the back of the truck afterwards, the sound of iron hitting the metal truck bed making a frighteningly deadening sound. As with many of the memories, I'm able to recall the beginning and the end, but nothing in the middle—the moment of entry into his world and the moment of exit always the easiest parts to handle. But I know there's still a big gap, the unknown part still waiting, and if I don't recapitulate it I'll have to bear the tension of it for another week. And so I don't hesitate, but go back into the memory several more times, letting it come in scattered bits and pieces, until I don't want to do it anymore. I'm so tired of it all. I don't want to go through another scene. I take the headphones off in disgust.

"Here it is only nine o'clock in the morning and I'm already exhausted," I say to Chuck. "I'm drained—drained and stunned."

Emotionally numb, I leave Chuck's office and meet with a real estate agent to go look at a house. It's a cute little place in a family neighborhood, affordable and not too far from my ex-husband; in fact the kids could walk to his house in the adjacent neighborhood. Still stunned from the morning's recapitulation, yet knowing that this is where I must live, that this is the little house I have imagined for us, I numbly make an offer. I qualified for a mortgage months ago, so there's nothing hindering me. I sit with the agent and fill out the paperwork with little feeling, except a mild sense of relief that I'm able to function at all. I notice that I'm emotionally drained, with no sense of joy, no sense of accomplishment as I commit to this transaction and set my new life in motion. Before the day is over the agent calls, saying that my offer has been accepted. In the evening, I bundle the kids into the car, telling them I have a surprise for them.

"See that little blue house over there?" I say, pulling to the side of the road. "Well, it's ours."

"Really, are you kidding?"

"No, I'm not kidding, I just bought it."

"Yay!" they shriek in utter, spontaneous joy, and they love it immediately.

"We'll make it a fun little house, we'll make it ours," I say. "See, it has a nice yard, a large garage, a newly paved driveway. We'll make it work. It's just the right size for us. It will be great."

I hear relief in their joyous cries and clearly see it etched on their smiling faces. I see tension melting away and I know that the idea of imminent closure is exciting to them. They want to know what's going to happen next. They want to know what their life will be like, that everything will be okay. They need to get settled, they need to be happy. I do too, but right now I feel how important it is that I make this move happen for them, for they are most important. Still stunned, but greatly relieved, I marvel at the way things are unfolding.

August 7, 2002

Thoroughly depressed, I don't want to get up. I just want to stay in bed. As I fight my usual morning inertia, I try to get excited about the house. There are so many things to do, loose ends to tie up: finalize the mortgage, lawyers, inspections, planning, repairs, and much more. But that's not why I want to stay in bed, that's all so simple compared to how the girls and I are feeling. I told them that I'm tired of the memories and that I don't want to go into them any more right now. Yesterday, as I recapitulated, I felt so bored by what my abuser had done to me. I'm tired of his games. It felt like the same boring things just happened over and over again; no wonder I left my body.

I'm empty, lonely, and sad, and even though I have the girls with me now, they're being very quiet, letting me do the work on my own, letting me find my way. They aren't pushing now, but I know they're with me. I can't linger here, depressed and sad, lost in a daze. I have to make decisions and forge ahead no matter what. I need to be a mother to my own two children, come out of my recapitulation and be here for them, dealing with this life, leaving the old stuff percolating under the surface. Let it percolate; it'll keep, it'll still be there, and my inner girls will still be there too.

It's time to get everyone up and start the day, get the kids to their summer camps, get to work, get planning what comes next, and deal with the emotions as they come.

"I just wanted to tell you that I'm happy about the new house," my daughter says, as she prepares to leave for the day.

"Yes, I know you are, honey. I know," I say, my heart going out to her, deeply loving her for taking this difficult journey with me.

I contact the mortgage broker, set up an appointment to meet with him next week, and then start gathering all the paperwork, confident that everything will continue to work out just as I've envisioned it. I'm surprised all over again how even in the midst of the dissociative state I was in yesterday, I was somehow able to make an important decision and buy a house, though I was barely present. The kids are happy about it, though it will be a few months before we move in. We'll be fine living there for the next seven or eight years while they finish school, then we'll see. A lot can happen in seven years.

In spite of all that I'm dealing with on a personal level, I had previously committed to curating a show at an artist's cooperative gallery that I've been involved with for several years. I've spent the past two days and nights setting up that show and it has given me plenty of good distraction. Last night, I even went out for a bite to eat afterwards with four other artist friends who are also in the midst of divorcing. We laughed and laughed, which felt really good, but a little pathetic too, hysterical almost. We're all on the verge of collapse while simultaneously open to embracing new life. None of us are sure what's coming next, but we're all in the same place: standing on the edge of the abyss, daring ourselves to take the leap.

August 9, 2002

In a dream, I'm walking through a dark forest with my two children who are small once again. Eventually, we come out of the woods into a bright green pasture. The setting is beautifully pastoral. Everything is etched in sparkling light, the colors vivid and clear. The field stretches off into the distance where it meets gently rolling hills. We're happily chatting as we step out into this peaceful setting. "Okay," I say, pointing off to the right. "We're going to walk across the field in that direction." We start running across the field, feeling totally free and unburdened. We're enjoying the vibrant beauty of the landscape when all of a sudden the field changes into a bridge. Now we're running on a bridge, though there's still plenty of green grass sloping down on either side and even growing in sections on the bridge. Every few feet there are metal grates that we have to cross. I'm a little nervous as I watch my daughter run ahead. This bridge doesn't feel as comfortable as the field had. It doesn't have the same quality of groundedness, nor of pastoral peace and beauty, in fact it feels quite derelict.

Patches of tall grass hide where the grates are and the only way to know that we are actually coming upon one is that we hear the sound of traffic coming from the highway beneath us. "Oh, we're not really in the country at all," I surmise, as I look down through one of the grates and see black asphalt far below. When I look up again, I see that a large suspension bridge has risen in front of us, and beyond that, clearly etched on the horizon, I see the skyscrapers of New York City. I'm a bit confused as to where we actually are now. Growing steadily more concerned, I watch nervously as my daughter leaps over a wide grate and lands on the big suspension bridge. I don't want to inhibit her sense of freedom and yet I'm extremely nervous. I'm not sure if it's really safe to be so innocent and happy. Suddenly, she takes three big carefree leaps and bolts right over the bridge railing, disappearing before my very eyes. I hear her screaming as she falls. Unable to do a thing to save her, I nonetheless want her to know that I love her. "I love you! I love you!" I try to shout as loudly as I can, but nothing comes out of my mouth. Then I hear a loud SPLAT and her screams abruptly end. I run to the bridge as fast as I can and when I look down over the railing I see her body lying on the asphalt. I know she's dead. "She knows I love her though," I think, "I'm certain of that, even if she didn't hear me calling out to her." I reach out and grab my son, fearful that he too will fall. As I clutch him to me, I wake up to find myself clutching my covers. I'm in agony. My mouth is open wide as I attempt to cry out, my daughter's screams echoing through me.

Try as I might I can't shake the dream and the terror of the moment. Distraught, I remember how Chuck taught me a long time ago that I could fix my dreams, so I decide the best thing to do is dream a different outcome. I fall back into fitful sleep and back into the dream, right at the moment of walking out of the woods into the field. Once again, I experience the freedom of running across the field of bright green grass with happy abandon, but as soon as the bridge appears I halt the action. "No, we're not going that way," I say. "It doesn't look safe." We turn away from the bridge and head back into the green field, walking in a different direction this time. It feels lighter and happier and not so uncomfortable now that the terror has been averted.

Even though I fixed the ending of the dream, I still spend the day with the horrifying image of my daughter flying through the air to her death. It replays over and over again, accompanied by her final screams. I can't get either the images or the screams out of my head. They plague me, even though I know the dream is really telling me something about myself and not her. I think it's about my fears, but it could also be about the little girl in me, finally daring to be happy after being so fearful and emotionally dead for so long. She's so carefree in the dream and yet I, the adult self, can't fully relax and enjoy the freedom. I carry too many memories of situations not being safe. The need to proceed with caution still instructs everything I do. In spite of the fact that I did something daring yesterday and bought a house and saw my own children react with joy, I wasn't able to release my old inhibitions and fears, even in the dream. Was the dream asking me to, or was it showing me what will happen if I do, that I will fail in some way? Or was it showing me where I'm still caught?

I think the latter, because although the dream started out with good feelings it soon turned bad, just as things usually did when I was small. I was feeling so protective and maternal in the dream, so happy with my equally happy children, and then I felt so guilty because I let something bad happen. In the dream—as I am wont to do in real life—I blame myself. And now I find myself caught in the horror of awful guilt. I want us to be happy; I want my children to be able to trust that I'm making good decisions for us, my inner children as well as my real children. But the image of my daughter leaping off the bridge has me stuck thinking that I've failed them all.

Perhaps my old fears just had to pop out in this dream because I so determinedly kept them at bay yesterday, leaving them in the dissociative numbness of recapitulation as I went ahead and took the next step into new life. One day, I anticipate that I will indeed leave the old fears behind, though not in dissociative behaviors but because I am totally freed of them and will no longer suffer either fear or guilt upon release of them.

As the day goes on, I return repeatedly to my dream. I notice the utter peacefulness and contentment of the moments of running in the vivid green field, and I let myself go back to them and thoroughly enjoy a few moments of bliss. A sense of lightness and awe are imbued in the stunning brightness of the fields, contrasting with the weighty darkness of the woods we've just emerged from. Once again, I realize that my daughter, in the dream, represents me as a little girl. Feelings of self-hatred arise again, as I despise myself for not taking better care of her, for not warning her, for not protecting her. I bear the sense of guilt that surrounds the momentary joy, the release of running carefree in the field ending in disaster. This is an old scenario: I'd let myself feel contented, let my guard down, and invariably something bad would happen. I hear the old voice once again, "Don't get too happy," it reminds me. "You get too happy and he'll get you; you feel too safe and he'll get you again. So don't let yourself enjoy too much. You're never safe. There is always punishment to pay for the experience of too much joy." I let that little girl down and I let myself down too. I am to blame—always. That I didn't protect her, didn't save her, is a persistent belief.

Okay, so in light of my own life story, I do know that I was too young to save myself and I could never have protected myself from my abuser. I didn't realize the danger; it was impossible to know of such evil at such a young age. To combat the negative feelings and beliefs that have arisen, I meditate into a dissociative state until I am totally detached. It's so easy, and it feels good too. I seek the distance and the utter calmness it brings.

August 10, 2002

In a yoga class, sitting in meditation, I suddenly gain a deeper insight into what is happening inside my heart center as I take this recapitulation journey. As I envision the door to my heart opening up, I'm led through an entryway and then down a steep stairwell that leads into a deeper central chamber. It's full of the warmth and soft glow of my deepest self. This is, I understand, my *energy center*. I basically have control over it, though I am also greatly influenced by what comes from without. I see its flame spark and spit when a disturbing thought arises and I watch as it returns to a small steady flame as I go calm again. I understand that as I do yoga breathing and postures that spark old issues or memories, my inner flame responds in accordance, flaring up at the least bit of tension.

I test the premise. Upon thinking of my abuser, I see my heart center turn heavy and dark while the flame immediately flares up. The rest of my body goes cold, numb, and unfeeling. I'm able to reduce the flame by changing my thoughts to all the little girls I hold inside, physically going lighter and calmer as I feel my love for them. I not only see the flame reduce, simmering down to a soft glow, but I also feel its warmth and calmness spreading throughout my entire body.

I understand that during especially demanding yoga classes the inner flame actually comes to my rescue. For instance, as I do yoga poses that mimic the old games I played with my abuser, such as being on all fours, my heart center might signal that it's time to erect a shield, a barrier to block feelings. It's an old technique, learned a long time ago to keep me from falling apart, though its far more devastating consequence is that I have suffered from an almost total lack of feelings. I push all feelings away in an attempt to thwart the ever-present threat of annihilation. I understand that in doing this recapitulation, I am not only reviewing repressed memories, but I am indeed learning how to feel again. The far greater knowledge I gain in this meditation is that I have full access to the control panel regulating my own feelings. I play with the flame a few more times, flaring it up and then turning it back down to a soft glow again. I understand how it works now. I realize I've always had access to it, and that my body and psyche made sure I was protected when necessary. However, I'm in a different position now, and learning how to personally regulate this main energy center is going to be a life-changing and extremely useful skill as I go forward on this journey.

I know that everything will be all right as I train this energy center and make it work for me, both as I do this recapitulation and as I do life in general. It's what I've worked with in meditation for years, though I never quite understood it as clearly as I do now. While poking around in my heart center, I don't actually see the girls, but I sense their presence. They're quietly staying out of sight, somewhere behind the flame, working the bellows and gently urging me to tackle the next issues that arise. I understand that they've presented me with this scene, that they're well-versed in how inner energy works, having had many years to study and utilize it themselves. I realize that they've been protecting me all these years too, that they've been taking care of me as much as I've been taking care of them—we've been protecting each other.

As I come out of the meditation, I clearly understand that the main issue I must face right now is my sense of guilt around the abuse, most importantly the sense that I somehow let it happen, as well as the strong judgmental premise that I should have somehow stopped it. The other issue that constantly arises regards my fears, which remain numerous. I'm still afraid of people, of having to deal with my emotions and feelings, and I'm still afraid of intimacy. In addition, I greatly fear the memories still to come.

Guilt is deeper than the rational mind's grasp of it. I cannot erase the guilt simply by intellectually understanding that it wasn't my fault. I completely understand that the abuse happened because I was groomed from innocent toddlerhood, and that I had no choice in the way things unfolded. Young and innocent as I was though, I still feel tremendous self-guilt. The guilt is not necessarily in thinking that it was my fault, so much as the fact that I partook in the abuse. I was a participant in deviant behavior, so by default I am guilty. Whether or not I had a choice is not the issue. For me, the greater issue is that I was actively partaking in disgustingly sick activities. I was there! I realize that at the time my feelings were deeply conflicted and confused. I didn't know how or what to feel, and so I sought to protect the most tender feelings and emotions that arose, thus allowing guilt to arise as a partner I could always count on. And so it emerged to play a necessary and important role in my life, perhaps keeping me safe from the real truth of what was happening, protecting me in a most unusual way.

Guilt is a known, tangible, easily talked-about cover for sin. If you are guilty then you have something to feel guilty about, thus you are indeed a sinner. I could give my bad girl self a sinful persona that fit into the Catholic mold. Guilt I could live with. I could pour all my badness into my feelings of guilt, masking what was really happening, the real unmentionable sin that there was no possibility of talking about—sex. In my guilt I became just a plain old bad girl. "I'm a bad, bad, bad girl," I'd tell myself as a young child, and it was true because I knew what a sin was—an everyday topic in Catholic school—and I accepted that I was indeed sinful. It was taken for granted in that milieu, as well, that we are all sinful until repentance and absolution of some sort are performed.

I was involved in the worst thing imaginable, the thing no one talked about. Sex or sexual abuse weren't acceptable subjects of discussion or normal dinner table conversation. And although the dinner table was often the place where my mother doled out her discipline—most often regarding such mundane matters as negligent schoolwork, laziness, or mischief we'd created in the neighborhood—and although she'd often zing us with something startlingly private, sex and the deeper issues of life and how to navigate it were never mentioned. It never mattered anyway. When I was in my childhood home, sitting at that table, the dark world of my abuser was completely lost to me. I simply knew I was a bad girl.

I think guilt became a most acceptable mantle, an almost saintly persona, something to wrap the trauma in, giving it a place to hide out. I could hunker down in tremendous guilt and stay that way, feeling justified that I was being rightfully punished for my sins, while simultaneously holding a place for all the bitter truths I just could not know yet. It may take a long time for those feelings to wash away, and just hearing Chuck say that it wasn't my fault, that I was groomed, that I had no choice, doesn't really sink in. No matter how many millions of times I've said those same phrases to myself, I still retain the bad feelings about myself.

Now, as guilt comes draping its dark mantle over me once again, I sink into a cavernous hole filled with murky black slime. I recognize it as the mass of disgust that sits in the center of my being, where it has long smothered the inner flame that I recently visited and enjoyed discovering. This cesspool is the badness, the tremendously guilty feelings that weigh me down. This cesspool of slime has grown and festered for so many years that it's become a monstrous black tumor that I must somehow remove, shovelful by shovelful. In each shovelful I must face the guilt I carry: I am guilty of not protecting all those little girls. I am guilty of letting them be tricked, kidnapped, and raped. I am guilty of letting them go back to him again and again. I am guilty of desertion and neglect. I am guilty of keeping them hidden, locked up to rot. I am guilty of starving and suffocating them. I am guilty of wanting to run away from them as fast and as far as I could. I am guilty, guilty, guilty.

This is not simple lightweight guilt. I know what that is. My friends and I used to steal apples from the orchard. We'd tuck our shirts in and then fill them with as many apples as possible. It was fun. There was a slight sense of danger about it because we knew it was wrong. Somehow we avoided getting caught and we always ate the apples and enjoyed every bite. Maybe I did feel bad about stealing the apples—for a little while. But that was easy-to-deal-with guilt. This other guilt is heavy, black hole-in-the-soul guilt. No matter what I say, no matter what Chuck says, I still feel tremendously sad and deeply guilty about what happened. "How could I have let it happen?" Guilt arises as soon as I ask that question. I wonder if perhaps the adult self is the problem here, the one who won't release the mantle of guilt. After all, it's the grown up self who keeps asking that question. Meanwhile, the child self was just trying to survive, to just get through the abuse, walk away and never let anyone know. Her intention was to go back home like nothing ever happened, pretending that everything was normal, to just be and act normal. It was her salvation, the thing that kept her together until the deeper forgetting came to the rescue.

Okay, so here I am now, the adult, full of guilt because I couldn't help or protect her, which is kind of absurd because I wasn't there yet. I had to grow up and become a thinking, caring, protective, loving, maternal person in order to come back now and take this journey of true absolution. So instead of feeling guilty, I should be forgiving and understanding, thankful that I'm here. I know I need to comfort that little girl self who survived, while at the same time, I need comfort too. But the adult me must find new, healthy means of comfort, and let the guilt go!

August 11, 2002

I went out again last night, after the opening at the artist's gallery, with the same group of people as the other night, the divorce group. We're all a little sad but very caring, and I felt us starting to feel safe with each other. I got home late, made some peppermint tea and read until two; I just couldn't sleep. I got up at four to let one cat out and the other in, then up at five again, then back to sleep until 8:30. Now I wake up feeling like I need to stay under the covers, but I get up and make some coffee. I bring it back to my room, telling the kids, playing video games together, that I'll be in my room all morning. I haven't been running lately—my knees have been cramping—and just as I started wondering if I was going to begin having knee problems I realized that the knee pain coincided with the emergence of the crowbar memory. I'm going to test that theory as I begin running again, but not today, today I'm staying in.

My work got a lot of attention at the opening last night and a lot of good comments; people seemed to really like it and derived pleasure from it. I've often enough pondered what the meaning and significance of my life could possibly be. Not much of anything has ever factored into the equation except the fact that I'm an artist. I always thought that if my artwork made someone happy, if it brought joy or offered a different perspective, or changed someone's way of seeing the world, then it was well worth it and my life was not a total loss. And so, when I saw how people were enjoying my work last night, I was satisfied with this artist's life I've cultivated. Perhaps there's meaning after all, I thought.

I noticed men looking at me last night too, someone's husband, a man who's interested in my work, a stranger or two. At the deepest level it made me uncomfortable, while at the same time I thought: "Yes, go ahead and look. I look pretty good! Even compared to most of the younger women here I look pretty good!" But to me the looks from men always feel so blatantly, nakedly sexual, as if they're undressing me as their eyes roam up and down my body. It's unsettling. And the idea of a man someday touching me is also unsettling, the thought of someday having sex—unnerving! I'm positive that if I had sex today I'd also have a major flashback, triggering the worst physical and emotional trauma. I see myself collapsing into teeth-chattering growling pain and probably having a mental breakdown as well. I'd be unable to distance myself from the intensity of the experience the way I used to. It's way too soon to even think about having a relationship. I'm deathly afraid of relationship and intimacy, afraid of feelings and closeness of any kind. As much as I yearn for it, I fear it like the plague.

I acknowledge that I was unable to be fully present, fully intimate and available with any of my sexual partners in the past too, unable to share myself completely. "Don't go there, don't reveal who you truly are, keep to yourself, safer that way," I'd often remind myself. "Don't get too close." My private self has always been so vulnerable and frightened; I've had to protect her. Even in my recent long marriage I kept her locked in, unable to share the deeper truth of who she really is. The door in the center of my heart that I've recently discovered was always shut tight. Hidden by debris and cobwebs, it has been locked up for decades. Now it's been pried open, but it could only be opened by me, and not from the outside, but only from the inside. This great opening had to be at the right time and within the right, safe environment so that exposure was as unthreatening as possible. So now, with the door open, the inner flame that gives me life and creativity, my innocence, is exposed for the first time in fifty years. It's taken major work to get that door open, and it's taking major work to keep the flame lit and safe. A fire needs air and fuel, it needs tending, and this is where my focus is now, though I find it's still too early to talk about this most vulnerable and tender self.

Being extremely busy this week has given me some relief from the onslaught of memories and some much needed quiet, as I've gotten some distance from the incessant battering that has pretty much gone on constantly for the past year or more. As soon as I elected to do this recapitulation, I opened a different kind of door, a door to the past, as cobwebby and dusty as the door to my heart, to memories so deeply buried I had no recollection of them whatsoever. But in opening that dark door to my most secret inner self, I also found my most tender self, my innocent self. I've been too distant from her. I'm glad to finally have that connection again; tentative though it is at this point.

It's strangely familiar and comforting to be in the position I find myself in, at long last connecting to a well-known self. Lost in the muck of the past, held captive by the traumatic events that I've uncovered, I must take her with me now and continue my forward trek. I sense deep satisfaction in this inner work, as difficult and disturbing as it is, and I sense it leading me to something far more eye-opening than the discovery of childhood sexual abuse.

I realize I've become quite adept at asking the recapitulation process to leave me alone for a while, to give me a break, by repeating my trusty mantra: "Not now, not now, not now! Let me do what I need to do, leave me alone for a while." I recently commanded that it back off and I was granted a reprieve, long enough to buy the house, to plan and do the practical things required, and I've been able to get out of bed every morning and proceed on this journey as well, even though getting out of bed is hard. Some days, like today, I just want to pull the covers over my head and stay in the womblike warmth they provide, a safe retreat from the outer world. But I also see the urge to remain in bed as part of my recapitulation, guiding me to remember what it felt like to be my child self, who found such safety under the covers. Now, as I linger in bed, writing these thoughts, I know it's time to turn to my inner girls again.

"Okay girls, so what do you have in mind for me next? Do I get a longer break, or are you going to hit me with something big?"

I sit and do the sweeping recapitulation breath, breathing in me, breathing out my abuser and his evil. Each time I exhale his energy I feel like rolling into a little ball. I want to curl up and hide. I'm in pain as I breathe him out, feeling guilty that it's my fault. "I know it isn't my fault, I'm a child," I hear my inner child say. "A child isn't bad. A child learns from adults. My abuser was bad and he made me carry his badness inside my body and my soul. He gave me the guilt. I didn't assume it on my own. He was bad, not me, not a little child." I understand this more fully now as I breathe back and forth, as I push through the feelings of pain and guilt, breathing the stench of his badness out of me. "I'm good and pure and clean and innocent," I say, as I breathe in my own good energy.

As I breathe, I imagine my heart center opening up and spilling out all the stuff that he put inside me, all of his tools, his sticks and ropes, his breath, his semen, his sweat, his smell. I watch as everything spills out the door of my heart, tumbling down the front of my body, gushing out, a river of ancient pain and torture. I let it run freely. But what do I do with it all? Do I burn it? Do I prepare a ritual fire and send everything up in smoke? I already have a fire going in my heart center; maybe I should just burn it right here? I could torch it as it appears, light it with the flame of my own rekindled life and watch it burn away, fanning the flames with the sweeping breath until I'm breathing like a flame swallower.

On second thought, I don't think I really want that evil destruction going on inside me or near me. I don't want to be contaminated by the evil air or the evil gases, poisoned by the blackened residue. Instead, I go back to his place in the woods as I do the sweeping breath, only this time I'm in charge. I hack away at the stumps he used, the trees he made me climb, the branches and beams he hung me from. I begin to pile everything up. I put the ropes, the tarps and blankets, the sticks, tools, crowbar, the hairbrushes, the bobby pins, the metal hair curlers, the pipes, the towel rack, and the doggy tail onto the huge pile and then I toss him, my abuser, on top. I realize I've just constructed his funeral pyre. I calmly step back and set it alight from my own heart flame.

WOOSH!

I fan the flames with the sweeping breath as the girls and I watch the enormous bonfire, with him in the middle burning and shrieking. The red flames lick the sky, reaching far beyond the treetops. He can't escape. He's weak and helpless, an old man with barely enough life left to hold his own dick and pee. We are stronger than him now, much stronger. As we feed the fire with more sticks, I suggest that the girls get rid of all those ancient bits of clothing they've been holding onto for fifty years. "We don't need any of it," I tell them. "We know what happened, we know why we had to keep them—to remind us—but we don't need them anymore. Toss them onto the fire. Throw those pearly buttons on, that shred of diaper, that white sweater, the little plaid summer dress, those turquoise pants, that stripped dress, all of it, including the pale pink graduation dress." The girls and I stand around, quietly watching everything burn as I continue doing the recapitulation breath, breathing in my own energy and breathing out the foul air of him. My intention is to keep the fire going for a long time, to make him burn in the hell he created for me. I want him to burn for a long, long time.

I stop the breathing and sweeping motion of my head and sit calmly, waiting to see what else emerges. I cover my face with my hands and close my eyes. In the warming darkness in the palms of my hands a small white face emerges, looking very much like a clay sculpture I recently made, glowingly white, its demeanor innocent. I sense that it's trying to tell me something. I take my hands away from my face but keep my eyes closed as daylight streams through my lids. A silhouette of that same tiny face remains etched on my inner vision. I cover my eyes again and the white face reemerges out of the darkness.

"Come on, follow me," it seems to be saying. I test this vision over and over again, keeping my eyes closed, but moving my hands away from my face then cupping them back over my face. I go from light to dark, dark to light, watching the face fading and reappearing, trying to figure out the message. Finally I get it. "Oh, she wants me to follow her out of the darkness into the light!" And once I realize this, the little white face disappears, mission accomplished.

I continue the covering and uncovering of my closed eyes, curious to see if I can learn anything else. I experience the same sensations of light and dark for a while, of black and white, but then I notice the white changing color, becoming an orange glow and the black softening to a deep purple. A small white moth flutters into the light, its delicate wings sparkling in the orange glow. I notice it fluttering in the darkness as well. As I cup my palms over my eyes, the white moth turns a pale lavender. Fascinated, I watch as it flits about in the velvety purple darkness. The moth appears to be happy, light and carefree. I allow it to draw me into the rich, purple-blue of the dark. I watch as it flips into a beautiful green color, as green as a well-tended lawn, a green that feels good and happy. Now the green spreads outwardly from the tiny moth, overtaking both the light and the dark. The orange and purple colors fade into green as I continue moving my cupped hands toward and away from my closed eyes. Suffused with intense green light, the amoebic energy of my vision grows and spreads, as the lavender moth happily flits about in its ethereal world.

The darkness shifts again and I sense an old evil darkness disappearing and a new beautifully good and safe darkness taking its place. The moth disappears and my vision is steeped in green, purple and blue, a lightshow playing out before my very eyes, closed though they are. I go toward the light, realizing I have the power to shift to the light. I'm also aware that I can keep the funeral pyre going for as long as I need to, that it's a necessary part of this recapitulation process. I can toss the memories onto it, put all the bad stuff there, and I can leave my abuser burning in that fiery hell for as long as I need to. Eventually, however, I will turn fully toward the light.

I wonder if the girls have merged during this process, into that one little face that called me out of the darkness. We all stood around the funeral pyre and watched the flames eating up the past, but that was before the experiences of light and dark, before the white face and the fluttering moth. Are we merged now?

As I come out of this experience, not sure what to call it, I realize I can feel myself again, my physical self. I can touch my skin and actually feel my fingers pressing into my flesh. I'm not a frozen zombie after all! I feel real physical sensations of pressure and release. I'm beginning to unfreeze as my abuser burns on the pyre. The more he burns the more alive I feel. I have this nice little warm body that I can actually FEEL!

August 12, 2002

Asking the memories to wait isn't working today, and yet I don't want to deal with them right now. I'd rather just bask in the warm glow of that funeral pyre, but I sense that I'm being pushed to keep going.

"*You have to,*" I hear a voice saying. "*You can't stop, you have to deal with the memories as they arise.*"

"But why? Why can't I wait until later, until tonight, or when I feel better?"

"*Because you need to get on with your life,*" the voice says. "*You need your life to begin and you will need all of you and all of your energy for that. Your children will need you; your work will need you. You have big things coming your way, but you will need to be free of all this old stuff to fully access them. You must get yourself to a place of calm and quiet, to a point where the recapitulation isn't the main thing on your conscious mind. You must get to a place where it isn't what you go to bed thinking about and what you wake up thinking about. But to do that you need to stay focused on it for a while longer, even more intensely than now."*

"How will I do that? It's already pretty darned intense!" I say, wondering if it's Jeanne Ketchel that I'm talking to, for this conversation carries the essence of her style of guidance.

"You need to let it take the course it chooses," the voice continues, definitely feminine in quality. *"You can't choose; it will choose and you will be taken along. You will learn during the unfolding of the process how to let go of the memories and how to release your energy that is now held captive by them. As this process unfolds you will be happier, naturally happy and energetically light. Right now you're in a physical and emotional lock with the past. It's gripping you so tightly that you can't budge, but even that is part of the process and ultimately very necessary. Until you acquiesce more fully to this process, and to the truth that it knows exactly what's right, you will suffer. Until you acquiesce you will not progress."*

"Okay you win! I'll let go of my old methods of holding. I'll release! You win," I say, acquiescing to the process. "Let's deal with it. Let's see how it goes. Take me where I have to go, you know I'll follow!"

Instantaneously, something happens. Inner tension and jittery anxiety, sure signs that a memory is emerging, immediately kick in and build to a boiling intensity. I give my permission to proceed and, Voilà! Off we go! I recognize this moment of acquiescence, knowing that I have no control—one minute I'm fine and the next I'm thrown deeply into recapitulation—but there is a part of me that still fights it.

"Please," I beg, "I need to deal with a lot of things today, some practical moving forward things. Can't this wait until tomorrow? Please?"

Apparently, once I declare acquiescence, I really don't have any control. No amount of bargaining is going to get me out of this one. For the moment, I feel like I'm wearing a body cast and I can't feel again. So, I get it, the girls and whoever is behind that voice seem to be pushing this thing along; they want this recapitulation done!

"She's right," the girls tell me, pretty much confirming my suspicions that it's Jeanne. "We need to move this along. You need to keep moving it along."

"Okay," I say, as I lie back down in bed and try to relax my body and let my mind go. "Take me, take me where you want me to go." Suddenly I'm back in the woods.

"Why are we here?"

"*Because you aren't done here yet*," Jeanne says.

"What is it?"

"*You'll see*," she says.

"Oh, the log."

"*Yes, the log.*"

There's a fallen tree trunk lying on the ground. I'm naked. My abuser tells me to shimmy along the log, scraping my crotch against it. He watches closely, very closely, as I swing myself along. He sets up small objects that look like pink doorknobs, attaching them to holes drilled into the tree trunk. I see that they aren't quite doorknobs, each one slightly larger than the previous one. He tells me to swing myself over them, like a monkey swinging along, hopping over the knobs. It's a game. The next time he tells me to drag myself over each pink knob before hopping over to the next one, until I've gone down the whole tree trunk of pink knobs, brushing up against each one. He continues to watch very closely. He then instructs me to lower myself onto each knob, pushing each one into my vagina. He pushes me down, bending over to watch, to make sure each knob goes inside me.

"Is it in? Is it in all the way?" he asks.

He's opening me up, each new knob harder to push inside me. After I've been opened up he makes me lie across the log and he has sex with me, in my vagina. Then he turns me over the log onto my stomach and I feel him putting things into my rear end.

"If I ask you to take me someplace else now," I ask my guide, "where would it be?"

Again, I'm back in the woods.

"Why are we here?" I ask.

"There's something else."

"It never feels good here."

I look around in the woods, in the memory. It's like being in a dream, but I have control to a certain extent. I can take my time peering into the darkness, into the gloomy shade of the trees, into the special place in the woods where my abuser has everything set up so we can play our games. I sense my abuser standing behind me, but then I see that there's another man here too! He has salt and pepper hair, an intense, nervous look on a thin face, with dark, deep-set eyes. I hear him speaking softly and gently to me, but his eyes are piercingly hard.

"What a pretty little girl!" he says, his upper lip quivering, his nose flaring, his breathing ragged, none of which are good signs. I'm wearing my sleeveless summer dress, the plaid one with the white collar that I wore in kindergarten. My abuser asks me to show this new man what I do.

"G'wan!" he says, encouraging me.

I stand there for a long time looking at the ground, trying to figure out what they want me to do, until my abuser breaks the silence.

"Take off your underpants and show him what we do!" he commands.

August 13, 2002

I meet with Chuck and tell him about the memory that began emerging yesterday. I say that I stayed with it as long as I could, knowing that I'd be coming to see him today. I put the EMDR headphones on and fill him in on what came through yesterday, and then I don't hesitate a second. I go directly into the woods and face the two men.

My abuser instructs me to hold up my dress. The new man watches intently, as my abuser tells me to go around the circle of things in the woods and show the man what we do. He tells me to show the new man how I hang upside down from the thick rope, how I shimmy along like a monkey and sit on the pink knobs, and get opened up. As I follow his instructions I hear him speaking.

"Trained her like a monkey," he says to the new man.

I see their faces, their beady eyes watching intently, and smell the scent of their greedy arousal. I see their quivering man-lips, as they hold in whatever desire is being aroused, until they can't control it anymore, and then they watch each other have sex with me.

"Where are you?" Chuck asks, as I pull abruptly out of the memory.

"I'm not sure. I feel dead." We sit for a few minutes in silence as I let the memory sink in.

"What was it that made me so vulnerable, that allowed me to become a victim, both then and now? Is it something in me?"

"You want the truth, the way I see it? Chuck asks.

"Yes, of course."

"It's not something in you, but something outside of you that has control. It's something that has a hold of you, of your energy, something you need to fight in order to release."

"Yes, it feels that way," I say. "It feels like I'm fighting something all the time."

"It's a pattern that started a long time ago, but you need to break it now, or it will consume you."

As Chuck speaks, I begin to understand what he's getting at. Although I've been fairly successful at releasing myself from the old patterns of behavior over the past several months, my abuser still maintains a direct link to my energy through the remaining memories and in the repetition of dissociative behaviors. Mostly, it's just a matter of being aware now of how I get caught and how the mesmerizing numbness of dissociation automatically puts me in a vulnerable position. I must not blame my child self; she's just showing me what happened, how the attachment was made a long time ago, and how I've been repeating an old dynamic for many years. Although there was great necessity in establishing those patterns of behavior at one time, Chuck is right, I don't want to be consumed by them. My intention has been set on releasing myself from this predatory energy for a long time now, so each time a new memory arises it carries the same message of intent: *Take back your energy from this memory!*

I tell Chuck about the time I got on a subway in Brooklyn, riding to meet a boyfriend in Manhattan. It was an early summer evening, still light out. I was in my late twenties. I sat down and pulled out a book. A young man sat opposite me, one leg up on the seat. After a while I noticed how fidgety he was and when I looked up I saw he was looking directly at me. His penis and balls were dangling out of his shorts and he was fondling himself. At this point in my life, I'd already lived in many cities and I was used to all kinds of behavior. Men had exposed themselves to me many times before, but this time something was different. I was caught on a subway car and I was paralyzed. "What is wrong with me," I thought, "why don't I move?" But I could not budge from my seat. Putting my face down, I closed my eyes, but this was not a good idea. Everyone else got off the subway at the next big interchange and now I was alone with the man with the dangling penis. Brazenly assured that he would not be disturbed as the subway train entered the tunnel connecting Brooklyn to Manhattan, he masturbated in front of me, ejaculating onto the dirty subway floor. As the car pulled into the next subway stop he smeared the semen into the floor with his sneaker and stood up. With his dick still in his hand, he wagged it at me, laughing crazily as he headed to the opening door. When he stepped off the car, still with dick in hand, an older woman caught sight of him and screamed at him to put it away. Why couldn't I do that? What was wrong with me?

I was mortified and ashamed, and I couldn't shake the incident for a long time. I was only slightly relieved to have not been raped. When it came time to get off the train I could barely walk. Stiff and frozen, I exited the hot underground tunnels shivering, as if it were the dead of winter. I knew then that something was seriously wrong with me; I just could not fathom what it was. Now I know that when that young man acted out in front of me, I was just a four-year-old girl again, numbly facing her abuser.

At the arrival of each new memory, I'm challenged now to refuse the habitual numbing response, rather than embrace it as I've done in the past, as well as to find new ways to disengage from my abuser's alien presence, including all that it has meant to me. I must not only identify how I reacted and still react to challenging, frightening, or disturbing situations, but I must continue the exorcism and break the stranglehold of this old stalemate between my abuser and my own energetic configuration. In a sense we have been locked in a lifelong predatory embrace, like a vampire and his victim. The fangs of this most despicable monster have been clamped into my neck for decades, while I, the victim of his desire, have been numbed into inertia and silence for decades, all of my ability to react drained long ago. Indeed, I became his slave in so many ways and I'll remain his slave if I don't wake up and learn how to defend myself.

As Chuck and I talk, I understand that I must constantly change how I ordinarily live my life. I must react differently now and take control for myself, because it's important that I no longer compromise my energy in the old way, immediately falling victim to the interests of others, ending up powerless in the process. I must challenge myself to take action now, rather than just accept what comes as my fate. I must not back off and hide, licking my wounds, waiting for the pain to subside, as has been my habit. Instead, I am being challenged to turn and fight, to fight the feelings of worthlessness, of not mattering, of not having control. I must fight the urge to fall back into being Zombie Girl.

"One of the old habits is to say: *It will be over soon, just get through it*," I tell Chuck. "I realize I still say that to myself, daily, because it's so comforting."

"But it's also deadly," says Chuck. "Don't do that anymore. When you do that it means you're letting someone else or something else take control."

"I get it! When I say that it means I have absolutely no control, no input, no say. It means I'm lying there inert, totally non-participatory, effectively dead. It's almost like I'm giving permission for the stuff that happened so long ago to continue happening."

"Yes, your energy is stuck there, being used *without your permission*."

"And I do it all the time! It's so easy. I just ignore things; I walk away. I'd rather do that than fight. I'd rather let someone run me over than fight. That's what it feels like when I'm in the middle of it. I feel safe in going dead and just walking away, like I'm protecting myself. But it really means someone else is in control. Even when I think I'm in control I'm not, because I'm acting from an old place of numbness. I became so used to doing what someone told me to do that I just followed along. I couldn't even *think* about protesting; I just acquiesced and then silently waited for it to end. I get it! It's as if, all those years ago, when he was taking over my body, something else slipped in at the same time, his energy, and took over my soul. An evil control-freak slipped in at the first vulnerable sign and took over."

"Exactly!" says Chuck. "And how easy was that, to slip into a two-year old and feel powerful?"

"Really! Not very hard at all! There was no one challenging what he was doing, because a baby didn't know how to say "Go away, you evil energy!" A baby doesn't know anything.

So, there I was at the age of two, possessed by a predator, in human form, but also in the form of evil energy. No wonder I've felt possessed my entire life! No wonder I've felt manipulated! No wonder I've always felt something else inhabiting this body! I believe this conclusion, because it *feels* so right. I leave the session feeling more empowered than ever, as well as much more deeply committed to, and aligned with, the original intent of this recapitulation: *to figure out as much about myself as I can, to find my way to healing myself.*

As I ponder the work of the morning session, the significance of predatory energy begins to make even more sense. I understand that this occupying energy is not something that makes me evil or harmful to others, it's only harmful to me. It feeds off me alone, as it parasitically attaches to my most innocent, vulnerable self and steals my energy. Many times, I have indeed felt as if I've been fighting something within my physical body—something real and tangible—totally known and yet totally alien as well. It keeps me isolated and alone, in a state of deep depression, far from my fuller potential. I even know what it feels like when it isn't present because then I'm a totally different person. But its numbing pull is as strong as sleep on a night of exhaustion and there's nothing I can do to stop it once it pipes up again. I hear it speaking, enticing me into its arms, whispering its soporific phrases: "Don't go, don't. Stay here with me," the evil energy says. "You're better off where you are. Don't talk, don't act, just keep quiet and everything will be okay. It will end; it will be over soon. Another day will come. Don't make waves and don't fight me either, I'm too strong."

"No, you're not! You're a weak coward, you Fuck-O!" I respond, finding a new voice in active imagination. "The only reason you're here is because you snuck into a toddler. A baby, for crying out loud! A frightened, uncomprehending, confused baby! You're not powerful at all. The only hold you have over me at this point is longevity. You've been around for so long and I've been brainwashed for so long that I automatically acquiesce to following your directions. I can literally feel your energy seeping into me, taking over, and how I disappear from my own body as a result."

Beyond that mixture of predatory confusion, beyond that whirlwind of feelings and memories inside me, something else lies waiting: *Me*. It's time now to nurture the part of myself that never cried out or even revealed itself, that hard embryonic knot waiting for this day of release. I'm taking over now. I'm taking over in every way possible. He is no longer in control. "You won't tell me what to do anymore. You won't be whispering words of caution and repression anymore. You are history! I'm going to get you the same way you got me—energetically—and free myself of your insidious, diabolical possession.

A tremendous creative surge, a great need to express myself begins to blossom as I go through this deeply challenging and life changing process. There will be a book some day, I'm sure of that, but just how it will unfold I have no idea. The other day I mentioned to my daughter that I had an idea for a book about children being controlled, caught in mesmeric states, but each of them with a hidden purpose, some of them born to lead, others to heal, others to be sacrificed; each with a destiny, each equally important, each with a major part to play. Even those who die will return in another form, but first they will have to live very difficult lives. Just talking about it sent chills up her spine.

"How about that book, Mom, when are you going to be writing that book?" she asked me again last night.

"I'm working on it," I said, for indeed this recapitulation is the basis of such a story.

"I can't wait to read it," she replied.

Ideas for a self-portrait are emerging too, a three-dimensional piece with a door to my heart, something safely ensconced inside—me inside and me outside. My art offers another means of recapitulation, another means of self-expression. As I experience how my spirit chooses to speak, whether in writing or in making art, I learn something new about myself. But I realize I must stop envisioning the recapitulation as a box filled with other little boxes, each one holding another secret, as has been my wont. In that vision all I see is an empty box at the end of the process, and that doesn't feel right. I don't want to end up with just an empty box. I'd rather envision recapitulation as something of endless value with endless possibilities, constantly changing, constantly fulfilling. And so, I know that I have to stop asking the recapitulation for a break, stop wondering if it's done, stop looking to see if the box is empty, because it's something that will just keep happening because there will always be new things to confront. I have to stop waiting for it to be nice to me too. There's no stopping it and there's no break from it. It's the call to new life really, and I have to meet it in a new way now too—openly!

"The recapitulation waves will keep coming in and you can stand there and let them take you where they will, or you can choose to do something else," Chuck said today. "You can ride them, you can dive into them, or you can swim out beyond them. But they will keep coming, just like the endless ocean waves, whether you are ready or not."

The next wave is coming. I feel the energy of it pushing against me, the undertow seeking to sweep me off my feet. Open to dealing with it—I ought to be good at it by now!—I close my eyes, relax my mind, calm my pulsing heart, and begin the sweeping breath. Almost immediately I'm recapitulating, caught in a mix of images. It's like watching a rapid-fire slide show, a haphazard collage of pictures, each picture overlapping the next, falling quickly into place and yet nothing is clear until all of a sudden something pops out, startling me: his belt with that shiny buckle!

Where am I, in the woods? I do the sweeping breath, clearing away the cobwebs of the past, sweeping my head, letting my breath part the veils of time. No, I'm not in the woods. I see more clearly now. I'm in the bathroom, standing by the towel rack underneath the windowsill. I see my right hand on the towel rack. I'm waiting. My abuser pulls down his pants and sits on the toilet seat in front of me. I have no pants on. He picks me up and pulls me onto his lap. I'm facing him, my nose in his chest hair, my lips pressing against a button on his shirt. He has vaginal sex with me. It hurts. I pant—then and now—I pant with the pain of it.

Aaaaaaaaaaaaaaaaaaaaaaaah!!!!!!!

Suddenly the scene shifts and I'm in the woods, hanging from a branch after I've shown the other man what we do.

"Are you open enough?" my abuser asks.

He pries my legs apart and looks. He licks with his tongue. I put my legs around his neck and push against his mouth. The other man watches.

I'm five years old in these memories.

August 14, 2002

This recapitulation is becoming increasingly fascinating! I've written pages and pages in this journal, even some words I have no recollection of writing. The day I suspected I was hearing the voice of Jeanne is a complete blank. I'd sat and written for a while yesterday too while recapitulating, as I do every day, but when I took some time to read what I'd written I was blown away by the process and where it took me, to places deep inside, utterly unknown. I become more acquainted with my lost child self each time I venture inward. Over time, what at first seems fantastical eventually dawns familiar. I know there is so much more to discover; and so, I am open.

"Where are we going?" I ask Jeanne, and my inner girls as well. "Where are you taking me next?"

Those questions alone are enough to send me into recapitulation and before I know it I'm back in the woods. I watch as my abuser unbuttons his plaid shirt and takes it off. Now we are both naked. My stomach clenches tightly as I wonder what we're going to do. Fear rises like a hot flame. Until I know exactly what game we're going to play a heightened state of near panic ensues. It's all I can do to withstand the heat of anxiety as I wait for the moment of disintegration—what I now know as *dissociation*—which I have no doubt will come. Once I know what game we're playing I'm able to deal with what comes, but until then I stand on the brittle edge of the abyss. Now that we're undressed the games begin.

My abuser stands before me with an erection. He tells me to lick his popsicle. I know exactly what to do. I'm small, and as I stand before him I'm right at the perfect height. I stroke and lick and squeeze. I'm the puppy playing with the daddy doggy. I'm having a doggy popsicle. We lie on the ground. I'm on top. We lick each other and he rubs me against him. He grabs my legs and rubs me hard against his chest as I lick and hold onto his penis.

I shift out of the memory. That's enough for now. I have a day to get through, kids to care for, and work to do. "Don't ask for a break," I tell myself. "Don't wonder if the box is empty or if it's the last memory. Just let them come, like the ocean waves."

I go out for a morning run, realizing that if I let the waves come crashing over me, dragging me down, then I'm giving the memories control, as Chuck suggested. If I show any weakness in handling this recapitulation process then I lose control and risk drowning, spiritual guides or not. That's the old way, to be swamped and silenced, but now I'm electing a new tactic. I'm choosing to swim beyond the waves, to go far out to sea beyond the memories for the time being, because I still have a life to live. So in my imagination, as I run, I simultaneously swim far out to sea, beyond the breaking waves, and when I get out there, where the sea is flat and calm, I turn around and shout back toward shore: GO AWAY! By the time I finish my run I'm feeling calmer, less haunted, and my knees don't hurt at all, they're perfectly fine. The pain dissipated as soon as I recapitulated the crowbar memory, for just as I had suspected, it was psychosomatic!

Successful at staying beyond the waves of recapitulation during the day, as soon as night arrives I toss and turn on the churning ocean of sleeplessness. I drift off eventually, but suddenly startle awake when a loud CRACK explodes over my head. Bolting upright, my heart pounding, I see a white shape in the air, hovering at eye level next to my bed. It looks somewhat like the ghost of a big white cat leaping through the air.

"What's that!" I shout, my heart pounding like crazy.

Whatever it is, as soon as I yell, it vanishes. It reminds me of when I was living in Sweden, going through a tough time after my first divorce. I woke in the middle of the night to find a woman in white standing next to my bed. She disappeared when I sat up and cried out. This didn't look at all like a woman, more like a ghostly cat with wings, but whatever it was, it freaked me out!

August 15, 2002

In a dream, I'm camping, on vacation somewhere. I volunteer to do all the work of setting up and cleaning up, saying that I'd end up doing it anyway. I constantly look at my hands, noticing how raw and chapped they are, swollen from being in so much dishwater. All through the dream I watch my hands, constantly moving, doing endless chores.

At six in the morning I wake up grumpy, feeling stiff and hard, like an empty shell. Inside I find nothing familiar, nothing to connect to and make me feel real. I am only a hard shell ready to crack.

I go to a yoga class, wondering if something interesting will emerge, if the breathing and physical movement will soften me and perhaps trigger something. Nothing happens during the class, but afterwards, the minute I cross over the threshold and walk into the studio, the walls disappear and I find myself in the woods of my abuser. I sense that I'm walking ahead of him, carrying something. When I look down at my hands, I see that it's a blanket. I slow to a stumbling walk, dragging my feet, reluctant to go too fast, deliberately stalling for time. I feel his hand pushing me forward. He bumps into the back of my head and his belt buckle catches my hair. The dead wood feeling comes over me as I take each slow step, creeping up my body until I am totally dead, as if anesthetized, already gone into numbness, just waiting for it to be over. He hurts me, so I react in the only way I know how: I cut the pain off. A scream begins to form, but I push that away too. Don't say anything, not a sound!

I come out of the recapitulation and find myself sitting on the sofa in the studio, a painful cry caught in my stiff, wooden body. I have no idea how I got from the door to the sofa, clear on the other side of the room crowded with furniture, worktables, and half completed projects. I've left the studio door wide open, and now, as I get up and cross the room to close it, I see by the clock on the wall that ten minutes have passed. Intent upon focusing now on work, I let the memory dissipate, just as the walls of the studio had dissolved a few moments before. As soon as the door clicks shut, I swim far beyond the waves of recapitulation, intent on staying there for the rest of the day. I'm able to concentrate on work, but every now and then I must remind myself to stay alert, to not get lulled to sleep. And so often enough, as the tide of numbness ebbs and flows and draws me in, I reassert my intent and swim back out to sea, far from the waves of recapitulation. I cannot deny, however, how in awe I am of this recapitulation process, for I cannot but marvel at the things that happen each day.

Back in bed at night I can't sleep. As I toss and turn, restless on the ocean of sleeplessness, I find myself lying on the doorknob tree, but there are no doorknobs on it this time, there's only me. Like Daphne of the Greek myth, I become the tree, a piece of wood inside and outside, a solid hunk of wood so he can't hurt me, so I can't feel anything, so I won't have to feel the pain. My vagina is a hollow wooden cup, carved just so. Outside, too, I'm so hard he could split me into pieces and stack me on a woodpile and I wouldn't feel a thing. But I do feel. Higher up, in the middle of my heart, I feel everything.

August 16, 2002

I wake at 5 in the morning after tossing and turning all night in the heat, the oscillating fan in my room offering little relief. Trying to recall a dream about kite flying, I finally give up, get out of bed, and wander into the kitchen to make coffee and let the cats out.

The kids are heading off on a camping trip with their dad today, leaving me wide open for experiences of the old stuff. I'll have lots of alone time over the next week, which I look forward to, but that's also when things come, when things seem to know I'm available. So my plan is to deal with it in the ways I've been dealing with it all week—let it happen, visit it, learn from it, and move on. Constantly back in the woods as I tossed and turned in the heat, I spent most of the night doing just that, letting the memories come, turning over and rolling into a tight ball with them, riding the waves, needing to cry—though, as usual, it was hopeless—I just couldn't. But I did discover an enormous, aching ball in the center of my being, in the area of my bruised heart, which I cradled tightly and floated along with until it eventually shrank into just a small hard knot. That small hard knot has been there all these many years and it's been growing again, bigger with each memory, awakened by this recapitulation process. I find that I still need to curl around it at night, but now I'm attempting to make sense of it, rather than trying to protect or stifle it. When I was a child it was just an intense, mysterious, bruised thing, but now I understand that it means so much more than that. That understanding, however, hasn't lessened the pain. None of this is easy.

Last night's memories return and begin to clarify as I sit down to drink my coffee. I remember more clearly my child self, in such pain that petrifying and turning into a hard dead piece of wood offered the only protection. Inside and outside, I became a hunk of wood, echoing hollowly with the sounds of my abuser's tools and wicked deeds. Indeed, I turned into Daphne.

In spite of the recapitulation work, I'm proceeding with life. I've secured a mortgage and completed all the paperwork necessary for the house closing. The kids and I anxiously await the day when we can move into our little blue abode. "You'll be happy here," said one of my brothers when he saw the house. "You'll be happy here."

My father is dying of bone cancer. I think about him sometimes and then try *not* to think about him. His prognosis is not good and by the looks of him he may not make it to Christmas. He resides mostly in confusion, depression, and pain, not clear on where he is, where he's going, what day it is, or what's really happening—kind of like where I am at the moment! I wonder if he'll be able to transcend the fog long enough to grasp that he may only have a few months left to live, long enough to say what he needs to say, or do what he needs to do. I realize his blankness is not unusual. He's been presenting us with it for decades. He checked out a long time ago. How do I say to him what I need to say? How do I penetrate the muffled distance he sits behind? Is it even necessary?

It's 6:30 in the evening and I'm still in the cool, air-conditioned studio. I've been working on new artwork for the two-person show that I'm participating in at the gallery in November, sharing the space with another artist. Up since five, and with little sleep last night, I'm pretty exhausted, but I'm almost afraid to go home because the old stuff will get me. I'm sure of it, especially with the kids away and the house to myself. Even now, as I state this fear, a visceral memory forms, creeping out of the past, and I feel my abuser grabbing my arms, pulling me towards him. I swiftly turn away and shake him off, vigorously shaking my hands and arms as I walk around the studio, until I've released myself from his grip. I go back to work on painting my self-portrait. I focus on pouring all the tension I'm feeling into mixing just the right skin tone and achieving just the right hollow look in the eyes that stare out at me from the wooden panel I'm painting on. The memory, however, is relentless. Every time I feel my abuser's hands on my arms, I put down my paintbrush and turn sharply away. I flick him off as I walk around my worktable, out into the hallway, even up and down the stairs a few times, before returning to painting. This goes on until I leave the studio at nine o'clock. I go out into the warm night air and head home to an empty house, hoping I'm done with *him* for the night.

August 17, 2002

It's early in the morning and even with no children to care for I wake early, with the birds. I don't mind. I have the luxury of staying in bed to process what comes without duty or guilt interfering. This time of day is good for me. I'm in good form for recapitulating should anything arise, in between the worlds of sleep and wakefulness, not fully present in either world.

How tired I am of being wooden! The myth of Daphne has been my own true holding state, but I'm done with that now—I'm ready to feel. I've drawn and painted hundreds of tree figures over the years, including little girls emerging from split trunks, representing my deeply hidden personal experiences and my secret desire for liberation. When I first heard the story of Daphne— sworn to virginity—I knew her story was my own. A free spirit, she lived in the woods, hunted, and enjoyed her freedom until Apollo became infatuated with her and unrelentingly pursued her hand in marriage. Begging for liberation from such a fate, she turned to her father, the river god, for help. He granted her wish, quickly turning her into a tree just as Apollo was about to capture her. And there she has resided for eternity, encapsulated in wooden bondage. Pursued by my abuser, I too turned wooden in an effort to survive, my true sexuality shut down in wooden response. In fact, I thought I *was* a virgin—such a funny thought now, the irony of it—and the last thing I was interested in was being tied down in a relationship, having to have sex! I never found Daphne's fate to be anything but delivering, and in the nick of time. Thank God, I thought, she didn't have to marry and have sex! Little did I know why I had such bizarre thoughts.

My psyche has been guiding me throughout my creative life, for many years asking me to go deeper into my imagination, into the mysteries of the unconscious, and return with the fruits of my labors clearly defined in line and color, in shape and form. Those girls that I have painted peeking out of the trees aren't wooden at all, just afraid, timid, wary of what life has in store for them if they leave the safety of the wooden trunks where they've resided for so long, protected in the solid womb of woodenness. They're just little Daphnes wondering if it's safe to venture into life now. As I contemplate this longstanding state of my true physical self—once wooden girl now grown into wooden woman—I'm thrown into recapitulation. I acquiesce to the insistent pull of body memory. As I turn onto my side, my bedroom and the present world suddenly disappear and I sense that I am somewhere else.

I'm a teenager, lying on the ground where my abuser has left me after prodding me with his foot, saying, "Get up, get out of here!" I wait until I'm sure it's safe, not moving an inch. I'm a dead piece of wood, a hunk of log, a fallen tree. Only when he's been gone for a long time does feeling begin to return, slowly coming back into my body along with the pain that sits at the core of my being. Suddenly, I snap out of woodenness. I get up and get moving. I get busy dressing and forgetting, so I can walk away with only the soreness between my legs a reminder of what just happened. I soothe the pain in my crotch with my hands, but then I push even that away and instead cradle it in the middle of my being, deep in my soul, far from the real area of pain. And so I walk away, forgetting, shaking it off, leaving it back there in the woods, in the barn, and in the past.

The ache in the middle of my soul has been there all along, sometimes silent, at other times calling out to me. Sometimes I'd hear it and wonder what it meant, but for the longest time I could only turn my back on it, too disturbing to investigate any deeper. It finally dawned on me that it was not going to leave me in peace. There came a turning point when I knew I could no longer push aside the stench of something old, putrefying within. That ball of pain in the middle of my soul is a major part of who I am. I'm aware that it helped me greatly, enabling me to somehow get up and get away, dusting off the dirt and the memories at the same time, helping me to walk away from it all. Now, at the age of fifty, I'm going back into the barn and into the woods, dusting off the memories, knowing that this time I can't just walk away, and that I can't displace the pain yet again. This time I have to experience it.

I know that the memories will eventually recede, that with time I'll work through them, as I also learn what I must about my past. But for now the memories must remain raw and fresh in my mind and body; they must remain viscerally, painfully present so I can talk about them. I still need to push them aside when appropriate, not completely away, as I once did, but only briefly, in order to get up out of bed each day, get dressed, and get on with my life. I need to do that *now*. Yet, the sad and hurt little girl part of me wants to reach out and call Chuck, but the alien presence is here again, my abuser's energy, making itself known, telling me not to bother him. "You don't need him, he doesn't want to be bothered. Don't call; don't be a pain in the ass!" The pressure of its presence is heavy, painful, and depressing. It wants to keep me to itself. It wants me to get to an old place again, where I won't ask for help, where it will have control over me and my energy as well. I have to fight it. I have to get away from it the same way I used to get away from what it did to me. I have to get up and shift away from it, forget it even exists, just as I walked away from the pressure of my abuser's hands on my arms yesterday.

I see more clearly now how my abuser and his energy worked in conjunction. They held me down and did what they wanted, one holding me for the other, one holding me mentally and emotionally and the other physically. I was, and still am, possessed by him. I'm not allowed to call Chuck. I'm tormented by this thing that has me, that's in me; this thing that holds me back, that teases and only let's me go so far before it pulls me back again. It doesn't want me to feel, because then there would be no place for it and no need for it either.

"*Something is holding you back, but it's not in you, it's outside of you,*" I hear a voice saying, Jeanne again, and I know she's right.

A great serpent lies nearby. As soon as a memory comes, so does it, wrapping me in a suffocating embrace, but then it lets me loose, just enough for me to catch a breath of air and think it's gone. And so I'm fully alert to its presence during the day, shifting, pivoting and abruptly moving in a new direction as often as possible to avoid its grasp. It plays with me, letting me feel my freedom. I'm even staying open, challenging it. Let it come, as it will, for this gives me ample opportunity to practice this shifting skill. And so it does. In quiet moments I feel it slithering closer, with flicking tongue, letting me know it's still here. Of course, I know it's still here. I *feel* it!

August 18, 2002

I'm being healed in a dream. I'm visiting a healer who tells me that I too have healing power in my hands. As soon as she tells me this I feel my hands vibrating with heat and energy. I learn that one day I will use my hands to heal others. "Your hands are so hot! Why are your hands so hot?" people ask. "They're hot with healing energy," I say, looking at my reddened palms. "I'm learning how to heal."

I wake from this dream realizing that my healing is in my own hands, literally and figuratively. At the same time, I'm still wrestling with the serpent that has me in its clutches and won't let me ask for help.

"You're not allowed to call for help. Don't bother Chuck! He doesn't care! You don't need him," it says, tightening its grip.

"You don't have control anymore; you are not my keeper!" I say in retaliation. "You have to leave. I'm changing; I'm different now. I'm making a new life for myself, and you aren't part of it. I'm going to fight you at every turn and get rid of you. All that old stuff that you keep saying—that I don't matter, that no one cares—is a lie! You don't like it when I call for help because you're afraid. You're afraid it means the death of you, and that I'm going to finally live."

"Be ruthless!" says Chuck when I finally break free of the serpent's grip and give him a call. "Stand up to him!"

"Okay," I say. "I can be ruthless. I'll go back and tell him that the game is over, that I'm not available any more, that I'm not keeping his secrets."

All this time, I've been convinced that it was the girls who were mad at me for breaking the pact we'd established a long time ago, but I realize it wasn't them at all. It's this serpent energy that has a grip on me, my abuser's energy parasitically siphoning the life out of me. He's the one who's angry that I'm breaking the pact and spilling the beans. Well, he'd better get used to it!

"I'M TALKING NOW!" I shout. "I'm telling Chuck all about it. I'm not going to be keeping your dirty secrets anymore. You are history!"

I've always felt physically restrained, unable to move forward, unavailable for what life has in store for me. And so I gave up so much, especially a budding career as a talented children's book illustrator. Terrified after several early successes, I retreated into places of safety, far from the grip of the public and the powerful old serpent. I understand that the challenge now is to wrestle this thing to the ground, to defeat it once and for all, and reclaim not only my energy but also whatever else life might have in store for me. I must not just try to avoid it, as I've done in the past, but do as Chuck suggests and stand up to it. I must lay down the law.

"NO MORE! GET OUT OF MY LIFE! I'm not yours. I don't belong to you; you can't have me. I belong only to myself. You can't touch me any more! I'm not running from you; I'm not hiding; I'm standing up and declaring my freedom. I'm standing my ground. Go away!"

"I'm not a little girl anymore. Don't underestimate my powers and determination. Don't underestimate me! You don't know anything about me; you're still back in the 1950s. I'm still young and strong, stronger than you now. You're nothing but an old devil, and pretty weak at that, just a weak, skinny old devil! Why have I been so afraid of you? You're just a sick old man keeping his dirty secrets. You were such a wimp; you had to steal a little girl's energy in order to live. Well, you can't have it anymore!"

"So weak and brittle you simply crumble underfoot. The terror is over as I stamp you beneath my feet. As I grind you to dust, I see you now for what you are and I'm no longer afraid of you. I realize I've innocently and unknowingly kept your memory alive all these years by failing to remember. But now, looking back, I realize the memories have been stronger than you ever were, in their needling effort to signal me to your energetic presence. To a child you were the embodiment of evil. To the grown up adult me, I see what a sad coward you are, a coward who had to do your evil deeds to a child barely out of infancy, a baby. Like a two-headed serpent you've followed me around, one of your mouths clamped on and sucking the life out of me for the past fifty years, the other whispering the same old lies into my ears."

There are no secrets now. This is wide open, as Chuck says. I'm going to start feeling again. Along with the release of the memories will come the ability to heal myself so that I can truly feel. No longer will I be wood—a petrified log—my feelings, my physical and emotional selves entrapped. I could push my abuser over like a toothpick. I could snap him in two. Like Quoyle's Aunt Agnes in Proulx's *The Shipping News*, I could dump his ashes into the latrine and shit on him. She, raped by her brother at age twelve, thought that if anyone ever found out about the rape she would turn to stone. Didn't she realize she had already turned to stone, immediately when it happened? When Quoyle mentions to her that he knows, it offers her the opportunity to chip away at the stone and turn back into a real person.

I know the feeling of turning into protective stone, though in my case it was wood. I turned wooden so I couldn't feel. Now I can't even feel a hug. I'm just a wooden statue, for I am Daphne. But in the nick of time, I'm discovering that I can actually uproot myself and walk into new life. I can think and act on my own, and I'm already experiencing what it means to feel. The spell once cast upon the mythological Daphne inside me is now being broken, as I recapitulate and split open the wooden tree trunk that has grown around me. Deep inside, the sap still flows. It's filling my veins, seeping into my heart, and beginning to reach deeply into my body. I'm waking up from that spell cast long ago, turning back into a human being, slowly awakening into life—real life.

I lie in bed at night, trying to sleep, but memories intrude, making themselves known. I knew what men wanted from little girls. I saw the way they looked at us. I knew they preferred us with our pants off, that they wanted to do things 'down there' with their mouths, hands, penises, with objects, tools, and sticks. The look of hungry lust in men's eyes made me angry. I hated the men who touched, who got close enough that I could smell their breath and see the sheen of sweat on their upper lips, as their sharp tongues darted in and out like snakes tongues, and their pink lips quivered in greedy anticipation. My abuser was like that, and when he got that way there was no stopping him.

Another hour goes by in endless tossing and turning. To shift away from more memories, I curl up into a ball. Trying to protect my little girl self from the onslaught of thoughts, I hold her close and breathe out the memories of invasion and rape. Sad and lonely, and with no possibility of sleep in sight, I finally get out of bed to ease the pain of that frightened little girl. I sit in the dark living room, drinking some of my husband's gin that I find in the freezer after searching the entire kitchen for something alcoholic. I pour a half-inch into a small glass and throw a slice of jalapeno pepper into it and take tiny sips until it's gone. Intent upon shifting myself, I establish a ritual: slowly sipping, slowly rising, slowly pouring more gin, slowly returning to the sofa, each movement and each step mindfully taken with focused determination. I feel my feet on the floor, my body on the sofa, my arm lifting my glass, staying fully present in each moment and each movement. Counting each step, I repeat this mindfulness ritual over and over again. I take just a little gin each time, wondering if it will be noticed, before walking the few steps slowly back to the sofa in the living room where I sit down and stare out at the moon. I watch the moonlight dancing with the shadows in the yard until I finally return to bed in the wee hours, hoping for sleep at last.

August 19, 2002

I wake feeling sad and exhausted, feeling like I can't call Chuck for help. What am I asking for anyway? Maybe it's enough to know that he's there, that I can reach out and find him when those memories come carrying the cloak of darkness that settles over me so heavily, reminding me once again that no one cares, that I don't matter, that I have a terrible secret to keep, a secret that I can never, ever tell anyone.

What will happen if I speak about the abuse now and what did I think would happen if I could have spoken about it back then? The only truthful answer is that when I was a child it would have taken the abuse out of its separate world and destroyed me in the process. It would have ripped down the iron curtain between the two worlds, shattering both of them, and I would have shattered as well. Keeping the secret has kept the two worlds apart, and it has kept me safe and sane. Now, as I face the challenge of revealing the truth of what happened when I was a child, I still feel the moment of annihilation towering over me, daring me to maintain the status quo or die in the process of breaking the silence. I can handle the shattering as well as the truth-telling now, though each time I give that curtain between worlds another tug I must deal, at the deepest level of my soul, with what it reveals.

I HAVE NOTHING TO BE ASHAMED OF!

I HAVE NOTHING TO BE ASHAMED OF!

I HAVE NOTHING TO BE ASHAMED OF!

I HAVE NOTHING TO BE ASHAMED OF!

I HAVE NOTHING TO BE ASHAMED OF!

I HAVE NOTHING TO BE ASHAMED OF!

I HAVE NOTHING TO BE ASHAMED OF!

I HAVE NOTHING TO BE ASHAMED OF!

I HAVE NOTHING TO BE ASHAMED OF!

I grew up in an environment where it was expected that I be ashamed of everything. It was part of growing up a Catholic, being ashamed of my body, my thoughts, my deeds. I look down at my body now in my attempt to annihilate the shame before it has a chance to annihilate me and I see only a human being, skin and shape. I see no shame sticking to me. The only place it sticks is in the memories. They are full of it.

I fight with myself all morning about calling Chuck and finally place a call around one in the afternoon, though he doesn't call back until the evening.

"Good for you that you called!" he says.

"What can I do? The anxiety is huge. I need help!"

"The shamans say walk, walk the memories out," he tells me.

So I do. I take a long walk at sunset. Of course, a memory begins forming almost immediately, triggered perhaps by my intent to do as the shamans do. I'm alone, minding my own business, walking across a field, many miles and many years away from my childhood home when suddenly I see my abuser, materializing on the path ahead of me. The world shatters completely and now I'm walking in a different world and I know he's coming to get me. "Come on," he says, as he pulls the curtain aside, and before I know it I'm entering the muffled darkness of his world. "I have something to show you."

As I walk into his world, I gain clarity on the memory of the fallen tree trunk with the pink doorknobs. Now, from my adult perspective, I see that they aren't doorknobs at all, but look more like wooden dildos. I hear my abuser talking to me from the past, telling me exactly what happened. His face is right in front of me, his voice in my ear, loud and clear. "Do it girl! Go on, girl, do it! Do it again, do it again, do it again, do it again," he commands, until I'm sore and wooden. And then I get up and walk out of the woods. As the curtain closes behind me, I find myself in the same field where I started from earlier in the evening, but now I'm walking in the opposite direction, back the way I'd come, heading home, the darkness of this world coming fast now.

"If you need me, you call me, all right?" Chuck said kindly, before we hung up today, in stark contrast to the harsh voice of my abuser.

"Alright," I said, but we're meeting tomorrow anyway, and I won't call him at night.

August 20, 2002

I awaken at four to the sound of heavy rain and the cats wanting to go out. Unable to return to sleep, I finally get up and make some coffee. I'm anxious and shaky when I meet with Chuck at eight.

"I couldn't sleep last night," I tell him. "I tossed and turned, the memory of the pink knobs repeating itself, as I felt it going through me in every sense. I finally fell asleep in the wee hours, but only because I was so exhausted."

"Let's see what happens when you go there now," Chuck says.

I put the EMDR headphones on and let the pulsing in my ears calm me and take me back into the woods once again where I clearly see the doorknob tree. I notice that it's all set up, the doorknobs in place, all planned ahead of time. I allow myself to replay the memory, looking for clues I've missed, looking for what I'm supposed to learn today. I come out of the memory, feeling like a little wooden girl, startled by the sound of my voice when I speak, for I sound like a five-year-old child.

"The tree turned you into wood, so you could survive," Chuck says. "The shamans say we should live in trees, we can learn a lot from them. They stay in one place, set down roots, can't move, so they're forced to sit and observe. What do you observe from where you are now?"

"I've noticed that every time I go into a memory now, I feel the fangs of the serpent in me, parasitically sucking my energy at the same time that the memory is emerging. It's like I'm having two experiences at once."

"Every time you go back now, you're in two worlds at the same time. And every time you retrieve a memory, you're also retrieving a small part of yourself," Chuck says. "Every time you defy the pressure to keep things to yourself, you retrieve even more of yourself. You need to keep retrieving those parts and not be afraid of him or of the memories. They're so important. Just let them be what they are, no judgments. Let the feelings just be what they are too. Just let them come."

"I haven't had feelings in so long, I've been wooden for so long."

"You deserve all those feelings, every one of them, so let them come," Chuck says. "Don't let him keep you from them."

"I have to kill the serpent."

"Yes, you do. It doesn't matter if the serpent is small or large, you still have to send it away, crush it, or kill it if you have to."

"Kill it or be killed," I say.

"There are things worse than death out there," says Chuck. "Don't let him be in control."

"I'm in control, I'm gaining back my power, I'm infinitely more powerful than he is, even if he tells me that no one cares about me and my silly memories. I care and you, as my witness, care. It *does* matter that I talk about them. Acknowledging the memories matters, retrieving myself matters. *I matter*."

"Fight him," Chuck says. "Don't try to get away, because you'll never get away—stand and fight."

"I've been trying to get away from him my entire life and I haven't been able to."

"Exactly! It's time now to turn and face him, no matter how big and frightening, no matter how powerful he may seem to be; it's time to fight. Kill or be killed."

"I've had enough of only being half alive. Now it's time to change everything, not just a few things, but everything in my life. I won't be afraid of the memories anymore; they are what they are. They aren't new either, not really. They're actually very familiar. I'm going back to get what I need from them, to get the little girl, to retrieve the energy from the pain and the fears and the experiences. I'm taking everything back now, making it into a new me."

I leave Chuck's office feeling stronger, more intent upon taking this journey without fear. I'm actually taking this journey to find myself, literally seeking the scattered bits and pieces of who I am, intending to mold them together and become the person I will become. I'm taking this journey so that eventually I can let the memories reside in the shade of the trees where they belong, without attachment. Once I'm done with my recapitulation, I won't need to go to them and they'll no longer draw me with the same power. I may occasionally have to go back to retrieve something, but the need won't be as great as it is now, for the greater part of the work will be done. Now is the urgent time, now is when it needs to happen. Now I am being called back.

Finding it hard to focus on work, I go out for a few hours to run errands and take a walk. Back at the studio again, the edgy anxiety settles even deeper and I find it increasingly difficult to stay present. Nausea creeps into my body and I just want to go home and right to bed, to sleep, or get back in the car and just keep driving until I feel normal again. My inclination is to just keep moving, while at the same time I wish I had a hole to crawl into. Fighting off an urge to vomit, I remind myself that I've promised to stand and face this now, to not run, and not get drawn back into an old place either. And so I turn my attention to getting some work done for my upcoming show. Without intending it, without even thinking about the conversation I had with Chuck this morning, I paint a tree. It's the same theme I've been painting and drawing forever, a theme I keep coming back to, the myth of Daphne manifesting once again.

The anxiety remains intense even while I paint, and the nausea persists. It's a struggle to stay on task and I constantly fight the urge to run out and do something else, to move away rather than stand and fight, yet I push through the urges and keep at it, not really wishing to stop anything that might come through. I wait for something to happen, but then notice that the anxiety hasn't gone beyond my physical body. It's staying contained, though it surges and recedes, on and off all afternoon. Like the waves of the ocean it ebbs and flows inside me as I focus on breathing calmly, trying not to throw up or splinter into a million splinters.

I wonder if I'm being tested, if my abuser's energy is testing me, and then I notice that the tree practically paints itself, and it looks pretty damned good too! It appears that I'm actually taking back my power by painting myself into a strong and beautiful tree, perhaps Daphne beginning to return to life.

"When you don't sleep, your defenses are weakened," Chuck said today, wondering if I would consider taking drugs to ward off the anxiety. "How can you fight when you're so exhausted?"

I know I'm being tested, that the energy is looking for compromise on my part, for concessions, looking for my weak points, but I won't give in. I've been shaking all day, but I refuse to take drugs, as I told Chuck. So I picked up some herbal remedies after our session and I've been drinking herbal teas all afternoon. Physically, it's taken the edge off, but I wonder what the night will be like after a day that's this bad.

August 21, 2002

In a dream, I'm looking at houses for sale with a woman I know. She's showing me many capes and cottages, pointing out their good and bad points, and I'm anticipating getting a good deal. At one of the houses I meet the owner, a woman named Margaret. At first she looks like a man, but then I see that she's actually a woman. She lives in a little cottage with some outbuildings made of stone. I tell her I like the outbuildings, that they'll make good studios. She tells me that she had used them in the past as pottery studios and that she sold her pots out of them. The woman I'm with whispers to me that Margaret is almost seventy years old, though she looks very young, and that she's "a drunk," which I take as an exaggeration—a rumor and of no consequence—for I immediately like her and feel good in her company. "Oh that's me, in twenty years," I think. "Me, alone but tough, maybe a little sad, but still young and independent in spirit."

"I wonder where this life will take me?" This is my first thought upon waking, and then I realize I slept from 11:30 until 5:30 without waking once. That hasn't happened in a long time! And so, to the music of the birds chirping good morning, I reconfirm my deep commitment to being open to what life offers; no more controlling on my part, if I can help it. I will let life unfold.

I decide to cut down on caffeine and drink only one cup of coffee. I then spend a quiet day with the kids—just back from their camping trip—doing laundry and a few chores around the house. As the day goes on, I notice that the anxiety is almost non-existent, though I sense its usefulness in driving the memories to clarity. Without it, everything is distant and dreamlike. With the anxiety pushing at me, everything is right here, immediate and real. I wonder if the anxiety being gone or lessened will interfere with my ability to recover the rest of the memories. How will I accomplish this recapitulation without the anxiety pushing me forward? Perhaps I speak too soon; perhaps there will still be plenty of anxiety and plenty of memories coming on their own.

"I know you'll be back," I say to the serpent energy. "I feel you there waiting in the shadows. Fine, but you won't win. You think you can make me believe what you tell me, but I know how to fight you now. You can test me all you want, you still won't win."

The type of anxiety, near-panic really, that I've been experiencing lately seems so familiar, the nausea and shaking reminiscent of being with my old boyfriend who was twenty years older than me. I'd often have attacks of extreme anxiety when with him, once while waiting for a subway, another time in a restaurant, and many times in bed while making love. I know now that I was experiencing flashbacks, though not complete memories.

I make a strong herbal decoction before bed, hoping for sleep. I'm tired.

August 22, 2002

I feel the anxiety immediately upon waking, stalking me, slowly sneaking up, waiting for the best moment to strike. Does it know when I'm tired and vulnerable? Should I keep my feelings tucked away so they aren't detectable and my vulnerable position revealed? Perhaps I'll just admit that "Okay, I'm feeling tired and vulnerable, but that doesn't affect how I'm going to stand up to you. You stalk me, you strike me, and I will stand up and strike back. No matter how I feel, I will fight you."

"You're a good soldier, a good warrior in every sense," Chuck said the other day, "but you still need sleep. That's your main job now, getting enough sleep so you can fight this thing."

By the time I arrive at the studio, I'm a little apprehensive about being alone all day, especially after yesterday when I felt my abuser's energy so insistently stalking me. His scent still lingers in the air. I know he's hiding in the shadows, waiting to strike, to draw me back into his world where he can have access to my energy again. I stand in the middle of the studio and reinforce my conviction to clear him out, to fight back by creating such an inhospitable environment that he won't want to stay. He's going to discover that I'm a formidable opponent. At the same time, I must fight old feelings that constantly seek to draw me back into dark places. Hurt and vulnerable, I just want to crawl into a hole and stay there for a while, but I don't think it's a good idea. Even if this battle is going on internally, energetically focused, it's better to not return to an old place physically. I must conserve my energy and prepare myself to come out fighting, but I have to do that in a new way. I must be a good warrior, but a well-rested warrior, as Chuck suggested.

In the evening, I talk to Chuck about the acute anxiety, and how debilitating it has in fact become. I'm not only not sleeping well, but I'm also not eating or working well, really not functioning very well overall.

"I'm scared," I say, as the conversation turns again to the possibility of taking medication to stem the anxiety.

"Don't be, it'll be all right, you'll be fine; it won't alter your personality or change you into another person," says Chuck. "You'll still be you."

I decide to call my doctor in the morning. The idea of gaining a sense of detachment over the next few months is pretty appealing. I'm not admitting defeat; it's simply an aid. I'm still a good warrior.

August 23, 2002

I wake feeling a lot calmer, realizing that Chuck is right, that the anxiety has a life of its own, independent of memories. It comes in huge waves that knock me down with trembling and nausea, sleeplessness, loss of appetite and the feeling that I'm going to explode. I have no control over this thing and even though I know it's part of the recapitulation—and that I must one day release Daphne completely from her wooden sarcophagus—I have to be able to function. The usual calming remedies won't work in the long run as I face this next, necessarily explosive part of my journey. I feel like I'd have to be drinking tea and downing herbal remedies constantly. This is too big.

I believe the intense anxiety I'm experiencing without a specific memory attached to it *is* a memory in itself. It's so familiar. I've had it before, but I've never understood it in quite the way I do now. I recognize the ill feelings triggering a need to just go home to bed, asking the world to just leave me alone while I curl up and feel bad for a day, or two or three. I realize now that when these feelings came over me in the past, memories were being triggered, suggesting deeply embedded trauma, though I just didn't know it at the time. The only thing I could do was resort to what my child self had always done and curl up in a ball of sadness, deeply depressed. And that's exactly what's happening now; I'm being triggered again. But this time I'm fully aware that I'm being given an opportunity to recapitulate and I won't let it pass this time. I won't go to bed this time; I'll face the anxiety and see where it takes me.

"I'll still be me. I just won't be so depressed and edgy," I say, shoring myself up with these suggestions as I make the final decision to take medication. "Okay, we'll see how it goes."

I meet with my doctor in the afternoon. We sit and talk about what's been happening. I'm actually able to tell him about the memories of sexual abuse that have been emerging, as well as the anxiety around the divorce. He immediately understands.

"That's the way it is," he says, "when one thing in life collapses it can triggers a whole host of things. I'm not surprised you're feeling overwhelmed, though it sounds like you've also been handling it really well."

He gives me a prescription for Paxil and I take the first pill right away, before I change my mind. After about eight hours I begin feeling nauseous, but it's light, not even as bad as the nausea I've been experiencing lately. I find it hard to relax though; I'm still a little nervous about leaping headlong into a world I never expected to go near: the world of synthetic drugs.

August 24, 2002

I dream that I'm staying at a cottage that I've borrowed for a few days. It's on an island in the middle of a lake. I have my daughter and two cats with me. When it's time to leave, I tell my daughter to wait outside while I go around the entire house straightening it up, not wanting to leave it without making sure that everything is in its place. I begin locking up the doors and windows, some from the outside, some from the inside. I'm worried about other people getting into the house and disturbing it while it sits unoccupied. I want it to stay in the pristine condition I'm leaving it in. I appreciate the calmness of the lake water and know I'll miss it when I'm gone. Suddenly the cottage turns into my abuser's house. I'm standing on his porch facing the front door that has a huge, rusty old lock dangling open from a latch. "Oh, that's where that key goes!"

As soon as I see the big old lock, I realize that the large skeleton key that's been hanging on a chain around my neck for years, in the dream, fits perfectly into the rusty lock. As I slowly close the lock and turn the key, locking the door, I become aware that someone is watching me. I feel a presence behind me, watching every move I make. After I lock the front door, I walk counterclockwise around the house locking every other door I encounter and by the time I've circled the entire house I'm back at the cottage on the island. I look inside the windows and see that I've locked the cats inside. I can't leave without them. They are too important and dear to leave behind, so I go back inside and get them. I'm also aware that I'll be returning tomorrow, but even so I'm intent on leaving everything in proper order. As I walk away, I try to relax about leaving the property alone and uninhabited, still fearing that it might be vandalized. "Let others do what they will to it, it isn't your house or your responsibility anyway; it belongs to others," I tell myself as I walk away.

I wake up in the wee hours and write this dream down. I'm struck by the symbolic key that I've been carrying around my whole life, the mysterious key that does in fact fit into the lock on the door of the house that belongs to my abuser. It's true that I've been carrying that key inside me my whole life, in the repressed memories. I just had to be ready to take it out and put it into the lock at the right moment. As I put the key into the lock and locked the door in the dream there was both an incredible sense of calm certainty that it was right, as well as the unnerving sense that I was being watched, but even that made sense, as if my abuser expected that I would someday return and put it all together. Everything made perfect sense.

Unable to fall back to sleep, I toss and turn until 5 when I get up and let the cats out. Back in bed again, I fall into a light sleep until eight. Upon awakening I feel calmer and more rested than I've felt in weeks. The medication shouldn't take effect for about three weeks, but already I sense a new lightness.

I've been feeling very sorry for myself lately. I started my work with Chuck knowing I had deep issues to tackle, but not really knowing what that meant and here I am a year later steeped in this awful past and on drugs. It's not where I imagined I'd be, though I do realize it's where I need to be. But even so, I'm sad and full of self-pity. I do see how I've grown, how far I've come in being able to trust another person. Even being able to admit that I'm feeling like this now is a total reversal of the old hard self. I've learned to trust Chuck implicitly over the past year. I can even tell him that I'm scared, something I've barely even been able to admit to myself before. I've really softened. I'm not really scared about being on medication. What I'm really scared about is the unknown, about where I find myself at this point and where this process is taking me. I know it's good for me, but frankly I'd rather just be dealing with moving into my new house and establishing a new life with my kids than have to deal with all this other stuff. Life in the present would be enough.

I take my second pill and shortly thereafter experience a definite reaction. I can tell there's a foreign substance in my body. I feel dizzy and nauseous, like a reaction to MSG.

August 27, 2002

I've been on Paxil for a few days now, the nausea coming in mild waves, but nothing like the first two days. I do feel a little spongy as I walk, like I'm floating along, but I don't mind that. I realize this is just another part of the journey, though it feels like a place I never wanted to go because I feel I should be able to handle everything, though I know I can't. Instead, I submit; I acquiesce. Pale and tired with exhaustion, I know I need to pay attention to my body now. It's tired too. It needs sleep, food, and attention.

I meet with Chuck. We talk about my dream and the fact that I have indeed had the key to my past in my possession my entire life—in what was locked inside me—but until the memories were triggered and the lock recognized, the key remained a mystery. I just had to find the lock that would trigger the memories. Chuck's insights broaden my understanding of the dream. As he sees it, in the first part of the dream I made sure to send my daughter outside before locking up the cottage on the island.

"She represents your innocence," he says. "Once fragmented and dissociated from her, you are now totally aware and protective of her."

Chuck suggests that I inadvertently locked up the cats, representing my feelings, until I realized I couldn't leave them behind either. I understand that I'm in the process of retrieving and valuing these two fragmented aspects of self, my innocence and my feelings, which I've been totally cut off from. In addition, this dream shows the great progress I've made over the past year.

Neither of the houses belonged to me, though I sensed their value, but, in the final analysis, as I said to myself in the dream, the houses themselves were not my responsibility. Although they had at one time been important to me, I could now leave them to vandals if that was their fate. There was nothing of personal value left in them. I found myself somewhat caught in an old place in the dream, wanting to leave everything as I had found it, so I would not be blamed should anything happen while they lay deserted, but in essence I gave myself permission, by the end of the dream, to let them go, as I realized they were no longer my concern.

I feel pretty calm as we talk, comfortable with the long quiet pauses as we dissect the meaning of the dream. I feel how perfectly fine it is to sit in silence, but at one point we start to talk about the divorce and I'm so uncomfortable that I want to leave.

"I don't want to talk about that," I say rather grumpily. "If we go there I'm going to get up and leave, even though my time isn't up yet."

"Okay, we won't go there!" Chuck says.

We talk instead about my experiences since beginning the Paxil. It hasn't really kicked in yet and lately the only side effects are a mild buzzing and a stiffening of the neck, except that I'm definitely calmer, not experiencing the heights of anxiety that precipitated my taking it, but I'm still deeply depressed and unhappy.

"I feel like I need to go to bed and sleep, just sleep for as long as I can," I say.

"Sleep will come," Chuck says. "I think it's good that you're on the meds. It may allow you to get to some of the stuff that's blocked, held back so hard by your not being able to allow yourself to go there."

"Yeah, last night I tossed and turned for hours, unable to allow myself to feel anything. It was the kind of night when everything seems impossible, that nothing will work out, and that I don't have any control. Today I just feel really weak."

"Maybe that will be good," suggests Chuck.

"It may allow me to let some things go, to not have to do everything and take on so much. That *would* be good."

"Save your energy for you," he says, as we end the session.

August 30, 2002

The memories reside in the shadows of awareness, giving me time to recuperate from weakness and exhaustion while I also get used to the meds. When I think about the abuse there's still a part of me that wants to deny it, mostly because I can't find a place for it in the life I remember. As I look back on my past I'm forced to revise it, write a new personal history, as the events of the past fifty years all take on new meaning.

How come I couldn't remember the abuse? Why now? How could I have survived all that happened? These questions come up repeatedly, my incredulous mind wanting to reject what I've learned, but deep down I know it happened and that there really is no denying it, as much as I might still want to. It's simply the life I got, the webs I got caught in, the paths I've walked and the people I've met along the way. Those abusive events defined who I became and they still do, to some extent, only now there's a new twist because by recapitulating they will define who I will eventually evolve into, the person I am yet to become. It's exciting to consider that I'm not really that frightened person I always thought I was, steeped in fear and just wanting to stay hidden. I'm actually someone else altogether! But whom?

I must become the warrior capable of driving the energy of the predator further and further away, until I'm freed of it, able to retain my own energy for myself alone. I must be well rested, as well as brave, if I'm to keep going back into the past to retrieve all the fragments of self, not just my innocence and my feelings, but every other part that's caught in the past. I can't let fear stop me. If I do, I'll never truly live. I need to go back into the muck of the past over and over again—no matter how bored or frightened or tired I become—and free myself. I must release Daphne from her tree and bear the incredible splintering process that will inevitably ensue as I go through this process. I must see and experience the past all over again, pay attention to all the signs leading me where I need to go, and bring forward a transformed self into a transformed world. I'm the only one who can do it. No one else can do this for me. I'm the one who lived it and so I'm the only one who can take this journey back into the past. I'm the only one who knows what to look for that has meaning. I'm the only one who knows what I'm capable of, now and in the future. I must have confidence in myself. I must be strong and alert, present in every sense of the word.

In high school and college I was outwardly calm, rather stiff, but nonetheless acting as if nothing bothered me, though inwardly I was in agony, constantly afraid, but I just kept going. And I've been going ever since, moving from one thing to another, needing change all the time, everything from the placement of furniture in a room, to my living abode, to my country. "Always change," became my motto. Now I know that I was running from the horrors of my childhood, wanting more than anything to find a safe little place for myself alone. I'd get to a new place and think that at last I'd found it, only to discover that it wasn't right, that it still wasn't what I was looking for. The search seemed endless. Now I'm back where I started from, finally able to face what it was that drove me. I'm finally putting the brakes on, calling off the search, and studying this perpetually driven self, studying what fueled me, intent now on staying put until my search is done. And I realize the search must be within myself, not attached to someone else. My place of safety must be within. I know I'll never find safety in someone else's life, only in my own, and only when I'm finally there—fully knowing and loving myself—will there be room for another, the right person. But first I have to heal myself. I will only be whole when I have discovered all there is to know about myself and when I have met all my own needs.

August 31, 2002

I'm so distant from everything today—even my own body seems so far away. I'm weak and wobbly, with large puffy circles under my eyes from so little sleep. I don't even recognize myself. Chuck feels at a distance too. Without the anxiety pressing on me so intently I don't feel so desperate, though the old stuff floats out there on the periphery, coming and going on the waves of awareness. I can still go to it, a bit like taking a walk along the seashore, the waves lapping at my feet, and it still bothers me when I do, so I know I'm not done with it yet. I know there's still so much more to understand, and maybe there are still more memories to discover too. Such a bizarre world, painful to contemplate, but I'm at a safe distance now. Like a wooden masthead on a ship, I'm sailing into the changing breeze, but deep down in the murky water below I see the glint of a golden purse nestled on the ocean floor. If I could just get down there and pick it up! It's just a small purse, but I know it's filled with everything I need; it's all in there. If I could just get down there, I'd open it up and everything would flow out into the water and surround me, and then I could release everything stuck inside this wooden body and become real again. But I'm just a hunk of wood stuck to the bow of a ship right now, and even though I see what I need, I'm destined to be Daphne in one form or another until I've resolved my past.

I spend all day in bed, feeling woozy, lightheaded, sad and depressed. I have a strong desire to curl up into a ball again and stay here for days. I don't care about anything right now, not work, or family, or anything. I just want to be alone with my sadness. I want darkness to come so I can go to bed for the long night hours and not have to talk to another person. I want to stop coping so well. I don't want to be the person who "does it all." It might be a relief to admit that I'm not feeling so capable right now. I feel like I've reached my saturation point. I am capable of no more.

Chapter 3

Groundless Doubt

September 1, 2002

I meet with my siblings to hike along the top of the mountain, back in the old neighborhood. We've come together to talk about our parents and their needs as they age, both what needs to be done now and what needs to be planned for in the future. As I drive up the hill to the beginning of the Appalachian Trail, passing my abuser's place on the way, I feel nothing, only distance from the abuse, though once again I note the drastic changes in the landscape of his property, as I had a year ago. I avoid thinking about the past and what happened there, but I can't deny how at home I feel in the familiar woods along the trail, the smell of pine and dry leaves comforting. I'm aware that at every turn in the path I could stop and get lost in the old stuff, but there are too many of us, and there's a different mission today.

Later in the evening, as I sit in my parent's living room listening to my talented brothers sing and play their guitars, I clearly understand my life as an intimately *personal* journey. I realize that as we take our solo journeys we are confronted with what we must be confronted with, in the context of our personal evolution. Once again, I face the truth that this is my own separate life that I'm piecing together, stringing the truths of my experiences into a perspective that makes sense, gaining insight that is meaningful for me alone. I also understand that this is an important moment in detachment. "Here I am amidst these people whom I grew up with, and yet they really know nothing about me," I think, "and it doesn't matter, even in this context of family. My role here now is as quiet participant and observer." I understand that although we once shared part of the journey together, I'm moving on now, breaking away, because my work here is done. I have other business to attend to, for me alone, and it has nothing to do with what ordinarily happens here or is happening in this moment, but everything to do with where I'm headed. And although just where that might be remains a mystery, I'm fully committed to going with the flow of it, to wherever I'm being led, for I feel that I am indeed guided on this leg of my life's journey. Perhaps I always was, but now I'm acutely aware of it.

By the end of the day, I'm grateful for the enjoyment of a few hours of respite from the intensity of the recapitulation; grateful also that I can be in the vicinity of where it all happened yet remain totally detached.

September 2, 2002

I wake in the morning shaky and uncertain, wanting to forget about everything and stay under the covers, hiding my pain and the heavy hurt that I drag around inside me. The past, the divorce, and all the uncertainties of the future have grown into one massive ball of contention, all begging for acknowledgment at once. Sometimes I'm able to push it all away and pretend nothing is there, so I can function, but I don't really want to be functional today. And so, instead of going to the studio I do laundry and spend most of the day reading in bed. The only time I go out is to drive my daughter to and from a friend's house. When my son asks me why I'm staying in my room, I tell him that I'm on vacation for the day, but really all I want is for night to come so I can lie down in the quiet darkness and wait for sleep.

I still cringe when I think about some of the stuff that my abuser did to me. Even though it was a long time ago and seems distant, it's still real. The smell of the woods, of him, and of my child self are strong. His commands, the deafening fear inside me, and the process of shutting down and becoming wooden are all still active inside me. While hiking in the woods with my brothers yesterday, just a couple of miles up the mountainside from where it all took place, I kept my eyes on the path at my feet, not daring to pause or rest, not daring to shift my gaze into the woods, though I was so drawn to. If I did, I knew I'd look right into the past, and it wasn't the time for that. My brothers pointed out a herd of deer, but I barely noticed them standing in the shade. At one point, I almost mentioned the spring in the woods where my abuser had threatened me, the words just sitting there on the tip of my tongue, ready to fall, and they would have if I hadn't bitten my tongue to stop them.

As I take this day of silent retreat, I feel the past starting to creep back in again. I allow my focus to turn to the woods now, no brothers to keep silent before. I feel the covers drawing up over my head as they did when I was a child, and myself rolling into a tiny ball, in acquiescence to the next phase of the recapitulation process. I'm ready to go deeper into the woods.

September 3, 2002

I meet with Chuck, but I'm so tense I can barely sit still. I'm shaking so hard that I get up and pace in the tiny office to cover my true state, but even walking is painful. After a few lurching steps I sit down again, determined to get to the root of what's bothering me.

"You're still holding," says Chuck.

"Yes, I am. How do you know?"

"I can tell," he says, "I feel it."

"I'm scared; every step is frightening."

We sit for a while in silence. I grip the sides of the chair in an effort to still my shaking body. I can barely find the energy to talk.

"Some of the old stuff still bothers me," I finally say.

"Of course it does, but don't stir it up," he suggests, "let it come on its own."

"Why do I still have a hard time letting go of it?"

"You'll let go when the time is right," he says. "You're probably still holding something, and as the anxiety builds around it you're going to feel it, even if you're not clear on what it is. Let whatever it is just sit out there while you retire and rest for a while. Deal instead with the depression and exhaustion."

"I am exhausted. I do need rest," I admit, grateful for the permission to retreat.

"So take it. There is no way you could continue to function while being driven by that anxiety. The past few months were bound to take a toll."

"I guess the old stuff will still be there, even if I take my attention off it."

"It isn't going to go away," Chuck reminds me. "It will be there when you're fully ready to go back to it."

"Even being busy with work hasn't diverted the depression, but maybe this week I'll feel stronger and better able to handle it," I say, still unable to stop shaking.

"Really, I just want to go home and sleep. I think I should leave," I say, even though my time isn't up.

"Then go home and go to sleep. Take care of yourself. Go easy on yourself."

I walk to my car, shaking at every step, and I shake all day afterwards.

September 4, 2002

Intense thunderstorms roll through the valley. Loud thunder and bright flashes of lightning keep me awake all night long and I wake up in the morning still shaky. I force myself to get up, feeling the weight of everything, wanting to collapse right back into bed. By noon I'm exhausted and unable to focus on work. I head home and as soon as I get there I go right to bed. "I'll just lie down and curl up for a few minutes and see what happens," I say, and as soon as I'm under the covers memories seep in unabated, and I am a child again.

My little girl body feels the big rough thumbs of my abuser pinching and pressing, hurting me, as I'm thrown into full recapitulation mode. Memories flash: Vaseline on the doggie stick tail, being in the bathroom, trying to reach something to hold onto, flopping forward, hands not quite reaching the floor. My white-knuckled hands grip my covers and my head throbs with a rush of blood as all time compresses into *now-time*, past and present one. I can't breathe. I look for something to divert my attention, to focus on so I can get through this. Rolling over in bed, I roll right out of the past and back into the present, landing in a pool of deep and quiet sadness.

September 5, 2002

I want stillness today, so I head out to an early morning yoga class, hoping to achieve some inner calm before I head to work. I've decided to keep listening to my exhausted body and give it some attention; so even before leaving the house I make plans to come home early again.

The yoga class definitely grants me a shift, for I am calmer afterwards. By the afternoon I realize the meds are kicking in too because all of a sudden I feel myself shift into a lighter frame of mind, the tired heaviness seeping away, as if I've walked out of a dark tunnel into the light of day. But wouldn't you know, the memories come sneaking back, taking advantage of the first opportunity to begin a direct onslaught. I realize just how close they've been sitting, just behind the heavy curtain of exhaustion, watching and waiting; ready to jump out at a moment's notice. As soon as I'm back home in the afternoon, the minute I lie down on my bed, I feel their dark energy and I go directly into a memory, more fully recapitulating what began emerging yesterday.

Once again, I'm with my abuser in the narrow bathroom in his house. I'm trying not to touch him, but I need something to hold onto as he grabs me from behind and rapes me. I see my hands flailing in front of my eyes as I reach toward the floor, too far away. I curl my hands so tightly that hard white knuckles form. And these are what I focus on as I slip into head-pounding despair, knowing for certain that nobody cares about me. My abuser knows that I don't have feelings, that you can do anything to me because he's trained me, like a monkey.

"She'll just get up afterwards and walk away. See? What'd I tell ya! No feelings," I hear him saying.

"Keep everything inside, don't talk, don't feel," the old voices tell me. "Don't say a word. Never tell—ever! Keep it in. Never tell anyone." And if she never talks, how will anyone know what she's feeling? Well, her walls are crumbling now. The old walls of the old self are coming down. I'm talking now and, in so doing, I'm personally and voluntarily destroying the walls I've been building around myself forever. I'm tired of holding them up, tired of keeping everything in, but I'm also discovering that letting go of the old walls and the silence they imposed is harder than I thought. Holding things in is how I operate, it's how I do things, it's my protection and at this point it's pretty automatic. As soon as the idea of "letting go" arises, I'm filled with dread and a desperate need to immediately replace the old walls with something else. I'm sure that I can't just suddenly burst through them either, because if I do that there will be no end to bursting. I'll keep on bursting until there's nothing left. Just as that memory in the bathroom suggests, I'm a child again, unprotected, scared and vulnerable, and I need something to hold onto, something to grab onto while I'm being obliterated.

Once again, I feel how alone I am as I go through this process, but loneliness is part of the recapitulation as well, for I am as alone as I was as a child. I also find that in the telling of the memories the details are far too disgusting to describe, and so even though I'm sharing them with Chuck, I can't fully speak of everything that was happening. Instead, I write down what I'm experiencing, asking myself to be strong, to not be afraid to take in all the details, so I can free myself of them once and for all. I must be the strong warrior that Chuck is teaching me to be. If I'm not strong for myself, I can't be strong for anyone else, nor expect anyone else to be strong either. Being a strong warrior takes work.

I can't help but wonder what I'll be like without the walls I've lived behind for so many years. I expect I'll be open and exposed, unprotected and vulnerable, a frightened little five-year-old child again. I'm afraid I'll freeze up and not be able to react to what life presents. I'm afraid I'll go numb, dumb, and dead again; that I'll be so raw and innocent that someone will hurt me again. I'm certain that I could still get hurt if I expose the real me, if I let down the walls and reveal the soft, scared person that I really am behind this hard outer shell. It's what I've been protecting myself against my entire life. I know no other way to be. I simply haven't found another way to be—yet.

I'm also afraid that what I hold inside me is far too much to ask another person to bear. I fear this may prevent my going deeper, as I'm growing increasingly protective of Chuck, fearful that even a small amount of the horrors I hold inside may be too burdensome. It's almost as if in sharing the horrors with him I'm asking him to bear the trauma of the rapes as well. But this may just be a projection, my need to protect him in the same way I protect myself, by avoiding and trying to hide from the truth, not going to a deeper level, though it's what I prepare myself for every day. At the same time, I have no one else in my life to talk to, no confidant, no one close enough, except this man, this therapist and shamanic practitioner, who sits so calmly and listens to my dirty tales of woe.

As I struggle to tell him of the things that come through me, I struggle also with feeling that I ask too much and I fear one day he'll have had enough. "I'm sorry, but I can't help you anymore," I fear him saying. "I can't do anything more for you." Where will I be then? But I'm also practical and I know this is his job, that he's been doing it for a long time. I also know that I'm going to have to keep asking for what I consider *too much*, as I continue telling him everything, because this is what I must do and there is nowhere else to turn. I will not evolve if I do not spill my guts, even though I fear that I risk being totally alone again. But on the other hand, I must expect him to be as strong as he is teaching me to be, and so I must continually open to this process with Chuck.

On a professional/client level, I respect Chuck's privacy and the boundaries of the relationship we share, but as a result of being so extremely cautious my entire life I don't take anything for granted. I don't believe anything until I actually see or hear what I need to see or hear. I need to see it on paper or spelled out, plainly illustrated or I'm doubtful. And I like Chuck too. I like him as a therapist, a person, as a man, a thinker, and I feel cautious because of that. Do I need him to like me too? Is that why I'm so cautious and holding back? Am I afraid he won't like me? As I've learned, if I allow myself to get too close—so close that I reveal my soft inner self, my tender self—I will soon be alone, for out of fear and pain I will run back into hiding where everything will be predictable and safe.

"You don't need him," the old voice returns, whispering in my ear. "You don't need him. You don't need help. You're fine behind your wall. Stay where you are, don't ask for anything. You're strong back here behind the safety of your strong walls."

I know it's just the old serpent creature, wrapping around my waist, squeezing tightly, as fearful of change as I am. "Don't bother him, leave him alone, he doesn't care about you" he says, his tongue licking my ear. "You're pathetic and lonely and you'll always be that way—alone, a loner."

How do I go from being strong and protected behind my walls—even though I know I'm also shut down back here—to being vulnerable and open to new life without walls, without suffering dire consequences? I do understand that dire consequences are often necessary as a catalyst to change. Learning to trust myself is part of enacting change as well. Learning to trust another person with my deepest secrets is another part of this dramatic change. As I deal with the process of making these real and necessary changes, including resisting the constant pull to *not* change, I must also encounter all aspects of taking this transformational journey, both good and bad. I must trust that this process will lead to good things as Jeanne hinted at in her missive to me last week, even as the ugly past must come to the surface and be made real again, its ugliness dealt with and exposed. As I suffer through the memories and relive the dire experiences that once posed so much risk to my sanity and wellbeing, I must stay connected to the good that will come of this recapitulation. I must remember that just as the divorce is good, so all these other changes will be good in the end too. But first, I must wade through the muck of the past if I am to reach higher ground, lighter air, and a prettier shore where no pain and no fear reside.

September 7, 2002

I desperately need to talk to Chuck, but I'm pushing myself to wait until I see him on Tuesday, trying to keep the muck of the past contained until then. So I set the intent to write, to release onto paper the old feelings that are returning with a vengeance. Here they are: *I don't matter. No one really cares about me. I have to keep everything to myself. I can't trust. I don't take anyone else's feelings about me for granted. I don't trust myself to accept help because it's too risky and it never lasts. In the end I'll be alone again.* I'm probably alone because I don't trust, and so I see the vicious cycle I'm caught in. Maybe if I could learn to trust and honestly confide, I wouldn't end up feeling so alone.

Yesterday, the old voices returned, taunting and telling me that I'm bothering Chuck, that I'm asking too much of him, telling me that he doesn't really care. I get caught by them. I fall right back into the grasp of their ancient rhetoric. However, the new truth is that I know he does care. After all, he's been with me every step of this journey. It's me; I'm the one who's afraid, as untrusting as ever because he shows me in the most caring of ways that he's available, that he wants me to heal, that he can handle anything I tell him. These struggles lead me to wonder where the girls are, for they feel so far away.

"Where are you, little girls?" I ask, coming out of my head, looking into my heart for a change.

"Waiting," they say.

"Yes, that I know, but for what?"

"We're waiting for you to acknowledge that we are just that: *little girls*," they say, "hurt, sad, lonely little girls who need you to let us release all that stuff we've kept in, all the pain you haven't acknowledged or talked about. We're waiting for you to give us permission to finally let it all go."

Why can't I? Why is it still so hard, and what am I still so afraid of? Am I afraid of needing help, of having to ask for it? Am I afraid of appearing weak? Am I afraid of my own feelings? Am I afraid to talk about myself? Probably all of these things are holding me back, because I've been trained to not talk about myself. I'm not supposed to be important, or consider myself before others, not supposed to have good thoughts about myself. I'm supposed to stay in the background, not draw attention to myself, not have feelings of accomplishment or pride. In fact, all feeling about the self appear tainted by old rules, old commandments, old judgments, and old world voices.

I was taught that I alone was responsible for every thought, word, and deed, and thus everything I've done in my life is a direct reflection of who I am, how I think, and what I'm made of inside. I need to start at the very beginning and find out who I *really* am, aside from the world I grew up in. I must strip down to the bare essence of me and somehow figure out where all these feelings and beliefs about myself came from. I must dismantle the foreign installation that the shamans talk about, the alien ideas implanted by others, especially my parents. This makes perfect sense to me the deeper I go into this recapitulation. For I do not know who I truly am, how I truly think, or what I truly believe. I only know what I've been taught, and that I've been stuck for the past fifty years in a world I just can't wait to get out of—that's the truth of it.

I always knew that I could tolerate any kind of torture, that I would never break down under pressure, like the saints that were burned at the stake or who had their limbs torn off. I always knew I could endure anything, quietly, and that I was very strong. So while my abuser was grooming me, I was also grooming myself to withstand whatever he did to me. It was my path, my own saintly test of endurance, to stand up to anything, to be as silent and as strong as I needed to be. Now I have to redefine the old endurance tests for what they truly are, shamanic challenges, as Chuck has been teaching me. But I must also understand that I no longer need to be my old brave self, for I am, in fact, re-grooming myself to live in a different world now. That is what I'm attempting to do as I take this journey. This recapitulation is a new grooming process, taken in full awareness this time, as I learn to live in a different world of my own creation, totally connected to my spirit's desire for life, unrestricted by the intentions and energy of others. I'm learning to flow with life by letting go of all my old strongholds, allowing myself to feel safe and protected within myself, in a new way, totally trusting and totally free. If I can only hang onto such enlightening thoughts as I proceed, I should sail through the rest of this recapitulation in no time!

It's pretty clear that I'm not done with the memories and the nightmares yet. I admit, I never wanted or expected to relive them, but here I am going back and examining them in minute detail. Even so, I can't say I really *want* to be doing this recapitulation work, but who would? It's so immediately painful and disturbing, so complicated and mixed up, even downright sickening, but I must visit all the memories that are still floating in the murky past, bumping up against me every now and then, asking me to grasp the significance of them. I feel like I'm not quite getting something though, not yet seeing them properly for what they truly offer.

I feel pretty good as I set out to attend an evening art opening. I set my intent to leave the recapitulation behind, but it goes with me anyway, thickly and heavily draped over my shoulders. I'm present, but not fully, as I try to make conversation with a few acquaintances, as I try to appear normal, but in reality I'm pretty spaced out. It's all I can do to walk around the gallery and look at the artwork. I don't stay long, the heaviness becoming increasingly uncomfortable, my distance from reality broadening. By the time I'm back home again, the cloak of recapitulation has pulled its hood back over my head, but I flick it off as I crawl into bed, begging sleep to take me instead.

September 8, 2002

Increasingly, I'm confronted with having to acknowledge that the memories are real. As long as I keep them to myself they remain my secret, and as long as they are my secret they're not real in this world. As emotions ride in on the energy of the memories, I fear their onslaught as much as anything, for their approach signals that the moment of annihilation is soon to arrive, bearing down on me like a raging river. They make me have to *feel* in so many ways, a wild torrent pushing against my weakening dam. When the dam breaks I expect chaos to ensue; I expect the walls to come tumbling down. I'm as fearful of what the flood will wash away as I am of what it will reveal, fearful of its devastating potential, as well as its cleansing potential. I strain against the inevitable bursting of my once so solid and indestructible walls, yet I also know that I must face annihilation now too.

September 9, 2002

Each time a memory comes up I struggle with having to tell Chuck, as if he hasn't been here all along, sitting through countless sessions over the past year. It's as if it's the first time I'm telling him about this stuff, as if he doesn't know anything about me. The same situation arises when I need to call him. Desperate to connect to someone in this world, I must confront the old self who won't call him, who fears he won't know who I am and why I'm calling. And so when I finally do call, I fully identify myself, stating my entire name, as if he has never met me before, as if he won't know me by my voice and my first name alone. On the outside, I'm a highly accomplished fifty-year-old woman, but on the inside I'm a tiny girl, curled up in a ball, full of fear. My bond of trust feels so fragile. It's better when I'm sitting in front of Chuck, but as soon as I leave his office I feel forgotten, like I don't matter or exist. I have to start over again at each session, feeling that I can trust, that I'm acceptable. But I also know that although the steps are slow and deliberate, each week I come a little further along this path of change.

I realize the depths of the abuse. My inability to trust that another person could really care enough to want to sit and hear my recapitulation week after week illustrates the amount of work still to be done. I find it hard to believe that people really care, even though they say they do. I'm in a perpetual bind around the issue, still expecting to be treated as if I don't matter and surprised when someone takes an interest or seriously considers my situation. By keeping the walls up to protect myself, words never reach me, as they simply hit against the walls, never penetrating. I'm so busy behind my walls trying to protect myself from further abuse that I can't really hear what people are saying. It's taking a long time for the full realization that I exist *now*, in a different reality, to penetrate those solid walls.

September 10, 2002

I wake feeling exhausted after sleeping only lightly, having fought with my inner girls all night over this recapitulation process, trying to break down some walls. The girls were pulling for silence all night, asking me to leave them alone.

"We've been fine all these years, just leave us alone. We don't want to remember anymore, it hurts to remember," they told me.

"I know," I told them, feeling their resistance. "It hurts me too. I'm feeling it, but we can't stay hidden. We have too much to do. We have too much we've been keeping down and we need to let it go so we can be free."

Even though sleep was fleeting I'm thankful that the dragging depression is gone, the meds apparently working. I have a session with Chuck this morning and I'm eager to jump right in, barge through my fears, and head straight back into the woods where a memory sits waiting for me. In spite of the reluctance of my inner girls, I'm going to push ahead and recapitulate.

"I'm with my abuser and his daughter, in the woods, playing the Doggie game," I tell Chuck as soon as I sit down. "We're two little puppies with long chains around our necks, rubbing our rears together, and then we share a wooden tail. My abuser sticks the two ends of a wooden pole into us; we're two little puppies joined at the tail."

"The girls are afraid," I say, feeling their resistance as I reveal this memory. "Which means that I'm afraid, but it's time now. I keep telling them we've waited long enough, that it's time to get out of this frozen state and be free."

We talk about the importance of my adult self being fully present at all times, willing to take over and guide the frightened girls through all the memories. At the same time, I, the adult, must also be fully available to experience everything—for as long it takes to retrieve every single tiny detail, until nothing bothers me—even my deepest feelings and emotions. As much as I want to resist along with the girls, I know it's not the way to go. I even wonder if they're really resistant or only making me face it on my own. And so while Chuck works the EMDR machine, I face the past, wondering what more there is to learn from this snippet of memory.

As I go back into the woods, all the unrealized pain and emotions wrapped in the memory begin to emerge and, difficult though they are to bear, I let them ride through me. Physically allowing them to surge through me, I cringe, whimper, shake, and shiver, as I plunge back into the woods over and over again, until I've released everything that comes up, until it feels like I'm empty, purged, fully done.

Chuck mentions how my out-of-body experiences, from a psychological perspective, allowed me to dissociate from the painful experiences, but from a shamanic point of view they offered enviable, valuable, and yearned-for experiences.

"It's a superb achievement," he says. "You were able to use the pain to your advantage and turn it into a lifesaving practice, but you also had the added benefit of learning a highly desirable shamanic practice. The shamans call it *dreaming*. In shamanic dreaming you find your energy body and intentionally journey in infinity. You found your energy body as a little girl. You left your physical body under the impact of trauma and transported your awareness to places of safety."

"I can still do it," I say, "but whenever I feel myself start to go, it still feels like a protective maneuver. Could I do it simply because I want to have the experience?"

"Yes, I think you can."

"I know how the saints and martyrs did it, how they were able to withstand being tortured or burned at the stake. They were able to do what I did—leave their bodies. I know the process," I say, suddenly understanding so much more. "We're so focused on the pain of dying. In recapitulating my childhood experiences, I've discovered that we pretty quickly transcend the pain. Our awareness is capable of leaving our bodies. Death isn't so frightening a prospect once you understand that. The saints left their bodies the same way I did, so they could withstand the torture, and then death didn't matter because they were already out-of-body."

"That's probably pretty accurate," Chuck says.

"I guess I thought someone would have already thought of that or written about it. It's pretty interesting when you think about it. I too was tortured and found a way to not feel, that was how I survived."

"I'm surprised you even made it out of childhood," Chuck says.

"Well, part of me didn't, the child part of me that's so afraid and untrusting, the part of me that's making this so hard, the part that won't ask for help or trust that it will be there when really needed, the part of me that doesn't trust that things can change. She's stuck back there. And she learned a long time ago that it's better not to ask for help. Better to just be quiet and deal with it in the ways that work so well already."

"I know it's going to be difficult to keep going through the memories, including the pain, but you'll only be fully released as you do," says Chuck.

"I do understand that. I *have* to do this recapitulation."

Chuck nods when I say this.

"I have to go to each memory, experience it, and move on. I won't be able to change anything about myself, or my life, until I do. If I don't energetically release myself from the past, I won't have access to my own energy and there won't be room for the new me in there either."

"The girls have to trust me," I say, as I prepare to leave. "They just have to let me take care of it now, to take over and rid them of their burdens. I am the ark by which they can be saved, by which they can be freed."

"Good work," says Chuck and, with my intentions renewed and strengthened, I leave his office and head off to a day of work.

In the evening, I revisit the sixteen frightened aspects of my child self, all those abused little girls still afraid of life. We meet in active imagination.

"You all need to trust me; if no one else, at least me," I say, pleading with them. "Let me bear all the torture and the horrors as we go through this recapitulation. I was there too. You need to give me the memories, so we can all be free. The memories are like invisible ropes tying us down, keeping you little children, when you deserve to be grown up. We all deserve to merge as one and become who we are meant to be."

"I'm not going to get rid of you—you are part of me. I'm going to treasure and love you. I vow to take your pain. Give it to me, so I can feel it after all these years, and then we'll let it go. We'll let the wind take it on its final journey into the greater universe where all things eventually end up. It's our destiny to become free like the wind. Please give the past back to me more fully, so I can learn how to feel and how to cry, so I can heal for us and continue growing for us, so I can take us places we never even dared to go before, so I can take us riding on the wind."

"You gave me the pain of a memory earlier in the day and I could hardly stand it, but I know where it comes from and why. You can give me that pain any time you need to—I *can* bear it. I'm old enough, and brave enough, and ready enough to bear it. Okay?"

Before long I'm tossing and turning in my bed, bombarded by flashbacks, embraced by somatic pain. Memories and objects intrude, and each time I roll away from one memory another appears. No matter which direction I face, my abuser repeatedly accosts me. Swollen and sore, I bear the pain of being pried apart, a nail being pushed up my urethra. I feel cold metal chains being stuffed into my vagina and wooden handles forced into my anus. I feel fingers and fingernails poking and pinching. In rapid-fire, a splurge of memories spill out of me. I experience hands holding my legs wide open, a penis shoving into me, hands grabbing my legs, fingers groping my vagina. I am raped anally. I feel pain and I latch onto it as my savior, while all the other feelings and emotions that I cannot bear smother in its insipid embrace.

September 11, 2002

"Do you still have any doubts that it happened?" Chuck asked me yesterday.

"Yes, sometimes," I said, "but less and less. Once I get to all the feelings, I think I won't have any doubts left. The feelings are so real and so raw that they leave no room for doubt."

As I continue putting the pieces of this mysterious puzzle-of-self together, I wonder how I can possibly still have doubts, but I also know that doubt and denial are old protective tactics. Such good friends, I know how they operate. They come visiting, asking me to question my motives. "Who in their right mind would want to have such horrific stuff in their past?" they ask. "Who would want to admit to partaking in such ugly acts? Who would want to carry such burdens, and why?" But I do carry such burdens and I did partake in such ugly acts. I can't get away from the fact that those two truths have been factors in my life forever, a very sad and heavy load to carry I admit, but mine to bear nonetheless. Now, as I face the fuller truths of that heavy load, I have the opportunity to lighten it considerably, if not free myself totally. By sharing it, by talking about it, I shed one thin layer at a time, almost flaying myself in a heart-wrenchingly painful process, but it means I get to live a new life when I'm done, to emerge encased in a new skin. It means I will finally be a free person, able to take on life without fear. These things I am certain of.

I recall my fearful child self, in kindergarten, so petrified of the other children and the huge playground. Afraid to run across it, I hugged the walls of the building. Though the teachers kindly encouraged me to try the slide or the swing, I refused to budge from my spot. I simply couldn't move. All I could do was huddle petrified against the brick wall. No amount of reasoning would unstick me from my spot in the shade of the building. It took many weeks of enticement and many reports sent home, questioning my behavior, before it was decided that I was suffering from socialization issues. My mother decided that I was just being difficult because I was forced to wear a dress—in those days the school dress code for all girls. She explained to the teacher that I didn't normally play in dresses and that was the reason I wouldn't sit on the floor with the other kids during reading time, or go down the slide. She said that in a dress I sat like a proper little lady, as she had taught me, never on the floor but in a chair with hands clasped in my lap and ankles daintily crossed. But of course the dresses weren't the reason, and no amount of enticement or reasoning could pull me away from my protective wall, until *I deemed it was safe*.

Yesterday, while working at the studio, I once again told the girls I would handle the pain and immediately I was struck with excruciating genital and abdominal pain. All doubt went out the window as I buckled under the intensity of it, fell to the floor, and rolled into a ball. A few years ago I might have gone to the doctor to have the pain checked out. Invariably, through all the visits I made, nothing was ever found to explain my symptoms. I now know that the pain I feel is something undetectable by modern means. It's only detectable by me. And yesterday's pain was very clearly and insistently telling me, in the most visceral way, that I had been sexually abused as a child. I accepted the pain on behalf of my child self, knowing that she still lives inside me, that she's still in great need, and that I'm the only one who can help. I'm the only one who knows what my child self went through, and she's letting me know that she's ready now, in the only way she can. She has observed the situation long enough and realized that she can trust me now. She feels safe enough. She knows that only I can help. Only I can listen. Only I can fix it.

September 12, 2002

During yoga class, as we focus on opening and releasing the hips, I sense that I'm accessing new memories, releasing them, being asked to listen to them, to believe them. I clearly understand that the pain I experience in my hips is ancient material from childhood, memories and trauma that got stored there when they became too much to bear. I am constantly aware, throughout the class, that this is the truth, that something in me numbed my muscles and sinews, cut off physical and mental capacities to remember, and used my body as a place of storage, with the intention that one day I would return, excavate the trauma, and relearn the truth. As I go through the class, I accept the truth of this intent, set so long ago. I ponder why I might still need to hold onto even a shred of disbelief. What am I still keeping from myself?

The class ends with a few minutes of meditation. Almost immediately I go into a vivid recapitulation. I am alone, sitting cross-legged in the sandbox in the backyard of the house I lived in when I was little. I am an extremely sad three-year-old again, at that age already leaden with the weight of adult-sized depression. Slowly and methodically, I shovel sand into a small metal bucket and then dip my hands into it, sifting the sand through my fingers. Suddenly, I dump the bucket, spilling the cool sand onto my shorts and bare legs. Filling the bucket again, I turn it upside down over my head. As it rains down over my face, I feel the grit of it in my hair, in my mouth, and running down into my shirt. I dump the sand over my head again and again, until I finally fill my pants with it, pouring shovelfuls of cooling sand down into my shorts. I'm aware, as I recapitulate, that I want to bury myself, but something else erupts and before I know it I'm tossing sand all over the place, even flinging it at myself. I'm angry! I'm fucking angry!

I come out of the meditation a little fearful that I may have actually gesticulated wildly, that my body may have acted out the recapitulation, but I open my eyes to see my hands sitting calmly on my knees, my back straight, my head perfectly still. I have not budged an inch on the outside, but on the inside I have traveled through decades and fully expressed my anger.

September 13, 2002

My inner girls are still hiding out, though I'm not sure why. Are they suggesting that I'm still in denial, not fully accepting of what happened to them? Or are they full of fear? I understand that they've lived with the trauma of the abuse for so long and that numbness has become a natural state, for the truth is that I'd sooner retreat from life than risk deep personal wounding. But even so, I've traveled far from that petrified little girl I once was.

"In spite of, or because you went through this traumatic abuse, you've gained an incredible ability to keep moving forward, to get on with life no matter what," Chuck mentioned the other day. So what's my problem? Why am I stuck here? Why the continued denial? Don't I want to get on with the rest of my life? I sense the girls sitting quietly, waiting for something from me, but just what that might be, I'm not sure.

It's Friday night. I'm not feeling too well. I lie rolled into a ball of old feelings in my dark bedroom for several hours. The pain of hiding everything within, of holding back, is so intense that I am reminded once again that this is the state of survival that I lived in for so long. I was a survivor, but I only survived by forgetting and pretending the abuse didn't happen. *It didn't happen.* At this moment, I realize that my continued denial is actually part of my recapitulation. *I am recapitulating the numbness of denial.* If the abuse didn't happen—my denial points out—I could go on and have a semblance of a normal life. I could grow up and move away, and do what I needed to do to feel like a normal person, for above all else I just wanted to be normal. Now, once again, I'm confronted with the bitter truth that I wasn't normal, that I never was, that my entire life was spent pretending I was something else. I made up the person I am today, mostly to protect myself, and I'm still trying to protect myself because otherwise I—and life itself—hurt too much.

Pretending meant survival. It became a life raft of my own creation. Carefully and painstakingly constructed, my pretend identity carried me forward into life. Now I'm giving up the old life raft. Constructed of pretend materials, it no longer serves its purpose. By dismantling it and tipping it over, I'm forcing myself to swim to shore on my own, finding out along the way just who I might be as I face the dark waters I find myself in. There are whirlpools, strong currents, undertows, and monsters of the deep to encounter as I swim along. Things I pretended weren't there are now clearly visible, all heading straight toward me, bearing down at full tilt. They carry painful memories, unrecapitulated feelings and emotions that sting and whip like the burning tentacles of poisonous jellyfish. The challenge I face at the moment is that I know it hurts and that it's going to keep hurting as I make my way through this recapitulation, so I'm denying it, still trying to pretend it all away.

September 14, 2002

I make a good amount of money at a big sale at the studio, which I'm happy about. Again, I note how being extremely busy has its benefits. I've been able to sail through the busy days fairly well, with little intrusion from the old stuff. At the same time, I feel the absence of it, the intensity of the deep soul-searching self noticeably missed on those busy days. I realize I need the balance that the recapitulation offers. My outer person needs my inner person to be in balance, both parts equally attended to, both given the same amount of attention.

I also need my quiet time, my alone time to roll up into a ball and let the feelings come, if I'm to make this inner process really productive. I value these moments alone—my trying to grasp it all times—and I can truthfully say that I yearn for them now. As painful as they are, I find that rolling up for hours, lost in the memories of some old aspect of self, often offers the most important moments of breakthrough and clarity. Sometimes I can barely wait for the day when I can once again say that I'm taking a vacation and hang out in my room, curled on my bed, my journal by my side, getting lost in another world.

I realize just how important it is for me to give this kind of time and attention to myself. I need it. I need to be able to wrap my arms around myself and let the pain echo down and through the hollow tunnel of time inside me. I desperately want to get to all the stuff that's buried in there, but I don't know how to simply acquiesce to it, for even though I'm gung-ho to do this recapitulation, more often than not I'm in my usual state of numb denial. It's so automatic that I don't even realize what's happening. I've always been so careful to push feelings away, *to not feel*, preventing further woundings my main objective. Now, however, I'm eager to feel all that lies pressed down inside me—so tightly compacted that I can barely budge it or scoop it out—but it takes such conscious effort to stay fully present and on task. To jolt myself I've begun asking, just like Chuck does in sessions: *How are you feeling?*

September 15, 2002

I dream that I'm sitting in my parent's living room, surrounded by a bunch of relatives. Everybody's talking about all the recent divorces in the family when my dad—much younger than in real life—gets up and comes over to where I'm sitting. "I've posted a guard in the bathroom," he whispers, leaning over me. I am so incredulously furious that I react immediately, screaming at him. "It's too late! It's too fucking late!" I say, my anger jolting me awake.

I'm glad I only have a few days left until I see Chuck again. Sleeping is better now that the meds are taking affect, though I still awaken each day feeling empty. During the day those fragile and shaky feelings gradually subside. By evening only heavy exhaustion fills my limbs. During the night, however, the emptiness returns. And so here I am now, once again feeling like I'm just about ready to crumble. In addition, I'm beginning to get stressed about filling my half of the gallery for the two-person show in November. I really need to be working continuously on new stuff, without distraction. I should get out of bed and get started on some new pieces right now, though I struggle with the deeper pull to just stay here all day, to roll up and vegetate, but luckily I don't have time. Duty calls. It's probably better that way.

September 17, 2002

I dream that I'm painting a huge ballroom. In one hand I hold a very valuable antique glass vase of a brilliant and beautiful cobalt blue color. I'm trying to paint with my free hand, which is nearly impossible. I teeter high on ladders, protecting the vase at all costs, while simultaneously intent upon being an impeccable painter. Indeed, an almost impossible task.

I meet with Chuck first thing in the morning. We talk about my dream, so fresh and visceral that I can still feel the shape of the vase in my hands and the weight of it in my lap as I describe it. I'm able to see that although I'm holding onto something precious, it makes it impossible to complete the painting job. In the dream, I do want to do a good job—in my usual exacting manner—but I just can't put the vase down. It's utterly important for me to hold it close and to protect it. I understand that the dream relates to my recapitulation process—as everything does of course—and that it's suggesting that I won't be able to finish the recapitulation if I don't release what I've always considered most precious to me: *my pretending that everything is okay, the real cloak of denial.* Chuck helps me to understand that in holding onto the last thread of what I have considered to be of value, I am unable to proceed; indeed I'm quite stuck.

"So, what do you think will happen if you let go?" he asks.

"Nothing will happen, I'll still be here and I'll also be free."

"What's keeping you from letting go?"

"My fear that something will get me if I don't protect myself," I say. "But I don't need to protect myself anymore, because the fear that I was protecting myself from is no longer there. My abuser is not a threat; it's only my own fear that's a threat. I'm keeping something that doesn't exist, and I'm protecting something important, the self, but the self is no longer threatened. Who is threatening me? No one. I'm learning to be free now, for the first time in my life."

When I tell Chuck about the dream of yelling at my father, he wonders if I could have a heart-to-heart with him.

"Could you talk to him about what happened?" he asks.

"It would serve me well, but I think it would only hurt him," I say. "He's dying, wrapped up in his own worries, barely present most of the time. Would I want to intrude and remind him of things he's obviously chosen to not address, like the abortion?"

"Something to think about," Chuck says.

"Mostly I'm angry at him. I think he knows something. I keep having a memory, seeing him walking away, a look of disgust on his face, but I can't place it yet. It's such a vague and dreamy memory, so long ago, but my own anger and sadness are clearly palpable whenever I go to that memory, as is my loneliness. The incredible loneliness hits me like a slap in the face every time I experience that memory, vague as it is. I think he may have known what was happening to me, but he chose to walk away. He couldn't handle it then. Could he handle it now?"

"Could he?" Chuck asks.

"I'm not sure I want to have a conversation with him."

"Why?"

"I'm afraid of what he might say."

"The memories are hard enough in themselves, though it might validate your experiences," Chuck says.

"Right now, I don't even like talking about it with you."

After leaving Chuck's office, I contemplate this new idea of speaking to my father. Is it right that I confront him? Do I really care? As I drive to work, I realize once again that I'm not doing this recapitulation journey for anyone else. I have no other agenda than to solve the mysteries of the deeper self. I also realize, however, that part of this process of self-discovery involves doing a dispassionate review and thorough investigation of my parents, both facing the truth of them and freeing myself from them in the process.

The private, inner person that I am would rather not involve anyone else in this deeply personal journey, but the evolving self, the one working on this recapitulation, knows that seeking ultimate truth would be extremely valuable. On the other hand, the pragmatic self knows that at this point in his life my father is a sick old man; that he is the way he is, long ago having decided to shut down to life. He's not interested in making amends, he doesn't think or act that way. He grunts his way through most conversations these days, and in the past our conversations rarely went beyond pleasantries. I remember having only a few deeper conversations with him, when I was in my twenties, but he was expecting something from me then, seeking advice.

As a teenager and young adult, I used to give my parents advice on how to better treat my younger siblings, for I saw how insensitive they were towards them, and so when he came to me later it didn't seem odd. My parents were rarely able to achieve any depth of feeling or emotion and conversations were cursory, messages bluntly delivered, as if they'd just rather not be parents at all. So tiresome and boring childrearing seemed to be for them, yet they had given birth to seven children! One day I knew I'd made an impact when my mother, after scolding one of my siblings at the dinner table for pointing out another sibling's faults, made the comment that advice would only be doled out by the parents and the big sister—me. I knew then that they took me seriously, for I often felt old and wise next to them, and it felt good to finally be appreciated. But at this point in his life my father is a sad old man, wrapped up in his own world. In the past, he just wanted us to tell him that he was a great father. He wanted his ego stroked and fed saccharin platitudes, true or not. Groundless declarations of love suited him well enough in the past, but never accusations, never questions and probings of deeper issues.

I find it hard to concentrate at work and finally give up and go home. I'm consumed by the question: Should I approach my father or not? I wonder what I could possibly say to him, though I'm aware that any conversation around the topic of sexual abuse might unleash something; perhaps even unravel the last little thread of life in him. I have to wonder what good it would do, except make him sad, and I don't see the point in doing that to him. I see him shutting down in the face of the truth as he and my mother have always done, pulling further away from reality, further into their no-feelings, no-emotions, no-truths emptiness, the same places they required that my siblings and I go. The truth is that they made their own choices a long time ago to live their lives the way they did.

I realize that in speaking to them it might speed up my process, but it may have the opposite effect as well and seriously stall my recapitulation. Whom would it benefit and whom would it harm, and what's the point of either? I don't require anything from them as I take this personal journey and I have no illusions about them either. I've chosen to distance myself from them most of my life, for they offered little to nurture my spirit or feed my deepest needs. I've had to look elsewhere for meaning in my life. I carry no resentment, nor do I harbor ill will towards them. I simply have no need or desire for any deeper relationship with them at this point. In the end, I simply don't know if telling them anything personal really matters.

September 18, 2002

Totally exhausted after doing an eight-hour painting job, I lie in bed at night and wait for sleep. As I teetered on ladders in reality today, that dream I'd recently had of holding onto that delicate blue vase while teetering on ladders in dreamland kept coming into my thoughts. The memory of being pregnant at age twelve and having an abortion of twins* simultaneously appeared and stayed on my mind while I worked as well. Are they related, the precious vase and the abortion, a symbol of the denial of the memories, as Chuck suggested, especially that one? As the day went on, the memory of the abortion became utterly real—there is no denying it. Do I really need my father to confirm it?

[*The original recapitulation of this memory can be found in *The Man in the Woods* on May 11, 2002.]

September 19, 2002

I dream that I'm out walking in a terrific blizzard, in the dark of night, along slippery, snow-covered mountain roads. It's impossible to stay on my feet. Buffeted by ferocious winds that have knocked out all power, I fall down repeatedly. Slipping and sliding along on the soles of my boots, I fly around curves and crash into snow banks as I make my way through the dark and snowy night. Though I tumble and fall the entire length of the steep mountain road, I am never hurt; I just get up and venture onward. It's actually kind of thrilling as I glide effortlessly along, and I'm warm and toasty in a long hooded down coat.

As I come out of the mountains, I see a farmhouse in the distant valley. I make my way towards it. I knock on the door and the man who lives there says he has no power, but that I can wait out the storm in his antique's barn or under the tents I see set up near it. I'm slightly miffed that he doesn't invite me inside where I see a cozy fire burning, but I'm thankful for any shelter, as it's a bitter night. As I make my way to the barn, I see rusty antique farm machinery buried under the snow. It's clear that it's been exposed to the elements for a long time and that none of it works, though I'm immediately aware of its value. A few other people come out of the storm, sliding down out of the mountains too. They stand and wait with me in the barn, wondering when the power will return. I tell them I don't know, but that we're free to wait in the barn as long as necessary. After a while, the electricity returns, slowly at first, dimly lighting a few light bulbs hanging in the barn ceiling, eventually getting stronger and stronger until it's finally on full force. Eventually, the sun comes out and begins to warm everything up. Slowly the snow melts and things begin to work again, and I know that everything is going to be okay now.

From this dream I go directly into another. A man stares at me longingly. I know he's in love with me, but I'm not interested. I'm just not ready for intimacy or any kind of relationship. "No, I can't deal with anything right now, no love, no sex, no intimacy. Go away!" I tell him, quite forcefully.

I wake steeped in the calmness of the ending of the first dream, knowing that it portends my future, for I cannot get away from the serenity I feel as I open my eyes. Even so, I know that I do indeed have a tough road still ahead. I'm fully aware that this recapitulation is still full of tricky situations; that I will have to let go of control and barrel along as if on icy slopes. I will have to learn how to let go to the inevitable flow of this process. This recapitulation is about power too, about regaining my own power, my own energy, and learning how to let it grow inside me. I'm certain that this recapitulation will lead to a better life, a better me, and that everything will be okay in the future. This dream underscores the process of revisiting old parts of the self, left behind unused and neglected, like the farm machinery I knew had value. It's time to learn how to deal with all the painful things that happened to me, recapturing all the forgotten emotions.

Instinctively, I knew that the other people I'd met in the dream were on the same kind of journey. None of us complained at having to wait out the storm in the cold barn. We took what was offered, knowing that our trials were necessary and that in the end the sun would come out and things would get better. The second dream seems to be associated with conserving my energy for myself, as I don't have any energy to spare for anything except my recapitulation. This is true.

I consider one last time whether or not to speak to my parents. I don't think they will be very open, but maybe I don't want to confront them because they might respond positively, actually be relieved by my acknowledging that I remember everything. Perhaps they'd confirm it and then I'd be faced with the bitter truth, spoken, made real in a different way. On the other hand, my father is so fragile right now, mentally and physically impaired. If he's in a good mood we're all happy, my mother is happy. Most of the time he's so removed and depressed; it tortures my mother, though she won't even acknowledge that he's ill. Never good at facing the truth herself, she'd rather keep it hidden. I don't think she really cares to know, to be reminded of the past, to have to go into her own feelings. No one must know anything personal. She doesn't even want others to know that my father is sick, even refusing to tell their best friends. She scolded me because I had mentioned it to a relative who called with concern and offers of help. I had to convince her that it was better for my father if people knew he was facing his death. I didn't mince words, though she instantly rejected this idea, making me realize she isn't facing his death at all. I realize that the telling of my truths, though good for me, would be devastating for them. I can't be cruel to them. It doesn't feel right. I decide to let it go.

I'm down to the last pages of yet another journal filled with memories; vivid pictures from the past and somatic sensations of the abuse unearthed in the process. I've filled these pages quickly. Now I need to go deeper, to where the feelings lie, long buried beneath the leaves and sticks in my abuser's woods, leeched out of me in my agony. I wish I could dig into the earth with my bare hands, easily uncovering the layers of feelings as I dig. But it's proving to be a harder task than that, more challenging than returning to the woods and what happened there, for inside myself lies the rest, as buried and covered in illusion as my parent's lives. Expecting them to shed their old ways and change how they relate to the world is just another illusion. For me, however, such a process has become a necessity. They taught me well, did their jobs impeccably, for I have survived as a result of what they taught me. Denial and illusion have kept me safe, but now it's my job to reject everything they taught me. I must try to live my life in the way that's right for me, truthfully, by shedding the illusion and becoming as honestly real with myself as possible. It's finally time.

Beneath the visual pictures that I paint lies the energy that drives me, the creative power so strong that I can't stop it. The amorphous energy of my spirit channels through my body, out my hands, and onto my painting surfaces. My emotions are deeply hidden and equally amorphous, needing to be channeled into human rather than visual form, needing expression in spoken sound and allowed to be felt in my body self, whether painful or joyous. I must use my creative talents to become a physical human being, fully present and functioning. I must plant my feet firmly on the ground and allow myself to be filled with the feelings and emotions that I long ago blocked. Everything must be acceptable; everything must be allowed.

September 20, 2002

I wake up hoping that today will be the day that I'll finally be able to get to that last little sticking point, be able to cry, release, and let go. I feel that if I could just cry then I'd be fine, everything would release and I'd be okay. Another part of me knows it's not that easy. The reality is that I'm still repressing, still holding back the unleashing of the sound and fury of my injured child self.

I begin yet another new journal as I write these words, the last journal ending with my wondering how to launch myself into the next phase of my recapitulation, how to let the feelings be expressed in my body, in sound and sensation, rather than in the color and form that I've always used for expressing my deepest feelings. I'm an expert at visual expression. My challenge now is to allow the pain and the degradation, the humiliation and the shame, to have *physical* expression, but I've been shut down, a zombie for so long. How do I wake up the zombie? How do I open up my chest, shake my heart, and wake up the sleeping child within? How do I set her free? How do I tell her that it's okay now, it's not your fault, so that she'll actually believe it, so I'll be able to move on and live a different life? How do I allow my Zombie Girl self to cry, to feel, and to react? I don't really know how to do any of those things, except when angry, but anger is most often negative. Now I'm searching for positive energy to carry me forward. Normally I shut down and just let things roll off me. I'd rather do that than deal with anything disturbing; to avoid is far easier to allow. It's what my parents taught me to do so well.

How do I express myself?

Oh God, a confrontation with my son! He's furious, yelling, big and threatening. We lock hands, pushing hard against each other, steam almost coming out of his ears; his eyes cold hard rocks glaring into mine, frightening because he's getting so tall. And then it's over and the tears come. I hug him, sit on his bed and hold him, and realize that this is what he wants and needs. He doesn't want to be angry with me; he just wants to know I love him and that everything will be okay. This is what I never got, but I can give it now to my own children, acknowledging their sadness over the divorce, their feelings of loss, confusion, and disorientation. They just want me to be the stable one, solidly present and available, not isolating them but receiving them, loving them no matter what the issues are. My son understands why things are the way they are, and that it will be better once we move into our own house. We're all a little unsure of our places right now.

"I miss you," he says. "All you do is hide out in your room."

"True," I said, thinking that we're all hiding in our own ways. "I know I've been absent a lot, I'm sorry. I'm doing a lot of work on myself and I know it takes me away."

"Could you at least sit and read in the living room?" he asks.

"Yes, I can do that," I say, and my heart goes out to him for taking this journey with me, certainly not a journey he'd ever bargained for.

He feels better after we talk. I tell him that I'm proud of him for being able to cry, to release in a way that I've never been able to do, that it's really good. I'm amazed at this confrontation with real emotion, on the very day that I ponder my own inability to react and be emotional! He reacted and he got my attention, proving that reactions get results. This was not what I learned as a child, where reactions were immediately shut down. Too disturbing to my parents, all emotional outbursts were stifled, pushed below the surface so that you'd never know there was a thing wrong in our house. We were all perfect little unemotional beings, a family of zombies. This is what I fight against constantly. This is where my recapitulation is taking me now, as I face the truth of the parents I got, who offered no emotional outlet. I turn away from them now and find my own way, for I am more certain than ever that confronting them is not the outlet to change—*I am.*

There are so many things that I can't tell my son right now, though I wish I could. One day perhaps he'll understand what all of this is about.

September 21, 2002

I can't get up in the mornings and run anymore; I'm just too exhausted to exercise. I feel a little guilty about it, but at the same time the exhaustion is so great that I feel it's okay to pamper myself for a little while. "Rest, don't push," I tell myself, though at the same time I think I might feel better if I do run. Instead, I take advantage of the time to sit in bed and write out the details of a long and complicated dream. The setting is a large sunny building on the edge of the ocean, an old warehouse now renovated into loft apartments. I've just moved into a second floor loft with my family. The view out the large front windows looks upon a wide street, then a boardwalk, and then the ocean. The dream is in several parts.

Part 1: I'm with my mother, passing through the lobby of the building. There's a dance studio on this ground floor, the door of which is wide open. We hear talking, the sound of loud voices spilling out into the lobby. I'm not really listening, but apparently my mother is because she goes into the classroom. I hear her asking the students if they know a certain dancer. I stand at the open doorway and look in at my mother as she holds court, standing in the center of a group of women students, speaking about this famed dancer. She's very knowledgeable about this dancer and as she talks the students become increasingly interested. The teacher asks my mother if she knows some of the dances that this dancer has performed and my mother proceeds to execute them impeccably, very gracefully, with perfect classical form. Eventually the teacher joins her. I watch as they dance for the students. I'm surprised, but at the same time not surprised to see this side of my mother.

Part 2: I leave my mother behind, and head over to the staircase leading to the second floor. As soon as I put my foot onto the first step, it flattens out and the staircase becomes a slippery chute that I slip and slide on, barely able to get a grip on the slick surface. I am halfway up when the chute suddenly drops away completely. I fall a long way down the empty stairwell with the walls caving in on top of me. I land unhurt in a dark pit at the bottom. I get up and start over, but once again, at each step I take, the staircase shifts and changes. After many attempts and many failures, I finally make it up to my second floor loft apartment.

Part 3: I'm getting the kids ready for school. It's their first day at the new bus stop. I'm a little nervous, since I don't know the area very well. My daughter goes outside to wait for the bus. When I hear it coming I look out the window and see her waiting with some other children. She looks up at the building and, seeing me looking down at her, waves, letting me know she's fine. I wave back, my fears for her dissipating. I then turn to tell my son to hurry and find that he's already left. I hope he too got on the bus.

Part 4: I start down the stairs and once again they completely disappear, collapsing beneath me. I fall through space. Wood and sheetrock tumble on top of me as if the entire building is crumbling. Finally, I land on the ground floor. "That keeps happening!" I say out loud, surprised and a little miffed, though once again I am unhurt.

Part 5: I'm standing outside on the sidewalk in front of the building when I hear a splash and someone screaming for help in the water. I run over to the boardwalk, thinking how I might go about rescuing someone, but when I get there I don't see anyone. I peer into the choppy ocean waves that splash with great force against the solid wall of the boardwalk. I wonder if I should go for extra help or if I should just dive in myself and see if I can locate anyone under the water, though the rough water presents the possibility of a difficult rescue. I keep peering into the water, but still don't see anyone. I also know that if I dive in and try a rescue that I risk my own life. It's a cloudy day. The water is rough and steely gray, and I'm aware that I might not come out alive, and so I'm reluctant to jump in. When there's no sign of a person in trouble, I'm greatly relieved that I don't have to go into the cold water.

Part 6: I go back inside the apartment building and head up the stairs, but as usual they trick me, abruptly shifting into a slippery metal chute again, which is hard to walk up. I keep sliding back even though I'm holding onto the sides, steadily pulling myself upward. I realize I'm not making any progress when the slide shifts. The walls of the building completely fall away and I find myself balancing on a miniature staircase suspended in space. The only thing left of the building is the ceiling, which floats directly above me. Balancing, as if on a tightrope, I bump my head on the ceiling as I crouch low and try to walk up the tiny stairs. It's an extremely precarious situation and I'm aware that if I'm not careful I might tumble off the edge and fall into the blackness below. Eventually, I get back up to the apartment—without falling this time.

Part 7: Now my mother is in the apartment, helping me get the kids ready for bed. We're all getting ready to sleep in one room that's covered with mattresses. My son wants to know where his bed is, and I try to remember if I had seen it since the move. I call out to my soon-to-be ex-husband who is in the kitchen, but he doesn't know where the bed is either. He gets flustered because we keep asking him if he brought our things. "We let you take over and do the moving, at your insistence, and we're just wondering where all our stuff is," I say. He finally confesses that he didn't do a very good job of packing, that he never checked the rooms and closets before he left, and that most of our stuff did not get moved. The kids tell him they're angry with him. I'm angry with him too, furious, though I don't show it in front of the kids. Instead, I walk out into the kitchen to talk quietly with him. I see that he's preparing food. A strange man walks into the kitchen to get a bottle of wine, and then I notice that there are other people in the apartment, laughing and talking.

"Are you having a party?" I ask.

"Yes," he says, "I'm having a party."

"Fuck you!" I yell at the top of my voice so that everyone can hear. "Fuck you!"

I can tell that the kids and my mother are glad that I'm doing this. I yell and yell, not caring who hears me, until the sound of my voice wakes me up, the words "Fuck You!" echoing through my dark bedroom.

September 22, 2002

In a dream, I show my kids what I've done with some sticks and stones I've found lying around. I've created a model village; built houses, streets, churches, etc., using every last piece, not leaving anything unused. I've created a whole new world out of the debris of an old world.

The other day, when I fought with my son and felt his rage, I responded with my own ancient, long repressed rage. I didn't want to hurt him or fight him—it had nothing to do with that—it was simply something inside me that leapt out and refused to back down. I saw the same thing reflected in the stone cold blankness of his eyes. "Oh," I thought, staring into his eyes, "he's not there." I didn't see *him* in there—my familiar child—for only bottomless darkness stared back at me and that is what I felt in myself, ancient darkness that is not normally present. I knew he wasn't seeing his familiar mother either, for I had no sense of self. For a few seconds I was as consumed as he was by that rage, as if we had simultaneously shifted into some strange yet familiar state of possession where only dark silence reigned. Our everyday personalities dropped away like the stairs in my dream and we became two ferocious beings. Reality dropped away too, as we were momentarily suspended in the timelessness of that silent darkness. And yet, we didn't fall completely apart, or hurt each other. We returned and met as mother and son once again, embracing in acknowledgement of each other and our shared frustrations.

September 23, 2002

I dream that I'm flying a kite, the string of it coming out of my belly button. The wind is strong and the kite pulls me slightly aloft while I try pulling it back to earth, tugging on the rope. Chuck is there, telling me to cut the rope. "Just cut it!" He hands me a large pair of scissors just as the kite jerks up higher. Suddenly, I'm being pulled out into space. "Cut the rope!" Chuck yells from far below. So I cut it and immediately plummet, twirling, falling fast, as the huge kite—freed of me—disappears into the atmosphere. Spinning toward the earth, I'm aware that at any second I'll hit with a SMACK! I imagine that I'll be dead then, the only thing remaining a giant hole in the ground. To my surprise I fall softly, landing gently in a huge pile of white goose feathers. Now I'm drowning in feathers, suffocating. The more I move, the further I sink. "If I stop moving," I tell myself, "I won't sink so fast." I poke my hands up through the feathers until I feel air, hoping that someone will see them and save me. "You're okay. You're okay," says Chuck as he pulls me out.

I wake up and roll over in bed only to roll right into a recapitulation. My abuser's penis is in my mouth. Gagging and choking, I silently keen. I am teary-eyed and drooling, aware that I'm crying, but at the same time I'm looking into a face, watching the tears dripping down it. "Who's crying? Who's making that noise?" I wonder. And just as I sit up and pull out of the recapitulation, I clearly see the little girl who's crying so softly, holding back, afraid that someone will hear her. She's very young. I wake up knowing that I've just looked directly into the face of my child self.

As soon as I begin dressing, I realize I can no longer have anything around my neck; even crew necks are too tight. I change my clothes repeatedly until I find something that's comfortable to wear, as anything around or near my neck suffocates me. I just cannot get enough air.

September 24, 2002

I meet with Chuck and he tells me that it's not about retrieving memories anymore, but that it's about letting go of control and unlocking the emotions now.

"Let the emotions come!" he says happily when I tell him about the tussle with my son, quite thrilled when I tell him I flew into a blind rage. "You have to find ways to not be in control, to let go of the old idea that you must be in control at all times, so that you can begin to allow yourself to *feel*."

He interprets the kite dream, its string like an umbilical cord, as being connected to the old way of being in control, underscoring that it's time to cut loose.

"It's telling you that letting go will be okay, you'll survive the loss of control. Just cut the damn cord!"

We spend a long time talking about the multifaceted dream I had the other night that took place in the oceanside loft apartment with the kids, my mother, and my husband. The ocean represents the source of all life and the deeper unconscious, Chuck suggests.

"It's important to note that there was something in the water you felt needed to be saved," he says, peering at me intently.

The stairs present difficulties along the way, while the dance studio below on the ground floor is where the joys and freedom of movement are happening. I saw a different side of my mother there, a confident and free woman, not the one I normally see. I tell Chuck that she was a good dancer and that at one time, when young, she had studied ballet.

"Perhaps, in the dream, she is just showing you a part of yourself that you will one day have access to, when you are grounded and free," he suggests.

The fact that I let my husband take over the moving, in spite of the fact that he did a terrible job, is also significant. Even yelling at him for his thoughtlessness in having a party with strangers in my new apartment, on a school night when I'm putting the kids to bed, is a good sign of release. The entire dream was about my unconscious offering me opportunities to let go, as well as tapping into the source of all life—the ocean just outside my window.

Although the water looked cold and uninviting, Chuck suggests that it may only appear that way because it's such a great unknown.

"I still can't get the sound of that voice calling for help out of my head. It's been haunting me ever since that dream."

"Who is it?" Chuck asks.

"I don't know," I say. "Me, maybe?"

"Maybe," he says, in his usual way of not telling me anything, and I know it's my job to figure out what my unconscious is trying to tell me, not his. So my assignment this week is to consciously let go of control, on all levels—to just be.

"Release the guards! Let them go home, they've been on duty too long," says Chuck. "Open the doors and let the joys of life in, let the rooms air out, let the sun shine in, be wide open and let come what may. In so doing, something else may come to guide you."

"I'm just not sure how to do that."

"You'll figure it out," he says, and so ends the session.

September 25, 2002

It's hard to get up today. I woke repeatedly in the night, finding myself caught in the throes of recapitulations, jolting flashbacks shattering every attempt at sleep. Over and over again, I'd wake to my own voice screaming and crying as I tried to get away from the grabbing hands of my abuser. I am once again faced with the contradictory dilemma of having to learn how to let go, while at the same time I must stay in some kind of control so I don't completely disintegrate. It's always been a matter of survival. Being in control, being able to quietly and strongly handle anything means I get to live. There is still a part of me that believes that I will die if I let go, if I lose control in even the most miniscule metaphorical way. I am confronted with my very survival when I hear Chuck suggesting that it's time to learn to let go. In fact, letting go means facing my own death.

In my long dream the other night, I felt caught in a distorted M. C. Escher drawing, the stairs shifting, narrowing and collapsing, going everywhere and nowhere, as I slipped and fell; the ceiling pressing down on me. It was frustrating, suffocating, and nerve-wracking to have no control over my environment or the situations I found myself in. I felt only trapped and tricked; forced into letting go rather than a natural release. I couldn't get away from that same trapped feeling again last night, as if I were stuck all night on that endlessly collapsing staircase again. The fear of falling to my death presses on me as I go through this phase of my recapitulation. I counter it with my old belief that if I can just stay in control I will be fine. It always worked so well before, why not now?

My other dream of falling from the sky promises that feathers will receive me, telling me that I'll be all right, but the old fears say that only annihilation, death, and more fear await. Control meant survival, so how can I give that up? And what is there to replace it with? I know there's nothing, and there should be nothing, but is *nothing* enough to keep me alive? On the other hand, I'm fully aware that nothingness implies emptiness, which implies possibility. In being empty, I'm aware that I'd have the opportunity to start over; an empty coffer I could fill or not fill as I please. It would mean I could finally let go of all the stuff that haunts me, rid myself of my demons, cleanse myself of the muck of the past still coursing through my veins. I could be open and alive. I could be a new me, a person who could feel, speak, move, be happy, cry and laugh, simply because I wanted to, because it felt right. Maybe I could learn to be kind to myself. Maybe I could even love myself.

Anxiety builds all day, forcing me to confront the old me who would like to run and just never stop. When I met with Chuck yesterday, he suggested that I practice letting go by going into complete relaxation and deep breathing, by gaining outer and inner calm and quiet. As he pointed out, I've already landed safely, my dreams guiding me to trust the process. I can no longer deny or entertain the slimmest doubt that I fought against death in my childhood. Although the threat of death was great at one time, death isn't threatening me in that same way anymore. My abuser is not here anymore, and so I must trust that I *will* land safely, just as I did in my dream.

I must face my fears if I am to experience what it means to be fully alive. I must turn and face head-on what comes to me, relax in front of it and breathe in the truth of it, knowing that it belongs to me, no matter what it is.

September 26, 2002

My abuser is about to attack me in a dream. I'm getting ready to just give in, thinking in the old way that I'll give in just to get it over with, but then I shift into a new way of thinking, and I react! "No!" I shout. "Don't give in! Fight!" I tell myself to just say no and walk away, and so I do. "NO!" I shout, loudly and clearly, and then I turn and walk away.

In another dream, I'm at a medieval festival. There are crowds of people milling about dressed in costumes, role-playing how people lived during an earlier time. I wander around talking to people I know, but I'm not participating, only watching, keeping to myself. I wonder why people are so excited, why they're caught up in this type of play, for it makes little sense to me. I don't see the point of it, but then I notice that they're having fun. Intimidated by all the activity and the carefree atmosphere of the festival, I withdraw. I don't want to be seen. In fact, I'd prefer to just fade into oblivion, but I bump into people—acquaintances and strangers alike—who tell me to get my fortune told. "You are the perfect candidate!" they say. "The fortune-teller is around here somewhere. Keep looking, eventually you'll find her." So I wander around looking for the fortune-teller, intrigued by the idea of having her tell my future, but at the same time I'm uncomfortable being around so many people. It's way too crowded for me.

In the morning, I realize that the dissociated self in the early part of the first dream and the non-participatory self in the second dream have been my true states of being, my personality dominated by these two characteristics of a deeply traumatized self. I've been quietly complacent my entire life, thinking it was just the way life was and that I should accept what was dealt me. Did I really think that men had a right to abuse me? Did I really think that I had no other recourse but to just let it happen? It's only now, as I do this recapitulation, that I realize my splintered, traumatized self could do nothing else. She was totally cut off from reality, caught in the nightmare world of fear and survival, the other two dominating forces in my life, holding my fragmented self together in delicate, tenuous balance. It's also only now—in my fiftieth year—that I understand that I don't have to take abuse. I don't have to give in. In my mesmerized zombie state it was all I could do, a survival mechanism that had already proven to work extremely well. I'm still alive to prove how well it worked. But now, for the first time really, I'm waking up to what it means to be abused and what a healthy personality might look and feel like too. I'm also beginning to realize that abuse of any sort is not part of a *real* relationship.

When I reacted in the first dream and stopped to notice how I was about to fall right back into an old pattern, the pause offered enough of a shift so that I was able to walk away from my abuser. Just as I had once kicked him in the face in a previous dream, fed up with the boring repetition of an old me, I felt empowered once again to act on my own behalf. Such a critical moment!

In the second dream, I was uncomfortable in the carefree atmosphere. I knew that I was only an observer, not a participant of the happy-go-lucky festival. I knew that I'd always lived my life as an observer, always watching on the sidelines. I also knew that I hadn't really lived yet and that there was the possibility for things to shift, and so the idea of seeing the fortune-teller intrigued me. It was curious to me that all the people I met implied that I was the perfect candidate. I wasn't quite sure what that meant, but each time I heard it spoken I felt new life stirring inside me. Perhaps the people in the dream were the real fortune-tellers, letting me know that I do have a good future to look forward to.

Up until a few years ago, I could live with the numb, dissociated self. I could live as an observer of life, not quite present, but simply wandering through life like I wandered through that dream. But the nagging feeling that things weren't quite right pestered me constantly, a reminder that my spirit was shut down, all but dead inside me for some reason. Now, as I recapitulate, I'm discovering that my life force, my spiritual self, is strongly interested in participating in life, quite urgently pushing me to live differently now: *to experience myself as energy and to FEEL!*

September 27, 2002

I felt almost manic yesterday, as a good mood kept me going while I worked on pieces for the November show, but as soon as I crawled into bed last night, the old feelings slipped in next to me. I immediately dropped into deep depression. I lay in bed full of sadness and needing to cry, but of course I couldn't. Still so blocked, I nonetheless continue to dare myself to investigate my past, asking for my truths to become known.

I know what happened to me now, though I admit I haven't let the full truth in. Feelings and emotions still remain trapped; though the longer I live with the truth the closer I get to emoting. I'm aware it's only a matter of time, but until then the old stoic self remains in control. At the same time, this recapitulation process comes with its counterattacks, which are directed squarely at breaking down the old commander-in-chief, the old me. It's like I've got two tornadoes brewing inside me, a tornado of sadness and a tornado of unspoken emotions building up the energy to go whirling out of control, intent on colliding. They have to. "The holding has been a holding on for dear life," Chuck said, "so of course letting go is difficult." Eventually, I know that I will let go. But I must convince all those old selves that it's okay now. It's what my dreams tell me.

September 28, 2002

I'm shrinking again, leaving my body, dissociating. I open my journal and pick up my pen in an effort to stay present by writing, to document this part of the journey rather than just disappear into the oblivion of it. It's been happening a lot lately, and I now realize that it's an escape from the emerging emotions. As soon as they start up, I immediately disappear. Without thought or intent something inside me reacts. My body bloats up into a large pillow and my awareness retreats. I experience a sense of zooming through time and space, going so far away that when I turn and look back in the direction from which I've come there's an immensely long tunnel snaking back to reality, just a tiny pinprick of light in the distance. Meanwhile, I'm so deeply and safely sequestered in numbness that nothing reaches me. From here, my body can be abused, but I can't be hurt because I'm not in it.

In one sense this is a comforting experience, but I'm also aware of the extreme loneliness that lies locked in this deeply cloistered place. That loneliness envelops me now and this tunnel no longer feels like such a great place to be. I intend to stay in my body this time, to experience what emerges as I face whatever is imminent. No matter how much it hurts, I plan on remaining fully present and aware as I acquiesce to this moment of recapitulation.

From a great height, as if I'm flying, I see a road winding into the woods. I zoom down until I'm in the woods, the autumn scent of dried leaves strong, and I immediately recognize the spot. I once hiked here when I was a teenager, at sixteen or seventeen years of age. A few friends and I were taking a shortcut down the mountainside, having gone off the Appalachian Trail that ran along the top ridge. Suddenly we came upon this strange little road in the woods. Everyone was so excited, for we who had hiked these mountains our entire lives had never before seen this road. I alone was overcome with terror. Shaking, doubling over with sudden severe stomach cramps and nausea, I was unable to cross the road. Fear gripped me as I hunched away, refusing to go a step further. For some strange and mysterious reason I could not cross over that road. It was as if a huge hand held me back or a magnetic force repelled me from taking one step more. One girl stayed behind with me, as I insisted we go another way, while the other two girls began walking along the road. Heading into the woods, they were eager to see where the road led. The girl who'd remained by my side urged the others to come back, for she saw how affected I was, though I could offer her no explanation.

"I don't know, something's wrong," I said, my voice cracking. "Don't go there! We can't go that way!"

"But it's just a road," the girl said, rationalizing, stamping her foot, jumping on the narrow road. "See? Nothing's happening!"

No amount of rational talk could sway me. I was overwhelmed by the imperative to flee, insisting that we take the shortest route possible back to our own neighborhood further down the mountainside, that we get out of the woods as soon as possible. At the time, I wondered why such a pretty little road in the middle of the woods would have such a violent affect upon me. Instinctively, I knew there was something sinister at the end of that road. It led to great pain and fear—that much I knew. No distinct memory emerged at the time, but the pain in my body was enough to signal that something horrible lay at the end of that road. Now, as I recapitulate, I know that the winding road led to a building, for as I let the memory guide me, I am with my abuser. He stops his pickup truck at his parent's house to pick up a key, and then we drive down that road, going deeply into the woods. I don't remember what happened there, but I do remember driving back out again. I remember him returning the key to his parents, and I remember contemplating jumping out of his truck to get away.

Now as I return to the memory of being in the woods with my friends, I recall how they reluctantly returned to me, finally convinced to go in another direction. I saw how disappointed they were, and yet I could not have put one foot on that road. I remember that I still had to cross over it to get where we were going and so I ran and jumped and took a flying leap, neatly clearing it. I never looked back. My pains subsided the farther we got from the road, until I felt almost normal again, except for the hollow awakening that remained like a dark and weighty bruise upon my heart.

Eventually, we hiked out of the woods. We emerged from the darkness of the trees and our next step took us into another world, for suddenly the woods fell away and a magical shimmering world of beauty and light appeared before our eyes. With the lightheartedness of innocent children we began running and shouting across golden sand that quite magically appeared beneath our feet. Sinking deeply into it, we ran clumsily toward a vast blue ocean, full of white-capped waves, that stretched before us to the very horizon. Hot after our hike, leaping with sheer joy, we shed our shoes and ripped off our tops, ready to jump into the inviting waves. Hooting and hollering, lost in the wonder and amazement of it, we paused for a second to ponder how far we must have hiked to be at this beautiful and mysterious beach! And then, all at once, everything shifted. In an instant the beach and the ocean disappeared and we found ourselves standing in the middle of our neighborhood, in a field not ten feet from one of my friend's houses. Surrounded by tall grass, golden in the sunlight, the blue sky stretched to the horizon as far as the eye could see. What had just happened?

Totally disoriented, we groped for an explanation, the wonderment of our magical beach dashed to pieces. The universe had tricked us, we decided. Like thirsty wanderers in the desert, we had seen a mirage! Rolling in the grass, laughing uncontrollably now, we acknowledged our gullibility. We couldn't believe that a second before we had been struggling to run over warm golden sand, throwing off our shoes and clothes, ready to leap into the waves when in reality here we were, standing in a field we had been in so many times before. But the truth was that in a few brief seconds we *had* experienced a totally different world, though we lived far inland from the coast. The mysterious thing was that one of the girls, the one who had seen how affected I had been a few minutes before by the road in the woods—the rational one—did not experience the illusion. She had no idea what we were yelling about, why we were ripping off our clothes, and what we were laughing about either.

"What are you talking about?" she called; totally confused in her own way, as she stood on the edge of the woods and watched us search through the field for the shoes and tops we had tossed off moments before. "Why are you laughing? What's so funny?"

The other day Chuck told me that I have to go through each memory, that I can do it now, that I have enough validation now that it took place. I do know that I need to feel everything, the wondrous moments of my childhood—like discovering that ocean in the middle of a field on a mountainside, where no ocean could possibly be—as well as the difficult moments like confronting the road in the middle of the woods that triggered excruciating pain only moments before. I *can* do this recapitulation. I will go through every joy and pain of it, in order to fully experience all that happened to me, recapturing every moment of my life and every person I've encountered until I am whole. He's right; I won't get anywhere if I don't allow the recapitulation to guide me.

"Even if it hurts, even if it's sad and lonely," he said, "because it's important."

September 29, 2002

In a dream, I'm hanging by my hands, trying to hoist myself over a high stockade fence, but my arms are getting tired. I tell myself that it's okay to fall, to just let go, but I still hold on tightly. Someone comes along on the other side of the fence and pries my fingers off. I fall, only to find that I've been hanging barely an inch off the ground. I land flat on my feet. "How silly I am," I say, finding myself standing upright; utterly surprised that it was no great distance at all. "What am I so afraid of?"

Again I dream. This time I'm vacuuming under a tall china cabinet. When I bend down and peak under the cabinet I see that there's just enough space for me to squeeze underneath. I crawl under the cabin and roll into a ball, wanting the rest of the world to go away; I just want to stay here. "You can't stay here forever," I tell myself, but I feel safely held in by the tight space, and even though I know I can't stay here forever I'm intent on enjoying it for a while.

I wake out of this last dream still encased in the need for comfort, so I stay rolled up in bed, aware that I confronted two aspects of my recapitulating self in my dreams. The evolving self urges me to let go, while the old self seeks an old comfort. More than anything I want to stay underneath the covers where I feel safe and warm. If I get up then I have to start living the loneliness of this recapitulation. I feel the turmoil and confusion of this recapitulation process weaving through my psyche day and night. There's a sense of imminent loss of control leading to frustration, though I know I have to go through it; it's the only way to salvation. In the end, I know the fall will only be short and gentle now and not the dreadful free fall that I have so feared. After a while I hoist myself out of bed, knowing I have to face the day and whatever may come.

The need to roll into a ball and hug myself confronts me throughout the day, the urge strong, no matter what I do to combat it. Luckily, I have a lot to do at work, but in my inner reality I stay rolled into that ball all day long, imagining myself small enough to be picked up and hugged, every bit of me held in a tight little ball of an embrace, small enough to fit into a pocket and be carried around. I gain some comfort, as I imagine this. But reality outside of that pocket cannot be dismissed, for the real battle that I face is that I am on the verge of splintering, of falling apart. I must constantly fight the urge to just go home and crawl into bed. It doesn't matter how beautiful the weather is or what needs to be done, my heavy comforter draws me to hide beneath it, where sadness and comfort wait to greet me, and where my splintering will be kept private and contained.

"You should follow your instinct," said Chuck the other day. "It's not a bad thing that you feel the need to stay under the covers." But I know it's such a depressing place, full of lonely little girls telling their sad tales. Meanwhile, the adult me is so tired of the tension of this recapitulation, my throat constricted with the effort to keep it all in, my hips still aching with memories. As I bear the increasing pressure, I constantly dare myself to let go, knowing that it will be the end of me in one sense but the beginning of a new self as well. But, just as in my dream, I still cling to the old self and the old comforts, gripping ever tighter against the incredible urgency to let go.

September 30, 2002

I wake to a dark morning and write my thoughts in the few minutes before I have to get the kids up. Again, the abortion I had at twelve years of age comes to the surface of my awareness. I clearly see my father leaving the doctor's examining room and a shockwave rolls through me as the bitter truth strikes home: It really happened!

I recapitulate my father walking out of the room over and over again until there is no doubt. I realize I just have to return to everything again and again and allow the truth of each memory to sink in even deeper. I know that in doing that I'll be able to gain the clarity I need, accepting the truth in the bargain, but that I'll also be done with each memory then as well. The urgent need to lie back down and curl up in a ball courses through me again as I allow myself to feel hurt and sad. My child self needs to be held and she needs to know that everything is okay now, but it's time to get up and take care of the other children now, my living and breathing children of this world.

After the kids catch the bus at seven, I go back to bed. I don't sleep, but instead lie curled up, allowing myself to go back into the memories that have been emerging. I walk down the little road in the woods and find the cabin where my abuser took me after getting the key at his parent's house. We drove down that long road going deep into the woods, the road that scared me so much when I came upon it with my girlfriends. I relive a somatic experience as I shake under the covers, my teeth chattering, and my body in pain. I realize that although my abuser hurt me such a long time ago, I'm still hurting; I've been hurting my entire life. In spite of all that I've done, I'm still that little abused girl in the woods. I lie in bed wracked with pain, inside and out, long enough for the memory and the accompanying physical experiences to fully go through me. As hard as it is, I finally pry myself out of bed at ten, more sure than ever that this new memory has been making itself known all weekend, loosening and emerging, beginning with the memory of hiking and coming upon the road.

And so I come to this final installment: being in the cabin. As usual, it was a game at first. We made a fire in the potbellied stove. He had me climb the bunk beds that lined the walls and jump down over and over again into his arms, and it was fun, except that I was naked. At some point I hit the back of my head on the edge of the bunk. It hurt, a bump the size of an egg growing quickly. I had to hide in his truck because he wasn't allowed to bring kids there, he said, the cabin was just for adults. He left me scrunched down on the floor of the cab when he went to get the key. I had to be very still and quiet so that no one would see me. It was our secret. He found things to stick inside me—a beer bottle and silverware. Lying on the top bunk with my legs hanging over the edge, the bump on the back of my head throbbing painfully, he started doing his thing.

Chapter 4

Between Worlds

October 1, 2002

In a dream, I'm trying to keep some bad men out of the house. I'm frantically running around, locking doors and windows. I hear them talking outside, their voices muffled. I can't quite understand what they're saying, but I know they're intent on getting in. There are other people in the house as well and, unbeknownst to me, one of them has invited the bad men inside. Now they're sitting at a table with us, eating a chicken dinner served on paper plates. The house is a safe house, a refuge, stocked with supplies, but we must be conservative, for they will only last so long and it's uncertain if we'll be able to get more. But now all of that has changed, because I no longer feel safe. "Who let them in?" I wonder, angry and resentful that these men are sitting at our table, receiving nurturance from our limited supplies.

I wake up angry, the dream tension and paranoia spilling out into the morning. I realize that this is what I do all the time: *try to keep the bad men out of my body-house.* It's a perpetual effort to not have to feel what's happening in my body, things that happened decades ago and things that happen now too. I constantly fight having to feel at all, but in the process end up suffering intensely anyway. It's my day to meet with Chuck and I need today's session more than ever.

"I want to get rid of this stuff, to stop holding it in!" I say, as soon as I arrive.

"Okay, so let the feelings take over," says Chuck, handing me the EMDR pods, suggesting that I dip into what's happening in my body.

"I can't do it," I say, immediately pulling back. "It hurts too much. It hurts to go there and it hurts to refuse to go there too."

"You have to stop fighting it in order to let it go through you. Release will bring relief," Chuck says. "Begin to relax your body. As you do, you'll open up to the possibility for new life to come in and help in the release."

"I know that, but it's so hard!"

"Let it just pass through and out," he says. "When you feel that white-knuckled tightness, release it. Relax your body so it can flow out."

I give it another try, and another, and another. Over and over again, holding tightly onto the EMDR pods, I incrementally relax my body.

"Relax your hands. Don't fight it; release it," Chuck encourages. "Relax your shoulders. Relax your legs. Relax your throat. Breathe and then let it go."

By the time the session is over, I'm exhausted, feeling wrung out and limp, as if something has indeed finally been released.

"I'm always amazed at how much I work through when I'm here," I say, as I open my eyes and hand back the pods. "Yet there's nothing to show for it. It feels like there should be piles of shit lying on the floor at my feet!"

"There *is* something to show for it. You're more present in your body now, you even look different," says Chuck.

"Yes," I say, quite amazed at how light I feel as I get up out of my chair. "I do feel like a new woman!"

October 2, 2002

I spend the day at the studio, but can't wait until I can go home and crawl into bed. If I pause for even a second feelings rush upon me, so I don't dare stop working. It seems that once activated they just want to keep flowing, but I don't have a place to put them right now—*now* isn't appropriate. I hope to ward off their pressure by writing this down, letting them seep out onto the pages of my journal. "Don't fight them; let them come; just relax," Chuck said yesterday, and I know that whatever seeks release is waiting for me to do just that, *relax*, for whatever it is lies just beneath the skin, ready to explode out of me.

I realize there are things that I just have no control over, and this may be one of them, and that scares me. But I also know, as Chuck said, that I have to let things go through me or I won't get any relief. While acknowledging this, I allow myself to make some quiet whimpering noises. This immediately leads to shaking and panting—a recapitulation—the intensity of it quite frightening. My intent to release only a *small* amount is not being honored. Even though I'm alone at the studio, I don't feel safe. Someone could walk in at any moment and I can't be found in this state. And so, I walk around. I go to the bathroom down the hall and throw cold water on my face. I will my shoulders and neck to relax, but to no avail. I realize I was alone when I was a child and I'm alone now, but at least now I've found a place where I can talk about it—at least I've done that for myself—as well as given myself permission to keep writing all of this down. But I must say, a padded cell would be rather nice right now!

"You're not alone," Chuck said yesterday, "I've been sharing this journey with you for many months now."

"Yes, that's very true," I acknowledged, "but it's ancient aloneness that comes to greet me."

"Keep in mind that you're actually in two places at once," he said. "You were sent into the future to be able to one day return and go through this, shot forward like a comet, but part of you was left back there waiting for this moment when you would return."

I try to keep these thoughts in mind as I meditate into relaxation, as I do the sweeping breath and allow this memory tension to go through me. "This is my destiny," I tell myself. "I was meant to get to this place of such intensity so I could go back and bring the two worlds together." However, the tension of those two worlds as they collide, which I conveniently avoided in the past by forgetting, is almost unbearable.

October 3, 2002

I stay distracted with lots of work during the day at the studio and then focus on the kids at home in the evening, but the intense need to curl up hounds me. Like a menacing dog, snarling and nipping at my heels, it follows me around. I turn to it throughout the day, repeatedly telling it that I will let it into my bed, that I will curl up with it under the covers, *but only at night.*

It's good stuff, Chuck told me as we ended the session the other day, and I know it's true. I'm heartened by the thought that I'm destined to go back into this past, though it's often difficult to have a rosy outlook when in the midst of it. I suspect it would help to be more open and accepting of it, but it's a little like leaping off a precipice. I don't know where I'll land. I have a memory of having briefly glimpsed the end of this process, but at this point everything is still steeped in darkness, with no end in sight. No lights guide my way, as I leap headlong into the blackness of it all.

As I go through the day, I pull out this diary, keeping the snarling dogs of recapitulation at bay by writing. There's a lump in my throat now, even when I'm not thinking about the abuse. Even when I'm laughing I feel it growing steadily bigger, the need to cry, just sitting there, waiting for its moment of release. I work on loosening my body and soul from whatever is inside me, doing sweeping breaths throughout the day, flicking off negative energy, but after decades of holding, this release is slow and painful, no matter how big the desire to let it all go.

The lump in my throat grows ever bigger as the day progresses, and by evening feels about the size and weight of a bowling ball. Firmly lodged, it constricts even my ability to fully turn my head as I do the sweeping breath, a sensation of choking accompanying it. I promise myself to loosen a little bit more each day, to relax my throat even though it may be slow going. This is really hard work. I assume that when I'm ready it will finally release of its own accord, though in the meantime, I bear the weight of it as best I can.

I soon find that the more I meditate, breathe, and physically relax, the more the pressure releases, just as Chuck had suggested. So many incremental releases are working simultaneously—I'm getting some relief at last! Writing helps too, just getting these thoughts down. It doesn't matter what they are, just the act of expressing what I'm feeling on a daily basis helps. Even if I'm repeatedly writing down the same endless thoughts, even it they're indecipherable, even if I'll never read them again, it helps.

Visions of pain and horror march across my vision, as a holocaust of terror courses through me. My known childhood is wiped out as these memories—long hidden in the annexes of my brain—come to light. Long buried fear and pain emerge now to mix in my body, becoming real again. Clutching screams of old, strangled into silence long ago, remain stuck. I once knew that it was not safe to make a sound, though now I long to free myself of the harsh demands of my abuser. Yet I am terrified of the painful sounds that reside in the depths of me; the inhuman howls that will one day escape through my tightly clenched lips, wrung out of me at last. And even though they don't really exist—not until I utter them—I feel their presence, discordant sounds locked in the dungeons of my soul. They wait for a burst of fresh air to release them into the universe and make them real at last. They wait to hear their own echoes too, the sounds of freedom reverberating through the atmosphere and beyond, echoing for all eternity in memory of the child I once was, and all the other children who have suffered the same suffocation of spirit.

"You can cry," Chuck said so gently the other day. "You can cry."

"When?" I asked, frustrated.

"When you're ready."

When the girls are ready, when I tell them we're ready to open up, then I'll cry. I look forward to the day when I am open down to the very bottom of my soul, the gates of my tortured psyche broken open at last. Then I will let the sounds, buried under moldy memories, pour out of me, purging myself of this ghastly childhood at last. "Look! Look at this, look at what happened," I'll say, again and again, until everything is released, finally made real in the awful telling of my secret childhood.

Perhaps I've lived with this trauma for so long that I'm used to what it's done to me. I'm so used to the way I am that I just accept it. I've always been like this. But Chuck made me realize that the way I am is because of the things that happened to me, not because I'm painfully shy or withdrawn, not because I'm bad or sinful, but because of what my abuser did. He explained that I was not born this way; that I have not yet lived as the person I have the potential to become. I still have the opportunity to be alive; it's never too late. Chuck pointed out that I had no chance; that I did, in fact, go far for someone so badly deceived by life, and that I still have far to go—that I have much, much further to go. Life is only beginning. I can get through all of this and still *live*.

"In the shamanic world," Chuck said, "what you went through is preparation for living a different kind of life, and that kind of life can be had when one is ready to view one's life as a journey of the utmost importance."

October 4, 2002

Gripping pain, rising from the depths of my abdomen, strikes while I'm driving. Between clenched teeth I beg it to subside, attempting to drive the car and drive the pain away at the same time. "Not now, not now, not now," I chant, seeking release in my mantras, hoping for a shift. "Wait until tonight. Wait until tonight. Wait until tonight."

"It happened. It happened. It really happened," I mutter. "Yes, yes, yes, I know, but not now." I acknowledge it, accept it, and push it away, though my stomach aches all day. I keep going; keep busy. I don't sit down once, but work the whole day through, though I want nothing more than to lie down in bed and cradle my wounded child self.

The kids are out with their dad for the evening and I have the house completely to myself—a rarity. I pop in a movie called *Monsoon Wedding*, featuring, unbeknownst to me, a pedophile uncle. I watch, my body frozen, triggered, my sadness weighing heavily, and yet I am unable to turn the movie off. As I watch the uncle selecting his young niece, I remember my abuser selecting me over his daughter and my legs cramp immediately. "It's your turn," and I'd so innocently go off with him, holding his hand, getting into his truck, knowing it wasn't a good idea yet unable to stop the inevitable, just like I am unable to stop the movie. I must watch it through to the end. "He's an adult, he rules, and this is what he does," are the thoughts that course through my head as I watch the movie, the same thoughts that coursed through my head as a child. "This is what I do when I am with him, this is what we do." There is no question of choice, for when he says, "Come," I come. And whatever happens is the way it is, no matter how I feel about it. How I feel never matters; I don't matter. Indeed, I become Zombie Girl once again as the movie triggers a recapitulation. I bury my pain and fear inside my stiff body. My emotions stir, welling up in confusion, as I try to figure out what's going to happen.

"Not today, please! Not today!"

"No, no, no, no, something else, please!"

"Not that! Anything but that!!!"

But it's already too late. By the end of the movie I am a limp rag of pain. It's all I can do to drag myself to bed and crawl under the covers.

October 5, 2002

I want to stay in bed this foggy damp morning, but the sun comes out and we have to get to the soccer fields. As I watch the girls on my daughter's team, I ponder a dream I had not long ago, the dream of being an observer, a non-participant in the festival of life. I notice that some of the girls play the game all the time. No matter where the soccer ball is they're constantly moving and anticipating, while some of them only play the game when the ball happens to roll their way. In my dream, I didn't want to participate in the festival at all. I only interacted when people approached me. Watching these girls helps me see just what I've been doing to myself: *I've been missing out on a fuller life*. "Well," I decide, as I watch. "I don't want to play the game only when the ball rolls my way anymore. I want to play the game all the time!"

Now, as evening rolls around—the dinner dishes done, the kids occupied—I have a chance to let the feelings that I've been deliberately holding back emerge and become real. Climbing into bed and curling into myself, I let them slowly reveal themselves until my arms are filled with their sad truths. "I'm waiting for Tuesday and my next visit with Chuck," I tell them. "We'll talk then. Until then I have you in my arms. You belong to me too, just as much as my own children belong to me. I have to take care of you and prepare you for release into life too. I know that."

Last night I was triggered, my legs cramping, as my body reacted to the implications of sexual abuse in the movie. As I clenched against the truth of sexual abuse in my own life, I felt myself falling into a dark pit. Now, as I recall the movie, I'm triggered all over again, falling again into a pit of terror, the same terror I felt as a child when I knew it was hopeless, when I knew that I was caught and couldn't do anything about it.

Swept up by such old feelings, I have no recourse but to recapitulate. All I can hope for is to fall through them and land safely, but it's like falling into a dark old well. As I tumble down, everything that lives in that old well grabs at me. I'm pinched and bitten as horrifying memories latch onto me. Scraped off the sides of the old well, they present me with awful flashbacks that are as real as ever. Terrorized by what I see, I know I must stay aware and keep one foot in reality. I must remember that in the end I will land in that bed of feathers, and a hand will appear to pull me safely to my feet. I stay focused on that idea as I tumble down, reliving all the stuff inside me, as the reality of it, though still muffled, makes itself known. Suddenly, I sense something telling me to stop the recapitulation, that it's enough. Screeching to a halt, breaking the fall into the dark well in mid-air, I return to the present moment.

"I must wait until I meet with Chuck," I tell myself. "He will guide me through the terrors I have yet to traverse."

October 6, 2002

I awaken early to a fuller realization that even though I know that none of what happened to me was my fault, all the old feelings are still alive inside me. Those feelings have sent out tentacles, now connected to so many other things, their energetic lines having penetrated all aspects of my life. Even though I know I wasn't to blame, blame and guilt have permeated everything, leaving me stranded and unable to fully live, for I think that I am not worthy of life, that I am to be blamed for everything, that I am guilty simply because I exist. Such feelings lie hidden in deep recesses. Once annexed to Forgetfulness Land, they now seep out as the memories come. Their power still impacts my life just as strongly as it originally did, no matter how many times I tell myself that it wasn't my fault, that *he* did this to me, that I never had a chance. It doesn't matter how old I am, or how much I understand and acknowledge, those old feeling still inhabit the far reaches of my soul, sticking to me like the leeches they are. I try to pluck them off, to fully understand them and then detach from the old significance of them, and yet I am only able to get to a certain point because more memories are triggered before I complete my task. Before I know it I'm right back where I started, lost and forlorn, falling deeper into the muck of it all, covered in still more leeches, blamed and guilty as charged.

My whole body holds memories, encapsulated in every part of me. As I write, my head hurts, my legs cramp, my crotch burns, and my stomach grips with the realization of them. Involuntarily, I roll into a tight ball, shaking and shivering as the painful sensations of memory after memory emerge and go through me. My teeth chatter and grind, my face contorts, my body writhes, while I softly moan and growl like the injured animal I am. My entire body, inside and out, is involved in this recapitulation process. I feel it—I definitely feel it.

I decide to stay in bed today, reading and writing on a cool Sunday, my day off. I am evermore determined to stay the course, to go where this recapitulation process is taking me. As hard as it is, I will not stop, for I see some light at the end of the tunnel now. The more I recapitulate, the more I understand that there will one day be an end to this horrific journey. In addition, being able to share this with Chuck and get his insightful feedback takes away the loneliness of the process. In speaking my truths, I disperse the intensity of the despair, releasing and lessening it, making room inside for new ideas to take root, just as Chuck once told me would happen. By releasing the power my abuser has over me in this manner, I am gaining back my own energy. I'm beginning to feel this new boost of energy in my body now. Even while I still wallow in the intensity of this recapitulation, I do feel a releasing of my abuser's negativity and a birthing of my own longed-for self.

The mornings are definitely the hardest time of day. I awaken stiff and sore, clenched in my lifelong protective sleeping pose—a tightly rolled fetal ball. In full acknowledgement of the truth of the abuse, I am now charged with unfurling and letting the horrors of my past flow out of me each morning before I even get out of bed. I must begin each day anew, present in my real body, even as I continually face my recapitulating self and my injured child's body. And so, each morning as I awaken, I must once again face the moment when my child self had to crawl out of her safe bed each morning and face the real world again too, most especially the world of the sexual abuser. The first step in letting go of the nighttime safety when I was a child, was to put on the invisible armor needed to face the outside world. Now, I'm faced with doing it differently, the recapitulation asking me to be brave in a new way, to become liquid, to flow into life unafraid, an adult now. Yet I am still fearful of that first moment upon arising each morning. No longer allowed to take the old armor out of the closet, I must face the world completely unprotected. And although I practice it daily, that first step is still frightening.

My resistance is definitely weakening. I put new pieces of the puzzle together each day, gaining greater clarity each time I recapitulate. When I emerge from a memory and find myself back here in this world, I must deeply consider what really happened in the past. From my adult perspective, I'm able to assess the truth and bring clarity to a once confusing time. And then later, when I have the opportunity to bring my experiences to Chuck, they finally make sense in a new way. As we discuss what happened from so many different angles, absent of the old judgments and demeaning self-criticism that once dominated my personality, I begin to see from a totally new perspective. I understand that it's really my choice. There is no coercion or salesmanship on Chuck's part. I am freely and wholeheartedly integrating what makes sense to me. As I do this deeply challenging work, I am electing to give myself every opportunity to grow, for I am hungry for change. As I pointedly and intentionally change my perceptions about how I think and feel, I am able to free both my child self and my adult self from the burdens of secrecy and blame that have burdened them for so long. Eventually, I hope the jigsaw puzzle of my life will be complete, and the greater meaning of all that I've been through fully revealed. Until then, I struggle onward through this process, focused on completion, for the sake of my soul.

"Open your mouth!" a singsong voice chants in my head. "Open your mouth and close your eyes. Open your mouth and close your eyes and you will get a big surprise!" Well, I did get a big surprise, didn't I? As these words reverberate, I sink into deep pain—Oh God, I hurt so much! I know why people do things to themselves to stop the pain, cutting and piercing. I understand completely, but I don't want to hurt myself or make the pain go away with another type of pain. I just want to be able to cry, to let myself cry it out. I want to let those little girls cry too, to let them weep for all those years of pain, for all the things my abuser did, for all the torture and horror, for the horrid games, for the things I endured and the things he made me do, for the way he treated me, for the humiliation and the guilt, for the shame he heaped on me with every touch, for all the feelings pressed down inside me, stomped tight like bricks baked hard in the sun, needing a sledgehammer to break them apart now. As I continue beating through the walls of the old self, I feel more and more each day like one big walking bruise, a hundred and two pounds of mashed pulp. Just touching my skin hurts now, where before I couldn't feel myself at all. I used to be able to touch myself and not feel a thing, neither a pinch nor a gentle caress. I was a dried carcass with no sensation whatsoever. Never having been fully present in my body before, I don't know which is worse, to be able to feel or having no feeling at all.

When I'm deep in the memories I forget that I'm not alone anymore. I forget that Chuck has been with me on this whole long journey. I'm so used to holding back, to keeping this shameful stuff private. When it all becomes so heavy and unbearable I forget that I do, in fact, have a seasoned guide to share it with. Even though I often don't dare to speak the horrible words, I know he wants me to be able to speak them. I know that speaking and saying how I feel are the ways to healing. I have to remember that Chuck has gone into the woods with me, that he's witnessed everything I've so far uncovered. Even though I may feel alone and abandoned while caught in those memories, I am no longer totally alone, and that is the difference between then and now.

As if spurred on by my journal writing, a recapitulation envelops me. I cannot halt it. Suddenly I am so little, afraid, confused, hurt, in excruciating physical pain, and no one in the world can help me. Fear covers me like the heavy quilt lying on top of me, and yet I'm able to reach out of the memory for the phone beside my bed and call Chuck, but I hang up without leaving a message. I don't know what to say, except that I'm lost in sadness and loneliness, so frightened and in pain. Rolled into a tight ball, so caught in the memories, I can't even get out of bed. Too much effort goes into getting out of bed, which involves forcing a sick and aching body to move, mentally motivating it, talking it through each tiny incremental movement. "Okay, move your legs off the bed, put your feet on the floor, and with great effort push yourself up to a sitting position. Okay, now stand. Now move! Do it!" And then all I can think about is crawling back under the comforter and sinking back into the world of memories, as if it were a good place to go and not a horrible place. But it's actually a place I must go, for it holds all the answers; it holds everything I need. I've waited all week for a day like this. It doesn't matter how beautiful it is outside, I need this day to curl up with the feelings and learn from them.

"It's good stuff; it's all good stuff," Chuck likes to say.

While I wait for my next appointment with Chuck, I must deal with the propensity to hold in—the most excruciating part of this recapitulation. I'm gaining greater clarity on how I've been doing it throughout my life, upholding the commands of my abuser and all the others who once dictated the rules, and how I'm still doing it now as the old memories emerge. Even as I write those words—*old memories*—my legs stiffen, the mere suggestion sending awful cramps coursing through my thighs, sadness and loneliness building on each muscle clench, looking for a means of escape. I know that everything inside me just wants to erupt. I feel the imminent explosion of all that once was.

I fear that I can't make it until Tuesday. Too many days pass between sessions and I find myself withdrawing from the feelings that arise, from opening up to the experiences, from wanting to share them, and from hoping. I sense that I'm starting to close up again, becoming afraid of everything again, as I feel a deeper recapitulation coming on. The need to conceal and keep the secret, even though I know it will destroy me, is more important at the moment than letting it go through me. I try to relax and let it flow, but my body fights, even though my far greater intent is to jump on board and let it rip. My old resistance is strong; I see that. My legs shake with cramps, my throat restricts, my shoulders hunch. My old armor comes out of the closet and seductively embraces me. Emerging simultaneously with the sensations of memory, I find it completely necessary, for there is nothing else that offers protection from the fear that rides in on this somatic experience.

I make a concerted effort to remove the old armor—by relaxing in tiny increments at first, and then more and more until I've shed it completely. Without the armor's guarded control, uncontrollable shaking ensues and I lose all sense of self. Although I know I must acquiesce to this recapitulation process and let the physical body disconnect from the old controls, it's a frightening prospect, for it means that annihilation is imminent. This is what my child self faced; I know the tension of it well.

I decide it's far better to perch on the edge of the precipice rather than fall into the black abyss, and so I pause the action, so to speak, and study where I am in the current moment. I find that my body wants to do one thing, my mind another. I decide to let my body have its way, to bravely disconnect from my mind and its old controls. And so I relax as much as I can and let my body do what it wants. As I do, something unfamiliar immediately takes over, and I feel possessed. I twitch and kick and feel angry—really angry! I go even deeper, and let it rip. I kick and stomp as hard as I can. That's good, right? I test it and find that if I hold back, I get leg cramps and my stomach hurts. If I kick I feel better. If I kick really hard I feel GREAT!!!

October 7, 2002

In a dream, my body is heavy, weighted down, increasingly difficult to move. I walk in heavy slow motion looking for an exit from the building I'm wandering around in, which is like Grand Central Station in New York City. Nothing about my physical movement is normal. I'm clumsy and awkward and find it especially difficult to climb stairs, as if I don't have the use of my muscles. I wander through this endless building with slow, heavy steps, dragging my heavy body around, looking for an exit. I traverse long hallways and tunnels. I keep coming up against blocked doorways and construction sites that are impossible to pass through. The exceedingly slow pace and the inability to move properly grow increasingly frustrating. I'm also looking for something to eat, but all the places I look into are so filthy that I don't dare go into them. Finally, I come to a marketplace where an old man is selling carrot cake. He cuts me a big slice, wraps it up and gives it to me for $1.20. In addition, he hands me a brown hooded-sweater on a hanger, gives it to me for free, simply because he likes me.

I wake up tense and stiff. I had woken several times during the night with muscle cramps and got through them by telling myself to calm down. I had wanted to call Chuck and tell him I wasn't going to do this recapitulation anymore, that I can't, that I'm done, but I just dealt with it. Now, as I wake in pain, a memory emerges as well, laced with anger and indignation, loaded with pain and fury. I feel it bearing down on me, a sense of total devastation coming with it. Too weary to stop it, I let myself go. Last night I took off my armor, perhaps for the last time. And so, as I acquiesce, I'm thrown into a fuller recapitulation.

There are at least three men; two are holding me down, one with his dick out. How old am I? Maybe I'm fourteen. They're talking. "Hold her down! Grab her legs!" I'm kicking, kicking, kicking! But they're too strong. They push my legs apart. Someone holds my arms. Someone leans over me. Someone's shirt is in my face. Then my head is covered by something, a brown hood or cloth bag. Then I go dead, completely lifeless. Then I find myself alone. I turn my head and look at my hand lying in straw. I feel dead inside. I feel dead outside.

I come out of the recapitulation surprised to find myself lying on my bed, my hand lying on the sheet next to my face. There's no straw here, though I still feel it beneath my flesh. My legs are tight with cramps; fury and anger boil inside me. I want to scream! I kick and kick and kick as hard as I can! Both legs kick in unison, my entire bodyweight thrown into each sharp jab. "This is the memory," I think, as I kick. "This too is the memory, and this and this and this!" And now I can kick as much as I want to. There is no one stopping me. I kick and kick and kick until I'm exhausted, until the anger is kicked out of me. The brown hooded-sweater, handed to me in my dream, does not escape my attention, perhaps premonishing this memory recall.

At the end of the day, I lie down as soon as I get home from work, heavy with sadness. The need to curl up and weep is great. The curling up I can do, not the weeping. The pains are still there, but I push them away as I prepare to go to an evening yoga class. During the class it dawns on me that, of course, the restlessness I've been experiencing over the past few days was the stirring of that memory. The rape experience was utterly familiar, as fresh as if it had happened just a few days ago; though in reality many decades have passed. After yoga, which was quite relaxing, I take a warm bath. Massaging my legs in the hot water, I pray for no cramps tonight.

October 8, 2002

I dream that I'm moving into a house that I've bought. It's cruddy and full of old junk, but I clean it up. Among the junk I find some things of value, which I keep. I also get rid of other things that I'm attached to but realize I no longer need. I clean so hard that I make the house sparkle. Now it's beautiful and everything is organized, inside and out. I feel very contented, with a great sense of satisfaction. A friend stops by when I'm finished. "Too bad the previous owners didn't do this before they put it on the market; they would have made a fortune!" she says. "Yes, but then I wouldn't have been able to afford it," I say. My kids and I are very happy in our shiny new house.

I wake up feeling happier, in a better mood. It's my day to meet with Chuck and I'm hopeful that the good mood will weather through the horrific stuff I have to face. When I get to his office I sit and wring my hands in silent agony, unable to talk for the longest time.

"How are you feeling?" Chuck finally asks.

"How am I feeling? I don't know!"

"What's going on?"

"It feels like my life is full of black holes, black holes that I didn't even know existed," I say, "places I've had no recollection of, horrible places, and it's so uncomfortable going there. It's better going to the forgetting places, where it's safer. The place where doubt still exists is safer, and the other place, the tunnel where I roll up into a ball with all the hurt, even that place feels comforting. But I realize I always carried those black holes inside me, even though I wasn't aware of them, even though they shaped my whole personality and were the driving force behind my every action. Now I'm exploring those black holes where no one else has ever gone, where I once went alone, and it's frightening!"

"No one could go there because no one knew about them," said Chuck.

"Logical thinking like that didn't exist when I was a child. I wanted to believe that some fantastic person, a stranger would come along and save me, find me to be this fascinating child who needed and deserved saving, simply because I was me. I didn't know I could save myself. That thought never crossed my mind, though in a sense I probably did save myself. Evil existed in my life, so why couldn't fantasy and goodness. Evil came and took me into its dungeon, but goodness never came to rescue me until now."

"Now you're learning to rescue yourself," says Chuck.

"Yes, with your guidance I'm learning how to rescue myself."

I tell Chuck about my dream of cleaning up the cruddy house. By the time I leave, the idea of rescuing myself is strongly linked to the sparklingly house of my dream. I sense happiness and contentment in my future—once the hard work of cleaning out my inner house is done.

October 9, 2002

I wake enfolded in quietude, but I don't have time to sit and enjoy it. As I get ready for work I feel a tremendous desire to finally let go of all this old stuff that has been pressing on me my entire life. "Come on, girls; let's let it go!" I say as I shower, feeling how good it would be if the horrors of the past could just flow right out of me, the way the water flows down the drain. Such release and such relief that would be!

My desire to finally let the past go is stirred to a new intensity as I realize I need and want to be a whole person, a whole woman, the one I've never been. I want to learn not only how to rescue myself but also how to enjoy my life. I want to learn how to love my body, to love the person I am, and to let someone else love me too. I woke up this morning and wished I had someone here to bring me a cup of coffee, to do something nice for me. I woke with a new desire to be in love.

Throughout the day, I experience sensations of spinning and falling, a dust storm of old memories and old things moving inside me, shifting and jolting me until I'm quite unsettled. I experience a tremendous need to cleanse myself of all this and be done with it, as if the energy of cleaning out the house in my dream is taking place inside me now, reminding me that it is indeed time to clean house. I try to relax, to let the tremendous whirlwind take place, to not panic or resist, but to sit back and accept it for what it is. It comes like a white tornado, and each time I sense its nearness I ready myself by breathing the sweeping breath. As it passes through me I'm left with a sense of awe, as if a tornado is actually spinning out of me, carrying the old me off in its dusty funnel. But even while inner cleansing is taking place, feelings of heaviness stir up too. Flashes of my abuser and his daughter intrude. I see us walking hand in hand, all three of us, but he soon says that it's time for me to do something special with him and that his daughter can't come. It's my turn.

Just as I let the tornado whirl through me, I let the memory come too. I'm very young. I'm aware that my abuser likes me. He's being nice to me this time. I'm pretty and he wants just me. He makes me feel special—until we're away from everyone else. Then the ugly game starts. Everything turns dark and scary. I close down my feelings to survive, to be able to handle the fear. I discover that once I've handled the fear it's easier to ignore the physical abuse. As I recapitulate, I sense I'm skipping things in the memory, perhaps things I don't want to face, and so I make myself go back and start over again. I'm there again, in the woods, walking into his chamber. He's leading the way, talking nicely to me, smiling fondly. I take all this in again, but notice more fully how fear begins creeping in. Soon panic rises in my chest, blocking my throat, a huge chunk of black terror so heavy I can't breathe. I'm tortured trying to decide if he's going to hurt me or not. I pull back, but he's holding my arm so tightly now I can't get away. He speaks calmly and playfully, trying to get me to relax. He tickles me. He keeps talking. We're playing a game. He undresses me. He talks incessantly, coaxingly gentle for a change. Maybe it's okay this time, maybe it'll be fine, maybe he won't hurt me. It's like I've forgotten the routine, hoping that it will be different, that maybe this time we'll just play. This is the hope that I cling to.

"Lie on the log," he says. He rubs my body with his hands. He tickles me. He talks quietly. He touches, touches, touches, and touches. He turns me over, still touching, flipping me onto my back and tying me down, my arms and legs spread wide. His fingers poke into me. He puts a stick in me. It hurts. He's breathing hard, talking quietly but excitedly. He doesn't sound so nice anymore. He's using that urgent don't-you-dare-complain-or-I-will-hit-you voice. He doesn't even notice me anymore. I don't exist; it's just him and his ugly breath. I see his sweaty lips coming closer and closer until his tongue is in my mouth and he's breathing down my throat. I hate that panting-like-a-dog sound he makes!

When he penetrates me with his penis, I immediately leave my body. I see what he's doing from up above. I'm in a tree looking down now. I see a tiny girl on a big log. The man with her has pants on, but no shirt. He unties her and pushes her off the log so that she falls onto the ground. I see her lying there in a heap on the ground while he puts his shirt on, looking at her. He pulls her hair and calls out *my* name! Then I am back there on the ground too, pushing him away. I want him to stop touching me. I hurt so badly that I don't want him near me. Go away, go away, go away, go away! He must hate me or I must be really bad for him to do such things to me. I promise I'll be good! I'll be good! I won't tell!

I stay there. I'm alone. I'm in a different world, not a real world. It's not the ordinary world of my parents and my brothers; it's someplace else. It's the world where bad things happen to me, a world that doesn't exist except when it happens, otherwise it isn't real. I go away to this bad place sometimes, but then I go back to my real life. When I go back into my own life I carry with me the heaviness of this shadowy world, the pain and sadness, and the incredible loneliness of it too. The sense of hope that I had at the beginning of this memory, waned after a short while. It was a very young hope, a naïve hope, and I knew it was a hopeless hope, but I had to have it nonetheless.

As this memory goes through me, I find myself sitting empty and broken, filled only with a deep sense of hopelessness, a most familiar aftereffect of the abuse. I relax, breathe the sweeping breath, and let the feelings pass through me, but more memories and feelings emerge as I do. After a brief peek at them, I hurry back into ordinary reality, though I sense my abandoned self still trapped in that other world, trying to get back too. The full transition back into the known self will come with sleep. I remember that. I know that my child self will hide out in bed, the covers pulled over her head, blocking out reality and memory alike, and that she will awaken the next morning and everything will be gone, erased from memory, taken away by the night. But it doesn't work that way anymore; sleep doesn't erase anything. Now when I wake up, I don't know who I am anymore. As I stop the sweeping breath and return to the present, I find that I am no longer who I was a few minutes ago either. Things are different now and some of the things about me that used to seem so normal and comforting just don't fit inside this body anymore.

October 10, 2002

I'm at my grandparent's house, in a dream. There's a big dinner party going on, for Thanksgiving or some other holiday. I'm sitting at the large dining room table. My grandfather, sitting at the head of the table to my left, is loud and overbearing, insensitive, as he could sometimes be in real life. I keep finding reasons to get up from the table. I walk around and do other things while the dinner is going on because I'm not interested in being near my grandfather's decidedly masculine energy. I make no effort to serve food or help at the table either, nor am I interested in engaging in conversation with anyone in the family. I'm just not interested in being involved. I'm utterly detached, and yet I feel a deep obligation to remain at the gathering.

I wake up in the middle of the night feeling the heavy weight of a great sadness. I wonder if this is what my child self felt like after the events of that last memory. Did she wake up in the middle of the night, feeling this sadness, pushing it away so it wouldn't still be there in the morning? Well, I can't seem to push it away now—

that doesn't seem to work anymore. Now the feelings stick around, challenging me to face them at last.

Heavy depression clings to me all day, like the overbearing attitude of my grandfather in the dream, and I constantly get up and move away from it, literally, much as I did in my dream. And just as in my dream, I don't really want to be depressed, but this is where I find myself now and so I accept the depression—for now. It must be trying to teach me something. In the evening, at a meeting of the artist's group, I laugh in spite of it. I notice that my fellow divorcees, whom I haven't seen in a month, look pretty depressed too.

October 12, 2002

I dream that my son has been molested. As soon as I see his haunted, vacant look, I know what happened. I see the abuse taking place, like a video playing in my head. I just take him in my arms and hold him, my desire to comfort him incredibly strong. At the same time, I wish that someone like me had been there when I was a child, and I wonder how no one noticed the signs of sexual abuse, which I notice immediately. I tell him all the right things: that it wasn't his fault, that the men were bad, and that I love him. I just hold him. Then, later, with a vengeance, I go after the men who abused him.

My dreams are about me, and this one is about recognizing what happened to me as a child, about caring for that traumatized child self and letting her feel loved. To hold my son and make him feel loved, safe, and not alone with his feelings felt like the most important thing in the dream. Also, in the dream, there was no denying, no concealing, no pretending that it didn't happen. It did happen. I couldn't make it *not* happen, but the important thing was to take care of the child, to see that the child got what he needed, to make sure that he didn't end up like me. I knew that the worst had already happened; now it was time to heal.

I had this dream on my son's birthday. I also note that lately I've been having somatic experiences—not being able to breathe, and having to gulp for air—at just the thought of my abuser. But I notice these sensations going away now, as well as the deep sadness that I've been lugging around, as I reflect on this last dream. I really am caring for my inner child now.

October 13, 2002

I dream that I'm a college student, packing up to move from an apartment to a dorm room. As I clean out my room I find jewels that I'd lost a long time ago. I hear sirens—police and ambulance going by on the street—and I'm aware that something tragic has happened. I gather up my belongings and go outside, taking the long lost jewels with me. I walk across a large square to the dormitory building I'll be living in and wait to sign into my room. Finally, I hear a woman calling out my name, telling me that I can go up to my room now. I begin climbing the narrow steps that lead upstairs. I go up the stairs and then back down again and then up again. I do this several times because all of a sudden I'm confused. I can't remember what's upstairs, where I'm supposed to be going, or why.

"I'm not sure where I am or where I'm going, I just know I have to keep moving," I said to Chuck the other day. "I'm confused. Sometimes I forget why I'm doing this recapitulation, but I'm following the protocol nonetheless."

"Yes," he said, "the two worlds are colliding. The body memory and the conscious memory are coming together, bringing the past to awareness, as the memories—caught in the body—are finally releasing."

The heaviness of not being able to breathe properly lifts completely, as I realize that Chuck is right, for I haven't been feeling right in the old world or the old self, but I'm not yet comfortable in a new world or as a new self either. His words make sense, grounding me, for I know where I am now: *between worlds*.

October 14, 2002

In a dream, Chuck leads me along a narrow, rocky mountain path. Up above us, in a steep field, I see *him*, my abuser, chasing a young girl who is screaming for help. I see that he's going to catch her. "We have to save her!" I say to Chuck. "We can't let him get her!" Chuck hands me a large stone and picks one up too. The girl is now climbing a cliff with my abuser close behind her. "NOW!" yells Chuck and we throw our rocks, each rock hitting my abuser dead on, so powerfully that he falls off the cliff and disappears into the valley below. I can't believe how easy it was! We tell the girl that she's safe now. We continue walking along until we come to an area of tall spiraling pines and deep chasms. My abuser's dead body lies across the path. A group of girls stands there looking at him.

"Don't worry, he's incapacitated now," Chuck says, and then he tells me to push him out of the way. I don't like the idea of coldly kicking him aside, even though I know who he is and what he's done. "It's okay, really; he's dead," Chuck says, encouragingly. I shove my abuser's body off the path and we stand and watch as it rolls down the mountainside, gathering dirt, creating a huge cloud of dust. Mission accomplished, we proceed along the mountain trail, Chuck and I keeping company with the girls now. Eventually, we come to a deep crevasse that must be crossed on a rope bridge. The girls are afraid to step out onto the rickety rope bridge that hangs suspended over a deep canyon, the bottom visible far below. "I'll go first, so you can see that it's fun," I tell the girls. I'm totally unafraid as I hop onto the rope bridge and swiftly glide over to the other side of the canyon. I'm physically light and mentally exhilarated, and this is how I feel as I wake up. For the first time in a long time I'm in a great mood! As Chuck says, I'm certainly working things out in my dreams!

October 15, 2002

I dream that I'm at a school gathering. I'm supposed to be at a certain place at a certain time, but I don't really care about anything, except withdrawing. I try to get lost in the crowd, to just do my own thing and not participate. I notice a lot of dirty dishes lying around, with rice drying on them. I stack them neatly, because I don't like the mess, but I won't wash them—it's not my job.

In another dream I'm visiting with friends. We sit around talking, but I tell them that I have something else to do. I'm not interested in participating in the conversation. I just want to withdraw. I've just returned from being with my abuser and I half expect someone to notice that I've been away or that something is disturbing me, but no one does. I get up, pretending that nothing is wrong. I soothe my discomfort by walking around the house, doing obsessively repetitive actions, such as stuffing things into small places. I stuff shoelaces into a kitchen faucet. I put necklaces into a small box in a wall that looks like a tiny locker. Then I wipe a large sheet of glass that's lying on a tabletop, over and over again, trying to get it clean, trying to wipe away all that just happened to me.

When I meet with Chuck in the morning we talk about these dreams. Going back into them in EMDR, I am so overwhelmed by a great need to lie down and curl up that I automatically slump over in my chair, my head falling onto my knees, my arms tucked in close. I feel very far away as I roll down into the deep tunnel inside myself. I feel Chuck's compassionate presence near me, hovering close, as if invisible hands are wrapping around me. It's good that he's here, I think, but I don't want him touching me, which he doesn't do. He seems intent on being near and I sense him just staying close, walking around, looking at me from all angles, taking in my recapitulation, as if he's never seen this before, covetous almost, making sure I'm okay as I go through this deeply felt recapitulation.

"What happened?" Chuck asks after a few minutes, as I pull my head up out of the darkness in my lap. I'm curious to find him sitting in his chair when a second ago I'd felt him standing next to me.

"I went somewhere," I say, a little puzzled.

"Yes, you did. What was happening?"

"Feelings, just feelings."

"That's right, feelings," Chuck says, nodding sagely. "It used to just be memories, but at this point the memories are almost insignificant as the feelings emerge."

"I know. When the memories used to emerge I couldn't feel anything. Now I feel. The experience just now was of falling headfirst into a deep pool of intense feelings."

"Good work!" he says enthusiastically, as we wind down the session.

"Did you get up?" I ask, unable to explain the sensations I'd had of a presence close to me. "Did you get out of your chair?"

"No," he says somewhat curiously. "I've been sitting here the whole time."

"Then who was standing next to me?"

"I don't know, who was?"

"Someone, someone was standing next to me," I say, somewhat confused, and then I realize it was Jeanne, but I don't know how to tell him this.

I don't know how to tell this kind man that his dead wife helps me through my hours and moments of pain; that she watches over me. Her presence was so real; I could have sworn it was a real person standing to my left, alive and breathing. Her vibratory energy hovered over me, utterly aware of what was happening to me, though I thought it was Chuck, watching me closely, making sure I was okay, but obviously he hadn't moved.

"I feel pretty safe here now," I say, blown away by the experience, utterly aware that something magical just happened. "I realize just how much I'm letting go of control and just trusting that I'll be okay. I can go there, into deep recapitulation in your presence, and know I'm safe."

October 16, 2002

In a dream, I'm working on a factory assembly line making thread with my bare hands, spinning wool between my fingers. Inspectors come around to look at the fine quality workmanship the factory is known for. The women on either side of me are acknowledged for the fineness of their threads. I feel no jealousy nor do I desire to be acknowledged myself; in fact I'm very happy for them. They're just quiet, shy, hard workers, doing their jobs impeccably. I'm so pleased that they're finally being recognized.

Each day now I wake up feeling different. I notice how much more real I am, how I talk and act differently. A huge chunk of ice is melting away inside me and I am more warmly present. My dream is true in a way; I have indeed been weaving together the threads of self—my past, present, and future selves—creating a new person in the process. In the dream, I felt happy for the other workers and completely contented with where I was. Not being singled out was fine; I just wanted to do my work undisturbed. Now, as I wake up, I realize that lately, whenever I look at myself, I don't recognize the skin I'm in. "What is this?" I think as I touch my arm, my belly, or my face. There used to be no feeling, no sensation except numbness when I touched myself. Now I feel not only the outside but also, even more importantly, *what's inside*. I'm reacting to things differently too. I feel like I really am the person I always thought I was, but now I actually exist. It's amazing to find that I'm real! I'm not just floating through the universe trying to avoid pain anymore. I'm actually feeling grounded. I am a real person!

"I'm alive!" I tell Chuck with great enthusiasm. "I'm real! Ever since yesterday I've been feeling different. I knew something was different and I'm changing even more today. I can feel hugs, cheeks, skin! Inside and outside, the ice is melting! I'm here like I've never been here before. I feel good things and bad things differently since yesterday."

"Welcome to the adult world, a re-birth into the world of adulthood!" he says.

"After a year of getting a hug from you every Tuesday, I finally felt it!"

"Well, don't judge it," he says, "just go with the flow of it."

"Oh, I am," I say. "I definitely am!"

October 17, 2002

In spite of obvious progress the need to withdraw remains great. After the kids go to school I go back to bed and stayed curled up for a few minutes. I go to a yoga class and want to stay curled up there too. The desire stays with me, the dogs of recapitulation shadowing me again. I put them off, only giving in for a few minutes at a time on the couch at the studio, letting what comes just happen—*allowing myself to feel*. I never used to let myself feel anything, but now I'm experiencing an almost minute-by-minute emergence of feeling, which in turn seems to be triggering a need to lie down.

October 18, 2002

I dream that I'm living in an apartment in New York City. I decide to be friendly to my neighbors rather than withdrawn and quiet like I usually am. I talk to everyone in the building. An older woman, whom I meet in the hallway, acts like I'm crazy to be so friendly and open. I frighten her so much that she quickly runs to her apartment and slams the door shut behind her. I hear two other women talking in the hall, sounding upset. "Don't worry," I say to them, "everything will work out." They bring their brother over to meet me, a very tall man. We say hello and then the women disappear. The next thing I know the man is in my apartment with the door shut behind him, towering over me, leering. "Oh no, not that!" I say. Quickly reaching behind him, I open the door and shove him out. I slam the door shut and go lie down. Then I hear a noise in my apartment. When I go out to the living room I find the tall man there again. This time he's setting up two large tables and hanging decorations for a party. As I stand and watch him, people start pouring into my apartment. It turns out to be a birthday party for the two women I'd met earlier in the hallway, the man's sisters. The sisters thank me profusely for allowing the use of my space, while I stand there wondering how this happened. I feel used and very disappointed as more people continue pouring in. I decide it's safer to withdraw and so I retreat to my bedroom where I begin working on some collages. Some of them are about keeping people out of my apartment, people whom I don't like. As I work on the collages, I decide I'm going to go back to the way I used to be; I'm not going to be friendly anymore. I determine that I'm only safe if I keep to myself.

The dream moves to a different venue. Now I'm in a car with my children, going to a gathering of some sort. We come to a parking lot full of cars and swarms of people. I'm immediately afraid of losing my children—who are young again—among the crowds. I'm suspicious of everyone, afraid because everyone looks like a potential abuser. I do lose sight of my son at one point and begin frantically searching for him. I keep visualizing where I'd last seen him, asleep in the back seat of a black car, but I can't find the car anywhere in the crowded parking lot. By now it's raining and muddy and my worry has escalated. I'm afraid to talk to anyone and ask for help. I keep thinking I'll find him on my own. I wander around the parking lot, envisioning him safely sleeping in that black car somewhere. We finally meet up and he tells me that he left the car when I didn't come back because it was too cold to stay there. I'm just so happy to see him and relieved he's safe.

The dream switches venue again and I'm back in my apartment where the party had taken place. Now there's a large social gathering of some sort going on. The collages that I'd made earlier are on display. A man rips them off the wall and tears them apart. They offend him for some reason. He leaves them in tatters. I feel extremely sad at this point. It seems as if none of this work at changing myself is really worth it. It's too uncomfortable and I just end up feeling depressed and hurt. I decide I'd rather go back to the way I used to be. I decide that I'm going to gather my children and go be safe somewhere back in my old world again. It feels like people only want to take advantage of me and destroy what's important to me as I struggle to change. I'd rather stop struggling and go back to what's comfortable and familiar where I'm not bothered by other people's opinions or needs.

I wake up more firmly committed to *letting go* of all that old stuff, for I know I must not be seduced into turning back to the old familiar world even though I strongly desire to do so in the dream. In fact, I'm really being asked to confront the changing self and accept and flow with the difficulties that arise as I go through this recapitulation process. However, I also have to accept that the desire to return to the old world is quite real and very unnerving. As Chuck said, I'm between worlds now where the familiar is safe, the unknown scary. In actuality, I no longer fit into the old world, and the self I once was no longer exists either. She has already changed too much.

In the dream, I struggle with becoming comfortable as my new self, in a new world, friendly and open to everyone. However, as the dream progresses, I feel hurt, ignored, and used, and then paranoia and suspicion set in, presenting the old comforts as viable options. Like the frightened old woman in the first part of the dream, I just want to go back into hiding. The man who rips up my collages seems to be telling me that I'm not allowed to be the old me anymore. In the dream, I'm pulled between the old and the new depending on circumstances, much as I am in my day-to-day reality as well.

And so I accept that this experience of forging a new self is extremely painful, just like a real birth. I'm keenly aware that I can't go back, that I've already come too far, and that I need to keep taking every painful step on this journey of change. My body very insistently forces me forward now too, much more so than before. I'm going with the flow of it as best I can, when I can. At other times, I'm struck by how I've physically changed, as if a new body really is being forged. Things constantly shift inside me as I do this work, triggering discomfort, but in allowing for the discomfort I'm discovering that I truly exist as a physical, feeling being now. I am no longer the dissociated, traumatized person I once was. Inklings of who I might become—lighter and freer—hints of the self I always knew existed are coming into being.

In some ways, I feel like all I do is complain and whine about this recapitulation, but I'm actually working very hard on it.

October 19, 2002

In spite of finding it hard to fall asleep last night, I awaken with a sense of having slept very deeply. I remain conscious of tension and seek to release it immediately. As the day goes on, I constantly drop my shoulders, unclench my stomach, and relax my neck, face, and jaw. Memories float in and out, old things, not yet clear. It appears that doubt is attached to them, but I expect that will release too, as the truth of each memory is fully revealed and understood. I wonder if there will always be vague or hidden areas of memory, but I'm also aware that I must stay focused on what I do recall at this very moment and deal with that, as it comes. I must not project ahead too much, but remember that whatever else is hidden will come up at the right time, when it's triggered and when I'm ready to handle it.

October 20, 2002

It's raining and dreary in a dream. I'm outside working under a tent with another woman. We're painting canvas floor cloths.

Another woman comes by and wants to know how to do it, but we're reluctant to give away our secrets. We very graciously show her some of our original designs and suggest that she get a book to learn the process.

In another dream, I'm in a house where there are birds flying freely, their cage doors flung open. They're fluttering everywhere, happily chirping and singing away. In the meantime, I'm taking care of other animals in the house, animals inside locked cages. Some of the cages are inside other cages, the animals deeply trapped.

Then I dream that I'm walking along a road with a group of people, the same friends that experienced the road in the woods and the mirage in the field when I was young. We are teenagers once again. We hear someone coming up behind us, so we jump into the woods to hide until they've passed. It's dark in the woods and I know there are old wells, so I'm constantly aware that at any minute I could fall into a deep hole. We see someone approaching from far away, but it's taking an inordinate amount of time for whomever it is to reach us. I sense the importance of this person and I'm aware that I must wait for whomever it is to pass by before I myself can proceed. At one point, frustrated with waiting, I go out to the road and peer into the distance. At first I don't see anyone, but then a tiny speck appears on the horizon. Eventually, it reveals itself as a tiny figure, running. I watch as the figure comes closer and closer. I anticipate that it will be an old lady, bitter and angry, a witch whom I will need to hide from. I'm certain that if she catches me I'll be lost forever, but I also know that I must stay and face this fearsome witch.

It takes a long time before it becomes clear that the running figure is not a witch at all, but just a little girl. She's running full tilt, barefoot, wearing a summer dress, and pulling a wooden cart piled high with barrels. She shouts something as she runs past. I gather that she's in a race, as there's a sense that others are coming behind her, but as far as I can see there is just this one lone little girl, running down the long stretch of road pulling her heavy load. As she arrives abreast of where I'm standing, I'm surprised to see that she's such a tiny little girl. I know, instinctively, that she's a good girl. "They're coming, everyone is coming! It's almost over, we're almost done!" she yells as she goes running by, strong and fast, out in front. She's winning, I think. "The end is in sight!" she shouts over her shoulder as she passes us. Then I realize that she's not in a race at all. She's not competing but leading the way for others. I know they're all headed to the same place, to a gathering place further down the road. I'm aware that, eventually, I too will get there.

As I wake up it's very clear to me that this little girl with the cart loaded with barrels is running *to* something, not away from something. She comes from a great distance and I stand and watch her approach for a very long time. I'm fearful that something bad is approaching and I'm ready to move on, to go deeper into the woods to get away from the mean old witch I think is approaching. But someone else says that we have to wait, that she's coming very fast, though to me she appears always to be far away. By the end of the dream, I fully understand that she's bringing me important information, and that she's leading the way for all the rest of my inner girls, letting me know that we're all heading toward something good.

I notice how my dreaming self went deeper and deeper as the night wore on, first confronting something from my everyday world of work, deciding that I must not give away my professional secrets, even though I am in the middle of a process where revealing all my other secrets is expected. The second dream took me deeper, into the two aspects of self that I've been experiencing lately, the new and freer spirit self and the still-caged feeling self. The final dream got to the real crux of the recapitulation. As I waited for the arrival of the running figure, I also had to deal with what was in the woods. I stood between worlds, the old still to be faced and the new fast approaching, but with the end already in sight.

The woods are dark and scary in the dream, cold and bleak, and I can't see very well, even though I've chosen to hide in them. There's thin ice covering the wells and I'm aware of how dangerous they are. In contrast, it's sunny and bright out on the road and the little girl is really happy, running towards something good. I sense I'm in the woods because that's what I normally did as a teenager. When someone came along the road I'd hide in the woods and wait for them to pass. In the dream, I finally realize that the woods are not safe, that they are actually full of dangers and I'm afraid and unhappy there. Even though I get pulled back into them as I recapitulate, I experience the old comforts as not really that comfortable anymore. I discover that it's far better and safer to be out in the sunlight. There's an overwhelming sense of relief in the dream when I realize that the girl is a good girl and not the evil witch I had at first anticipated. This is also what I must face about myself, that I am good.

It's Sunday. I spend the whole day at home with the kids, restful and quiet in many ways, much needed, but I also focus on recapitulating. I spend time cocooning, curling up as the need arises. I crawl under my quilt and allow myself to feel. Some of the things I feel are fear and loathing, mixed with pain and anger. On top of that, I have unexplainable physical sensations. I let myself FEEL them, while I simultaneously finally admit that things *are* bothering me, and that I actually *have* needs. This is a big step for me.

As much as I release, something still holds back the deeply buried sound and fury that I sense needs to be expressed in so many ways. Perhaps there is still lingering disbelief, though more than anything I yearn to get beyond doubt, out of the proverbial woods, away from thin ice and deep wells, out of the dreary darkness and into the happy light.

My dream has been a big help to me, as I've carried the energy of that little running girl inside me all day. Now, as night comes, I go back to bed, this time to sleep—I hope. However, I sense something stirring, unknown feelings that I can't even articulate— things contained in those big barrels pulled by that little girl perhaps—so old I don't even know of their existence.

October 21, 2002

In a dream, I'm looking at dresses and skirts on a rack at a store. I keep going toward the skirts, but then I think, "How about something different? How about a change, something new, rather than just a skirt as usual?" I wonder if maybe some of the dress styles might look good on me. I want to try something on, but the store is closing. I notice a large bear, a huge seven-foot-tall bear, standing in the store posing as a guard. I know that he's also there to protect me and that he's watching out for me. Then he takes his head off and inside there's just a little man with a tiny face smiling at me, and I'm so disappointed. I feel like I've been tricked because he isn't what he appears to be. He isn't fearsome and protective at all; he's just a nice little man.

I wake in the middle of the night and realize that the little man is showing me something important by revealing himself, asking me to face the illusion that I need protection from outside. I must find it within. As soon as I think this thought, I'm gripped by old feelings and my first thought is that I must get them out. I must rid myself of them. I toss and turn for a long time as the beginning of a memory comes over me. In wave after wave, the memory comes in physical release and, as it does, my mouth opens wide, like an alligator's gaping jaws, before snapping shut. This happens over and over again. Without forethought or intent, of its own accord, my mouth silently opens wide and then suddenly snaps shut. This goes on for hours, until my jaws ache, until I finally realize I'm trying to scream and nothing is coming out. By the time the sun is rising I'm in agony, my body releasing deeply held memories, one after the other, faster and faster, not only through my jaws but through my entire body, as I shake and shudder and writhe like a crazy person. The momentum of this release has a life of its own, and it's unstoppable. Suddenly I experience a great need to push, like the moment of giving birth when there is no stopping it; the moment when you know you just can't hold the baby back. I struggle to birth the memories right out of me, pain searing through me.

After spending half the night and most of the morning in this extremely restless and painful place, I finally force myself to get up and go to work. But I'm so uncomfortable that I leave after only a short time and head out for a walk. The pain stays with me for about a mile, but eventually I walk it off. By the time I return to the studio I'm quite exhausted and, with little ability to focus, not much work gets done. When I tune into my body and ask how it's doing, I find myself in tatters, shredded into a million tiny pieces. Nothing quite fits together anymore.

October 22, 2002

I dream that I'm standing at a large window, open like a set of double doors, on the fiftieth floor of a high-rise building. I lean out the open window and dump out a small plateful of dead yellow jackets. I watch as they very slowly float down toward the ground, which seems to take forever. As they flutter lightly through the air, I ponder what would happen if a person were to fall. A person would probably fall a lot faster, but it's still such a long way down. You'd have time to think, I imagine, to change your mind. There's a sudden shift and now I'm *standing* on the window ledge. How I got here I don't know, but my awareness is heightened. Everything I see is crystal clear and vividly lit. I'm staring straight down into empty space, keenly aware that I could fall, that with just one false move I'd go over the edge. I quickly hop back off the windowsill. I wake up sweating and with heart pounding, immersed in the panic of knowing that I was a mere shaky second away from falling. It's 3 a.m. and I lie in my bed trembling, aware that one day soon I will have to let myself go and take the plunge into that most frightening abyss.

October 23, 2002

I dream that I'm standing at the back door, looking out at my two cats who are lying in the sun on the stoop. Two small dogs appear in the yard, a mother and her pup. "Who are you?" I ask. Then two more dogs appear, another mother and her pup, and again I ask, "Who are you?" Then two more dogs appear, and again I ask them who they are, as two more dogs, a mother and a pup, appear. This goes on and on, until the whole backyard is filled with hundreds of dogs. I want them to stay; I want to take care of all of them.

In another dream, a landlord is showing me an apartment on the top floor of a sprawling Victorian house. He points out a wall of large windows, like doors, that lead onto a shady rooftop. There's a nice yard too, which is visible far below. The shady roof garden is really nice, but I'm aware that it's not suitable for babies—a baby would fall right off the roof. Downstairs, on the first floor of the house, is a bank. I have some checks to deposit. I go in and talk to the teller, mentioning that I've just been in the apartment upstairs.

I walk out of the building with very pleasant feelings, and I wake up with good feelings too.

I immediately interpret the animals in the first dream as representing my true ability to feel deep affection for myself. As I ask my feelings to reveal themselves they will emerge more fully and become totally acceptable to me, just like the dogs in the dream. I have no qualms about taking ownership. In spite of the fact that there are hundreds of dogs, I want to keep them all.

The second dream is a little puzzling, especially as I'm about to sign the contract on the little blue house in real life. The closing has been delayed so many times for one reason or another and now the present owners have asked to stay on while they wait for their contractor to finish building their new house. I've agreed to let them rent the house until December, but then I want them out. It's a huge imposition, but I feel obligated to be kind, the old me numbly feeling like I can't make demands that benefit myself, as if I still don't matter. I notice how passive I'm being about the whole thing, just going along with the process, which is indeed the old way, but at the same time I have so much going on right now that I don't really care. I know the kids are anxious to move, as am I, as the situation in the house we're all sharing is getting increasingly uncomfortable. This dream seems to indicate this discomfort—the baby isn't really safe—though overall I'm banking on eventual happiness and a new sense of security. In reality, I've already felt a new sense of independence blossoming as I take control of my life and make this move happen. And it feels so right, buying this house, not only reasonable and affordable, but a place where we will indeed be happy, like in the dream.

In spite of having an extremely busy day, the nastiness of the abuse sinks ever deeper into consciousness. I cannot escape the truth of its brutality as memories intrude while I work. I finally acquiesce to their insistence. I take a break and sit on the couch at the studio, allowing for a few minutes of inner work. Even as I accept the reality of the abuse, letting in what comes, a tiny voice of denial remains persistently present, whispering constantly of doubt. I know enough to refuse it, though I also acknowledge its presence. "Yes, I know you are there, but I'm not focusing on you today." I'm aware that such needling denial is similar to the physical resistance that automatically sets in whenever a memory seeks to emerge. I push them both away and slump down on the couch to await the onslaughts of whatever memory has been hovering around me all day.

Tension builds as my body pushes to recapitulate. I can't help but react, wanting to fight it off in some way, just as denial fights the truth. But I'm aware that I must no longer refuse what is on the verge of surfacing—I must acquiesce if I am to heal. And so I accept that there is no more denying anything. There is no turning back either. Too many things have changed. I've changed. I've already splintered apart. The truth is that I've already fallen into the abyss of my dream, already taken the plunge out the window of the fifty-story building. Now the struggle is really with remaining fully conscious and aware as I return to those painful years, as I repeatedly plunge back into a time I'd vowed never to return to, that I sought constant escape from, in one fashion or another.

As a child I escaped by forgetting, by blocking things out, by creating distractions. Still later, I expanded my options—running, swimming, walking great distances, and traveling. Finally, I moved as far away as possible. But a mysterious unknown self always haunted me—hinted at by the flashbacks and triggers, as well as the nagging feeling that something wasn't quite right with me—suggesting that I was somehow damaged. Acceptance of the sexual abuse, and the fuller realization of its bitter truth, does ultimately involve going back to relive what happened, taking the plunge into the abyss of my body and psyche over and over again. Sometimes it's like watching an old movie, but, as details emerge, I actually feel everything that's going on in that movie. In full-body, extrasensory experiences I become my past self. Sometimes I'm stunned by what comes through. "Is that me?" I ask. "Yes, that is me, that was me! Yes, I remember. I remember being there, and I remember feeling that too."

I tire of the self-analysis as I sit on the sofa now, the intensity of the process all of a sudden too much, though I know I must stand on the edge of the ever-present abyss and face what is coming. Looking for distraction, I pick up an old magazine. Flipping through it, I come upon an article about a pedophile, a serial rapist. A five-year-old girl whom he had raped—described as being delicate, with chin-length dark hair and ivory skin—describes my five-year-old self perfectly. It's like reading about me at that age, and in *Good Housekeeping* for crying out loud! I force myself to read the entire story. Even though every word sends me deeper into depression I refuse to put it down, the significance of it not to be missed. I know I must not only face the truth of my own past, but the truth that people do rape tiny children. Having memories of being raped as a child is not my secret alone, but a dark secret that inhabits many a human soul. I must accept the abysmal truth that such aberrant behavior is rampant in human nature; children are raped every day! I must also face myself and the shameful memories of my own rapes, at five and even younger. If I can't face my own truths, how can I expect the world to face this most bitter truth and take action to do something about it?

As I finish reading the article, I am suddenly released from the tension of denial. I still sense resistance in my body, though not in my mind. The abuse happened. I accept it as a fact of my life, but as my body struggles to go into recapitulation mode I have the distinct sense that I'm still resisting something. I suddenly realize that the resistance I've been experiencing in my body is a recapitulation of long ago resistance to what my abuser was doing to me. I go deeper and allow my body to remember. I feel myself pushing my abuser away, fighting and kicking. As I recapitulate, I gain the clear understanding that this is the reason he tied me down. My hands were tied because I fought back. Full of angry indignation, I struggled then, and I struggle now, against the restraints he used to keep me where he wanted me.

As I come out of the vividness of the memory and back into the present, I can't deny the realness of such sensory, experiential episodes. Much more real in a sense than visual memories alone, they encompass everything. For a long time now, I have indeed been able to accept that what the memories are telling me is the real truth of my past, but it's still hard to go back to a childhood where I didn't want to be most of the time anyway. As I return there in recapitulation, I must face the brutal truths that I've spent my entire life running away from. As memories emerge, I am charged with bringing back into clear focus what I have tried so hard to erase. I must accept that my childhood was a nightmarish existence that I attempted to cancel out by forgetting, achieving balance of a sort by trying like hell to lead a normal life.

The abuse didn't just happen once or twice, but occurred many times, perhaps hundreds of times throughout the most impressionable years of life, the formative years. This realization was once too much to bear—impossible to fathom that I had been under someone else's spell for sixteen years without remembering a single thing about it—but now I'm ready to understand it on a deeper level. And, so, while I suffer through this painful recapitulation process, on one level regaining my memories and letting them go through me, I'm also suffering through a much deeper desire and need to thoroughly fathom what it all means for me as a human being. I want to know more about myself.

I cannot push away or discount the resistance I feel either, because I realize now that it's part of the process and not just the resistance of my present self to experiencing the awful truth, as I had at first perceived—at least not this time. This time the resistance comes from the intense anger brewing inside me, the fighting, kicking, and biting anger, and the frustration of trying to scream in a body that has totally shut down, is frozen in silence, incapable of uttering a word. That is what I was experiencing when I woke up the other night and snapped my jaws for so long. As I go through the memories of rage, I must now more fully accept the truth of the intense brutality. I must also be compassionate toward my child self, who found protection in shutting down, in hiding in the tunnel of darkness and loneliness, for it was the instinct to survive that sent her there. To get to this acceptance, I must confront being tied down and held against my will, knowing that I am caught, yet hellbent on resisting anyway, even though I'm aware of how futile it is. I must also acknowledge that in some fashion I've been fighting back ever since.

While Chuck is away for the next two weeks, I must deal with this on my own. I must stay grounded in this world, even though that old world is very potent, with such a strong pull, especially when I'm experiencing a string of memories. As they arrive in rapid-fire assault, they catapult me into another world, somewhere between the past and now. I may land there for days at a time, and in that vague place, living can be dangerous, driving hazardous, and my mind forgetful.

October 24, 2002

In a dream, I'm standing with a group of relatives. We're watching several boys drive their cars, full force, into a little cottage, totally destroying it. The sound of the cars crashing into the building is deafening, and upon impact debris flies everywhere. Everyone is upset at what the boys are doing, but no one seems to be able to stop them. I talk to my uncle who is schizophrenic and has not spoken in years. He's a young boy in my dream. I tell him that I understand his silence, but that I'm glad he's decided to come back to reality. More relatives arrive until a huge crowd has gathered. We all stand around watching, not saying a thing to deter the boys who continue slamming their cars into the small cottage.

The significance of the dream does not escape me, though I'm disturbed by the lack of direct response to obviously alarming activity. This was commonplace in my immediate family, though there's no denying that it's actually taking place. I've pretty much handled what happened to me according to the family practice of silent denial, pretending it away—until now that is. And so, the boys crashing their cars into the small cottage cannot be stopped, for like the rage inside me they must fully vent. As I acknowledge the silent uncle in the dream, the little boy who has decided to finally speak, I'm really addressing my own child self, finally facing the truth of what happened, finally daring to face reality and speak too.

On and off throughout the day, I let myself feel, taking time to lie on the couch at the studio and tuck into a ball. I hold myself tightly to keep from disintegrating, but I don't hold back the somatic experiences or the feelings that ride in on them. I go home late in the afternoon, exhausted and bothered by the intensity of the recapitulation, and lie under the covers for a solid hour. The physical sensations, now allowed fuller expression in the privacy of my own bed, ripple through me in endless release. The intensity finally dissipates, though feelings continue to percolate, spilling out as I let go, for I am no longer able to hold back. By the end of the tirade, my throat is sore with a clutching need to cry, but nothing comes. No sound escapes and no tears fall from my eyes.

On the bright side, tomorrow I go to the closing on our little blue house. The kids are as thrilled as I am that the end of this stage is in sight.

October 25, 2002

A heavy red velvet curtain falls on top of me as I come out of sleep, burying me under dusty memories. I find myself lying on my side, in limbo, enveloped in a sense of nothingness. I scan my body and discover that none of me exists, nothing, except the tip of my thumb. It's the only place I feel present. There is no sensation whatsoever in the rest of my body. In fact, there's a total absence of weight and awareness of being. I don't even feel the usual state of numbness that often accompanies these moments of dissociation. I'm aware, however, that I could slip into numbness at any second, and yet I don't. I *hear* myself breathing, yet it's a little freaky to discover that I can't actually *feel* myself breathing! The only body part that feels alive is the tip of my thumb. I feel it rubbing against the blanket, and it feels enormous, as if my entire being has crawled inside my right thumb.

Enveloped in this eerie feeling, I realize I've been here many times before. However, this time I'm aware of what's going on, as if the recapitulating adult self is standing off to the side, observing. I lie in unearthly stillness, unable to energize my unfeeling body, yet somehow I'm able to lift my thumb to my face and rub it back and forth against my unfeeling top lip. After a long time I begin to feel the softness of my skin, my sense of presence spreading from my thumb to my lip, as if the tip of my thumb carries access to reality. Now I feel these two tiny spots on my body, my thumb and my lip, but nothing else. The rest of me still doesn't exist. The rest of me is gone; drowned in a dark red velvet sea of nothingness. I notice that sadness and loneliness coat me as well, as the heavy red velvet curtain tucks in more tightly around me, firmly asserting its weighty presence.

Waking up to this makes me wonder how I'll manage to get through the rest of the day, but I have no time to dawdle. I have to buy a house today! I find that I can roll out of bed and so I do. I land on my feet and make my body move by placing one foot in front of the other. I take a breath and tell myself to just keep going as I walk towards the bathroom. If I can just keep moving everything should be okay.

I shower and dress and drive to meet up with my lawyer at her house so we can travel to the closing in a nearby city together. It's an unusually warm autumn day and I'm extremely grateful when she offers to drive. I'm in my usual daze, trying to stay present and focused, though after my strange morning it feels harder than ever, as if I'm constantly swimming up out of that red velvet sea of nothingness. The world is muffled and distant, until I finally surface and remind myself that I'm supposed to stay in this world now. As we drive, my lawyer compliments me, saying that I'm one of the most intelligent women she's ever worked with, clear, concise, and strong.

"You're a rare breed," she says.

I thank her. I accept the compliment and tell her that it's really nice to have the feedback, especially with all I'm going through at the moment, getting through the divorce and basically becoming a single mother as I prepare to live with the kids on my own. I realize that while the recapitulation has brought up so many old ideas of myself, the last year has monumentally built up my self-confidence and sense of inner strength. I've stepped out into the world in so many new ways, finding my footing after many years of hiding behind shyness and low self-esteem. Indeed, I do feel stronger than ever.

In spite of the morning's recapitulation, I arrive at the closing feeling much clearer and more present, though it takes me a while to feel physically comfortable. We sit around for a long time waiting for one thing or another to be faxed over, but it's over fairly quickly. I feel much lighter and happier as we head for the car, a new homeowner. Even though I won't move in for a few months, just the thought that the end is in sight is enough to keep me cheered up for several hours.

Once back in my own car, I pick up some lunch and head to the studio. I'm aware that I'm really too keyed to concentrate on work, but eventually my focus returns. Before long I'm involved in work projects, my ego somewhat spurred by the feedback from my lawyer.

The kids are with their dad for the evening, his night to cook and hang out with them, so I'm able to work late. I spend the afternoon and evening on getting work done for my upcoming show. The old stuff tugs at my heart every now and then, attempting to draw me into its sad and lonely depressive state, but I refuse its call, and yet I notice how it automatically asserts itself into the new work I'm doing. As I let my unconscious lead the creative process, I find myself sculpting a tiny white clay baby. Before I even realize what I'm doing, I plant her inside an assemblage of sticks and other found objects, in woods, buried under snow. The little baby girl, pale and waxy, is reminiscent of the twin fetuses that swam up out of my recapitulation last spring, perhaps bringing something unresolved a little closer to reconciliation. I know there are deep feelings that I haven't gotten to yet, regarding not only the abortion but also surrounding the entire incident. Maybe I'll resolve them in this new body of work, though I wonder if I'm really ready to hang it on the wall and let the whole world see it.

I head home at 10:30 and spend some time with the kids before I turn in for the night. I wonder if I'll be able to sleep, but once my head hits the pillow I find myself easily drifting off. I half awaken in the middle of the night with intense cramping in my hips. Caught somewhere in dreamland, I'm unable to fully grasp what's going on. The painful physical sensations and the vague dreamworld I'm in neither merge nor totally split apart, and so I wander in nightmarish murkiness, visionless and lost. Tossing and turning, I wonder where I'm supposed to go next.

October 26, 2002

It happened. It happened. It happened. These are the words I awaken with and as they reverberate through me I awaken more fully to the truth: *the abuse did happen.* I find that I must keep repeating this to myself, reaffirming my intent to fully recapitulate. It happened. It happened for years, year after year of brutal assault after brutal assault. If I need confirmation, all I have to do is notice how my body reacts to triggers and thoughts, to the memories that arise. This small woman's body holds many years of painful abuse. Now it releases, very slowly, one painful memory at a time through mind and body, yet my throat remains closed off. A heavy metal door blocks entry and exit, through which no sound penetrates. I haven't been able to remove that door yet.

I meditate. I sit and do the sweeping recapitulation breath. As I breathe, I change form. At first I'm a dead baby lying in the woods, but soon I transform into a wolf. My pale white, hairless baby arms and hands become powerful wolf legs and paws covered with fur. My jaws grow large and long, full of sharp teeth. I snarl and snap at the air and feel the primal nature of my animal self, but something shifts again and suddenly I'm aware that I'm injured. I drag my heavy body along the ground, my entire back end bloody and paralyzed, the fur matted with blood, dirt, and leaves. I drag myself to my cave and lick myself clean. Strong and powerful, I sit patiently. I calmly wait to heal. I am aware that my injuries are severe, but with time I am confident that I will fully heal and be strong again. I will hunt again one day. I will hunt him down, and I will howl at the moon again, in both anger and joy.

While I meditate, I sense my human body tightening and clenching. I feel sadness sitting heavily inside, in a deeply primal place. As I transform from injured and yet powerful wolf back into human form, I am more fully aware of the extent of my injuries. I understand that the wolf is showing me that although I have been mostly numb, unable to acknowledge the pain of my injuries, the sight of the blood demands that I accept the truth. I cannot deny that I am injured, though the first sight of my bloodied and useless legs surprises me, as if I have not noticed them before. But once I get to my cave, I realize I've been bearing the weight of my injuries, dragging them behind me for a long time, my powerful wolf legs useless. I am fully aware that I am in need of healing. As my wolf self sets the intent to heal, I simultaneously begin to *feel*. The reality of years of pain, sadness, and loneliness sink in, until I feel actual pain. As I let the pain go through me, my body reacts, clenching as it both fights and releases. I sense my wolf body and my human body in alignment, both knowing that this time of healing is essential.

As restless energy courses through my human-wolf body, shifting and vibrating, it reminds me that my injuries are not centered in just one place, but that my whole being has been traumatized and that every part of me needs healing energy. I do realize how hurt I am. As I return my attention to the wolf in the cave I am instantly in pain, a howling kind of pain. But also, like the lone wolf intent on survival, I know I mustn't cry out—I must not draw attention to my woundedness. Thus my body bears the tension, while I sit firmly in my intent to continue this healing journey.

Like the wolf alone in the cave, I am alone at the studio again tonight. I'm intent on getting the last of my new work done in time for the opening of the two-person show next weekend. I feel strongly centered and sure of my abilities, the new work expressive of the deep inner process I've been experiencing, its very execution offering healing release. As I work, I accept that I can't cry, but I also accept that I've learned to speak to and through my body in a way I never could have before. As I ask it to tell me what it needs now, and why, I find myself like the wolf in the cave, settling in to lick my wounds clean. I am intent on fully healing myself, so that I may regain full access to my, as of yet, untapped powers.

October 27, 2002

I dream that I'm at a friend's house, framing several large pictures for him. He comes into the house and tells me that there's going to be flooding along the river that runs nearby. I'm a little nervous that I won't be able to leave, but realize that with the threat of flooding I should just stay put. I tell him I'll delay my departure until all danger has passed. I ask him to set me up with more work to do and settle into staying busy, trying to relax about having to stay longer than I'd expected. The truth is, however, that I'm feeling pretty anxious. I go out to my car to get something and find it vandalized. The tires are slashed, the steering wheel has been cut off, and the windows smashed. I try calling the police, but can't get through to them. It's already raining heavily. The ground is wet and slippery with mud, and I'm nervous about being cut off from help. I show the damaged car to my friend, telling him that someone has been following me and that this kind of damage has been done before. He says it can be fixed, but when he sees how nervous I am, he lends me a small scooter so I can get away from my pursuer. I thank him and set off immediately, not caring about the rain or flooding at all. Before long I'm hopelessly lost. When I stop at a gas station and ask for directions I'm told to take the main road, which will be faster, but that I should be very careful.

I get back on the scooter and go in the direction that was pointed out to me. Eventually, I arrive at the intersection with the main road, but as soon as I see the speeding cars and trucks, hear the noise, and consider the dangerous exhaust fumes, I decide I don't want to risk traveling in such heavy traffic on the little scooter, especially as it's still raining heavily. It just doesn't feel like a good idea, so I turn around and go back, hoping to find a calmer, less busy route. After a while, the road ends abruptly and I am confronted with a maze of steep ascending and descending stairways, much like the steps of a Mayan temple. I remember these stone steps from other dreams. Intent upon tricking my pursuer, I abandon the scooter and start climbing up the steps. Before long I duck down out of sight and backtrack to another set of steps going in another direction, keeping low so *he* won't see me. I do this a few times, backtracking and ducking out of sight, following the steep stone stairs until they eventually end at a boardwalk. It's the same boardwalk I had dreamed about a month ago, in front of the building where I had a new loft apartment and where I had heard the cry for help in the raging ocean water.

As I step out onto the boardwalk I find myself walking along beside my abuser's daughter. I'm extremely nervous, feeling exposed, sure that *he* is nearby. It's raining so heavily now that we duck into an entryway and enter a movie theater. I roll myself up into a tight ball in a seat, curling up so *he* won't see me if he comes in, but I still feel so exposed. Finally, I tell my abuser's daughter that I'm going home. She's very annoyed that I'm leaving her alone, but I quickly turn from her and hurry away. I leave the movie theatre and begin running along the boardwalk as fast as I can. I wake up, still feeling like I'm being followed.

I work long hours getting ready for the upcoming show, from 8:30 a.m. to 8:30 p.m. with barely a break, going strong on adrenalin and caffeine. I paint a small canvas and find that I love the feel of it, how it gives and receives, much better than painting on hard wood as I've been doing for so long. And then suddenly, I am struck by an intense desire to work as large as possible, the creative urge kicking in, asking to be given expression. It's too important to ignore and so I call up my studio partner and ask to borrow a large canvas she's had sitting around for a while.

"I'll replace it tomorrow," I tell her. "I can't stop, something is driving me. I just have to keep going."

She doesn't hesitate, but immediately tells me to take it. Before I even start painting, I envision a large tree, the trunk split wide open and everyone who has been trapped inside flying out and away, all the little girls inside me set free at last, done with hiding.

October 28, 2002

I spend the day working on the large canvas I'd started last night. I'd painted the background and left it to dry overnight. Now, I paint an enormous tree. I watch as it grows and branches out, as it becomes more and more colorful, as it changes and takes shape. I work quickly, the brush flying through the air.

While Chuck's away I've been going to a lot of yoga classes and keeping things at bay by concentrating on work. I keep music playing at the studio because if I turn it off the old stuff creeps right in and demands attention. I have moments when I feel like I need to go lie down, curl up, and lick my wounds, like the wolf in my mediation. I push these recapitulation moments away and focus on work during the day, but in bed at night the old stuff comes sneaking in, clutching at me, wanting to tell me more of its secrets. I push it away as best I can, begging for sleep, licking a wound or two, but really trying not to indulge it in anyway. It just feels safer that way.

My children miss me. I've been so busy getting ready for the show, taking advantage of their dad's willingness to help out, but it means I've been away a lot more than usual. They understand the circumstances, but it's been hard for all of us and I know they need me.

"Even though we talked about it," my daughter says, "I need you, and I want you when I want you."

"You're never around," says my son, seconding her feelings.

They feel better after I tell them that this busy time is almost over, that I really appreciate how good they've been, and how much I'm looking forward to moving into our little house together. I tell them that we'll be together the whole weekend, that we'll go to the opening of my show together, that they can help out, and that we'll have time to relax and just be together, the three of us.

It's time for the day to be over now. Everyone is in bed and asleep, though I'm simultaneously revved up and exhausted, still going strong after running all day on adrenalin and too much caffeine again.

October 29, 2002

In a dream, I'm standing with my two children on top of a mountain. It's raining heavily, the rainwater flooding down the mountainside in swift torrents. As I watch, the water washes straight down the side of the mountain and goes swirling right into a hole in the ground far below. I've been searching for this hole throughout the entire dream, certain of its existence, but unable to find it until now. Now, as I see the floodwaters rushing into it, I experience great satisfaction. I wake up feeling that same sense of satisfaction, as if something important has finally been verified. I sense that all of my scattered energy is gathering and rushing into the center of my being now—where it belongs.

October 30, 2002

I'm sitting in a classroom in a dream, observing a class that a man I know, a doctor, is teaching. First, he teaches a dance number. The students all stand in rows and some of them get the dance steps while others don't. Then the doctor holds a small white bowl in one hand while adding powders to it with his other, explaining how a chemical reaction works. When he's done with the lesson I take the bowl and some other things to wash in a sink. The doctor comes over to inspect the cleanliness of the bowl. His last lesson of the day is about not using credit cards anymore. "Spending has gotten out of hand," he tells me. "It's time to conserve."

In a second dream, I'm in an art school. I walk into a painting studio and see a boy painting a group of odd, abstract shapes on a large canvas. As I walk closer, I see that they are actually human and animal body parts. I tell him that I like his work.

I am constantly drawn to lie down and curl up in a ball, but I have too much to do with putting the show together, just three more days until the opening on Saturday. I take the advice of the doctor in my dream to "conserve spending" as meaning to conserve my energy, as I do feel as if I've overextended myself. The paintings depicted by the boy in my second dream are the truth behind my own works of art; the bloody remains of a dissected self. It's not surprising that the essence of my abuser looms over the entire event. How could it be otherwise? Most of the work I'm exhibiting is based, in some way, on my abusive past, having emerged so succinctly out of this recapitulation process.

There's one more week to go before I meet with Chuck again. In the meantime, the tension of the past still lies heavily upon me. The red velvet sea of nothingness drapes over me like a heavy cloak, tied too tightly. My neck cracks every time I turn my head, the heaviness quite apparent as it seeks to drag me down into the depths of its smothering darkness. Luckily, I have much to do! The paintings are getting done and the show is going up. This is a very exciting time!

October 31, 2002

In a dream, I'm walking down a sidewalk in New York City with a friend, pushing her two children in a baby stroller. We're glancing in shop windows as we walk along the avenue. "You are so quiet!" my friend suddenly exclaims very loudly; at which point her children disappear and the stroller is suddenly empty. Wondering where they are, we turn around and head back in the direction from which we've come. Eventually, we find the children sitting on the steps of a building with a young girl, a babysitter who knows them well. The two children are happily hugging each other, oblivious to having been missed at all. We are so relieved to find them safe.

I wake up with a stiff neck, feeling sad and tense, weighed down by such heavy feelings. They sit on my chest, pinning me to my bed, asking me to acknowledge them. "Not now," I say, turning away, knowing that the children in the dream disappeared because they felt threatened by their mother's challenge to me. The silent little girls inside me just didn't want to be confronted, yet again, by their reluctance to speak and so they took off. In real life, an energy healer has repeatedly offered to treat me, tenderly challenging me to deal with my emotions. She clearly feels the energy of them boiling inside me, but I'm not ready to trust another person; it's not safe yet. At the same time, I know it's imperative that I attend to my feelings and emotions, to let them become known, to let go of the old mantra that still sticks: *People let me down; people can't be trusted.* Until I do trust more readily, I am like the children in the dream, running away, disappearing to an old childhood comfort, their babysitter. In my case, that means running to my bed and curling up under the covers.

I acknowledge that some of the feelings I have yet to investigate on a much deeper level are related to loneliness. I acknowledge that I want romance and intimacy; even though I also know I'm not ready for that yet. I'm still afraid of people, not ready to trust, not ready to trust my own instincts or desires even, because I fear I may make the wrong choice in a partner, and in the end I'll be alone again—wounded and withdrawn. Far better to not even go there at this point. At the same time, I know that I must get out of this hard tree body that I've lived in for so long and experience new feelings, new desires, and new relationships. I must leave the shelter of my tree self—so tough and brittle—for a softer, gentler abode, a caring place within myself.

Chapter 5

Stalking A New Self

November 2, 2002

I'm with my daughter in a dream, walking on narrow trails that wind through steep and treacherous mountain passes. The paths are dangerous and I'm aware of how careful we must be as I look for safe means to descend from great heights. I keep stopping to ask people we meet along the trails for directions, making sure we'll be taking the best routes available. My daughter, seemingly oblivious to the danger, jumps from great heights, like a little mountain goat. I, on the other hand, pick my way along, stepping gingerly, very slowly and carefully making my way down the steep slopes. "How did you do that?" I ask, each time she takes a giant leap down the mountainside and lands safely on her tippy toes. "I just do it!" she says, as she flutters lightly to the ground.

The dream stays with me as I go to the artist's gallery early in the morning. The two-person art exhibit opens tonight and I still have some last minute things to attend to before then. As I stand and stare at the large painting of the girls flying out of the tree that I'd painted the other day, now hanging on the back wall of the gallery, I think about my inner girls one day being as free as my little daughter in that dream.

"Okay, you can go now; it's safe," I whisper. "Fly away, be free! Your spirits are free now! I'll take care of the rest. Go, go, go!"

I notice that the last little one is still reluctant, still untrusting, even of me, not quite ready to go forward. "People are still not trustworthy," she seemed to be saying as I painted her. "I'm better off alone. I'm better off taking care of everything myself, not being involved with others, safer alone and separate." I encourage her to let go, to get out of the tree, knowing that I'm challenging myself to do the same, with this painting especially, but also as I do my recapitulation. I acknowledge my daring self, thanking her for this process that has allowed me to be as revealing as I am with the work I've hung for this show. I walk slowly through the gallery before I leave, taking in my inner world, now exposed for all to see. I'm pleased with how everything looks and, so far, the weather is good, which bodes well for a successful opening tonight.

Back at home I take a few moments to write some thoughts, noting how being so busy these past few weeks has certainly helped keep the recapitulation manageable, especially important while Chuck has been away. Without our regular session time it was critical that my focus be centered on other things, even while *it*—the old stuff—crept in. Although I've expressed and released it onto canvas and wood, into collage and assemblage over the past few weeks and months, I feel it still waiting for greater release. Much like my dream of last night, I've picked my way carefully through the past few weeks, aware that I must continue along the treacherous path, but also aware of not inviting too much danger. As I write, every muscle and pore in my body seeks a means of expression, as if aware that Chuck will soon be back. I look forward to the moment when I can open my mouth and speak out loud again. Until then my artwork speaks for me.

Memories stir. In the achiness of my hips and shoulders, in the tension and cramping of resistance I hold them back. It's so difficult to fearlessly release these deeply held physical memories when I'm alone, the ones still buried in the tissues of my body. I note that I have no cognitive memory associated with this pain, only visceral memory, deeply embedded. I feel as if I'm teetering on the precipice in the second before the inevitable plunge, and yet the fall doesn't happen. Seized by fear and somatic pain, I hang suspended in the moment before going over the edge, in frozen anticipation.

Like my daughter in last night's dream, the little girls inside me are leaping fearlessly now into the unknown, at my insistence. And yet a small part of me is still afraid, a vestige of reluctance still wants and needs to curl up and hide, like the last little girl in my tree painting. Yet, at the same time, I must go where this journey takes me. "Let it carry me back into the past," I pray, "so I can go through whatever it is that still obstructs the flow of my life, so I can get it out of my body and move on to fuller healing." As in my dream, I still prefer carefully picking my way down from the precipice, but I realize that's controlling, no longer a viable practice. I know that I too must leap like my daughter in the dream and like the girls in my painting, reluctant or not. My body knows it, my mind knows it, and my spirit knows it. It's time to let go, to just go with the flow.

I intend to be observant at the opening tonight. I wonder if anyone will understand the truth of what my unconscious has been saying for the past year. It's all there in my artwork.

November 3, 2002

The opening flew by last night, attended by an enormous crowd, the gallery filled to capacity, our work enthusiastically appreciated and supported. Both the other artist and I emerged from the event grateful and satisfied. It pretty much went just as Chuck had predicted. When I had shown him some photos and described the work I was doing, he suggested that some people would be disturbed by what they saw and he was right. I got such an array of comments, from "Mysterious!" to "Chilling!" One very tall woman in a brown fedora just grunted and stared at me all evening. My mother said nothing. My father, weak and ill, sat on a chair in the gallery, looking haunted, barely able to take anything in. An acquaintance, a woman psychotherapist, appreciated my sense of humor, understood the feminine, maternal, and little girl aspects, but she just could not go near the disturbing aspects, which surprised me. Either she was refusing to take them in or she just didn't quite get it. My yoga teacher didn't say too much, but I noticed him pondering deeply, standing quietly for a long time in front of each piece, peering into the painted boxes and paintings that reveal the rich reality of my inner world. At one point he caught my eye and nodded. He got it.

"This is what art should be," one of my brothers said, his voice cracking. "It gives me chills and makes me want to cry."

"I know it's all about something else," an acquaintance said, prying a little. "I don't know you very well, but what I do know about you is that you won't tell me anything. We'll talk sometime, but I know you won't divulge."

November 4, 2002

I'm not sure how to handle the touchy-feely fondness coming from an older man; it makes me nervous. I sense he wants to know me in a deeper way, but I'm keeping my distance. He found my work very moving and also very disturbing, asking, almost pointedly, what it was all about. I don't feel comfortable around him. He's that age, the age of my old boyfriend, the one who was twenty years older than me, and close to the age my abuser would be now. I feel the tug of a pattern, and it scares me, though I know I'm in a different place now. But even being in a different place doesn't take away the fear that I could easily fall right back into that old place. I have to be careful. I know this is a test and yet I sense there's a need that's not being met that pulls me towards older men. What is it? Hopefully, he's not contemplating a sexual relationship, although I have been aware of him looking at me in a most interested way ever since I first met him several years ago. I don't like it and I don't want it, whatever it is. Yet the way he looks at me and talks to me draws me to him in an almost perverted way.

I know Chuck would say that it's *him* all over again, my abuser, so don't go there! Don't go to his house; don't go out with him; stay away! The intensity of the pull is ancient, a familiar concoction of tension, fear, intrigue, and desire. Yes, there is even desire there, sucking me in, inviting me to take a sip. How am I going to deal with this? I need to tell Chuck about it, but I'm afraid to, because if I do I'm admitting that I still have issues, that I'm not over it, that I'm not done recapitulating yet. The last little girl, reluctant to leave the darkness of the tree, the safety of the old place, is still inside me, and still under the spell.

That's what it's like, it's like being under a spell, and I hate it. I hate it because I'm losing control. *It* is trying to take over again! I'm fighting *it*, the old monster; the old snake in the grass, the petty tyrant that comes out of nowhere, the alien energy that gets me, again and again.

November 5, 2002

Chuck looks rested. Just back from a *tensegrity* workshop, he tells me about the shaman's proclivity for using movement and breathing as tools to release the self from old patterns of behavior.

By setting the intention to remain consciously aware of our normal body postures we can learn to quickly shift out of our habitual stances into new and energetic ones. In being aware of how we stand, sit, walk, hunch, etc., we discover how we've traditionally carried our issues in our bodies. We discover that in continuing to maintain old postures we also create an untenable situation where nothing ever changes. Our comfortable body postures are not particularly helpful as we engage in processes of change, such as this recapitulation, and I understand the truth of this as I sit in the chair opposite Chuck. My shoulders are in their normal hunched position, signifying fear and withdrawal, and I admit that I feel rather diminished and powerless as a result.

When we no longer offer the same resting places for our fears, worries, and deeper issues, Chuck tells me, we offer our entire beings the opportunity to transform. By training ourselves to constantly change our ingrained postures we break the normal chain of events and thus invite different outcomes. In electing to pay attention to my posture—in everyday activities, as well as during every recapitulation—I can achieve certain physical, mental, and reality changes, Chuck explains.

We talk about the importance of doing tensegrity movements and focused breathing exercises as I face the intense scrutiny of the older man coming so synchronistically, just when I must face down a different older man whose energy has inhabited my body and psyche for most of my life. As I face the issues and patterns of the abuse, no matter where they arise from—inside of me, from the past, or outside of me in the people I meet—I understand that I can train myself to change how I think, feel, and react. In breaking my old patterns of holding, I offer myself new opportunities to be in the world in a totally different way. Perhaps I'll even begin to actually feel real, present in my body, and more powerfully decisive on my own behalf. It's quite thrilling to imagine that such simple shifts—how I physically hold myself, and how I breathe—can have such a big impact on my life, and my entire outlook on the world. I know this concept from my years of yoga, but I've never received such practical guidance in how and where to use it as I do in this moment.

Chuck suggests I go into an old posture to experience the process, to study what happens as I go there. I immediately roll into a ball. The comfort of the pose envelops me, but I also sense the greater necessity of it as well.

"It feels good," I say. "It's a place that no one else can enter and I feel warm and safe."

"What else do you notice?" Chuck asks.

"I'm barely breathing and my stomach is clenched."

"Okay, can you breathe into your belly?" he asks.

"Yes."

"What happens as you do that?"

"It feels looser, calmer," I note.

"What else is happening?"

"I feel quiet in here. It's like I'm hiding," I say. "Even though I know you can see me, I feel totally alone. I'm really protecting myself in this pose. It feels like it's the only sane place to be, like going to sleep, to dream."

"It's similar to a shamanic dreaming position and you enter a dreamlike state when you go there," Chuck says, "similar to the altered state the shamans enter when they go into other worlds."

"Well, even though we're talking about learning how to shift out of old familiar places this is one I like going to," I say. "I think I still need to hold onto it because it's also where I go to recapitulate. It's an essential part of the process."

"Yes, we have to accept that you can go there very easily and quickly, and that it's a good ability," Chuck tells me, "but it's also associated with the past and being traumatized, so there are aspects of it that aren't particularly helpful. You'll have to learn to use it when appropriate and to shift out of it when inappropriate; even just breathing into areas of holding may do it."

I get up out of the chair as Chuck demonstrates a shamanic breathing pass that he calls the "belly-releasing breath," similar to the HA breath of yoga. He explains that it helps to purge and clear out what's been stored in the belly, a place where we tend to keep stuff that isn't useful after a certain point. We stand with feet apart, legs slightly bent. Inhaling a full breath, we hold it for a second before bending over, exhaling fully and forcefully through the mouth while simultaneously pushing our stomachs and all that they contain earthward. From this position we send old energy down to the ground, releasing through our bellies, into the floor and beyond. We practice this simple breathing exercise a few times.

"You can still maintain the important aspects of that dreaming pose to do recapitulation and also to access other worlds, but first get rid of anything that might stand in your way by releasing it forcefully out of you and down into the earth," says Chuck.

As if some blockage has indeed been removed, the belly releasing breath leaves me in a pleasant dreamy state. I notice it as we finish up the session, as I drive to work, as I eat a bagel and drink a cup of coffee. An hour later, I feel like I'm still in that dreamy place, perhaps recapitulating something, only half present as the morning progresses. Finally, around noon, something triggers an awakening and I emerge to find myself back in the present, my head full of cotton. I have enough presence of mind to bend over and do the breathing pass that Chuck taught me this morning, releasing from my belly whatever may have been stirred. However, I just can't shake it off and before long restlessness sneaks in. No matter how many times I do the belly releasing breath I just can't get free of its hold.

I end the workday early and go for a long walk, aware that I do indeed need to change my posture. I also know that walking often stimulates a shift and, true to form, it doesn't take long for something to happen. Within a few minutes, I walk through whatever has been blocking my way and into clarity. As if I am peering at old photographs, a memory of being with my abuser emerges in crystal clear images. I see him sucking on an icicle and then inserting it into my vagina. I am sickened by the sound of his laughter. As these flashbacks appear, seemingly out of nowhere, I notice just how tightly I hold my entire body and how violently I shiver as the chill icicle of recapitulation pierces my present reality. I realize there's still plenty of old stuff I haven't recapitulated yet. Sitting somewhere deep inside me, it surfaces slowly of its own accord. Perhaps the belly-releasing breath really is having an affect, moving more old stuff into fuller consciousness.

I do yoga when I get home, take a bath, then do more yoga. I notice that if I stay in table pose too long, it brings up unpleasant memories. Even being on all fours for thirty seconds is too much. I shift into child pose, curl up on the floor, and let myself go back into the memory that arose while I walked. As I allow it to emerge more fully, I find that I'm a little girl again, standing in the snow, naked from the waist down. My snow pants are bundled around my boots, which are still on my feet. I'm holding my jacket up and out of the way. I'm cold. He does what he wants to do and then cleans me off with snow. I see that it doesn't matter what time of year it is, snow or no snow, if he has a need he finds a way to get it filled.

I realize now that I had previous access to some of the memories, but I couldn't relate to them directly. I always experienced myself alone in the strange flashbacks that came to me throughout my life. No one else was with me, and so I simply thought I had conjured them out of my own perverse imagination. But now, as I put it all together, I realize that it wasn't my own strange imagination that I was experiencing, but the perverted imagination of a pedophile. I'm also more clearly aware now of how patiently my abuser groomed me, how planned and set up everything was. I hear his voice, his instructions so precise. I hear him being nice in order to get me to play the games, keeping it fun, just the two of us playing a special game. But he also hurt me. He hurt me so much that it didn't matter what he said, and the games always turned from being fun to games of survival.

As hard as it once was to deal with the abuse, it's equally hard now to bear the emergence of these memories. Even so, I'm determined to heal, to release the poison that now sits like painful tumors in my shoulders and hips, in my legs, genitals, and stomach, in my throat and neck—my abuser's poison—hard plugs blocking access to the truth. While Chuck was away I went into an old holding pattern. I knew it was a dangerous place to be, an old coping mechanism dredged up and brought back to life. But it was also necessary in order to do what I had to do, to get my work done, to put up the show at the gallery, to take care of my kids, to sign the contract on the house and prepare to move. Now that Chuck is back, the unclenching begins anew. The work we did today offers new insight into the practice of letting go, into unblocking, so that healing can take place, but it also opens the door so that memories can more easily flow too.

Even now I sense a new memory encroaching. The yoga I did this evening and the anxiety and restlessness that have been building all day signal that something is about to explode to the surface of awareness. I just need a catalyst to trigger the longed for glory of release that I know the revelation of the memory will eventually bring. It's funny, but I don't fear the memories as much as I once did. I don't particularly look forward to them with delight, but I do know they carry so much more than just horror and terror. Healing energy rides in with them too.

November 6, 2002

I'm with my abuser's daughter in a dream. We're riding subways all night long, counting out piles of coins to pay our way at each token booth. One time we put handfuls of fish through the window slot of the booth and ask for tokens in return. A group of children is with us and I fear for their safety on the crowded underground subway platforms. My abuser's daughter completely ignores them, but I tend to them carefully, never taking my eyes off them, herding them close in an effort to keep them safe.

I awaken stressed out, caught in the throws of fear, in spite of how I felt last night about the emergence of more memories. What am I so afraid of? After all, this is a *healing* process. Is this holding back a control issue? What do I think will happen? It's something Chuck asks me all the time. "What do you think will happen if you let go, if you let the memory come, if you feel?" he asks. "Nothing will happen; I'll be free," I always say, and it's the truth because I've already experienced the sense of freedom that ensues.

So why can't I let go? Do I still need time to absorb it all? Do I need more time with the memories? Did the last two weeks of holding back on the recapitulation hinder my progress, set me back? Maybe now I'll be able to release to it, let it all out—now that Chuck is back, now that I feel safe again. Do I feel safe? What do I really feel? What am I so afraid of? Am I still afraid of falling down the spring, into the dark blackness of the spring in the woods? When I think of being held over that spring I'm a little girl once again, flooded with anxiety, fearful of being dropped into that hole in the ground where no one will ever find me. If I keep quiet, if I never tell anyone, I'll be safe. But if I whisper even one word, I'll be thrown into that black hole in the ground, never to be seen again.

"No one will ever find you!" were the very effective words my abuser spoke so often, what he threatened me with. So I thought not of dying or being dead, but of being down in that well forever. I imagined living in that hole in the ground, up to my neck in black water, alone and afraid, breathing in the musty dampness among the snakes and spiders, forever lost and forgotten. "No one will ever hear me," I imagined. "No one will ever find me." Is that the threat that keeps me from letting go? Is that the reason I'm afraid of falling, not just a symbolic but also a real fear, long ago embedded? Am I still afraid that I'll tumble down into the dark well and suffer everlasting loneliness, abandoned for all eternity?

Now that Chuck is back and we've begun our sessions again, I feel looser. Already my shoulders are relaxing, my neck is less clenched. The yoga and the bath last night really helped, as well as yesterday's walk and the new intent to remain physically aware. I'm trying to be mindful of my hunched shoulders and clenched stomach. It's harder to attend to the clenching in my throat, signaling a deep need to release all the sound and fury of fifty years, still buried inside. My mindful self, however, stays connected to my physical body by doing the belly-releasing breath as much as possible.

Flashbacks assault me as I sit and write these words of healing intent. Once again I'm being held over the open spring in the woods above my abuser's house, a black hole in the ground, large enough for my small body to fit into. He holds me upside down, while I stare wild-eyed into the darkest of water, the tar black sheen of it visible far below. I smell the musty, mossy odor that rises from the ground and with it comes so much fear that I go numb. I'm a little girl again and I can't handle it, but the flashbacks continue marching in front of me and I know I must face them. In the light of their flashes, I see my abuser having sex with me, just a tiny little girl lying on the ground, peering down into the spring. As I watch the scene play out from above—indicating that I'm out-of-body—the motor of the pump installed in the spring suddenly turns on, as loud as a lawn mower, freaking me out. Shrieking with fear, I'm jolted back into my body. I see my abuser's face, ugly and distorted, looming above me. Evil laughter comes out of the smelly black hole that should be a mouth, as black as the hole in the ground. "Is fear of letting go directly associated with this memory?" I wonder, as I pull away from the alarming blackness of those two holes.

I'm having a hard time fathoming the enormity of the abuse, the duration of it, and that it actually happened to me, yet there is no denying it. And even so, I can't feel anything for myself. I can't seem to get any feelings to relate to *me*. Feelings are obviously emerging with the memories, but I can't seem to connect them to myself, although intellectually and consciously I know they belong to me. I know they are my own feelings, my own fears, and my own devised methods of coping. I know I must work on connecting all of this: the memories, the fears, the feelings, the physical pain and mental stresses, as well as the dissociated, fragmented parts that still hover somewhere in the air above the well, the woods, and the barn. I must find a way to pull them all together, to write the history of my life and apply it to the person I am now, because the person I once was couldn't.

In order to survive, the old me elected to remain distanced and dissociated from everything that happened, but I understand now that she did this out of dire necessity and that I must not be so hard on her as I go back into the past. As I become my child self again, I must gather all these seemingly disparate issues that have been safely ensconced in their separate compartments of forgetting—independent of me and yet totally belonging to me— and fit them into a new picture of who I am. By dissociating, fragmenting and compartmentalizing what happened, I left everything scattered, though at the same time very carefully packaged away, determinedly placed out of sight, never to be touched again. It's as if I too threatened myself with the same charge: "No one will ever find you!" And so I had no reason to value anything from that time, for everything was encased in the threat of life-everlasting in the darkness of the spring in the woods. I realize that even though I never spoke of what happened, and I never ended up in that spring either, I have lived out that threat anyway. I have lived as if it really did happen, for I have been alone in the darkness of my own well all these many years. In keeping promises made under great physical and mental duress, I endured the same kind of exile that my abuser once threatened me with.

I should probably stop thinking so much, just let it all come together using all the tools at my disposal—yoga, magical passes, breathing, meditation, relaxation—to release the holding patterns and the old body postures that keep me so stuck. In getting to the specifics of the abuse, I'll eventually get to the deeper feelings and emotions too. Making the feelings and emotions of my child-self real and applicable to *me*, owning them as my own experiences, is so difficult, though it's my life's task now. It's much easier to think of the abuse as happening to those other little girls that I watched from above, safely dissociated from what was really happening.

I'm not so afraid anymore to go into my cocoon, into my dream ball where I encounter the memories; I've gotten good at handling the onslaught of the past. I'm not so shocked or negating of the reality of the abuse. It happened. But now I'm also curious as to how else I might use this so-called "dreaming" ability. Aside from going there to recapitulate, to tap into feelings and rediscover my lost self, I've had hints of so much more waiting to be discovered there. I'm not afraid to explore. In fact, I'm fascinated by what I might encounter as I dream in the shamanic sense, the way Chuck talks about the shamans dreaming. I wonder what he really means when he speaks of the ways of these shamans, and where it might lead me, though at the moment I'm still confused. For although I have no greater sense of whom those shamans might be, I'm certainly gaining a greater sense of their valuable insights.

November 7, 2002

I dream that a predatorial sniper is pursuing me. I'm desperate to get away, but I run into all kinds of obstacles: stairs, traffic jams, and crowds of people. I must, however, keep moving. I must not become a sitting target. I run and run, moving as quickly as possible, feeling how close he is, just one step behind me. I run up a set of familiar stone steps and onto an oceanfront boardwalk, both of which have been in recent dreams. I see my abuser's daughter, sitting by a bandstand, listening to music. She's totally oblivious to what's going on with me. She wants me to sit with her and listen to the band, which I find loud and obnoxious. I can't pause for even a second—it isn't safe. I tell her that I have to go. I even blurt out that I can't stand the music, but more importantly that the sniper is looking for me. She's angry that I'm leaving her behind, but I don't care. Once again I feel the sniper closing in, honing his gun on me. In the urgency of the moment, I take off running again. I run along the boardwalk, farther and farther from the crowds, with the ocean on one side and beach houses on the other, intent on getting to a place of safety.

I wake up before I get there, my heart pounding, as if I have indeed been running, the sniper of my dream still in hot pursuit. Unable to calm the anxiety, I talk to Chuck for a few minutes, needing support and input. He suggests that I just allow the process to unfold, to just let it go where it wants to go, to let myself be taken. He suggests that it's the only way I'll resolve any of this; not by refusing the call of my spirit to figure this out, but only by fully acquiescing to the journey it's leading me on.

"These are very deep-seated fears," he says, telling me to be patient and to use all the resources I have available. "You are breaking old contracts, and as a result the fears are full of discomforts. I've listened and witnessed your process over the past year and a half, and it's very clear how deeply rooted it all is. You have to give it time."

"I understand that," I say, "but it's the intensity of the fear and the feeling that it's happening *right now* that's freaky. It's the fear of falling down the well and being left there for eternity that I'm dealing with. I'm acquiescing as much as I can."

"Do the sweeping breath and the belly releasing breath. Do yoga and yoga breathing. And remember that it's not now. It happened a long time ago and you're just going back to capture the details. Get the details and come back to now. We'll process them when we meet."

I hang up the phone and go into my body, asking it to help me, to speak to me and tell me what it knows. It tells me that these deep-seated issues are what cause my shoulders to hunch, my hips to cramp, and my stomach to clench. The fear of falling down the well, the feeling of needing to curl up and hunch away from my abuser are all still strongly present in my body and my psyche. Even my dreams are revealing the depths of my physical and psychological trauma, and the switching back and forth between this reality and the past are creating a lot of the discomfort too. Sometimes the two realities only merge when I bring them together by talking to Chuck, otherwise I'm half in and half out of the past, part of my conscious mind always there, assessing, trying to figure out the truth of what really happened to me as a child.

I realize that my physical body has always been compromised by the trauma that I suffered as a child, but that it has also been highly invested in utilizing what it learned as well. For I see now that as I learned how to block things out, hiding them from conscious knowing, I was learning the means to remain sane and alive. And so my body did its work well, locking down and locking out that which was intolerable, so I could survive. Now I'm picking all the locks, learning to release and let go, though my body still upholds the original shutting-down mechanisms, so deeply instituted. In its knots and cramps, aches and pains, it does exactly what I trained it to do. All of this should help me realize, as I revisit these places in my body, that yes, these things really did happen, and the repression was indeed a very arduous but necessary task. Further success will come as I allow my physical body to tell me more of what it knows.

I've already attained a semblance of release in the physical activities that are a big part of my normal life. As I work, paint, run, walk, do yoga, etc., the details of my past coalesce. In physical movement, the bigger picture emerges; it's always been that way. I think and learn with greater clarity as I move. I was not a good student, the long school days sitting at a desk unsuitable to my personality type. Inactivity dulled my brain. It was only in hands-on-activities that I became fully engaged in the learning process. Now, I am like my child self, finally allowed to get up from her uncomfortable desk. Part of my brain that otherwise lies inert is awoken as I do the sweeping breath, and as I move through my day too. Details clarify, my whirling thoughts settle, and I am brought the truth. And eventually, I hope, peace of mind.

In yoga class we work on the fifth chakra—the throat chakra—loosening the shoulders, throat, jaw, and mouth. I speak during the class as we discuss our experiences of the breathing exercises we're doing. I speak all day after that too. I'm chatty, but even more important, I'm forthright, clear and articulate, not my usual tongue-tied, quiet self. I'm proud of myself! All day afterwards I'm aware of releasing my jaw, which in turn releases my neck, which releases my shoulders, in the kind of chain reaction of release that Chuck and I talked about in our session the other day. I see the intent I set that day now in action, as the yoga and the shaman's suggestions to constantly shift the body, even by incremental relaxation, come together, working hand in hand now. And I'm quite amused that, as a result of all this work, I can't stop speaking the truth!

A memory emerges as I try to sleep. I shake violently as I go into a full somatic recapitulation, totally immersed in something that happened in the past. Anger boils out of me. Enraged and frustrated, I grind my teeth, furious at hands that hold me down. I fight back, kicking and gnashing my teeth as I thrash out at my unseen enemy. I am a tiger, fighting for my life. As I try to drift back to sleep, I'm jolted awake by yet another emerging memory. This time I see a snake coming out of me, being pulled from between my legs. Encased in the horror of it, I sense something horrific being removed from inside me. A snake? Why do I have a snake coming out of me, a slimy ugly snake? How did it get there? Then I see the babies, the one on the table and the other one at the end of the snake—but they're only dolls. I'm totally confused and still the snake is being pulled and pulled. In clenching pain, my abdomen contracts violently.

As I roll over in bed and out of the sensations of this memory, I realize it isn't a snake at all but the birthing experience that I'm recapitulating again. It's the umbilical cord I see, the contractions of the uterus giving birth that I sense, as well as the afterbirth being expelled from inside my twelve-year old body. The anger I felt in the first part of this recapitulation may have been related to being held down, tied onto the examination table, though I sense there is still more to be recapitulated. It's still too misty and foggy. But, as I've sensed before, I don't think I'm totally finished with this memory.

November 8, 2002

I wake to a thumping noise, a persistent rhythmic sound. As the darkness lifts, the source is finally revealed, a deer mating ritual taking place right in the back yard. The buck stamps his hoof into the ground, THUD-THUD...THUD...THUD, and then the same pattern repeats over again: THUD-THUD...THUD...THUD. The doe keeps her distance, skittering sideways, almost playfully teasing and snorting, lightly thumping back. Each time she moves, the buck moves parallel to her, mimicking her playfulness. The kids and I watch, spellbound, as the day grows lighter. The buck seems to be showing the doe how strong he is, the two of them moving in ritual dance, him stomping out his romantic yearnings, she moving shyly away, though clearly captivated. This looks like it could go on for a long time, so I send the kids to get ready for school while I make breakfast and pack their lunches. Suddenly I notice that something is missing, no more thumping! I look up and see that the buck has mounted the doe.

"Hurry," I call to the kids. "Look, they're mating, he's mating her; they're mating! They're fucking! Fucking deer in our back yard! Nature procreating in our back yard!"

It's all over in ten seconds. The deer move apart, muttering to each other, as if suddenly embarrassed after their hours-long infatuation. With only a brief backwards glance they take leave of each other and bound off into the woods, heading in opposite directions.

I still feel the effects of the fifth chakra work from yesterday, bringing the ability to release pent up words and emotions. The person inside me is speaking the truth, strongly, intelligently. The words coming out of me after so long are right, clear, and full of insight. I am no longer the cowering individual I'd gradually become through the years of a long marriage that had lost its spark a long time ago. Even the past, repeatedly laying its heavy red velvet drapes of mystery over me, constantly calling my awareness into unknown realms of self, is no match for this truth-speaking self. I even said "the deer are fucking" to my kids. It's unusual for me to swear, but since they were present and clearly captivated, I wanted to take the mystery out of the word. I wanted them to grasp that "fucking" is natural, that it's good, that it occurs in nature, and that nature is in all of us. Perhaps a part of me needed to hear and understand this too, my little girl self, so traumatized by the vicious acts of fucking once perpetrated upon her innocence.

I'm delighted at meeting this new self. Another level of feeling, another new ability emerges, another means to grow, as I discover a new tool: *my own true voice*. I'm opening, releasing myself from my tongue-tied past, and I want to keep opening and releasing the sounds that are so stuck inside. Even so, sometimes I just don't want to talk about another memory. I get so tired of them, simultaneously bored and sad, as I feel another one emerging. "Oh God," I think. "More? How can there be more?" It's unfathomable almost, except for when I take in the reality of the amount of years I lived under the spell of my abuser, from the age of two until I was eighteen. Look at the amount of stuff that was repressed!

November 9, 2002

I'm driving in a dream, down the same road that the little girl pulling the cart loaded with barrels had run down in a dream several weeks ago. I'm on the way to the meeting area up ahead, the same place the girl with the cart was heading. I'm forced to stop in the middle of the road because my abuser and my old boyfriend, the one that was twenty years older than me, are blocking my way. They tell me I can't pass that way, which makes me angry. I refuse to turn around and go a different way. "No! No more!" I yell, fully intent upon mowing them down. And even though I flinch, I don't for even one second regret what I'm doing as I hit the gas pedal and drive right over them, flattening them into the pavement. I drive off exhilarated and triumphant, leaving them lying flat on the road like two squashed cartoon characters.

I feel pretty good when I wake up too, though my jaw is tightly clenched and I sense I've been grinding my teeth all night. I consciously relax my jaw and neck, then my shoulders, allowing for deeper release. The fifth chakra work has definitely allowed me to speak out and stick up for myself, to say what needs to be said, in dreams and reality. In this last month of living in the shared house with my ex-husband, I am no longer afraid to give voice to my feelings. For a long time, I thought it didn't matter, that we were done, moving on, and that what I had to say would be insignificant at this point. But I realize I've been holding a lot back and so I have been able to say what I needed to say.

The belly releasing breath that Chuck taught me is significant in combination with the throat chakra work. As I speak words of release through my mouth, I also release pent up energy from lower down in my physical body, sending it out into the earth. I love the feeling of giving it all away, of purging from both ends in a sense, letting old energy flow out of me in rivers of release, being taken by Mother Earth deep into the recesses of her own body and then beyond, into the vastness of infinity where it will no longer cause disturbance.

Body memories surface as I do yoga and as I consciously shift my body out of old postures. My feeling is that I'm not quite done with the memory of the twin's abortion, that there is still unfinished business there, as my body is definitely hinting at unrecapitulated details. As the flashbacks occurred the other night, I noticed how they focused on my actual feelings at the time and what was happening *in* my body, as opposed to the out-of-body perspective I'd experienced during the original recapitulation of the memory. This time, as I recapitulated what happened in the doctor's office, it didn't matter so much what my father was doing, or how those babies looked, or even the intense loneliness that had enveloped me while in the original recapitulation. This time the memory was focused more on the physical and emotional aspects of my *in-body-experience*, which, for some reason, surprises me. I guess I thought that since I had gone *out-of-body*—viewed the scene from outside of my physical self—that I wouldn't be able to feel what was simultaneously happening *in* my body. I'm not actually sure how I could be in two places at once and retain memories of both experiences, but that does seem to be the case.

As repressed as these memories were, it's fascinating to find them now slowly emerging. Two different segments of this experience lie side by side now, as I struggle to integrate the truth of the entire experience. I understand now that my psyche was unable to handle what was happening at the time and that it did indeed fragment the experience, breaking it up into manageable blocks, compartmentalizing it. That's how I've been recalling it too, in bits and pieces. At each recapitulation, another strip of fragment is laid down, like torn shreds of paper, out of which a clearer picture begins to form. Out of nothing comes a story, my story. The truth that I have indeed lived a most numb, unfeeling life, and why, is clearly being revealed as I do this recapitulation.

I can't help but note that this is a fascinating journey! I realize that I came out of this terrible past a strong, determined, and resilient person, preparing all along to arrive at this time and place where I would be able to venture into very deep layers of my psyche. I'm fully able to dive into the shadows, into the frightening glimpses of darkness and horror within, where most people never dare to go. I'm lucky!

November 10, 2002

In a dream, I'm about to enter a boarding school. My abuser's daughter and I are to be roommates. She's trying to convince me of something as we prepare to move our personal belongings into our new room in the dormitory building. I've lost my glasses, so I can't see clearly and I'm carrying too much stuff. My arms are filled to overflowing and things are dropping all over the place. I want to make as few trips as possible, so I'm trying to be efficient, but the truth is that I can't possibly manage all the stuff I'm carrying. Things are falling out of my arms and tumbling down the stairs behind me as I make my way upstairs to the second floor where our room is located. I try to pick up as much as I can, but every time I pick something up more things fall. In the end, totally frustrated, I leave everything lying in a heap on the stairs, except for one very large, delicately crafted, frosted glass bowl in the most beautiful shades of blue and yellow. It bothers me that I'm leaving the rest of my stuff lying on the stairs, but I figure I'll go back and get everything later.

By this time I'm totally lost and confused. I leave my abuser's daughter on her own, no longer sure where I'm going or why, but I must keep going at all costs. I know I cannot room with her and so I climb up and down stairs and along many corridors looking for the right floor, for the place I'm really supposed to be, but I'm unable to find it. Suddenly, I notice that all the rooms aren't intimate little dorm rooms but instead large, impersonal classrooms. I decide this school isn't very attractive or inviting and

I wonder what I'm doing here. In one room, a graduation ceremony is about to begin and I realize I'm supposed to be graduating, but without my glasses I won't be able to see properly. I refuse to graduate without them. Someone hands me an old pair of glasses; the glasses I had when I was twelve. They were my first pair of glasses and they were so ugly that rather than wear them I squinted through my middle and high school years. The only time I wore them was in the dark of a movie theatre or to drive. Now I realize just how old they are and how meaningless at this point. As I put them into my pocket, I suddenly realize that I'm already wearing new glasses. I've been wearing them all along and I can see perfectly well.

I go back to collect my belongings, and see that people have begun going through the piles of stuff that I'd left on the stairs. I yell at them to leave it alone, wanting to protect my things, but I can't stop them. They're going at it like vultures, sorting and removing things that are important to me. At first I feel violated, but I don't want to have to be confrontational. In fact, I just want to hide so no one sees me. I want to find my room and hole up there. I want to find a place to put my beautiful glass bowl, which I'm still carrying. At the same time, I sense that I know all these people; they're the boys and girls of my childhood, now grownups. They were once my friends and I know they are compassionate beings. I'm aware that on a certain level they know me intimately, and that they really mean no harm. In a sense, I know I can trust them.

I wake with a stiff and achy neck, aware that I've kept it rigid all night. Lying in bed, massaging my neck and shoulders, I think this dream is about not seeing things clearly, about not understanding things correctly, about being lost and confused, unable to find my way because of this inability to see clearly. The crick in my neck seems to uphold this idea, but after I get out of bed and move around, as Chuck suggested I do to allow for a different perspective, I discover that this dream is about how much I've really changed.

My old childhood glasses represent the fearful self-conscious child I once was and the old way of seeing, being, and acting. No longer helpful or appropriate, they actually represent what I once chose not to see, specifically the abuse, as *I never wore them*. I didn't want to know what happened to me, but I'm changing now. I don't want to stay attached to an old means of seeing, deceiving, or perceiving of myself in the world. Once I realize I'm already wearing new glasses, my whole outlook shifts, most specifically as I come upon people going through my belongings. At first, this seems like a violation of my privacy and I want to hide, but suddenly my perspective shifts and I no longer take it personally. Even the belongings themselves no longer seem that important, as I understand that they have no real value or meaning.

I also suddenly perceive people differently too, no longer to be feared, but as compassionate beings with the same underlying feelings as I possess. Suddenly no longer threatening entities, they appear as kind, gentle, and compassionate people, and I'm aware that we are all like this at our core. The only thing of lasting value seems to be the glass bowl, which is actually something new, as it did not belong to the old me. In fact, I'd never seen it before this dream. It's as if my psyche is attempting to alert me to the fact that I don't belong in an old school of learning, that, in fact, I've graduated to a new level of awareness. As mysterious as the glass bowl is, it's the only thing worth salvaging. I can let all the other stuff go, as I'm already holding what is most precious and good. And so I'm able to walk away from everything else, totally without attachment.

My abuser's daughter has been in several dreams lately. Why does she appear and what is her role? Perhaps she's a symbol of the reality of that past, representing the old defense of denial that I no longer accept. We sometimes talk in the dreams, but mostly I ignore her, or find her unappealing and bothersome, as she gets in my way or pulls me to stay with her. I'm energetically separating from her, declaring that I don't want to uphold the old secrets. Only what is most important goes forward with me and in this dream it was the beautiful bowl. The dormitory building was brand new, with the feeling of gritty construction dust still remaining on the floors. It had the sense of being a recently renovated place, the old cleared out and what was left made new, like this process of recapitulation. But it's not a place I intend to tarry in for long, for I am indeed moving on—graduating, as the ceremony implies— leaving everything behind as I transition into a new phase. I'm moving on into new life with a new way of seeing the world, as represented by the glass bowl and the new glasses. Interesting that both of them are glass, and thus breakable. This is a little disconcerting. I wonder if even these things that I consider to be of such value now will one day be found unsustainable and eventually of no importance, breakable as they are. Perhaps everything that is now known will be left behind in the end, not just at death, but in the remainder of this life as well.

The releasing poses I worked on this week have been wonderfully helpful. I feel lots of things coming to an end, but I also feel pretty confused because I have such a cauldron of feelings bubbling up right now. Strong creative urges are flowing while at the same time I have new physical and even sexual awakenings. I'm unfreezing as I release, but at the same time I'm growing and changing rapidly, and with new feelings come new desires and needs. I'm seeing things more clearly and gaining a fuller understanding of who I've been, but at the same time the new feelings are coming fast, and I'm not sure where they're taking me. I should do as Chuck suggests and just let the process lead me, stop trying to control and figure things out. I should just release to the experiences and see what happens.

While Chuck was away everything seemed to return to a certain degree of intensity. All the old fears, the hunched body, the need to hold in, the feeling of not being in control, coursed through me once again, and the old me responded in an old way to the advances of an older man. The vulnerable me was more present then, acting in an old protective way, but also reminding me that it's a style of vulnerability I no longer engage in—for the most part. I'm in a different place now, but it's clear that plenty of old dynamics are still deeply embedded, still needing to be excavated and dealt with. And now that I'm back in the swing of the recapitulation again, going to regular sessions with Chuck, I feel strong again, more sure of myself, and more alert to dangerous situations where my vulnerable self might be threatened.

I realize that avoidance is okay, to a certain extent, but it's better to confront old behaviors and get to a different inner place, like in my dream, to a stronger position where my wounded child doesn't rule. I wonder if I'll ever get there, or if I'll always have that wounded child inside me, perpetually in need of protection? I also wonder if my wounded child gravitates to abusive people and situations because she gains comfort of some sort, for I recognize now that I do have a wounded child inside me. It has taken all this work for me to know this, for I would never have been able to acknowledge this as my old defended self.

November 11, 2002

I jump! In a dream, I run and bolt over a high balcony railing without fear or hesitation. I hang for an instant by one hand before easily and gracefully dropping to the ground, landing lightly on my toes. I determine that taking the winding stairs from the balcony level down to the main floor of the cavernous ornate old building that I'm in will take way too long. The steps seem so arduous and time-consuming. I see that there's another option and quickly take it. Two men watch as I leapt over the balcony railing, one standing at the top of the stairs and the other at the bottom. "How did you do that!" they ask in amazement, as I easily sail over the railing. As they speak, I am reminded of my recent dream when my daughter leapt from great mountain heights and I asked the same question. In that dream, I picked my way slowly down the mountainside, but this time I have no patience for such timidity and so I easily and lightly hop, just as I had watched my daughter do. Things certainly have changed!

In a second dream, I hike along a road with my daughter and her friend. Once again this is the same road that has appeared in several dreams, most notably the road the little girl with the cart full of barrels ran along. Now the road has been dug up and there are huge puddles of water everywhere. The ground is muddy, the road surface scraped bare, and the forest that once lined the road has been cleared of trees. At first, I'm amazed at the destruction, the tangle of vegetation and downed trees, the holes, the barrenness of everything, as if a massive tornado has come through. Then I'm aware that this is not the result of destructive forces, but in fact a new road being built—this is new construction.

In a third dream, I'm sitting packed into a car with a large family. I'm in the back seat holding their infant son who is sleeping on my chest. The baby is not in a car seat and when we see a policeman we collectively hold our breaths, hoping that he won't see the unprotected baby. Then everyone else gets out of the car and I drive it from my seat in the back, sitting behind the driver's seat. I'm aware that I don't have my license with me and that this is a strange way to drive. My feet go under the front seat to the pedals and my arms stretch to reach the steering wheel while the baby remains asleep on my chest. Suddenly there's a policeman in the car, kneeling on the driver's seat facing me, a big blond bully type. "You can't do that!" he shouts at me, but I just shout back, telling him that his feet are in the way and that I can't drive properly while he's blocking access to the pedals. "Move your big feet! Get out of my way!" I yell. "I've gotten this far and I can darn well keep going! I'm going to do this my way, no matter what you say, because only I know what is best for me and the baby."

I awaken to my usual painfully stiff body, as stiff as it has been every morning for months now, possibly even longer than that. Even though I've been working myself into looseness every day it doesn't seem to last very long, as I return to the grip of tension each night. As I slowly unclench, I note how my dreams constantly replay important lessons, taking me through familiar settings, offering insight into my progress. In the first dream, I experienced the joy of pure release, what it really feels like to "let go," something I have feared greatly. In reality, it's really quite exhilarating and perfectly safe! I then noticed that the road I've been traveling along in so many recent dreams is being totally reconstructed, representing the truth of all my hard work as I go through this recapitulation process. I come away from that awareness and into the third dream only to be confronted by a policeman, a conventional sign of authority, an old guard from an old world. I'm fully aware that he's attempting to thwart my progress, a petty tyrant seeking to prevent me from going where I have to go, as I continue this recapitulation process. Just as in the dream of the other night when my abuser and my old boyfriend blocked my path, he too gets right in front of me and threatens me.

I've used this old guard to protect myself in the past, but I'm now seeking to sever the old patterns of behavior. I'm determined that nothing will get in my way as I take this inner journey to deeper and deeper levels of self. In addition, I will do anything to protect the innocent baby, the little boy asleep in my arms in the dream. I'm aware that the child is really mine and I'm tenderly loving and protective of it. At one point in the dream, I ponder if this baby is related to my concern about those twin babies, as I've begun to wonder again—in waking moments as well as sleep it seems—if they were really born dead. I still see them as originally recapitulated, stiff, waxy, and underdeveloped, only a few inches long, plastic little dolls, their arms and legs curled inward. Quite lifeless, they looked very much like the white clay baby that I unconsciously formed last month. Barely aware of what I was doing, my hands shaped the clay and the next thing I knew I had a tiny baby in my hands, as if I were giving my memory life. But then I placed it in a cold forest, a snow-covered setting. Perhaps my unconscious was guiding me to understand that the babies were born dead after all, but how do I really know that? Is it possible that I have adult children somewhere in the world? I can't help but ponder such a possibility.

I lie in bed and reflect on where I am now in this process, so incredibly full of stuff—old memories and new perceptions all jumbled up—trying to make sense of it all. I'm overwhelmed by the content of my dreams; they seem so significant right now. In addition, what has emerged out of the act of recapitulation itself— the signs, symbols, synchronicities, memories, pain, as well as the creativity that is pouring out of me—is astounding. Once I opened the door to all of this, it really did take over. And, as Chuck suggested I do, I'm letting it lead me now.

The dream of the other night with my abuser's daughter in the new school building becomes even clearer now as I do the sweeping breath, beginning with the parts of the dream that I remember. My breath, like a broom, whisks away the gritty sands of sleep, clearing my vision. I sweep my head back and forth until the details come into sharp focus. And then I remember that as we walked into the school building my abuser's daughter was attempting to convince me to stay with her. She was mad at me because she knew I was moving on, getting on with my life, graduating, seeing things differently, and that I was going to leave her behind. She went to her room alone, while I moved my things up to a higher floor. That's why I was attempting to carry everything all at once, so I didn't have to go back. I knew that the fragile blue and yellow glass bowl was important and that it had real value and meaning, and I also knew that the rest of the stuff was just baggage, cumbersome, difficult to handle, and totally unnecessary—I could let it go now. As I left my abuser's daughter, she turned away and stomped off to her room. "I thought you liked me," she called to me in an angry huff, "but I guess you don't want to be my friend anymore."

November 12, 2002

In a dream, I'm with my daughter. She's a baby again, about a year old. We're at the ocean and I'm letting her put her feet into the water when suddenly a strong undertow pulls her into the water. I frantically grab for her, fearing she'll be dragged out to sea. When I bring her up out of the water she's not breathing properly. In near panic, I watch as she struggles to take a breath. She can't fully inhale nor can she make any sound. I slap her on the back over and over again, and try all the things that I can think of to help her get her breath back. No one else notices us, though I see other people on the beach. Then I hear these words: *the gift of life, the breath of life, the breath of love.* As soon as I hear those words, I breathe a very gentle puff of my own breath into her mouth and as I do she immediately revives. She doesn't cry or act as if she's been under any duress at all. She just smiles very sweetly at me and I hear her thinking these words: *the gift of love.* I hear her thanking me, a tiny wet baby, alive in my arms.

I wake up from this dream when I hear my daughter go into the bathroom adjacent to my room. Afterwards she comes into my dark bedroom. Quietly tiptoeing over to where I'm lying in bed, she puts her tiny hands on my face and kisses me very tenderly on the lips. Without a word, she turns and goes back to her room. Wow! I wonder if we're dreaming, but I know I'm wide-awake.

I fall immediately back to sleep and into another dream. Now I'm being taught a step-by-step method of total relaxation. I'm instructed to let go, a little at a time, to pretend as if I'm sipping water through a straw rather than drinking the whole glass at once. Slowly, as if taking little sips, I let go little by little. I wake up in the dream. I'm lucid, feeling totally calm, all the tension gone. My neck, shoulders, and hips are incredibly loose and flexible. I sway, feeling so alive and present in my body. I feel great!

I get the kids to school and get ready for an appointment with Chuck. During the session, I relay a memory that came to me during a yoga class last night. In the class we were working on spreading our toes, preparing to do some standing poses. All of a sudden, I very clearly remembered that I had been paralyzed as a young child and that I became expert at picking things up with my toes. The memory went no further at that point. Details emerged more fully in the fifteen minutes of meditation that ended the yoga class. I tell Chuck that I called my mother last night after the class and asked her why I had been paralyzed at the age of six. She explained that it was the result of a long bout with the measles that turned into "brain fever," what meningitis or encephalitis were commonly called, each illness manifesting in its own way, though in extreme cases paralysis may occur.

"I remember waking once, in and out of consciousness," I tell Chuck. "I saw my arms flailing about in delirium and heard myself talking gibberish. I remember dealing cards and playing a game with someone sitting at the foot of my bed. When I asked my mother who played with me, she said no one had been in my room, but I clearly remember a woman sitting with me, keeping me company, talking softly and playing Go Fish. She taught me how to shuffle a deck of cards—after that I was quite expert at it. I remember waking up feeling as if I had been asleep for a very long time. I had no sense of time. I felt strange. It was dark and I could hear my mother in the kitchen, preparing dinner for the rest of the family. My room was right off the kitchen, a tiny room, barely bigger than a walk-in closet. It was then that I discovered I couldn't move. No matter how much I wanted to use my arms or legs I couldn't budge them. I couldn't speak or call out even. I just lay there, listening to the noises in the rest of the house. It was as if I were lying in a dead body."

After the fever went down I was allowed to sit in a big old armchair in the living room next to the fireplace. My father carried me there. Soon I regained some movement on the left side, but my right remained paralyzed. My brother brought my homework from school, which I attempted to do by propping a pencil into my left fist, but it was frustrating and mostly unsuccessful as I am naturally right handed. My small motor skills were completely gone and I had only minimal use of my limbs. I remember the doctor visiting, testing my legs and arms, practicing some exercises with me to get the circuits reconnected. At the time, I thought I was being punished because a stick was stuck in me. I envisioned a huge splinter stuck into the base of my spine, causing a festering wound, a pus-filled infection that I attributed the paralysis to. Whenever the memory of this paralysis came up, I instantly recalled that there was something wrong with my vagina; that something had happened down there in that place between my legs. It's funny that I always had that memory, but no clearer memory of the abuse.

The paralysis took a long time to wear off. I sat in that chair in the living room for weeks while my right side remained totally immobile. I remember reaching for things on the hassock in front of me with my left foot, my brother having placed them there. Once again I see my brother watching intently, willing my toes to work, as I struggled to grasp the erasers and pencils and sheets of paper he'd placed there. I relive willing my hands, my feet, and my toes to work. I remember lifting my dead right arm with my left to move it out of the way. I'd often collapse in angry frustration, my mother telling me it would go away in time, that with practice I would regain full use of my limbs. The most embarrassing thing of all was not being able to walk and having to be carried to the bathroom by my father. One day, a boy from the neighborhood was playing with my brother and he wanted to know why I was being carried. "She can't walk!" my father exclaimed, and I was mortified that the boy would think I was a baby, but he surprised me. "She's lucky," he said. "I wish I could be carried everywhere!" And that made me feel better. I smiled at him, and it didn't matter that he'd seen me in my nightgown, another big embarrassment.

I couldn't relate the paralysis to illness, it never occurred to me that it happened because I was ill and susceptible. I thought I deserved it, that I had done something to cause it. I recall sitting in that chair fearing that I would never get better if the stick didn't come out of me. I thought I would remain permanently paralyzed, split right down the center of my being with absolutely no movement or feeling on my right side and the floppy inadequacy of my left side. Once, after the doctor had visited at the beginning of my illness, my brothers were sent to stay with our grandparents for a while. Meanwhile, I spent endless days in bed and then endless days in that chair. I was jealous when they returned with new pajamas, robes and slippers, new toys, bubbling over with the excitement of having been away.

After I'd fully recuperated, my parents got rid of the chair, it stank so much. I'm sure it was greatly soiled after having supported my sick body for weeks or even months. I don't know how long the illness lasted, but I remember watching my father plunk the chair into the wheelbarrow and cart it up the hill behind our house, to what we called the 'back-backyard,' where he set it on fire. I felt responsible for its deteriorated condition and was even sad to see it go; it had been a special place. While I was sick and sitting in it I felt safe, offered sanctuary from what I knew not. I watched the chair burn for a few minutes, until the black smoke that poured out of it and a sense of deep sadness drove me away.

"You may still have more memories, or even more dreams, about your abuser," Chuck says as we end the session.

"Yes, probably," I say, giving a long sigh. "The memories seem endless, but I really like the dreams!"

November 13, 2002

I dream that I walk out of my studio and into a world filled with flower petals raining down from the sky like giant snowflakes. It's springtime and the scene is so wondrously beautiful and magical that I immediately feel light and happy. The scene suddenly shifts and now delicate blue eggshells are falling from robin's nests, fluttering to the ground like tiny blown jewels. I want to collect them all because I want the perfect one to go inside the bird's nest art piece I'm working on. I chase after the fluttering eggshells as they fall, but they are so fragile that as soon as I catch them they crumble to dust in my hands. But even this doesn't stop me and I'm still trying to collect the beautiful shells when one of my brothers appears and asks me what I'm doing. "I'm looking for the perfect eggshells to represent birth and new life," I explain. He points to some on the ground that look pretty good, sturdier than the ones falling from the sky. When I pick them up, I see that several are stacked together so they won't break, a shell inside a shell, inside a shell. "Perfect!" I say, as I pick them up and take them inside the studio building. I go upstairs and into a huge art studio crowded with easels. Two men are in the room. It's fairly obvious that they're trying to have a private conversation and when I enter they go off into a corner to talk. Ignoring them, I go over to a group of easels on the left side of the room, placed so that they form a small square. I drag large sheets of plywood over and place them up against the four easels, like four walls of a house, creating a small private room. I crawl inside and sit down in the middle of my little private house. I need to be alone with my eggshells.

It's springtime in this eggshell dream. The feeling is of birth and new life and lots of energy, and I'm very happy as I catch the gently falling eggshells. It's very important in the dream that I find exactly the right shells, the perfect ones among the thousands that are falling. It doesn't feel like an impossible task and even though many of the delicate eggshells crumble as they fall into my hands, I'm not dissuaded or frustrated. I am simply happily experiencing the blissfulness of carefree innocence. Eventually, I find what I want. As soon as I do, I'm struck by a strong urge to go inward, to experience the joy and contentment of my beautiful prize on a deeper level. The easels and the plywood form the walls of a personal mandala—a small, geometrical, energetically charged shape—a private space into which I crawl with the eggshells, allowing me to be shielded from intrusion while also offering the solitude I seek.

I wake feeling very calm and happy, aware that something new is anchoring inside me. I'm not sure what it is yet, but it does indeed imply a sense of new life to come. A shift is taking place in this recapitulation process and I feel much better as I progress each day. Today the stiffness that I've woken up with every day for so long is totally gone. Calmness stays with me all day. The sense of bliss I'd experienced in the dream provides a new undercurrent, one of hope and expectation.

In the evening, I go to a meditation class. We begin by sitting in a circle. After a few minutes of sitting, I begin to feel myself dissociate, going into my puffy body mode. My awareness retreats into the top of my head and I notice that my breathing is light and only minimally noticeable, as if it's coming from a tiny pinprick of a hole in the back of my throat. I open my eyes in an effort to stay present. Bringing my focus back to the room, I sense a warm mixture of breath and energy swirling in a counterclockwise direction, coming from the group of people. I'm aware that I can breathe into it, that my breath will join the flow of energy and that it will flow endlessly, effortlessly, as naturally as my own breath flows. I send my breath and my intent out into the river of energy, feel it merge and get pulled into the gentle current of it, circling around and around as we sit and meditate, our energies merging in the counterclockwise flow that I both see and feel. Again, I'm aware of the energy of a mandala, this time created by all of us, a spinning wheel of breath at the center of the circle, within an outer circle of people sitting in a square room. Each one of us creates a spoke of the wheel with our breath. As the spokes meet at the center hub, we send the wheel spinning and our collective energy spirals upward and out into the universe—sent as a peace offering, the intent of this meditation session. I imagine it joining with the energy of all the other meditation groups meeting on this ordinary night, in such a simple and yet extraordinary endeavor to give peace a chance.

After the sitting meditation we get up for twenty minutes of walking meditation. It's difficult at first. I lurch unsteadily, feeling uncoordinated as I walk on stiff stick legs, feeling the weight of my pelvis, heavy from sitting. Focusing almost entirely on my feet, my eyes only slightly open, I finally get into a rhythm, walking slowly, pacing myself by the person in front of me. Suddenly, I am a woman walking through the desert at sundown. The last rays of sunlight warm my bare feet as I walk, each step leaving its mark in the sand. I'm aware of my unusual clothing, a long dress and a thick blanket shawl. I live here in this desert; both it and the surrounding country are exceedingly familiar. There are mesas in the distance, the reddish color of the rock formations deepened by the setting sun. I'm aware that I've been on an important mission and that I'm walking home now. There's a sense that I've attended a death, and now my work is done. I walk calmly and steadily; there is no need to hurry. I am deeply contented, sure of myself, calm and unafraid. I am strong.

At the end of the walking meditation we return to our seats for a final few minutes of sitting meditation before the group disperses. The river of breath appears once again, cooler now, and I'm able to tap into it immediately. The session ends with quiet talk of our experiences. I mention the wheel of energy, but I keep the desert experience to myself, too private and mysterious to share. I need to savor it alone. Afterwards, I go home with two friends, to stay the night at their house. Easy to be with, they cook and fuss over me. Matching my quiet, we spend an extremely pleasant and relaxing evening together.

November 14, 2002

In a dream, I'm traveling with a little boy and a woman friend. We're in a foreign country, walking on old cobblestoned streets packed with crowds of people. We're on our way to a gallery where my painted furniture has been on display. The show is ending and I need to have my work shipped back home. I'm dealing with the logistics of packing and figuring out the best method of transporting it. Afterwards, I tuck the little boy safely into bed in a room at the guesthouse we're staying at. I still have more details of the shipping to attend to and so I leave the room. At the door I turn to see my friend sitting beside him, telling him a bedtime story.

I wake out of this dream to find myself curled into a ball. I see and feel this from two different perspectives simultaneously. I am both at home in my own bed and I am the little boy in my dream as well. At the same time, I'm still *in* the dream, standing and looking at the little boy I have just tucked into bed. As I gaze at him from across the room, I'm aware that I am also him, a small child-sized ball, so familiar and so comfortably safe. I'm aware of my deep love and caring for this innocent child. For a few minutes I'm caught in a strange glitch, in several places at once. I'm still dreaming, but also standing in my own room, though I'm not there at all but in a guesthouse in a foreign country. In actuality, however, I'm asleep in a guest room at my friend's house. I see myself lying asleep, both an adult and a child at once, both my dreaming self and my real self. As I wake up and roll out of my fetal pose, I feel strangely familiar and yet totally unfamiliar at the same time.

I've slept well in the calmness of a foreign dream house and in the house of my two friends in this world, and I wake feeling calm too. I sense my impending move to the little blue house in this dream, the packing and preparing I've been doing, the logistics of it all, as I've been deciding how best to get everything moved in next month. I'm aware of the importance of this inner work, caring for my innocent child self, accompanying her on her journeys while also asking her to take my journeys in this world with me. I'm ever mindful that she's a wounded child with many needs and that I must take care of her no matter where I am and what I'm doing. I must keep her safe, even as I urge her forward into new life too.

We rise early and I thank my friends for their hospitality. On my way to a yoga class before work, I wish for better luck with my car. One thing after another has been happening to it lately. I'm acutely aware that I must keep up with things and not let them get so bad that they can't be salvaged. During the yoga class I feel very light and airy. After last night's meditation class and the gift of a quiet retreat, I sense the real possibility that life could be this dreamily pleasant all the time.

November 15, 2002

All night long, I dream of children, with little recall of any details, except the sense that I am caring for them, protecting them, tucking them into cozy beds, loving them. I wake up late, get my own kids up and ready for school and go right back to bed after I send them out to the bus. I lie there and let something, some horror I can't quite make out, go through me. There's no memory associated with the sensations that rattle through me, just a feeling of terror as my body curls up and shakes. I have a strong desire to pull the covers over my head and just stay in bed all day. It's what my body wants, but I have other things to do.

As I drive to the studio, I recall that after I'd recapitulated the paralysis memory and talked about it during my last session with Chuck, my whole body simultaneously released the somatic pain and tension that arrived with it. I felt quite light and pain free after that, and both my body and my dreams have been reflecting this new, calmer state. Now, however, I sense a gathering of the crows of recapitulation, coming to pick my bones again as new tensions build. I anticipate that something will make its way to clarity as the day goes on, but whether it will manifest in feelings, smells, or visual flashbacks is unknown. I only know what I feel and sense, based on what I've already felt and sensed as this recapitulation has unfolded.

Part of allowing for this process to continually unfold is to acknowledge emerging tension and pain, usually the first sensations indicating the arrival of a new memory. Indeed, something new is clearly brewing; I had an inkling of it this morning though I haven't quite captured the fuller picture yet. It's like trying to recall a dream that resists coming into focus. In addition, as these somatic sensations arrive they send me into that in-between world—into muffled confusion laced with pain, anxiety, guilt and terror—with little clarity as to why. To experience this daily, for months on end, is excruciating. I keep thinking I'm getting to the point of no more memories. "Certainly there can't be more," I think, but here I am again, wallowing in the murkiness of yet another mystery, and I can barely move my neck again.

After a morning of struggling to focus, too restless to work, I head out for a walk. As I walk, I contemplate all the signs my body has been giving me lately. My mouth went numb last night and at first I thought I must have gotten an allergic reaction to something I ate, but then I had the sensation that it was connected to the paralysis memory. Last week, I noticed how my body felt like it was shutting down, literally going into a state of feverish illness and paralysis. I didn't eat much, barely went to the bathroom, felt drugged and distant, and I slept a lot more than usual. Indeed, I felt empty and numb, with cold sensations of paralysis, my neck stiff as the memory came through. It's amazing how much I've stored inside this little body and how this recapitulation process really works within the physical parameters, offering full-body participation. Quite amazing!

As I continue my walk across a field, I'm suddenly alert. Perhaps it's the proximity to the woods on the far edge of the field, or a whiff of something caught on a breeze. I don't know for sure, but a sense of my abuser rides into my awareness. I realize I could never get away from him; he was everywhere, just as he is now as I take this walk. I acknowledge that I suffered deeply, emotional as well as physical pain, and that it still courses through me. As much as I was able to repress it, it remained inside, a festering secret wound. Now, I'm picking away at it, cleaning my wounded being. I'm neatly picking my bones along with the crows of recapitulation, intent on leaving them pure and white, my innocence exposed at last. In this process of cleaning, rinsing, and drying my entire picked-over being, I will evolve.

Even though I reach this clarified state of awareness, by the end of the walk I'm shaking with fear, feeling like I'm being pursued. Someone is going to get me! Holding back unshed tears, I suffer through an overwhelming desire to flee. There is imminent danger and yet I will not run. I continue walking, wondering if perhaps I've stirred something—a predatory energy—with my intentions to heal, with my thoughts of crows and recapitulation and pecking at my bones. As I hurry along the last leg of the trail, I know I must face the truth. Glancing over my shoulder, I fully acknowledge my one-time pursuer, the predator in my long-ago childhood. "It's not now," I tell myself, slowing down, for indeed there is no one behind me, "but it was once true."

I believe everything now. I was sexually abused in a most vicious way as a child and I need to let myself completely feel what that means. I must face the entire truth of it without fear. "It's okay; everything is okay." I whisper to myself as I walk on. "Everything will be fine."

I must allow myself the freedom to feel everything there is to feel about this past that has unraveled and revealed itself in such visceral fashion, or there will be no end to my sufferings. I need to go all the way back, as deep as I possibly can, or I'll never be picked clean enough. Whether I have the help of the crows of recapitulation or not, I'll never reach my innocence if I am not thorough in my research. If I don't give in to the healing potential of this process I'll never evolve, and I'll still have *him* in me somewhere, in some tiny crevice, and that would be deadly. Any tiny remnant of my abuser, any speck, any atom, any energetic attachment, and I'd be parasitically contaminated. For the rest of my life I'd remain impure, hampering my potential to evolve.

As I head home, I more firmly commit to this recapitulation process. I am strengthened by the insight that I am on an endless journey of constant change and growth and, hopefully, real spiritual evolution.

November 16, 2002

Merely an essence of dreaming remains as I awaken to a wintry Saturday morning, cold and grey. Freezing rain shimmers down, making a soft swishing sound as it falls past the windows. The memories, more real now after yesterday's walk, sit heavily upon my chest, taking precedence over dreams, staring me in the face, asking for attention. I also feel the pull of the new me, the changing me who's really beginning to feel, not only within my body but also in the energy of the world around me.

As I learn about energy—my own and that of others—as I learn to *feel* energy, I'm more able to sense energy that resonates with my own. As I exercise and utilize this skill to my advantage, I open myself to meeting new people. I'm beginning to recognize the kind of energy that I'm drawn to, finding it both within and without. I'm strong enough now to resist energy that I'm not truly compatible with, though it still seeks closeness. Instead, I intend to cultivate energy that resonates. This really means that I'm learning to pay attention to how I energetically feel when I'm with another person or as I make decisions. As I allow my energetic reactions to become factors in my decision making process, and actually let them guide me—yes, *this feels right*, or no, *this doesn't feel right*—I make better choices.

This new method of navigating the world really involves paying attention to signals from my physical body, as well as inner signals from my deepest self, as I strive to listen to the knowing of my soul. It means learning to distinguish between habitual or patently ingrained reactions to something or someone, and really feeling my way to a different understanding of why I react the way I do, finally letting my feelings guide me to new and even perhaps unusual reactions. As I practice this energy reading skill, I'm in better alignment with my true self, making right choices for myself on a deeper level, even if they sometimes feel daring or frightening. In the past, I might have responded to negative or incompatible energy by going cold and dead, turning inward and shutting down, leaving my body to bear the brunt of it. Now I'm learning that I don't have to stick around and just take it; I can even reject it, turn and walk away from it. I can say no.

As I navigate energetically now, I'm aware of my sense of direction coming from deep within, from a new place of calm and quiet, so different from the old quiet numbness of dissociation. Chuck once told me that by removing the old energy of my abuser from my psyche, I would make room for new energy. I sense that new energy now like a calm pool, my own, still and deep. There's more room for it now, and my own energy is taking precedence over the old shutting down energy of fear. This recapitulation is turning into an open, more welcoming process now, workable in a new and different way.

I understand this journey better now too, this changing process, as I dare myself to keep going. I understand that there will be unimaginable future possibilities now too, not just dreams or fantasies of what I'd like in my life, but a new reality. It's already manifesting. And I envision new life unfolding more rapidly now as my own energy is retrieved and becomes involved. I can truly say that life is no longer just a tiny pinhole of light at the end of the long dark tunnel where I have mostly resided. Now I see my life being lived out in the open, for I have more than poked my head out of the tunnel. Expansive vistas of far-reaching possibility and unlimited growth are in clear sight, but only because I am open to experiencing such a life. I'm ready now.

I turn my attention to more fully removing the negatives from my life, not only the people, but the thoughts, the judgments, the decisions based on an old way of perceiving the world and myself. I find that a lot of things I once automatically said, thought, and did, were not really based on my own truths, were not resonant with who I truly am, but were rather things I'd been taught. The truth is that I've simply been living my life like a puppet, mimicking what I've heard others say, acting not on personal beliefs but on old ideas implanted while I was sleeping. I was long ago mesmerized by my parents, the world and, of course, the man in the woods.

I'm learning to dismantle the world I once lived in and my mind along with it, that foreign installation, as the shamans call it. And, in deconstructing it, I'm faced with questioning, sifting, and feeling my way through everything, deciding if it belongs to me or to someone else. I'm having to confront what I *really* think and believe, and why. The shamans, as Chuck tells me, consider this a major aspect of the process of recapitulation. Only in dismantling the old world can we open ourselves to the possibility of new worlds. This is what I'm experiencing right now.

I wonder if it's possible that this life was laid out before I was born, that I accepted it as a sacred contract, that I *selected it*, as Caroline Myss suggests in her book *Sacred Contracts*. Did I know that I would build strengths that were invaluable as I took my journey through a childhood of sexual abuse? Was I so farsighted that I knew exactly what I needed in order to fulfill this journey's true promise of growth? I'm trying to get my conscious mind around all these possibilities, finding this both enlightening and confusing. What do I believe? Will my beliefs constantly change with new discoveries and new experiences, as has been the case? Where am I going?

New people are coming into my life, making their interests known, wanting to befriend me, men included, but I'm not ready to go out with anyone or be intimately involved. I just want to continue my inner work. I want to dig deeper and find out what's still there to discover. This process of exploration is, at the moment, all that I can handle and all that I wish to be involved in. Opportunities to engage in interactions with new people will still be there later, and if they aren't, if those people don't stick around, then I don't feel that I've lost anything important. The important ones will remain.

Nonetheless, I'm drawn to ponder some of the relationships that are being presented to me, for they seem to be part of this self-exploratory process. I know I must encounter others, new acquaintances as well as old, and that I'm charged with learning something important from each encounter. Everyone I meet has something to offer me, this I'm certain of, but just what that might be takes time and reflection. For instance, some people are intrusive, wanting to know what's going on inside, prying, and their interest in my inner world frightens me. I sense them detecting something interesting deep inside me that *they* want.

I'm not ready, if I ever will be, to share with just anyone. My inner world is too private and I feel too fragile still, though such prying people constantly rake through the coals, looking for what I may have left behind. Right now there's nothing for them. I have barred my doors; for I fear that if they find a way in they will take everything that I have worked so hard to gain. Their prying energy feels so needy, so greedy and self-serving. I fear they will totally deplete my newfound energy store, the energy that I've so recently taken back from my abuser. It's as if they can sense its virgin goodness, and they want to steal it for their own purposes. I need to protect it, and myself.

Such predatory energy feels dangerous and yet so familiar—I absolutely recognize it. I'm aware of what it can do, of how devastating a relationship with it could be. And even though I'm not interested in a relationship now, I can't deny that certain people have been approaching me with just that possibility. I'm uncomfortable with such interest, and yet the sexual, physical, intellectual, and spiritual components seem so utterly familiar. The attractions are all there, but the people are all wrong. And so I urge myself to not get sucked in, to not be alone with them, though they are constantly thrown in my path. I bump into them all the time, feel their draining need and hunger for connection, as if they sense my good energy growing. In turn, I feel their pull. I'm strong enough now to resist, yet there still remains a certain amount of fragility that makes every encounter frightening.

These are my tests, tests of my inner strength, of my inner process, of my conviction to keep changing, to keep confronting what arises. At the same time, I've noticed that such disturbing energy is increasingly countered by other more positive energy, coming from people I immediately feel comfortable and safe with, without desire for anything in return except my own positive and comfortable energy in companionship. With this good, compatible energy I don't have to talk or answer to anything. I'm accepted for who I am and where I am. There is no probing, no digging, just total acceptance; and I feel the healing possibilities within that nonjudgmental acceptance. At the same time, the negative and disturbing energies are utterly familiar, while the resonant energies that I'm meeting for the first time, though comfortable, are completely unknown.

I gain a deeper understanding of how energy works as I ponder these people coming into my life. If I feel uncomfortable, I need to acknowledge to myself that I feel that way, acknowledge that I'm not in a healthy situation, and give myself permission to turn my back on it and walk away. I must give myself permission to not play games in any way, but to act decisively, keeping in mind that I'm changing, that I'm not doing my life the same way anymore. "Don't even toy with the idea of playing an old game," I must tell myself, "because it will only invite the negative energy in. If it senses an opening it will take it, so don't even get in the position to have to deal with it. Just don't do it!" As I continue this journey, I can and must make choices that are totally right for me, based now on how I *feel*. I sense that I'm beginning to make some real headway at last!

November 17, 2002

So many insights and realizations bombard that I feel a need to be alone, to go inward, to contemplate and let things sink in. I must also honestly admit that I'm feeling the stirrings of desire now, after so long—I've been so dead for years. This tells me I truly am starting to heal, though I know I still have so far to go. But at least I'm beginning to feel my body again, and a real connection to it this time.

I did battle with a Midas muffler franchise last week, regarding a faulty alternator they'd recently put into my car, and I won! In the midst of recapitulating my broken child self I had to go out into the real world and confront a powerful adversary to heal my broken car. First my car conked out far from home and I had to have it dealt with, leaving it at an unknown repair shop. As a woman who obviously knew little about cars, I sensed that I was totally being taken advantage of. I didn't know what kind of battery I wanted or even if it really had to be replaced. Deeply depressed, just struggling to stay present, and with no other alternative, I let myself be overpowered. I acquiesced to letting the mechanic at the Midas shop determine what needed to be done. The alternator and battery were replaced—at great cost, I might add—but I still had problems. When I had a mechanic friend look at the new alternator he declared it defective. Not only that, he whistled loudly when he saw that the four bolts on the alternator had not been properly tightened, in fact two were falling out and two were missing! "Take it back and have them replace it," he said, tightening the bolts that remained. By then I knew that I had been screwed.

There was no way I was going to have the same Midas franchise work on my car again, for I felt that their shoddy workmanship had put me, and my kids, in danger. I don't know what would have happened had the alternator fallen out while I was driving. My mechanic friend said they'd never give me my money back, but suddenly the energy of the warrior stirred inside me. I knew it was the same energy that failed to come to my rescue when I felt inadequate—a woman who didn't know about cars—but once awoken there was nothing that was going to stop it. It was magically coming to my rescue, from somewhere deep inside, just when I needed it.

"You are invincible!" a friend said to me and that did it, for indeed I felt like I suddenly had Midas's golden touch. And so I went to battle. I drove to the Midas franchise that had put the alternator in and let the quiet, complacent self make the first contact. They told me no refund; they could only *replace* the alternator. I calmly listened, but then the warrior inside me emerged and spoke. In a very even but firm tone of voice, I told them the work was shoddy and that I wasn't comfortable or willing to have them do the work a second time, that I didn't trust them. I was forceful and convincing, citing the safety of my children as paramount, telling them that a mechanic friend had looked at the work too and declared it inferior.

The mechanic who had done the work, simply turned away without another word, talked to his manager, and then came back and went right to the cash register and returned all the money I had paid. I left victorious, elated, proud of myself, knowing that for the first time in a long time I had stood up for myself in *this* world.

Recognizing and utilizing that warrior energy is important. Not only does it support my badly depleted ego, but I now also realize that I've always had it in me—it's been the key to my survival. In fact, it's stronger than I ever imagined. But it's also the same kind of energy that makes me stick with a bad situation. Having often appeared in the guise of the stubborn warrior, I'm utterly familiar with this other side. More often than not, when the stubborn warrior emerges and plunks down, I end up sitting in fuming stagnation, clinging to a bad decision with the fierceness of the warrior, even in spite of what I might clearly know and see. Now I'm learning how to use it to my advantage, in an energetically appropriate way to gain stability in a world I have long avoided— everyday reality—though I'm also aware that its ego-boosting power has the potential to consume, as I could be swept up in an inflated sense of self-righteousness. For I feel rage, deep-seated rage at the bottom of this warrior energy, and I'm afraid of losing touch with my tender self, my goodness, if it takes over. I'm also afraid I might hurt others, and that I won't care if I did.

I've used this angry energy to my advantage in the past, and I know its power—I've let it take over often enough to know just how dangerous it can be. It can quickly tip me off balance, and so while I feel and desire its presence, I can also forget who I really am when in the throes of it. I'm fascinated by it and afraid of its powers at the same time, though I still dare myself to tap into and utilize its strengths. Perhaps I'm just not trained enough in the warrior's way to be able to handle the fierceness that I feel brewing inside me. At the moment, however, I must acknowledge that I do feel strong. I have indeed defeated Midas, including the long-held-back Midas inside me, allowing her to release at last and speak the truth. Now, as this golden self emerges more powerfully, I know that nothing will stop me from continuing this changing journey; in that sense I *am* invincible.

November 18, 2002

Recent happy dreams focused on organizing and preparing for the move into the new house have deserted me and my sense of invincibility plummets as I awaken lost in pain, totally deflated, back in an old place. The snow and ice covering everything outside my window reflect my true state. I have tumbled from my mountain; my Midas touch has frozen everything.

I did yoga last night before bed, trying to release the burning pain in my hips, as the deeply embedded need to cry revealed itself quite clearly. The heat of long held-back tears seeks escape and I sense this pocket of misery is about to be set afire. Tiny flares burst forth as the pressure builds. Like a volcano about to erupt, I feel it shifting deeply inside my body, under the crust of me, the first warning signs of what is to come.

The paralysis memory seems to have had quite an effect on me, the repercussions still reverberating through my body. It wasn't the memory of the paralysis itself, but the confusion of my child self that was so starkly apparent as the memory emerged. She very clearly made the assumption that the illness and subsequent paralysis were due to the splinter she envisioned stuck in her spine. This suggests the deep wounding, and the subsequent belief that what happened at the hands of my abuser was embedded like a virus, causing symptoms that I had no other explanation for.

The intensely real physical symptoms of the memory brought everything back into focus. I am amazed at how viscerally real the entire memory was as my body took on all the symptoms of illness and paralysis in a stunning effort to alert me to the truth of what happened to me as a child and how that child self managed to rationalize it. What came through in the memory was a real shock, both the confusion of the little girl I once was, and what she really bore. If there was any last little bit of me that was holding out in disbelief, I can't ignore the truth that my body so clearly impresses upon me. I have to stop pretending that just maybe the abuse didn't really happen. Why can't I let go of that idea? Do I need any other sign than the pain I feel right now in my body, in the tightness of fifty years of mental and physical distress, in the shame, guilt, and burden of secrecy that I still carry?

November 19, 2002

When I meet with Chuck I am so dazed I don't even know what we talk about or where I go. I emerge from the session still lost, with little awareness of reality. When I leave his office I don't drive well at all. I keep zoning out and almost have an accident. I remain fuzzy and vague all day, lonely and sad, fearful of my absentmindedness. I start a big job tomorrow, painting a large kitchen and family room, and there's a lot to organize. I have to pull together all the materials, load the work van with ladders and equipment, as well as make arrangements for scaffolding to be delivered. It's a real challenge to stay mentally present and focused.

November 20, 2002

I must be careful and alert today, mentally sober and in this world, especially after yesterday's struggle with reality, a very weird day to say the least. Fogged in, unable to gain footing in either the past or the present, I floated between worlds. It was a very dangerous place to be, and so I'd turn inward in an attempt to figure out what was going on, but I just kept ending up in some vague otherworld. I simply couldn't find a foothold anywhere. It was freaky, like being stuck in a dream that I couldn't wake up from, and it could have been pretty disastrous.

Seeking stability for the day ahead I do some grounding yoga, *Tadasana* (Mountain pose) and Sun Salutation. Breathing deeply, I ask for the gift of presence today, as I face the stressful day of work ahead. The morning routine offers focus and anchoring. I make mental notes of anything I might have forgotten to pack up for the job while I dress and get the kids up and ready for school. I make breakfasts and lunches, and soon the kids gather their things and head out the door. As soon as I hear the bus driving off down the road, I too head out.

I gather last minute items at the studio, pick up my work partner, and head to the job site, a large, sprawling house off a rural road. I remind myself that I must stay present in the moment, be in this world, and take everything slowly and carefully. We arrive to find the house empty and within minutes of our arrival the scaffolding, which I've borrowed from a friend, gets delivered and promptly set up. Once it towers above us my partner realizes she can't handle the height, so I have to climb the thick wooden boards while she works on the walls and trim below me. It becomes another fear to conquer, because frankly I'm afraid of heights too, but the warrior in me takes over, very soberly telling me I can do it, to just be cautious, to feel every step, to not move until I test my balance and check my perception. *Be careful. Stay present and in the moment. Stay focused. This is a test.*

For the rest of the day, I dangle from the twenty-foot scaffolding, painting beneath a two-story high cathedral ceiling. Luckily the ceiling only needs touchup work or my neck would be suffering more than its usual tension and pain. While I work, my thoughts go to the river of forgetfulness that Caroline Myss speaks of in *Sacred Contracts*, a book I've been reading. She proposes that we go through this river of forgetfulness the instant before we're born, when we lose connection to our past life and begin a new one. I wonder, however, if we go through this river of forgetfulness every time we experience a traumatic event in our lives. For it seems that I certainly went through it often enough, as I forgot about the abuse, leaving my wounded child self behind in order to survive, in essence birthing myself forward into new life many times. Each time I was jolted out of my body I experienced a kind of death and upon return a new life, and so it certainly feels as if I've gone through that river of forgetfulness often enough in this lifetime alone, simply in order to survive, to remain in this life. I can just about feel myself swimming through it now, as I seek to remain present in this moment, in this world.

As I ponder this idea, it seems most likely that Caroline Myss did not suffer from PTSD, for if she'd been out-of-body as often as I have she might perhaps have a similar perspective. I base my theories on my personal experiences—what I learn as I go through life—and thus perhaps she does as well. I realize that because of this recapitulation and as I begin to really think for myself, as I break through my old ideas of self and the world, my theories about life and death are changing too. A bigger picture emerges as I experience my energetic self; I sense an interconnectedness with all things that I've never quite comprehended before.

I understand that I was catapulted out of my body and into other worlds by blunt trauma and that, as Chuck tells me, this out-of-body experience is possible to achieve at anytime with training and intent. However, at this point, I'm simply intent on figuring out what's been wrong with me, so I can figure out what I'm supposed to be doing here. I haven't really figured that out yet. I still have a long way to go before I fully grasp the shamanic concepts of the energy body and out-of-body exploration.

I've always questioned whether my choice of career, as a lonely artist, writer and illustrator, had value. I felt I needed to justify my choice, find some greater purpose in life besides choosing to be a freelancer because my deeply introverted self needed the solitude and safety of the occupation. Would my work benefit humanity, I wondered, contribute to the greater good, make a difference in the world, or really have impact? Eventually, the only thing I could come up with was that yes, it was a good career choice, because I figured that if my work helped even one person to see the world differently, if it gave joy or new meaning to someone, or if it even made an unhappy person smile just once, then it had value. I decided that if my work could do any of those things then I was not just keeping myself ensconced in a safe career, albeit in something I did well, but I could also envision the possibility of there being a greater purpose to my life in general. I wanted my talents to be used for something really meaningful, but frankly I don't think I've really found meaningfulness in my work yet. I think there's more to come, though I have no idea what that might be. I just sense that I'm not yet done with searching for my true purpose in this life.

In fact, I'm intent on making choices based on a new set of rules now and so I no longer feel the need to hide myself away in my studio, hunched over my drawing board, creating my own idea of a safe and happy world in the pictures I draw. Now I'm more interested in what's coming. My fears are gradually leaving, being replaced with excitement. I already know that life is full of having to make choices and decisions, some conscious and some not, some frightening and some not, some easy and some not. I've learned over the past couple of years to more fully trust in synchronicities, allowing the unfolding of events in my life to guide me, and I've shed so many old fears as I acquiesce to this new source of guidance. As I come out of the fog of my old self, trusting my journey to lead me on, I see things more clearly, and I'm more certain than ever that my life does have a higher purpose. Someday I'll discover what that is.

I pull myself back to the present throughout the long workday, focusing on where I place my feet, taking care that the scaffolding boards are firmly anchored before climbing higher. I work at a deliberate but careful pace, always aware that I'm high off the ground. Luckily, I keep the recapitulation at bay while I work. I don't, for a moment, let my guard down, for fear of losing my balance. It's an exhausting day, physically and mentally, and my shoulders and neck bear the tension of it. As the day nears an end, I look forward to an evening meditation class, and a relaxing bath followed by sleep.

This has been such a dreamy, introspective, full moon week. My eyes feel as if they've been turned inward, as if they're actually sitting incorrectly in the sockets now after such intense inward peering. I desire sleep so I can close them for a long time, long enough for them to settle back into their normal position. As I ponder where I've been lately in my crazy inner world, I realize that even though I'm being supported and guided in so many ways and on so many levels, only I can call the shots. Only I will be able to recognize which choices are right. Only I will recognize just who the real me is as I do this work of self-discovery. No one else can do this work for me. I'm in charge because I have to be.

I feel more objective about who I am and how I choose to act, less defended. I used to be so scared and guarded, so careful to keep to myself, always afraid of being scolded, blamed, or shamed into feeling that I was doing everything wrong, or that I was simply unworthy of being here on this earth. Life was too hard that way. I slept tightly, walked tightly, talked tightly. Now I seek release from that old scared self, and yet I still seek greater understanding of why I was that tightly inhibited and controlled person to begin with. Even more so, I seek the release that is sure to come as I deeply change my very being.

November 21, 2002

While painting red walls I think about what I'll do with my new discoveries about myself. I think about possibly turning all this inner work into something good and fulfilling, because I need to share it somehow. Not my story or my pain so much, but what I've learned. I need to share how it's possible to overcome painful, fearful traumatic episodes and devastating life experiences, and emerge whole and transformed. It's possible to change from a defended, angry, bruised being into a person who is enlightened, contented, and happy. It's possible to find new life. Even though I'm not totally there yet, I know that life can be good, as long as you have the courage to seek new life, to let go of the old self and dare to find what is really out there for you. I see how long and crooked my journey through this life has so far been, and how relatively short my period of real self-discovery in comparison.

I truly believe that everything will work out just fine, and that anything is possible.

November 22, 2002

Today I start yet another new journal, my seventh since I began this journey. The journals seem to always end and begin at turning points, so in alignment with this recapitulation process. I sense this even now, as there has been a definite shift since last week. I notice how I'm turning away from the dark past more often now, heading in a new direction, moving more fully into who I might become. In fact, I'm going forward with some degree of excitement now, even though it's largely into the unknown. A definite transition *has* occurred and this is so heartening after so many months of pain. I feel better about things. I've even decided that it's time to care about myself, to allow myself to be pretty, to admit to wanting to look nice, and to admit that caring about myself is really okay.

November 23, 2002

In a dream, I'm in constant danger, pulling my legs out of the way so they don't get run over or trampled. Although I haven't recapitulated much this week, I guess my dream is alerting me to the fact that I've still got more work to do and I'm doing some of it while I sleep. In fact, I *did* keep pulling my legs up and out of the way as I slept, keeping out of the way of whatever was after me.

I've worked long hours this week with barely time for much else, no time for curling up and letting things happen. Being very busy has kept the old stuff away, and I don't miss it at all! The break from it has been nice, giving me a chance to do and think about other things. Tomorrow the big job on the scaffolding will be finished and I'll also be taking the show down at the gallery in the evening. It's time for the dismantling of everything, the month in the gallery gone by so quickly.

November 24, 2002

This is the second time this week that I've had this dream. I recognize it as soon as it begins. I'm high on the scaffolding at the job I'm currently working on, standing on the narrow boards. Someone hands up five-gallon buckets full of dead babies and body parts of little girls. "Okay, I believe it. Okay, I believe it," I say, over and over again, each time they hand up a bucket. "Stop, you can stop now, I believe it." But even as I grab another bucket and take in the enormity of the bloody masses of tiny limbs and aborted fetuses, I must still convince myself of the reality of what is being handed to me. It's almost as if although I *see* what it means, I still can't *feel* what it means or take in the blatant, bitter truth of it.

"See? It's true! Believe it," I tell myself. "You have to believe it or you'll never get down off the scaffolding. You have to believe it or you'll stay perched here on the scary precipice forever, having to be so careful and guarded." I constantly wonder what's so wrong with me and why I can't believe it, even when I'm handed the evidence. I take bucket after bucket and line them up along the scaffolding until every board is filled with buckets of bloody body parts.

November 25, 2002

I wake up sore and quite exhausted after working for twelve hours yesterday. We finished the big painting job. After we cleaned up, dismantled the scaffolding, removed all the equipment, and unloaded it back at the studio, we then took the scaffolding to my shed. I then headed up to the gallery to remove the show. I didn't get home until midnight.

I conquered the fear of falling, or sort of did, as I climbed that scaffolding every day. Even so, I realize I'm still trying to deal with the truth of what happened to me as a child, still trying to get to a place of acceptance. Why is it so difficult, why am I so resistant? I already know everything there is to know. There aren't really any surprises left as new memories emerge. In a sense, it's just more of the same kind of abuse, like those buckets of bloody body parts sitting on the scaffolding in my dream, row after row of the same thing. There's only so much that someone can do to a little girl, right? So why do I still hold out? I wonder if it's the habitual fear still reigning. Physically and mentally, I trained myself to be guarded and distant from the reality of the abuse, both during and after. In repressing memories and in dissociating I found safety and protection. Now I'm asking my physical body and my psyche to stop doing what they've always been doing. I'm asking my recapitulation to release me from the secrets, from the deeper reasons that my child self was so dissociated.

I wonder if my child self is still afraid to let it all go, or perhaps my adult self is reluctant. Part of me still thinks, as did my child self, that if I admit to the truth then everyone else in the world will know about it as well. I'm afraid it will show on the outside and I'm afraid of what people will think. I'm embarrassed and ashamed, disgusted, sickened, fearful of accepting the truth. Even after all these years the fear of exposure is so great that I don't dare let go of my old protective devices. My psyche and my physical body won't let me either, for they learned a long time ago that it meant death. As I face this truth, I realize that fear of death still rules. It grips me tightly. Even as I write this, I feel its hands circling my throat, reminding me once again of the pacts I made with my abuser so long ago, and with my frightened self too.

It's not just fear that I sense on the brink of emergence, but the bubbling presence of pure terror. There's a shield between what I'm recalling and what I'm feeling. I've been aware of it for some time now. When I'm on the scaffolding in my dream, I see all the evidence, the body parts, but I can't get to the feelings that I know I should have regarding them. There's something blocking access, a great solid wall between what I know and what I know I should feel, but I just can't seem to get through it. Knowledge and truth fail to merge; my body itself steels against it. Is the terror of the truth so great, or is there just so much of it? Maybe I'm just stuck, clogged with a massive blockage that needs to be removed so my feelings can naturally flow and the truth become acceptable. But exactly where is the blockage, and how do I remove it? Is the blockage my old pact with my abuser? Is it fear of him, old terror of what he will do to me if I tell, that has me so dammed up?

I lie in bed, curled up tight, my stomach pulsing and clenching with pain, my second chakra hurting from the tangled web of memories that still reside there. It's lonely here. I want and need to be held, to feel the warmth and presence of another human being. But I have to get the kids up for school and then go to work, so I unfurl my body from its lonely pose, force myself to stand up, and just get going.

November 26, 2002

I'm walking to a restaurant with some friends in a dream. As we enter the restaurant a rough looking guy dressed in a white chef's outfit, sitting with another chef, both of them fat and sloppy, asks me if it's my first time here. "Yes," I say. "Well, damn!" he exclaims. "We'll have to do something about that!" Our group splits up into several smaller groups and I take a seat with a woman friend at a small table facing the wall. I sit looking directly into a mirror. Reflected behind me I see everyone else in the restaurant having a good time, but I feel disconnected, lonely and sad. The food arrives, two pieces of meat on a plate: a dry piece of chicken and a hamburger patty. My friend and I eat, not talking much, picking at the dry chicken. Two men sit at a table to our right and I notice that the one facing the mirror has turned his chair so that he's no longer looking into the mirror. "Oh, what a good idea," I think, but I can't move my body or turn my chair around, I'm stuck in place.

The chef who'd spoken to me earlier comes over and sticks his fat index finger up my nostril. He digs around until he looks satisfied then sighs audibly before walking away, laughing loudly. I'm very aware that I don't react, that I'm stuck in a daze, a numb and frozen old place, and that *I just let it happen*. "Why didn't you react? Why didn't you stop him?" I scold myself mercilessly. I'm angry, but at the same time I realize that what the chef did has jolted me out of my depression. I immediately sense a thawing taking place. My body begins to loosen its tight clench, and I'm able to turn my chair around so I'm not facing the mirror anymore. I go back to eating and notice that the hamburger isn't properly cooked. "Don't eat it," I command myself. "You don't have to eat it. You don't have to protect anyone from the truth. The truth is that the food sucks here."

Now I notice that other things have shifted too. My friends have left the restaurant; even the friend who was sitting with me is no longer sitting opposite me. I also notice that the two men at the table next to me are holding a baby now. As I get up to leave, I notice the woman who had been sitting with me at a different table, ordering another glass of wine. I'm slightly miffed that she moved away, wondering if I was just not good company. I tell her that everyone else has already left and that we need to go too. She takes out her credit card to pay, but at the reception desk discovers that someone from our group has already paid for our meals. As we leave the restaurant, the fat chef asks me how I liked the food. "It was terrible and I'm never coming back," I say, quite honestly, suddenly pleased that I'm being so forthright because my first thought had been to lie and say that it was okay, to give a noncommittal answer like I would have done in the past. I leave the restaurant feeling pretty good about myself.

I reflect on this dream. When I look into the mirror, I'm uncomfortable. I'm confronted with the true state of my sad and lonely self, how distant and out of touch I am with my own feelings and life going on around me. When I notice that it's possible to avoid looking into the mirror, I can't do it at first. I must sit and face the frozen truth of myself. It isn't until later, after I'm jolted out of my depressed state by the chef actually abusing me in public, that I begin to thaw out. Abuse itself offers the trigger to change, much as this recapitulation of abuse is helping me to change. It's in the public exposure that real release comes. Only then am I able to turn from the mirror. And once I've confronted the truth, I'm able to be honest about everything. It's also then that I notice a general thawing going on around me, for as I change, the world changes as well: others move on, the two men have a baby, my friend is drinking wine at a different table, and my debt is paid. Only then do I begin to speak the truth, and only then do I feel good about myself. The dream is telling me that I must still sit and face the uncomfortable truth in the mirror, but eventually I will accept it and be done with this recapitulation process.

Last night, as I was trying to fall asleep, I thought about why I continue to maintain that solid barrier—appearing as that shiny mirror in my dream—keeping the true horrors of what happened to me as a child from my feeling self. I wonder if it's the horror itself that's too frightening to feel. I know that all I really have to do is go back to the memories, drop my defenses, and go through each experience more fully, but even the thought of doing that is frightening. Am I so afraid of the deeper feelings that will arise as I continually face what actually happened? Do I fear the feelings of suffocation and dying that I know accompany the memories? I taste the terror as it begins to emerge. Like a monster in a cave waking up after long sleep, its foul breath permeates my nostrils and its stench fills my mouth. Like the fat chef in the dream, it's heading right towards me, threatening and horrible, and there's no getting away from it! I am the only person it wants.

In a difficult meeting with Chuck, I face the uncomfortable mirror of my dream. I know I must deal with *believing*, yet I sit frozen in a cathartic, frightened state, my hands clenched in tight fists. Suddenly, my knuckles begin knocking against each other, automatically bumping together *harder and harder and harder*. I have no control over my fists as they smack loudly against each other. I'm angry and yet I have no sensation in my body. I battle a strong desire to smash the invisible mirror in front of me with my fists, to shatter the frozen images of a frozen self, yet I can't even feel my hands knocking against each other.

"If I can just physically feel pain then maybe I can release something," I say, "but I just end up feeling frustrated and sad."

As Chuck hands me the EMDR pods, I enter the old world of my child self where no emotions were allowed, where expression of feeling was curtailed, dismissed, and ridiculed. Such cold and impersonal requirements, imposed at an early age, resulted in a stiff inability to appropriately release any feelings and emotions whatsoever, as it was always inappropriate to do so.

"My child self doesn't know how to express what she's feeling," I say, growing increasingly uncomfortable. "And for my part, I can't let the child self speak for herself because there's no room inside me at present."

"Why?" asks Chuck.

"There's only room for frozen avoidance," I say. "Like in my dream, I can't turn my chair or move out of this state. I'm stuck."

As we probe deeper into this stalemate, I run smack into the wall that is holding back all that has been separated inside me for decades. On top of that solidly constructed wall a covering of shame lies smothering my feelings—feelings about myself as well as feelings in general. For deep down inside me, I believe that I will be scolded for inappropriately expressing myself, as well as for drawing attention to myself. I am not allowed to draw attention to myself in any way. I'm supposed to be good at everything I do, but never in any way that puts me at risk for exposure or even a hint of self-importance. I know there is a very fine line between being talented and being inflated about it. I'm taught to excel but never to show it or be proud of it.

"I realize I was never encouraged to feel any sense of self-worth or self-confidence," I tell Chuck. "My parents never gave any positive feedback. If anything it was mostly negative. In fact, they withheld things that would have certainly changed my personality had I been differently encouraged."

I recall my parents once telling me when I was an adult that I had been quite a talented swimmer, Olympic material, they said, but I have no recollection of this. I told them they were confused, that it was my younger sister who was the talented swimmer, for I remember talk of her swimming abilities when I was away at college. "No," they said. "It was you! You!" When I'd asked them why they never told me, they answered that they didn't think it would be good for me; they'd feared I'd suffer a 'big head.' For my part, I was stunned by this admission. I realized how valuable such information, if acted on, could have been to the depressed child I was at the time, when I was eight or nine years old. It took me a long time to understand just how damaging this omission was on their part, and how much of a disservice it is in general to withhold such information from a talented person. How could someone not alert another human being, especially one's own child, to the presence of such innate potential? How could someone not support such promise?

As I stand on the brink of smashing through that wall of shame and worthlessness, I'm also aware that I stand on the rim of annihilation, expecting severe reprimand. Having decided long ago to remain silent to appease the angry adults in my life, I cannot separate this moment from the fears of my abused child self. There remains a deep sense of shame around what happened at the hands of my abuser, but there is a deeper sense of shame stemming from the rules of my family of origin. Once again I am a child feeling ashamed of needing attention, for needing someone to take care of me. I am even ashamed of my desire to shatter the wall that blocks me from taking the next step in my recapitulation.

"The shameful truth is that, yes, I wanted someone to rescue me," I tell Chuck. "I wanted someone to come and save me, take me away, and I was utterly ashamed of desiring that, of even fantasizing about it. I was even ashamed of needing a mother, of wanting a mother who would absolve me of being the dutiful, obedient, perfect daughter who never complained, who silently crept through life, careful to not ruffle a feather or bring attention to herself."

As I admit to all of these things, red-hot shame immediately flares up, burning my face as it did when I was a child. I was ashamed of my most basic needs, a child's needs. Even now, as an adult, I still hear the harsh tone of my mother's voice inside my head, scolding me for wanting, for desiring, for asking, for needing.

"I'm supposed to be perfect, I'm not supposed to want or need anything," I tell Chuck. "But at the same time I'm not trying to get attention! I never was. I do have needs!"

"Of course you do, it's perfectly normal," says Chuck. "Yes, having needs is normal, and you need to allow your inner child to know that it's okay to have needs, all kinds. And it's even okay for *you* to have them too!"

"This is progress!" he says enthusiastically. "And on that happy note, our time is up!"

November 27, 2002

In a dream, I'm with a man, a stranger, though he seems to be a partner or a friend. We're living in a small house. A hobo is lurking in the shadows. He's everywhere I turn, inside and outside, always there. "Go away! I'm sick of you! I don't want you around anymore!" I yell at him. He goes into the woods and stays there hiding. I'm ashamed of him and yet I feel sorry for him at the same time. I keep his existence a secret from a woman friend. My male partner, however, knows of his existence and goes along with me in keeping him a secret. He knows how important it is for me to have some kind of control over the hobo.

Once again, I am confronted by the deeply wounded child self. I treat her feelings like the old hobo in my dream. I'm ashamed of them, keeping control over them. When I go to her and question how she feels, I discover that she's still deeply ashamed of everything. She's not even allowed to think good thoughts about herself. She's ashamed of her good accomplishments and she's ashamed of her perceived bad self too. Anything that has to do with the self or the ego is bad. She has to hide everything. Fears are feelings too, and feelings are not allowed. So fear must not be confronted either. These are the things that come to me from this dream and this interaction with my child self. I'm in such a quandary, feeling such a split, so ashamed and simultaneously so sorry for my despicable hobo self, my poor silent feeling self. I also know I'm being challenged to work on this and I admit that I'd rather this feeling self went away, taking her buried feelings with her, that she not confront me with her shameful secrets. At the moment I don't really care about her, while at the same time I genuinely care about others. I feel deeply for others and fully expect them to show their feelings, which I accept as necessary, but I'm never allowed to feel or express my own.

I see this split played out in my life too. I know the truth of who my parents are, for instance, and yet I always expect them to act differently, to have somehow miraculously evolved into beings capable of showing some emotion, some kindness, some thoughtfulness and compassion as they've aged. No longer a child, I expect them to treat me differently from the way they treated me as a child, but then I'm confronted with the truth of who they really are each time I meet them. I'm floored by how confined they remain, how emotionally stifled they are, and how they cannot relate in any real way. They have not softened one bit, and so all relationship with them is still bound by their old world concepts, values, and rules. It's a dead world to me now. I've spent my entire life trying to get away from it, breaking through its taboos by becoming a kind and compassionate being, and I guess I expect others to have evolved too. It's still a bit surprising to discover that my own parents are clearly uninterested in changing themselves and how withholding they're choosing to remain.

I must face the truth that people must choose to change and that many will never make such a choice. Each time my abuser approached me I hoped that he would treat me differently too. Why do I still keep hoping that the abusers in my life are going to suddenly be good, kind, thoughtful, and caring? It's such a false hope. Abusers treat people badly; they inflict pain! It's their job! I question why I still hold onto my childish hope for a different outcome. Why do I want to protect the abusers in my life, constantly hoping that they aren't really abusers? Am I really that innocent or is it because I'm ashamed of them?

The truth is that I'm deeply ashamed. I'm ashamed to admit that *I* was involved with a pedophile. I'm ashamed to admit that *I* was abused. I'm ashamed to admit that *I* wasn't aware and that *I* let bad things happen to me. *I let it happen!* Another part of me knows it must question whether I really believe that. Do I really believe that I could have been stronger, that I could have prevented it in some way? Am I really ashamed of myself for what happened in my childhood? Am I ashamed that I got caught up in someone else's issues and that, yes, I made some terrible mistakes in my innocence that got me into their evil clutches? But I was raised under certain standards of perfection, and a perfect person does not make mistakes, and by not being perfect I let people down. I shut myself off from all feeling because it was expected that I do so and, as a result, any time I begin to have feelings now I'm so ashamed of them that I continue to shut them down. No sadness is allowed, no anger, no happiness, and no feeling good about myself. So, yes, I'm ashamed of my past. It's impossible to release the shame, to feel happy, to feel good about myself. Instead I'm stranded in an old place, a child on the verge of annihilation. Someone is clutching my heart, twisting it in a painful, claw-like grip, waiting for it to burst.

I want to feel sorry for everyone else, but not for myself, for myself I have nothing to offer. I even feel sorry for the abusers.

November 28, 2002

I'm distracted by the Thanksgiving holiday today and the fact that my daughter is sick. We stay home, watch movies and have a quiet time together while my son goes off with his father. Now it's later in the evening and the old stuff sneaks back under my skin. I automatically clench against its invasion, tightening my neck, shoulders and legs, holding them stiffly. I haven't been running lately, but maybe I need to start again, if only to release this memory tension from my body.

All I have to do is close my eyes and I'm in the field in front of my abuser's house, the grass is high and golden; it's the height of summer. I reach up and take his hand and walk down into the woods with him and into a memory. I'm tied up, lying on my side, my hands bound to my ankles, an animal that he's caught. A stick tail is stuck in my rear end. I wait for him to finish his preparations. He's making something. Using a hatchet, cutting saplings, he makes a small rack, like a sawhorse. Untying me, he makes me crawl on hands and knees over to the rack. My stick tail falls out. Lying on my back, my legs draped over the rack, I hear the scraping sound of metal against metal. I don't like to look at what he's doing to me down there. When he's done and the game is over, I have no sense of self.

As I lie in bed and recapitulate the moment of release from his game, I have no sense of being, no sense of ego, none whatsoever. From this place of nothingness I go immediately into another old place where I recapture the deeply shameful feelings of my child self: I am nothing; I simply don't matter; I am not allowed to express or feel; I have no power, no needs, no place nor person to turn to. I recapitulate hiding my feelings, stuffing them away as deeply as possible until I no longer have access to them. It's only then that I know I will survive, only by rejecting what little sense of self I have, and so I simply stop feeling.

I hear that tiny girl inside me, deciding that she will never ask for anything. She doesn't need anything from anyone. Determined to be a solitary being, a stoic unit against the world, she is set to fight her own battles. She already knows there are no safe places to go for help.

November 29, 2002

I want to let go! I want to fall! I'm so tired of holding onto everything, tired of being in such pain that I can't move. I want to fall and fall and fall. But even so, I'm afraid, not of the falling itself, but of the loneliness of the fall, and the vast nothingness that I'm heading into: *the great unknown.*

I've lived my whole life in fear of being grabbed and taken away to a place where horrible things would be done to me. Ironically, this fear just served as a cover for the truth, which was that I *was* actually grabbed, taken away, and horrible things *were* done to me as a child. But I've also lived my entire adult life caught in the grip of that same fear. I'd always hoped that the older I got the safer I would feel, but the fear of abduction has never left me. Now I know I have to confront it, that the only way I'll ever be safe is to fully face it, not duck and hide from it, but relive it and then store it in the archives of my memory, fully resolved, without attachment. And so I dare myself to peek into the woods again, to recapitulate.

I do the sweeping breath. As I enter my abuser's chamber I immediately realize that by the time I am naked, tied up, and lying on the ground I'm already tuning out, already disappearing, tumbling down into the tunnel deep inside myself. From this inner place of safety, I watch my abuser in his ritual setting up, his methodical constructing of the set. It's like watching a scene through a viewer. I experience what's happening outside of me as if I'm peering through binoculars, watching from a great distance. Sounds are muted and feelings so distant as to be completely cut off. Everything is faraway, even my body. I am safe in a state of numbness, as if I've hypnotized myself in order to survive. As I exit this moment of recapitulation and my abuser's chamber in the woods, I reestablish that I really do want to let go of those faraway experiences that hold me so silent and withdrawn, though right now, at this very minute, I just feel like giving up and staying in bed. I feel like curling up and staying here for days, not moving, but I know that if I do that I'll simply stagnate.

I tell my child self that it's okay to want to curl up with the pain, that it's okay to feel sad and lonely and afraid. It's okay to hate him. In this case, hating is okay. If it makes it any better, then hating is okay. Everything that arises is okay because it's part of the recapitulation process, it's also part of being human. Everything must be acceptable, investigated for what it truly is and then properly shed, through deep inner work. I must understand everything that happened to me on the deepest level and go forward only with what is of value. And so, I will not achieve full healing until I release everything that my psyche is holding back from my greater awareness. I must be fearless as I let it unleash its truths.

November 30, 2002

The kids and I spent the greater part of yesterday together. The distraction and attention placed on others was good, for the most part taking me out of my inherent sadness. We watched a James Bond movie last night, *On Her Majesty's Secret Service*, in which a ski chase ends when several people go over a precipice with an incredibly long, long drop. Watching it was excruciating. At the same time I felt such a need to allow for the same kind of plunge, to let myself go off the edge and just fall and fall and fall, as I so yearn to do in my inner reality. I'm aware that this kind of letting go carries its own excruciating moments, that it's like falling off the edge of that steep mountainside, knowing that you have no control and that you are plunging into the abyss, certain death awaiting. In my case, it will be the death of the old, and though I look forward to it, something still holds me back. I keep reminding myself that I must be fearless anyway.

I realize I still have memories to confront; that I'm not done is so obvious. The memories ask me to feel, to experience emotions and confront not only what happened to me, but also to break through what is holding me from leaping off the invisible precipice. The challenge is becoming clearer now. I must let go of the old need to hold everything back, break through the shield that surrounds me, and knock down the wall inside that keeps me from truly feeling with full emotional involvement, from truly taking the leap into the abyss of release. I must get to the feelings that are trapped inside the buckets of bloody little girl parts that my dream showed me so clearly. Until I sort through those buckets and handle the horrific truths of the dismembered little girl self, and suffer through a full emotional outpouring about what really happened, I will not heal.

Chapter 6

Moving

December 1, 2002

I awaken from a dream in the middle of the night, stuck in a tight body clench triggered by something I can't quite grasp. The stubborn need to hold onto the old stuff—for the most part conducted by my unconscious—appears to be much greater than I'd thought, and even though I've made a *conscious* decision to release the memories, it doesn't seem to matter. The physical holding is like an ancient curse and I haven't yet learned the magic words to break its spell...

I must have fallen asleep after writing that because suddenly I'm startled awake. The sound of my own voice crying out brings me back to consciousness. I awaken in pain once again, to the dull warnings of more pain to come, to the coldness of the morning and the weakness of the sun at this time of year. Barely risen, it does not bring warmth with it today.

I think about not going to yoga class, but my body leads me there anyway. As the class begins, I acknowledge the dream-triggered pain still coursing through my achy hips, but notice that I'm stable and strong nonetheless. Even so, memories constantly seek entry as the class proceeds. I push them away, but it becomes increasingly difficult to detect them conniving their way in during certain poses. They sneak in unnoticed and suddenly it's too late—I'm flooded with ancient pain and fear. On my back, in a submissive pose, knees bent, with pelvic floor wide open and exposed, I am overcome with panic. "It's only a memory," I tell myself, as burning anal pain sears through me. "This is a yoga class. The memory will still be there later. Relax, relax, relax; don't let it get to you." The pain releases as I incrementally ask myself to let it go for now, promising that I'll deal with it later. I also know that if I forget, the pain—never shy about reminding me of my promises—will return of its own accord. But I do forget. I head to the studio after the yoga class and work intently all day until it's time to pick up the kids after school. The evening too is busy, as I give my attention to the domestic scene at home, and so I'm able to keep the murmurings of more-to-come at bay.

I'm more anxious than ever to move on the twenty-first. My in-laws have purchased our house, allowing me the financial ability to move on. They will share the large house with their son, my husband. Unwilling, however, to wait until the kids and I have moved out, they've descended upon us like a pair of old geese, their decades old habits taking precedence. It's a bit too crowded; too many generations and personalities with too many disparate needs under one roof, and there's conflict. The formerly agreed upon stasis that had prevailed between my husband and I has totally dissolved, and I'm forced to partake in the troublesome domestic scene that now reigns. Protective of my children, I constantly shield them from the new energy that has taken over what was once our home, gathering them to me like a mother lion protecting her young. I don't want them hurt any more than they already are.

"I don't like it here," my daughter confided to me this morning.

"I don't either," I told her, unable to contain myself, "but it will only be for a little while. We'll get used to it and, before you know it, we'll be moving into our new house!"

Meanwhile, ancient fear, stirred in the morning yoga class, raises its ugly head again as the evening progresses into night, sending me searching for a safe place. I find no peace in this house anymore, but I have to get away somehow, for the need to go as far down into the tunnel as possible is urgent. At the same time, I force myself to not dissociate. While I wash the supper dishes, I remember Chuck reminding me that I must observe everything that happened to me in the past, but that I must stay present too. After I finish cleaning the kitchen, I go into my room and shut my door, telling the kids I'm going to rest for a few minutes while they finish their homework.

Intent upon exploring what my body is attempting to alert me to, I let myself recapitulate. Conscious that I'm lying on my bed, I quickly sink into the past. I let myself be drawn in until I find myself on the ground in the woods, tied up like an animal, my hands and feet bound together behind my back. Inwardly, I'm shrinking, going deep inside myself. Suddenly I'm swirling faster and faster, sinking down into the safety of nothingness. I have no control over what's happening and in spite of my desire to stay present and aware of my environment, I disappear completely. But then I notice that I'm able to look out from this faraway place. I peer through the telescope that I have become, out a tiny aperture in the distance, no bigger than a pinhole. I'm far away—a great distance from what's happening outside of me—trying to protect this tiny little bit of "Self" from harm, the only bit of awareness that still exists.

As I come out of this memory and back into the present, I realize I'm experiencing this recapitulation process on a different level now, with greater detachment. That sense of detachment must spread to other areas of my recapitulation as well now, to not just include the memories but every aspect of my changing self. Although I experienced deep abandonment as a child, and although I feel deep resentment toward my parents, I realize that I must detach from wanting or needing anything from them now. I must let them go and not hold them accountable. If I don't, I'll remain stuck in an old place. I must also more fully embrace that solitary child that I once was, for she does hold all the powers of detachment that I seek. I see that now. I don't want anger or resentment to hold me back anymore, polluting my personal energy or my recapitulation process either. I must also more fully embrace the truth offered by my past and take the dissociative skills of my child self to a new level, utilizing them with *awareness* now, as Chuck once suggested, for I envision the possibilities these skills might afford more clearly now.

If I step back and look at my parents from a distance, quite dispassionately, I see them almost as characters in a movie, strange people I'm not particularly attached to. If I'm honest, I do harbor some vague feelings about them at this point, but I also feel that to leave them to the choices of their own souls is the best thing for me to do, while I attend to the care of my own soul. If I'm willing to seek change, to keep going with this recapitulation, I will no longer have to fear being like them, as I've often dreaded in the past. But if I refuse the call to change, then yes, I may end up like them, as closed and boxed-in as they are now and as I myself have been up to this point. In doing this recapitulation, I'm breaking away from them and their influences, from what both shaped me and kept me captive. I have my own voice, my own heartfelt knowing of what feels right, and when I listen it tells me to do what I know is best: *to trust my heart.* And I already know that when I'm open and receptive, I receive guidance from the spiritual guides who are assigned to me. I have long been aware of their existence, yet under the auspices of the old world I could not find my way to them very often. As I let go of the past, of my parents and all they taught me, I'm finding my own way. I'm evolving into a spiritual being—and it's right *for me.*

I do recapitulation breathing, breathing out my abuser, breathing out my parents and my past, making room for me, preparing myself for the inner birthing of the new me. I am my own mother now, and my own father too.

December 2, 2002

In a dream, I'm setting up a huge art show. Other artists arrive to help out. We prepare artwork, frame paintings, and get everything set up. A person makes a comment that nothing looks ready, insinuating that I won't be able to open as scheduled. I refuse the implication, look her straight in the eye, and very calmly say, "Don't worry, I'll be ready."

In another dream, I'm setting up for a meeting of a historical society. I look around at all the tables that I've set up. Everything is neatly organized and exquisitely laid out. I'm perfectly satisfied; everything *is* ready.

I'm up and out early, getting everyone to school and myself to the studio. The dreams underscore just the way I feel at the moment, soberly confident, as a lot of things come to closure. I am indeed ready for the challenges that lie ahead. Even today has been well prepared for with lots of work, but still time for myself. The kids will be going out to dinner with their grandparents this evening and I'm planning on working late. I'll end the day at an evening yoga class. The long day alone offers me time to gauge where I am at this point in my recapitulation process, as well as the opportunity to do some inner work before I meet with Chuck tomorrow.

I sit in the early morning calmness of the studio, in the quiet before too many people arrive in the building, and allow myself to meditate on this process of self-change that I've been so diligently working on. In the beginning, my main need was to address my dying spirit, long shut down, practically ignored for decades. I'd almost forgotten of her existence, but now she's been revived and is being brought into new life. As I take my next steps, I must reassert my priorities and once again determine just what it is that I seek. As this journey has progressed over the past year-and-a-half, I've discovered so many needs, feelings, and desires. Long denied, they were once deemed so unnecessary and too selfish to attend to. As I've faced the truth of them and begun to accept them into my life, so many other unknown parts of myself have emerged and journeyed with me, asking to be included too.

I must constantly address what arises each day and now I must face the latest priorities that have arisen, those of my spirit again, for the truth is that my spirit seeks still greater freedom yet. That freedom must be untarnished, uncompromised, freed of the past without fear of retaliation of any sort, totally freed of shame and guilt, and without the threats of punishment once imposed by my religion, my parents, and my abuser. That freedom must come from being completely relieved of not only the trauma and subsequent burdens of the abuse—from PTSD—but also from everything that I once valued as important. For I understand more fully now that I must completely leave the old world and enter a totally new world of my own choosing. To do so, I must continually change how I view the world and my place in it, how I react and live, how I think and feel. I must totally transform myself. Out of this recapitulation process, this is what has evolved as my true mission now: *to totally transform.*

At this point along the journey of transformation, I am further confronted with detaching from the parents I got in this life and from the expectations I've had of them. I'd always supposed them to be good parents. Even though it's clear now that they sorely lacked in parenting skills, and even in basic communication skills, I nonetheless expected things of them. However, now I see my parents fairly clearly, as lost souls without a clue, not dishonest or valueless, but merely incapable of taking life by the horns and wrestling it to the ground, as I'm attempting to do. And so, I find that I can no longer uphold my old expectations of them. In fact, I no longer have any expectations of them at all. Now, as I view them with adult eyes, I see them as avoidant and fearful of life. I also find that I'm not angry with them anymore. I'm more saddened by the choices they've made, but even that I must let go.

I must accept who they are, not expect anything from them, and no longer wait around for them to change. I must move on now with compassion for them, devoid of any attachment, always aware to not repeat their mistakes. It's imperative that I choose differently now, that I break with the old rules of their world. I must rid myself of the old habits and old behaviors once foisted upon me. At all costs, I must constantly dare myself to continue this life-shattering recapitulation. I must barge ahead, unafraid now, yet always remain aware that I could easily slip back into the familial addictions of denial and avoidance. In training myself to detach in this manner, I am keenly aware that I am doing so for reasons other than out of fear. I don't choose detachment out of fear anymore, but only out of a far greater need to free my spirit. I'm choosing to face the darkness, to break through the silence of secrecy and learn what it means to be *real* in the world. I choose to rebel! I choose to fully live!

As I come to this critical point in the recapitulation process, I feel I must address my inner child and let her speak again. I sit in the still early morning quiet of the studio, pen in hand, and invite her to join me in conversation.

"What do you want? What do you want, my wounded child?" I ask her.

"I want love expressed so that I understand that it's real, accompanied by genuine affection. I want to experience true love," she replies, and I sense I am speaking to my articulate, sensitive teenage self. "I want to be held. I want to feel safe. I want someone to notice me, to notice that I'm too quiet, too good, too lonely, and too afraid. I want someone to listen, *really* listen to what I have to say. I want to be able to trust, to be able to speak honestly, and I want to be allowed to cry. I want to be told that it's all right to be afraid, that it's all right to need other people, and that it's really okay to be sad."

"Someone did some very bad things to me," she continues. "It wasn't my fault, none of it. I couldn't stop him, no matter what I did. He was a very strong adult and I was a tiny child. I don't need to blame myself. I felt the way I did because I thought I was bad. Now I know I wasn't. He was bad, not me. He tortured me, a tiny child, until there was nothing left in me to torture. And then I snuck away, deep inside, until I found a place of emptiness. And then I went even deeper into that emptiness, as far down as I could go, to the total absence of everything."

"Why? Why did you go there?"

"Because he hurt me, he frightened me, but it was more than that: he *terrorized* me. To him, I was not a little girl but a vagina and an anus. I was flesh only, a pliable carcass with no little girl inside it, because I was gone. I was hiding from the sticks and ropes and tools. I was hiding from the pain, from the sadness, from the loneliness, from the terror, but mostly I was hiding from him, the man in the woods."

"He could get your body, but he couldn't get your thoughts or your soul," I remind her. "He couldn't take away your determination or your will to survive. He could hurt you, but he didn't want to kill you; he needed you. If you died, he'd have to start all over again and train someone else, another little girl. He liked the one he had."

"Yes, you're right, he needed me," she says, "but I felt so helpless. No one ever came to help me. I wanted someone to look at me and know everything that was happening, without me having to explain anything. I wished for an angel to come down and save me. I wanted comforting, and I still want comforting, someone to hold me in a tight little bundle and tell me that everything is okay, that I'm a good person, that I didn't do anything bad and that I'm not bad either. I'm good and pure and clean."

"There's nothing to be ashamed of," I say.

"I know. None of it was my fault," she says, "and I'm not going to get hurt by him anymore."

December 3, 2002

I am wracked by feelings too great and inexplicable. Like a caged beast I need an outlet for this sudden build up of energy inside me. I need to do something physical. I feel destructive and then immediately angry with myself for feeling this way. While driving, it suddenly occurs to me that I could drive right off the highway, that I could replace mental pain with real pain. How easy it would be!

I'm scared; I'm scared of myself.

"It's not uncommon to feel this way, but you're not going to act on it, are you?" Chuck asks when I sit in session with him.

"No," I say, but Chuck doesn't look convinced.

"Look, I promise you I won't hurt myself. I can't do that," I say emphatically. "I have too many responsibilities, too many people depend on me. I'd never do that."

"Okay," he says.

"The funny thing is," I say, "that although I'm feeling this incredible distress, this mental anguish and turmoil, it doesn't feel like legitimate pain. It's not real enough. It's so foreign, as if it doesn't really belong to me. I don't like pain that doesn't have a name, this invasion of feelings that I can't connect to anything. I want to substitute the pain for something tangible and real, that's all. And on top of it, I'm exhausted. I'm just tired."

"A shift is happening, that's what this is all about. A shift is happening and something wants to hold on, something is resistant to change," Chuck says, "but change is good. Change is good."

"Change is good. Change is good," I repeat. "But what could be resisting? What is it that wants me to be in such pain? Maybe it's trying to show me something, perhaps something to do with that memory of paralysis that I keep getting drawn back to."

We do EMDR around the memory of illness that I had recapitulated last month. Even though I'm drawn to explore it more deeply, I hear Jeanne's voice giving me permission to refuse the call, to renege on the urge. "*You don't have to be here in this memory; you don't have to go there anymore.*" At the same time that I acknowledge the advice, I let myself go a little deeper, just to see what happens. Suddenly, I'm standing beside the burning chair, the one I'd sat in throughout the long illness. The smoke is so thick I can barely make out my father standing on the other side. In a little girl voice, I tell Chuck that burning the chair is wrong, that it's polluting the air, that it's dangerously toxic. I actually say something to my father to this effect, about the smell of the black smoke, even at six years of age aware of its poisonous fumes. I cover my face, then and now, so I don't have to breathe in the stench of it.

"It smells really bad," I say to Chuck, gagging as I recapitulate, "but it's like everything else is burning up with it, all the splinters of memory are going up in the putrid flames too."

As I recapitulate, my six-year-old self looks up and sees the sun shining high in the sky, far above the black smoke pouring out of the chair. My awareness shifts back to now, back to the power of my adult self to change things and, with renewed intent, I fling all the toxic stuff of that sickness memory into the sun's fire, where it incinerates, the same way my father incinerated the old chair. As I send the memory up in flames, I sense a total cleansing taking place. I finally release the pain and twisted sentiments embedded in my body since I was that six-year-old child.

"I don't have to go back to this memory anymore," I say, as I come out of EMDR. "But even though I know this is true, there's still something that wants me to have pain. Something is strongly suggesting that pain is normal for me. How can I give it up? If I give up the pain, I'm sure I'll still need to substitute something, put something else in its place, though I know that's not really true. I don't need pain. I can be free of it all; free of mental pain and physical pain too. I can just let it all go and be pain-free."

"You are being pulled back there," Chuck says, "because it's familiar. Change is frightening."

"Yes, as I begin to let go, even just a little, I feel the old familiar comforts so strongly. Even pain and depression are deeply comforting. Everything is known, and I'm okay with it. The truth is that right now I'd like to just stop in my tracks and stay all cozy in that tunnel inside myself, depressing as it is. Something is tugging at me to stay there. Something doesn't want me to change. I think the fear inside me just wants me to stay where I am—accessible."

"Tell it that you're okay now, that you'll be okay, that all parts of you are okay and you can go on. Work on that," says Chuck, as we end the session.

I know that where I'm headed is a much better place than where I am now, a much happier place. I conclude that I can leave the memories behind when I'm done with them, incinerated into ashes by the fire of my intent and the heat of the sun rising on a new day. Eventually, I'll be able to leave the woods and everything they remind me of too. I just won't need to go into that lonely quiet tunnel inside myself anymore.

By the end of the workday I'm exhausted, my energy depleted, but my heart is overflowing with love for my two children. Such deep affection for them has been stirred by my own complicated past. I am so thankful for them, perfectly acceptable the way they are, so complex and yet so innocent. I'm grateful for all they bring to me and to the life we share together. I treasure them. I just want to be near them so I can take care of them and pour all my love into them. I head home with this tender intent uppermost in my mind.

December 4, 2002

I dream that I'm in India, staying with a very wealthy family of hotel owners. They own a large sprawling hotel that's been totally wrapped in mosquito netting. The hotel rises high into the sky, incorporating several different architectural styles, everything from ornate onion domes and intricate spiraling wooden structures to minimalist concrete walls. The hotel is vast, monumental in scope, and sits on the edge of a calm wide lake. The men in the family are domineering, sexist, totally carefree, and blatantly rude. The women are servile, restricted by numerous rules. All the women wear saris, including me. When we females sit on chairs or sofas we have to cover them with thick cloth first, so that we don't contaminate the furniture by touching it directly with our skin. Between the hotel and the lake lies a sprawling garden of ornate fountains and stone walls with seating areas covered with rugs and pillows, all surrounded by plants and fruit trees. I sit in the shade of a tree, observing the scene before me through a camera.

There are other people sitting and milling about—men, women and children. I'm taking pictures, but also observing everything through the camera lens. The women are bubbly, talkative, and seemingly accepting of everything. They accept the restrictions placed on them by the men, and the men take full advantage of their dominance over the women, touching and pawing them, even me. It's clear that in this country women are for men's enjoyment. I don't say much as I continue observing through the camera lens, but it annoys me that the women are so accepting of their roles. Meanwhile, a man sits down close behind me. He keeps touching me. Then I feel him putting cold red cherries down my back. I'm annoyed. I try to ignore him, hoping he'll go away when he sees I'm not interested, but he's very persistent, aggressively so, and I am unable to dissuade him from this activity or fend him off. I'm aware that he's just doing what's natural in this country, but I keep hoping he'll see that I'm not of his culture and leave me alone. I ignore him as best I can.

Peering through my camera, I notice a young Western girl on the other side of the garden. Dressed in jeans and a short crop top, she's sitting and talking with an Indian man. "She's brave," I think, "to come dressed like that." I admire her non-servile attitude, her self-confidence and determination to be who she is, even in the face of such ardent tradition. Inspired by her, I stand up and walk away from the pawing man with his cherries. Turning my camera toward the lake, I notice how very still and calm it is, like an enormous reflecting pool. I have the impression that the monsoons have recently passed and that they've left the water in the lake higher than normal. When I step into it, however, I'm surprised to find that it's very shallow, only coming up to my ankles. Holding my long sari out of the way, I slowly walk from one side of the lake to the other, calmly and contentedly wading in the placid water. When I turn from the middle of the lake and pan my camera back toward the hotel, I notice the tightly wrapped mosquito netting once again. I'm struck by how odd it looks—as if the artist Christo has wrapped it—yet I also understand the necessity of it in this tropical climate.

I wake up from this dream certain that Chuck is right about there being some small part of me that is resistant to change. Some part of me wants to stay in the tunnel, captive forever like the women in my dream. The rules and behaviors are clearly spelled out there and everything is pretty predictable. There are no surprises, and even though I'm not in control—even though I am totally dominated by what my abuser did to me if I stay there—it has become a sort of safe haven. Fear took me there a long time ago, to an exotic place much like the hotel in my dream. Like the sari I wrapped around myself in the dream, I let fear embrace me. I let fear keep me hidden away in my tunnel of self, while I kept things hidden from myself as well. Now, as I prepare to leave that tunnel, the place that in the midst of terror became a safe haven, I am terrified all over again. Even though my dream takes place in an exotic environment, I'm still in captivity.

Is that really where I want to be? Is that as far as I want to go? The fact that I'm looking through a camera lens through most of the dream seems to indicate that I'm only visiting. I'm an observer, documenting a strange yet, in many ways, familiar world. I must keep taking this recapitulation journey to its very end if I am to break the spell of captivity, if I am to fully evolve to a new, *truly* exotic place. This dream seems to portend that I will, for even as I wade out into the water and gain yet another perspective, I know I don't really belong here and that my visit will soon end.

During the day, I find myself constantly glazing over. The tunnel tugs at me, pulling me back into the dream, reminding me what it's like in the safety of captivity. Experiencing a certain measure of detachment, as if I still have the camera in front of my eyes, I find it easy to wander around the hotel grounds in my imagination. I experience a certain level of calmness, especially as I wade in the calm lake. Memories of complacency come out of the dream suggesting how predictable captivity is, so easy to acquiesce to once you've gotten used to it.

As the day goes on, I fall for the numbing enticement of that dream world and allow inertia to take over. I know it's not the best choice to make, but I can't help myself. As if my energy is suffering in the suffocating heat of an Indian afternoon, I cannot resist. Yesterday, as I drove down the highway and felt that old urge to remain where I am for the rest of my life, in the deeply familiar comfort of pain, I had to fight against it with all my concentration. It would have been so easy to just let go of the steering wheel and let the fear of change take control of my car. It's that fear of change that I'm fighting right now too, fear of the unknown. My constant companion, it dug me that tunnel of safety, separating me from my once traumatic experiences, while successfully keeping me from living a fuller life as well. Last night, as I lay in bed, I made a concerted effort to physically let the fear go, for I truly don't need to carry it any longer, but the tightness in my body refused to release it. We fought, jerking and shaking and, unfortunately, I woke up this morning still wrapped in its tight embrace.

Chuck recommended that I use drawing and painting to rid myself of all that's bottled up inside, both the physical and the mental stuff. As soon as I imagine expressing what I'm feeling through my art, my body comes alive. I feel big expansive strokes swirling inside me, ready to unleash in a freedom of stark expression. I feel broad, definite strokes, big splashes of bright color set in motion by my moving body, so in contrast to the controlled techniques of painting and illustration I've done in the past, as I've hunched stiffly over my drawing board. I think Chuck is right that this is the perfect outlet of expression, as I sense a deep stirring to actively paint out my anger and my pain in abstraction now. I anticipate finding freedom in such physical release, as I channel my multifaceted and multileveled spirit, giving it fuller expression. But I also feel the need for sound to erupt. Long held back, it too seeks release. More than anything I want to yell and scream, but I can't! Afraid to make even the tiniest sound, I must remain silent, a little quiet mouse hiding in my tunnel. This fear of verbal expression dominates every thought of release, reminding me that I must stay silent because then I'm safe, because then I'm in control. At least that's the false premise I've lived under and, in fact, survived under for my entire life. Obviously, it isn't working any longer!

Each time I contemplate giving up my safe places and my old comforts—presented as so exotically beautiful in my dream—I find myself glazing over and disappearing into my carpal tunnel body where I am securely in control, everything locked in tight. This is what my dream was showing me too, while it was simultaneously showing me the frustration of being held captive. As soon as I find myself back in that tunnel, I get drawn back into the memories that are so connected to that tight place of safety. I counter this by trying to relax, reminding myself throughout the day that I'm safe, that I can relax my guard now, that I am no longer a child being abused. I refuse the call of the tunnel by constantly changing my posture. I get up and move around, like I did in the dream.

I do yogic and shamanic breathing throughout the day as well, especially the recapitulation breath, to loosen my physical hold, to discourage my habitual control. I journal and use meditation to shift my awareness, but the clenching is so automatic that it creeps right back in. Each day, as I awaken, I must start over again, talking myself through the releasing process yet again, telling myself to relax my jaw, relax my neck, relax my shoulders, relax my stomach and my hips and thighs, to loosen my hold innerly and outerly. In the end, perhaps I do let go a little bit more each day. Time will tell, I guess.

At three in the afternoon exhaustion hits with a dull thud, almost knocking me down. The urge to lie down and curl up is powerful. I find that lying flat on my back, melting into the hard wooden floor, helps avert the old draw to roll into a ball. While lying on the cold floor, I remember Chuck suggesting yesterday that maybe my dosage of Paxil wasn't high enough. "NO!" I'd immediately shouted back at him. I'm suffering from major denial mixed in with rumblings of fear—that's the concoction that's the main problem here, not the dosage of the meds! I'd told him that this recapitulated stuff just doesn't fit into the life I've been living. I can't find me, and I can no longer find my way back to the childhood I once remembered either. It doesn't exist anymore, for everything that once was has disappeared—collapsed, gone! On top of that I can't believe I so totally blocked out so much stuff!

It would be so much easier to assign this total annihilation of all-that-once-was a higher dose of meds, but it won't solve the issue. It would be so much *easier* if none of this recapitulation had started, if I had just never remembered any of it, but my life didn't go that way. And so now I'm confronted with everything changing, and with the fact that I've totally blocked out huge hunks of my life experiences. I'm faced with having to rewrite my entire life story, putting together two separate lives, one known and the other completely unknown. That's why I'm going crazy!

December 5, 2002

In a dream, a wasp is trying to sting me, diving and attacking. I run down long hallways, and up and down staircases in a large institutional type building, trying to get away from it. Not only is the wasp chasing me, but a man with a baseball bat is after me too. He's even trying to hit a baby over the head with the bat, so I swoop up the baby into my arms and run with it. I'm trying not to draw attention to myself, but a woman notices that I'm in a bit of a pickle. "Are you okay?" she asks. "Yes, I'm fine," I say, as I dodge the swings of the bat, fend off the wasp, and try to save the baby all at the same time. This chase goes on all night long.

Maybe I'm finally allowing myself to feel, to comprehend and, ultimately, to believe, because the denial factor is coming on strong again. I am inclined to just say, "Forget it, I can't believe any of this stuff!" The difficulty in believing, at this point, lies in the fact that what I've recapitulated so far is such a different life from the one I thought I had lived. It's pretty difficult to fathom that such disparate lives were being lived simultaneously, and trying to merge them is nearly impossible. Trying to fit the recapitulated memories into the conscious life I lived is a bit like trying to put a square peg into a round hole. I'm discovering that what I thought was real wasn't real at all; it was made up to accommodate the brutal facts, the trauma of the repressed life. I'm trying to place the memories in some kind of context, attempting to interweave them into the fabric of my known everyday reality, but the whole picture, the whole story needs rewriting as a result of all this new data. Such cognitive dissonance shatters my world.

At the studio, I try to focus on work. I fend off anxiety, which pesters unrelentingly, buzzing inside me like the wasp in my dream. Suddenly, I'm overcome by a need to be held like a little child. The only thing I can think to do is lie on the floor, curl up in a fetal position, and wrap my arms around myself. As I lie curled up on my yoga mat, I realize that I've spent most of my life with this needy child inside me, wanting to be held, so in pain but not sure why. This is what the girls were alerting me to in our conversation the other day. Instead, I became the girl who was so aloof, seemingly independent, the girl who never needed anything, largely because nothing was offered. The truth was that I'd often escape to the privacy of my bedroom and curl up on my bed where I'd go into a dead zone, into the tunnel of no feelings. Now I realize that I was really finding my own means of comfort, a way to deal with all those unmet needs. Sometimes I'd stay there for hours, taking a respite from what-I-knew-not, though now I certainly do. Like the pesky wasp in my dream, something inside me was always trying to take me back to remembering, trying to jumpstart a recapitulation, an inner revolution. And here I am now, finally recapitulating, going back to my child self to hold and comfort her, consciously aware that it's exactly right that I do so. I've used this fetal pose to comfort myself many times before, but this is the first time I've fully separated the child from the adult self. This time, I'm not comforting my adult self, I'm holding and loving my child self—I can actually feel her in my arms!

As I lie on the floor, I sense the guy with the baseball bat from my dream hovering nearby, looking for an opportunity to interrupt this tender moment of reconnection, seeking to drag me back into that old place of fear. I go back into my dream to empower my frightened self and, in waking awareness, I dream a new ending. I turn and attack the guy. Chasing him with a club of spikes, I whack the bloody hell out of him, stick the club up his ass, and then take a knife and hack him to pieces.

Horrified and yet utterly relishing every second of this rush of brutal power, I allow it to take over. Long repressed anger is allowed full expression, totally absent of my usual inhibitions or any form of biased censorship. I simply give my deeply repressed self full permission to act out her rage. As she does, a sense of unburdening simultaneously takes place inside me, my inner load lightened by this roleplaying. I find this exercise both empowering and exhausting, as the tenderness and love I'd felt one minute abruptly flips to violent behavior. The two sides of my deeper self are finally in alignment, working together on this recapitulation process. I've broken through something!

Getting up off my yoga mat, I contemplate the pain I've experienced as I've gone through this torturous recapitulation. It's not like having some little scrape on the knee. This is like having your belly ripped open and your guts wrenched out.

As the day progresses and things emerge, I get down on the floor repeatedly and hold my poor child self in my arms. I know she needs an adult to help her deal with what's been stirring. She has been given permission to unleash and yet she also needs me to keep her together as the moment of disintegration, so long feared, now seems so imminent. At one point, I find myself biting my hands and before I know it I'm spinning down into memory.

Taken into recapitulation by my little girl self, I remember biting my arms, pulling out my eyelashes, picking the hairs out of my head—I'm angry! I do hurtful things to myself until my mother tells me to stop, that I'm disturbing her with my awful behaviors. I recapitulate the time I awoke in the night, screaming and drooling, my hands grabbing my crotch.

The old lady who babysits comes into my room. She shakes me by my arms and yells at me to stop, to go to the bathroom. I can't stop screaming. I'm awake but not awake, in my bed and in my room, yet not in my bed or room at all. She panics, tries to get me out of bed, but I can't stop screaming. I can't move or totally wake up either. I am frozen in some strange inarticulate state, out of control and yet locked in a body that will not respond. In the middle of this tirade my parents return home from a night out. They come into my room wanting to know what's wrong with me. I hear the panic in the old lady's voice; she sounds scared. "Just woke up screaming like that!" she tells my parents, and even though I'm holding myself like I have to pee, I refuse to go to the bathroom. I'm glad my parents are home, but I can't communicate that either. Unable to give a coherent answer to all their questions, I simply tumble back down into my bed and burrow under the covers. I just want everyone to go away and leave me alone. "What was that all about?" my mother asks in the morning. "I don't remember," I say, but I do remember—it's just too confusing to sort through. I just know it wasn't about having to pee. Now I understand that my two worlds were colliding; the curtain between worlds had fallen and the moment of disintegration had come.

The little girl inside me has waited all this time for someone to come along and help her, and I'm the only one who can do that. I'm the only one who knows why she needs help. She doesn't even have to say a word, I just know. I am the angel, the fairy godmother she always wished for, come to save her at last.

It's snowing heavily, the roads slippery, as I head home at the end of the day. As I drive slowly along the snow-covered streets, I sense that I'm about to lose control as I head into the next phase of this recapitulation, my sense of groundedness going, my whole world changing even more than it already has. In fact, the snowflakes swirling dizzily out of the darkness, flying straight into the windshield, seem to underscore this prediction. It feels like I'm about to lose my equilibrium, as if I'm in a slowly orbiting space capsule about to spin right out into space. I grip the steering wheel a little tighter and thank my adult self—forged strong and stable—for staying soberly present and getting me through this rough day. I ask her to stay with me as we head into the darkness of outer space too. Glittering brightly, the white snowflakes gather around me like brilliant stars come to light my way, as I drive right into the great unknown.

December 6, 2002

I dream that I'm at an art exhibit, which I've also curated. Some of my own artwork is on display as well. The exhibition rooms and hallways in the building are filled with people and artwork. There are lots of little girls in pretty party dresses running around. Several repairmen are busy fixing plumbing problems under the floors in certain areas and there is other construction work going on in the large building. I speak to a tall pretty woman with curly hair, wearing an expensive looking fur coat. She doesn't speak in return but only nods. I walk around, hearing bits of conversations, aware that the show is successful and everything is running smoothly. After a while, the tall woman in the fur coat follows me outside. We walk down a long tree-lined drive. As we walk she reveals that she's deaf. Tucking her hair behind her ears, she shows me that she's wearing a large white hearing aid on each ear. She says that she doesn't usually tell people, but she feels such a connection with me. I understand that I'm being allowed access to her private world, but I'm not sure why. As we walk into a building the woman looks for a bathroom. She takes off her heavy fur coat and hands it to me to hold for her. When she returns, I feel a sudden urge to get away from her, for I feel that she wants something from me in return for having revealed her deafness. I tell her that I have to go, that I have to make sure the little girls are okay. I'm worried about them with all the construction going on, that it's dangerous, and so I leave the woman.

As I walk back through the various art galleries I notice that I'm still carrying the woman's fur coat. I decide I'll return it later, for I'm on a much more important mission: to protect all the little girls. As I walk through the building, I constantly shoo little girls away from the areas where the repairmen are working. One little girl with long dark hair asks me where Lily is. I point to the room that I'd just seen Lily scamper into. We enter the room together and are shocked to find Lily lying on the floor, naked, bruised and dirty. Her hair, arms, and legs are displayed as if someone has purposely laid her out just so. In fact, she looks dead. It's hard to fathom how this could have happened so quickly, in just a matter of seconds, but part of me knows that a second is all it takes for someone to be abused.

I tell the dark-haired girl to run and get Lily's father. When he arrives I sit him down and place Lily in his arms. She lies there draped over him like Jesus over Mary's lap in the *Pieta*. He talks and laughs, seemingly unaware of his daughter, not even noticing her condition. "Lily," I call softly. "Lily." The other little girls are all gathered around, worried looks on their faces, as I stroke Lily's body trying to warm her up, trying to wake her up. She just lies across the unemotional father's lap and I realize he doesn't really see her. I tell the other little girls that we need to leave Lily and her father alone, so they can have some private time together. Though I'm reluctant to do so, I know I must give the father a chance to connect with what has happened to his daughter.

I take the other little girls outside to play some games. As I walk through the building, I find Chuck in another room looking at some of my artwork. I tell him I need his professional opinion. He mentions how powerful all the artwork is, how surprised he was when he first saw it, but now it all starts to make sense, he says. "The deeper meaning of it." He says that people see my self-portrait and all they see are the bare breasts I've painted. If they look closer they'll find the deeper meaning, but to go deeper scares a lot of people and they'll never get beyond just seeing the body. While he talks, I lead him down the hallway to Lily. "There's a little girl, I think she's dead, she won't wake up," I quickly explain, afraid that Lily's father will think she's dead and take her away before I can get back there with Chuck.

"She doesn't need him; that's not going to work," Chuck says, as soon as we enter the room and he takes one look at the father. "I want *you* to hold her, Chuck," I say, certain that he'll be able to revive her. We get Lily away from the father, slipping her easily off his lap. As if he doesn't even notice he's been holding her, he simply gets up and walks away. Once again I notice that I'm still holding the deaf woman's fur coat. We gently place Lily in the coat and wrap her up—folding her into a fetal position—and then both Chuck and I hold her between us.

"I want you to get in there with her," Chuck says after a while. "You need to do it; you are the only one. I can guide you and help you, but you need to be the one to give her life." So I get into the fur coat with Lily. Wrapping my entire body around her, I gently hold her close to me while Chuck folds the fur coat around us and holds us in his arms. "Don't go. Don't go. Please stay," I say to Chuck in a little girl voice. "I'm here," he says, "I'm right here." We stay like that, wrapped around Lily. I know it will take time, that there is still more work to do, but that eventually she will come back to life.

Upon awakening, I see how the inner work I did yesterday, as I lay on the floor of the studio, has spilled into my dream world. It's as if my unconscious—seeing how well I did with the angry and frightened parts of my child self—has decided to connect me with another part of myself to work with in the same manner. In this dream I am introduced to my innocent self, another part to hold in my arms and love.

When I was a child, my best friend and I often pretended we had prettier names than our own, and most often I chose to be a girl named Lily. In addition, I'm not surprised that my unconscious has selected just this name, both when I was a child innocently playing with my friend and now in my dream, for the white lily flower symbolizes innocence and virginity. It's often associated with innocence being restored upon death. In the dream, I'm aware that Lily isn't dead, but that she just needs tender care and the opportunity for new life. I'm so angry at her numbskull of a father, who doesn't lift a finger to help her. He merely looks away, incapable of dealing with the troubles of his daughter, stuck in his own world. I realize this was the experience I too suffered through with my parents, as they were incapable of dealing with me, their own troubled daughter. I too was at risk of dying but, as I've now learned, I had many means of survival. My innocence, however, was tampered with, just as Lily's was, and although I now know that I was a virgin only briefly, as I work to bring my child self back to life, I look forward to fully restoring that innocence, virginity or not.

It's cold this morning and hard to get out of bed. I'd like to stay here all day rolled up in that fur coat, feeling safe and warm, but I have another life to live, so I force myself to stand up. As soon as I'm on my feet, I shift into autopilot. Breathing in the crisp scent of new fallen snow, I make coffee, get the kids up, and prepare breakfasts and lunches. With its predictable and known routines, the morning is easy to ease into, and in the time that it lasts I'm able to forget the past. I'm busy at the studio during the day too; on the phone with clients and writing estimates for upcoming jobs while people wander in looking for things to buy for the holidays.

As often as possible, I roll out my yoga mat and lie down on the floor in a fetal position. Partially hidden by my drawing table, I pull a small blanket over me and imagine that I'm wrapped up in that fur coat of my dream with Lily, always aware that she's waiting for me to return to her, needing so much, needing me. Now that I have a name for her it's easier to imagine her as a separate part, as a small confused child, half-dead with fear and loneliness. It makes it easier to deal with the state she's in as well. I'm the strong adult, knowledgeable about how the world works, capable of making decisions and caring for her own children, so I know how to do this for Lily too. However, as the day goes on, I notice how the child's neediness sometimes overpowers even this strong adult self that I am and I feel my groundedness undermined as Lily's needs take precedence. Just as I sensed my equilibrium leaving me as I drove home in the swirling snow last night, I now sense how important it's going to be that I—the adult—always remain aware, whether I'm swirling in outer space or not. If I can succeed in staying alert, and the child gets soothed, a state of balance will develop and we'll soon be in perfect symbiosis.

As the day goes on and the needs of the child stir more often, becoming known in a more visceral way, I get thrown out of my adult state and lose the tenuous balance I've been working so hard to maintain. Although I remain peripherally cognizant of being an adult, the stronger pull is into the lost child state and before I know it I'm deeply submerged in the world of the abused child. There's a critical moment, when I'm fully aware that I'm about to lose touch with my adult self, but there's nothing I can do to stop it. As if I am indeed spinning into another world, I feel myself turning inward as I once did as a child. I hear my voice changing. I have a child's voice again, my thoughts those of a child as well. I find that I'm confused, trying to figure things out, but attempting as well to distance myself from what's happening. These moments of mergence with the child last a long time before I sense my adult self again.

As I go in and out of these two states, something else begins to happen. I gradually lose my sense of self. Neither a frightened child nor a determined adult, I simply *am*. All my fears slip easily away as I sense myself merging with a great timeless sea of awareness. Gently rocked and supported, I float in this inviting ocean. I become one with the vastness of it all. Without thought, simply *knowing*, I gain clarity on just what my child self has had to deal with. I understand that although a lot of stuff got repressed, fear was always with me, a known and useful entity. Both a protector and a constant reminder, fear kept me safe in the world. I became a solitary being, a lone wanderer navigating through life on heightened alert. Now I understand that, in the long run, the fear kept me alive as well, as I certainly survived and even thrived under its vital and incessant energetic presence. However, fear need no longer play this role.

With these new insights grounding me deeper in this process of recapitulation, I take Chuck's dream guidance to go under the fur with Lily seriously. He also told me, in the dream, that it was going to take some time to heal. With the calming experience of the vast sea of awareness fresh in my mind, I set the intent for this healing to become a priority. And so, I notice that each time I roll up in a ball under the fur with Lily throughout the day, a little bit more of her fear seeps out, some of her physical tension releases, some of her mental pain is relieved too. As if I am indeed a child being held and comforted under a fur coat, I too become more relaxed and feel a little lighter each time I stand up and go back to work. I actually experience how being under the fur in this very dreamlike state, rolled into a fetal position, *is* healing me, allowing stuff to flow through me without attachment, setting in motion a new process of release and change. I actually feel myself healing, one small release at a time.

At one point, I'm suddenly aware that, as strong and innerly defiant as I've always been, my victim personality has long dominated—in my relationships, in my interactions in the world, in work as well as personal situations—as I've just followed along, letting fate drag me onward. Not that long ago, I would have balked at the notion that I was a victim, the idea abhorrent to me, but now I realize that I have lived under the spell of victimhood for most of my existence, my own energy seriously depleted and unavailable. What little I had went into just keeping myself alive. I must also acknowledge that for the first time since I began this journey, I'm beginning to experience myself as a spiritual being, more fully tapping into this long-lost connection. As I release all the things I've repressed, my long-denied spiritual needs and desires unblock as well. These are not church-oriented or religious needs and desires—the things I learned as a child—but my own innate senses of wonder and magic.

My personal awareness that life can truly be experienced on a magical level has been buried under the heavy, negative gloom of the past. Influenced from earliest childhood by my upbringing, by the worlds I was exposed to, by my choices in relationships and the paths I've elected to take, my innocent spirit has remained hidden somewhere in the complex world of my inner darkness, trampled down by reason, denial, and long-term neglect. Now I'm actually allowing magic into my life simply because I believe it *can* happen. Alongside the horrific memories, it has waited for me to return to it, to reconnect with it, and bring it into new life. Funny that two such disparate energies have resided in such close proximity all these years, in the shadowy regions inside me, and that they are emerging simultaneously; the horrific with the ecstatic, the devil with the saint, the negative with the positive, two sides of a coin, two opposing forces. But perhaps you can't have one without the other; perhaps that's just how it is.

Based solely on my personal experiences, I do believe that energetic forces outside of us assist us, whether we are aware or not. Such connection may be beyond our control and beyond our normal perception, but I fully acknowledge such activity in my own life. I have indeed been in the presence of energy that is good and kind, but I also accept that there is evil energy at work as well. I'm aware of my abuser as one of those entities working on the side of evil.

I have yet to fully understand just why I had to encounter him, but I hope that one day I will arrive at a satisfactory conclusion. On the other hand, my experiences of good energy have led me to understand that we all receive assistance, possibly at all times, but especially when we need it the most. In my case, I've had profound experiences of Jeanne Ketchel appearing in her energetic form when I have been at my most broken.

Although I've experienced the mystical, I have to say that I've never encountered an entity, good or otherwise, in a church setting. Though I spent my Catholic childhood searching for angels to guide and protect me, I never found them in the church or school I spent so many years in. By the time I went into the public school system at the age of fourteen, I realized I would have to look outside of the church for the spiritual connections I so strongly desired, and so I turned my face upward at night and prayed to the moon shining brightly into my bedroom, for I could find no other entity to connect to. Now, I find that what I needed existed all the time, within the context of everyday life, within myself; for in my experience we are all spiritual beings surrounded by other spiritual beings, seen and unseen. When we are ready and open, we may have powerful, deeply profound experiences that cannot be rationally or otherwise explained. We are always given ample opportunity to accept or reject what comes to us—we always have a choice. I believe that even people who get swept up in evil, taken into the darkness, have made the choice to do so for some reason, whether they are aware of it or not.

I've always been open to the possibility of magic, enchantingly *good* magic, for it has always intrigued me, and I've often fervently wished for its healing salvation. However, it's only now, as I more fully accept my own personal experiences of magical energy, and as I take back my innocence, that I'm ready to declare this a true possibility for all beings. Though I've suffered greatly at the hands of evil, I absolutely believe in the goodness of humankind. I am aware that all people are inherently good. It's in the masses that we lose sight of this, in ourselves and others, but if we take the time to understand each other, one person to another, we will find this to be true.

I've always wanted to be good. At times, however, it seemed to be the most difficult thing in the world, the most distant of possibilities. But now I feel goodness stirring inside me, nurturing me, cultivating a new good person, a totally different person. I am becoming aware of myself in a new way.

December 7, 2002

In a dream, I'm an overnight guest at a hotel when I discover that my car got towed in the night. I'm sitting around talking to a group of other hotel guests in someone's room, talking about how unfair it is. There are no warning signs posted anywhere letting people know that their cars might be towed. The group starts collecting money to pay for my towing costs. They sincerely want to help me, but I say, "No, I'm fine." Over and over again, I refuse the help, even though I really do need it. They seem to know this, so they collect money secretly. I get my period. I don't have anything with me and I don't ask anyone if they have a pad or tampon, but instead keep running to the bathroom to wipe the blood off as best I can, worrying that it will seep through my clothing. Eventually, we all make our way down to the hotel lobby. The stairs we take are extremely long and complicated, winding inside and outside the building. After a long and frustrating descent along this cumbersome route, we finally arrive in the lobby.

I decide to talk to the manager. I notice that the bookshelves in her office, tall cases with glass doors, are full of fossils and petrified objects, deer poop and other animal droppings among them. The shelves stand back-to-back like rows of library shelves. As I open the door on one of them and reach my hand in, to pick something up, the bookcase begins to tip forward. I catch it just in time, but then notice that the case behind it is now about to tip over. I run back and forth catching first one bookcase as it starts to fall, then the other. I see what the problem is: they are top heavy. I call for the manager to come help me. After much yelling she finally hears me and sends someone to help. I'm very surprised that she hasn't already detected the problem herself. I'm also surprised that I have to explain it to the maintenance man who comes to fix it. I show him how to brace the bookcases to make them more stable and secure.

I wake up bleeding and in pain, my dream perhaps warning me of just how engaged in this recapitulation process my body is. This is the second time I've had my period in ten days too, so I can't ignore that it's a sign that I'm going through the beginning stages of menopause as well. I refuse to get caught up in it as something to worry about, as a medical issue. I consider it just a natural aspect of the cyclical nature of being a woman. I recognize some of the symptoms as being similar to those I had when I was a young girl getting my period for the first time. My body needed time to adjust then, and so I intend to flow with this changing physical process now as well, just as I elect to flow with this recapitulation process. I will not attach to old world ideas about my changing body, and so I choose not to worry.

I did plenty of worrying in my dream, however, which I found so frustrating as I attempted to juggle everything and stay in control. I had to confront my victim personality straight off, however, the one who felt wronged, the one who was blaming the management, the one whom others felt they had to take care of. The constrained adult self refused to accept their help, though the truth was that I needed it to get my car back. So there is a sense of having to disperse the tensions between these two selves, the poor-me self and the controlling adult self. As I learned in my sea of awareness experience yesterday, the only real way to do that is to let go of *all* that controls the self.

I wonder what else this dream is trying to show me. What if I were to just let the bookcases go crashing to the floor? They aren't really my concern, though I am inordinately concerned about them in the dream. I just will not let them go down, yet at the same time they are totally inadequate, flimsy at best. Maybe the petrified poop is signifying that I'm trying to save something that is basically meaningless, just a lot of old shit? The truth is that I do have so many people and things that need my attention right now. I do feel very much like I'm running around trying to take care of everything and everyone: attending to the memories, comforting my two children as we prepare to move and leave their dad, all the problems associated with the divorce, attending to the feelings of so many family members, and taking on the move itself. Even the cats, aware that change is happening, want attention! No wonder I'm so tense! Yikes!

I talk myself into calmness, telling myself to just let go, to just float on the ocean of awareness, though my whole body is screwed up, feeling the stress. "It's okay, just let it go. You don't have to hold it in, just release, release, release. It will feel good to finally let it out."

I have no energy. My enlightened self has deserted me. I lie on the couch at the studio all day. I can't move. I finally eat some leftover Chinese food I'd left in the fridge the other day and make a cup of coffee so I can go do my stint at the artist's gallery. When I arrive, the previous attendant tells me that it's been a quiet day. There's very little activity and for the next four hours I have the place mostly to myself. At nine o'clock, I finally close up and go home.

"Before you sleep, tell yourself that in your dreams you will ask for help," Chuck had suggested the other day. So that's what I do. I set the intent to ask for help in my dreams.

December 8, 2002

I wake to find my neck a solid steel pole, stainless steel at its core, and the rest of my body as tense as steel too. I can only relax the outer layer of skin as my body staunchly refuses my normal calming suggestions. I fell asleep out of sheer exhaustion last night, still fighting the stress, which now fully envelops my body, solidly taking over. I woke once in the middle of a dream in which there was a lot of struggling going on. In spite of asking for help, none came to my rescue.

The kids are handling things at home a little better now, though both remain extremely sensitive, stressed by the situation, feeling lost and displaced by the intrusion of their grandparents and the extra demands being made on them by such elderly people in poor health. I feel such protective love for them, wanting to give them the emotional support that I never got as we weather through the final days here. I leave them asleep on this Sunday morning, the house quiet with everyone else still sleeping too, and head out to a yoga class, intent on working on the bottled up tension.

While sitting in meditation at the beginning of the class, I contemplate how I'm finally reawakening and reconnecting with my spiritual self. Sitting peacefully, eyes closed, feeling a good silence inside and out, I realize just how distant I've been from sensing myself as a spiritual being. I accept that my spiritual disconnect wasn't anyone else's fault, though in the past I've tended to blame everything on someone else, from how they were treating me, to what they did or didn't do to me or for me. But the truth is, there is no one else to blame. The connection to my spirit was almost severed because I just couldn't go there for a long time. It wasn't that I was rejecting my spirit, but it confronted me with things I just wasn't ready to face. I see that now. I've only been able to handle certain things, and sometimes that has meant totally absenting myself from my inner world, leaving it for long stretches of time. Any spiritual yearnings that did emerge or sought my attention had to struggle against my personal issues—my feelings of deep inadequacy, my state of victimhood, of not being good enough or deserving of anything—the deprecating aspects of self that have played such an important role in my life thus far.

As I continue meditating, I recapitulate how occasionally a bit of that vulnerable inner world would emerge in my artwork, but it wasn't really until the past year that I finally dared to let my spirit speak more fully, even in that manner. For a time, when I lived in Sweden and was married to my first husband, I embraced the magic of that cold, mysterious country, with its folklore of little people and fairy helpers, incorporating it into my artwork. Having run from my past, it was a time of breakthrough for me in many ways, a very important time, but once I returned to the States, I let the magic recede. For the most part, I was unable to incorporate it into the self who emerged upon return from that exodus into foreign lands, as I forged a new self so different from the young woman who had left nearly a decade before. More often than not, the voice of my spiritual self was drowned out by the louder expressions of dismissal of such concepts by others, overpowered by the doubters—the rational ones who "knew" that such things as magic, psychic powers, astrology, reincarnation, ghosts, angels, and fairies did not exist. And so, I suppressed my own spiritual inquisitiveness and deep hunger for knowledge of such things. Unable to accede to the idea of it being mere childish fantasy or delusional imagining, however, I never allowed it to totally die. Somewhere inside me it slumbered.

As I meditate, I feel a new acceptance awakening that, yes, it *is* true: I do have a very receptive spirit and a deep spiritual hunger. Suddenly, I am given an image of tiny winged spirits emerging from the ground, like seventeen-year locusts, and I watch as they fly into the woods to revive a tiny sleeping beauty, a little Lily wrapped in her fur. I see that she is very needy, but I know that eventually she will fully awaken to embrace a new life, and I will too. This magical image fades as the class begins. I realize I met my husband seventeen years ago. The long incubation period is over—I have awakened, and transformation is indeed taking place!

After the yoga class I go to the studio to get some work done, but to no avail, for I am unable to forget the magical image of the tiny winged creatures. Much like the large painting I had done for my recent show, of the sixteen winged little girls flying out of entombment in the colorful tree, I sense that they are asking me to take this message from my spirit seriously. And so, once again, I lie down on my yoga mat and roll up into a comforting ball with my inner wounded child, my little Lily. Pulling the imaginary fur coat around us, I let her know that I'm here. I tell her that I'm sorry it took me so long, that I had to go away for a while and learn how to grow up, so I could come back and get her. I tell her that I know she felt abandoned, forgotten, but now I'm back for good. I tell her that I love her and I'm so proud of her. I tell her that she's so brave and strong, and I know she needs me. I know she desires that I never leave her again, but in order to do that she needs to learn to trust me, so we can go on together now.

"I was there too," I tell her, "We can leave the past and go on from here, making new memories for ourselves. We can live a new life, with new people who love and understand us. We don't have to stay in this sad and painful place."

"Don't turn your back on me," I say to her. "You and I need each other. We can't go anywhere unless we go together. You can trust me, you have to, because you are me—and I am you. We belong together. Let me hold you and warm you and make you feel again."

"It's safe to come out of hiding now, to come out of the tunnel, up to the surface for air and breath, light and love. Be open with me! Come up to the light with me! Come up and find new life with me! We'll settle into our little house and take care of ourselves and our kids and our cats. We'll settle in and learn a new way of living, being open and unafraid."

"I've been busy finding safe places for us to go," I tell her, "to Chuck's, to yoga, to the studio, and the gallery. There are dangers along the way, but we're aware of them now, and we know how to trust our instincts and intuition. We know how to save our very souls, how to turn and attack the demon when necessary. And I can stand to watch him suffer now, even while I feel disgusted and triumphant, horrible and proud, ugly and beautiful! And I can do it over and over again, and when you feel like it, I invite you to help out if you want to."

In spite of the potential for new life that now feels so tangible, I end up feeling lost and sad as I lie on the floor, ready to cry, to have a long jag of release, but I can't get anything out. Instead, I end up feeling miserable, suddenly full of fear again, as I lie on the floor whispering these things to my child self.

"I need to shift away now," I tell Lily. "I have other things to do. I'll come back later. I'm going to try drawing, to see if I can get anything out in visual expression."

I sit with my feet tucked under me and draw for about an hour and then turn to meditation again, the morning experience pulling me. Suddenly, I am out-of-body, no longer sitting on the sofa at the studio but transported to my grandmother's house. I am myself, the adult me, as well as myself as Lily, a little girl of seven. I'm sitting on a little footstool in front of the fireplace. It's Christmas day and I'm wearing a white blouse and red plaid kilt that my grandmother made for me.

"I love you," I, the adult, say to the little girl sitting so primly.

She looks at me, then turns back to face the fire. I know she needs someone to love her. I suggest that she lie by the fire and get cozy and warm. She looks at me again, and I know what she's thinking. "No, he'll get me," she's thinking. "I have to sit up straight, with my legs and ankles shut tightly together. If I lie down he'll get me. I'll be exposed and vulnerable and he can poke a stick inside me." I know this. I know she's afraid because I am too. I'm afraid that he'll get us. He's still lurking in the past, waiting for us to walk by. I know I have to get rid of him.

I pull back into the present, though I am still in deep meditation. Once again I feel the sofa beneath me. I am sitting in the studio again. My breathing is deep and long. Memories come to me and, as they do, anger erupts out of me, fueling another violent reaction. I decide to put my abuser on his own homemade rack, the one he made for me. Now I am an abuser. In my imagination, I shove him to the ground and onto his back, stake his arms to the ground with his legs hanging over the rack so his private parts are exposed. I apply clamps and wrenches to his genitals and I stick a hammer handle up his ass. I plug his mouth with leaves and dirt and I leave him there, alone and vulnerable, to experience the stench of fear. Later, I burn him over a grill—for a long time. I toast him until he's blackened on both sides, and then I feed him to the lions, the ferocious kind, the kind that make your heart shake inside you when they roar. Then I bash his charred remains with a stick until they are pulverized into ash so that there is no possibility of him ever coming back to life. I have to totally destroy him so he won't be able to come back and haunt us, so we'll be able to innocently lie on the floor without fear of intrusion, so that we can do a simple little thing like lie by a fire and get warm.

As I come out of the meditation, I am somewhat horrified at my vicious attack on my abuser, and yet it feels right. Nothing else will do. I realize that, in some sense, I still feel that he's a threat. I haven't killed him enough times yet. There are still memories to deal with, and some of them are still fresh and painful. I need more time to process, to recapitulate, and to get rid of him, to rid myself of him. If I don't exorcise him, the memories will continue to fester like old wounds, getting re-infected over and over again. Every time I crawl into the tunnel to lick my wounds, the dirt from the tunnel will keep them painfully alive. It's time to thoroughly clean them. It's time to expose all the wounds, to allow air and light to heal them, so that one day I can lie on the floor without feeling vulnerable, without having to protect myself, without having to constantly be alert.

I know that all I have to do is take my abuser's hand in my imagination and walk into the woods with him and a new memory will emerge. But even the ones that have already emerged are still so powerful, so fresh that I have to be careful that I don't freak out when in yoga class. Some yoga postures continue to trigger me. Immediately, I revert to a vulnerable little girl, and although I know he can't get me it still feels like he can. When triggered, I am no longer simply lying on the floor in the yoga studio. I am also back in the woods with him, the smell of dirt and leaves strongly intrusive. I hear the clank of his tool box being set down by my ear, and the panting of his breath. I know how Lily feels, sitting by the fire with her legs clamped shut. I still do that too, my legs aching from the effort of being clamped tightly shut for the past fifty years.

Part of me wants to get this process over with, to hurry to the next level, but the memories keep pulling me back, reminding me that I'm not done yet, that I have to take my time, allowing them to guide me. The little girl sitting by the fire isn't afraid of me, I realize, she's afraid of him—my abuser. So I'll sit beside her and we'll go through the memories together. We'll go through the feelings and the fears, slowly, one step at a time until we feel good about moving on, when we can do so without him coming along with us. At this point, I realize we're still attached to him. Until we recapitulate everything, we're still upholding the pact we made with him so long ago.

Just thinking about my abuser opens the door to a memory. Ropes are tied around my waist, between my legs, cutting into my crotch. He is pulling me along as we walk the dog. I am the dog and we are playing the Doggie game. I feel and smell the ropes. I feel the earth beneath my hands and knees. I smell the dirt and leaves in the woods. I am a puppy. I see a rope swing contraption hanging off the branch of a tree in the woods. He walks me over there and hangs me in it, tying me into it so that my legs are pulled apart, my genitals exposed. I am helpless. He lies on the ground beneath me, poking sticks into me.

"I'm opening you up!" he says.

December 9, 2002

In a dream, I've been selected to go on a special trip in a spaceship. I'm only allowed to bring a few items along on the journey. I bring a few dolls, some doll clothes and tiny doll shoes that belong to my daughter. While in outer space, I have to go outside the spaceship and make a repair. Clinging to the outside of the ship, hanging by a few wires, I am attacked by some kind of mite that gets inside my spacesuit. Once back inside the spaceship, it's determined that I must go through a cleansing ritual to get rid of the mites before heading back to Earth. Part of the ritual entails walking along a very narrow and precariously steep staircase to enter the delousing chamber. Once deloused, I will head directly back to Earth.

I'm allowed to bring only a few things back to Earth with me, whatever I can carry. I select a few of the doll items that I'd originally brought with me, while the mites burn my skin, biting voraciously. The doll items are very important to my daughter and I don't know how I'll tell her that I had to leave some of them behind. I begin climbing the steep staircase that leads to the door of the delousing chamber when I suddenly realize I'll never be able to make it with my arms so full. I need my hands free so I can pull myself up by the railings. It's the only way to climb the narrow, rickety staircase, and so I start dropping a few things at a time. One by one I let them fall to the floor below. People standing in the vestibule below start yelling at me as the doll items rain down on them, telling me that I have to hurry or it will be too late. "Go, hurry, just go!" they say. "You don't have time to waste!" With their urgent cries ringing in my ears, I toss all the doll items away and quickly climb the last of the stairs, wondering once again how I'll explain to my daughter that I had to leave her things on a spaceship in outer space. As soon as I enter the delousing chamber I am deloused and sent back to Earth. I have only been gone for a few days, but it seems like a much, much longer time.

In a second dream, I meet a woman who is a jeweler. I watch as she prepares to exhibit at a large art show in a new arts center. I'm aware that the new center is not going to be built in time and that she will be disappointed. I feel deeply sorry for her because I know how excited she is and how important the art show is to her. This reminds me of the long wait to move into my little blue house.

I feel a similar frustration as I wait for the previous owner's new house to be built.

In another dream, I have two dogs. My kids and I are walking with them when a large dog comes running up to us, barking loudly. My two dogs are frightened, cowering and whimpering, but my kids protect them. We are headed to the train station to take the train into New York City. To get to the train we have to walk down a long flight of steps that are covered with children's books. At first, I try to read the titles of the books as we walk past, but soon realize that there are too many, way too many, and that I will never be able to read them all. In the end I step over them, kicking them out of the way, so we can get to the train platform on time.

We get onto the train, which is very long and crowded. I see Chuck sitting in a seat, nodding and smiling encouragingly, though he doesn't say anything to me. Even here the floors are covered with children's books, making it difficult to walk. As we make our way down the aisle, a group of boys gets between the kids and me. I lose sight of my son for a few seconds and when I find him again a man is molesting him. I scream at the man and beat him up. "Good, you reacted!" I tell myself, feeling strong and invincible.

The kids and dogs and I walk to the very end of the train, to the last car where there are big windows, where it's light and airy and very sunny. But then I notice that the train doesn't end here; in reality it never ends, it keeps going and going. As we speed along, I see many, many cars leading into the bright distance ahead of us. Even here it's really crowded and there's no place to sit. "Come on," I say, "let's keep going." We continue walking onward, passing through one car to the next, through the endless cars, all of them crowded. I'm aware that it's imperative that I not lose my kids and dogs in the crowd as we walk through this endless train. I'm also aware that there is no need to go back or look back, the only thing that matters is to keep going. I must, at all costs, keep going, keep moving quickly through this speeding train.

I am still riding that train as I awaken. As I open my eyes and sit up, I see it heading right into the endless brightness ahead me, straight into oncoming time, right through the wall of my bedroom. I know, for certain, that it's the right train to be on. In spite of the risks and challenges, I am in a most positive state as I ride this train, undaunted by anything. I'm aware that this positive state is just what I've been working so hard to achieve as I do this recapitulation. When I was on the spaceship and had to pack up for the cleansing ritual, I was less sure of myself. I wanted to take everything with me that I had brought, because I only brought what I thought was important to begin with, but a group of women standing nearby laughed at me. "Look at her," they said, "she thinks she can take all that back with her." They told me to just leave it all, that I couldn't take any of it with me. "You don't have time, it's too much to carry," they shouted to me. In the end, I had to let everything go. I was so disappointed at first, but I worried mostly about how to explain to my daughter—to my child self really—that I was leaving her things behind. In the end it didn't really matter. I'm fully aware that if I am to truly transform, I must do so with complete detachment.

The middle dream seemed to be about now and dealing with the frustrations of moving. I'm making all the right preparations, though part of me realizes that other circumstances, beyond my control, may arise. Can I go with the flow? In the final dream, I finally felt good, sure and strong. Stepping over the children's books, as I entered the train station, seemed to indicate leaving my childhood behind, this time for good, the contents of the books known, reckoned with at last. Chuck showing up in the dream and nodding encouragingly seemed to indicate that I was on the right track.

I wake up from this trilogy of dreams aware, however, that I won't be free to take the journey if I don't complete this most important task of recapitulation. Only in shedding everything will I really be able to understand and embrace new experiences as I go forward. I'm learning patience as I let the recapitulation process lead me deeper into my inner world, but I'm still able to look ahead and see the light at the end of the tunnel. I am assured that one day I will exit the tunnel. After this dream, I'm fully aware that the light up ahead is endless and that I am about to tap into an endless flow of energy.

December 10, 2002

"I'm suffering!" I say, tense and shaky when I meet with Chuck early in the morning.

"What do you feel you need to do for yourself?" he asks.

I elect to lie down on the floor, but what I really want to do is kick and scream and cry. "Why can't I express this need?" I ask myself, full of self-hatred for my inability to be honest, to speak the truth about what I'm feeling and to act on it. It seems such an impossibility, that's why. The prospect of actually putting myself in a vulnerable position in order to carry through with fully expressing myself is frightening, impossible even in the privacy of my own home. There's no way I'm ready to do so in the presence of another human being, and so I suffer through the emergence of deeply entrenched feelings, now becoming known as *real feelings*.

A big old crying jag might offer some relief, but I can't even do that and I don't want to bite, pinch, or hurt myself anymore either, which I've been resorting to lately. I want to learn how to feel and express myself in a healthy way, but for the moment I simply lie on the floor and let my physical body do its own thing. In desperate and confused turmoil, I resort to the usual. I automatically roll into a tight little ball and push everything away, just as my child self always did. I lie with my cheek pressed into the hard floor, listening to Chuck's voice, steadily resolute, telling me that I don't have to clench anymore. He tells me that my abuser can't get me anymore, and, as much as I know this is true, my body cannot stop protecting me. It behaves as it always has, tensing against the inevitable probability that I will be assaulted, that out of nowhere will come the man who abused me. Even though it has been many decades since he was actually anywhere near me, my body holds the violence of the past in its very fibers.

I am somewhat present, but mostly gone, already in my usual state of semi-dissociation before Chuck has spoken many words of encouragement. I become more fully aware that I have not yet connected with this physical body that I walk around in every day. It does not really belong to me. I make it move, talk, eat, sleep, etc., but I do not really reside in it. I am an enigma, half woman, half ghost, wandering aimlessly, looking for a place to rest. Now, lying stiffly on the floor, I listen to Chuck's voice, his warm intonations directing me to acceptance of what is so clearly true; that my abuser never really got to *me*; he didn't get to the tremendous inner strength. I have to go back and find that strength again in order to move on now. I know it's what made me invincible, what enabled me to live into adulthood and become the person I am today. That invincibility resides inside me still; it's what I'm constructed of. Although I cannot find a connection to it in this body at this moment, I do know that I still hold, somewhere within me, the strength that my child self tapped into in order to survive, to forget, and to move on.

Chuck's voice calms me. I acknowledge to him that I know my abuser can't get me anymore. I know I don't have to hold my legs tightly together anymore either. I don't have to clench and wonder when he'll pop up in front of me. *He won't get me anymore.* My mind accepts this. Now I must let my body know the same, so I can let go of the ever-present fear of kidnap, violation, and penetration. He can't do it anymore. Even if he's still alive, he doesn't have the power anymore. And in the end, he only had a certain kind of power over me because he could never fully own me, he could never totally absorb me. I survived his cruel and totally self-obsessive behavior.

With Chuck's voice providing a calming overtone, I turn and go deeply inward, far back to the survival instinct, tapping into the tremendous power that kept me alive. I acknowledge that this base instinct has totally impacted and usurped my body and psyche for fifty long years. I acknowledge that though it once kept me safe, its work is now done.

"You don't have to clench, you don't have to keep fighting," I hear Chuck's calming voice saying. I accept this truth: *my body's work is done.*

"He's no longer here; you can let go. You're free of him forever. He can't touch you; he can't ever, ever, ever get to you again. You can let go of the hold he has over you; just let it go. Stop holding it in. Let him go. You are in control now. Let him out, and you will be free," Chuck says, and I swim back to the present, the sound of his voice so gentle and calm.

"That's the irony of this whole thing!" I say, as I emerge from deep within, to the sunlight on my face, a smile breaking the surface of my usually sad and serious demeanor. "After all these years of being possessed by him, my life controlled by him, I've had the capacity within me to let him go this entire time. I just didn't know it!"

"Yes!" says Chuck.

"You make it sound so easy," I tell Chuck, as I get up off the floor. "You make it sound as simple as falling asleep. But we know how hard that can be sometimes. Sometimes we just can't do it."

"Don't dwell on it," he says. "Believe it. And, as frightening as it was, believe what happened in the past too, and then let it go."

"I know. I have the strength to do that; I've already proven that I have the strength," I say, the session over.

As I leave, I wonder if there are still more memories that I haven't accessed yet. Do I really have to go through them in order to heal, to become clean, to no longer feel dirty and defiled, to become free, as Chuck suggests? As I drive to the studio, I confront, with utter clarity, the bitter truth that my abuser had no respect for me as a child or as a human being, that he was a brute of the worst kind, insanely cruel and vicious. Just thinking these thoughts makes me clench, but I realize that Chuck is right. I need to let it all go—the thoughts, the memories, and the physical clenching—in order to heal. And the only way to do that is by confronting it, facing the truth of it, and letting it go through me.

I have to learn that I'm fully capable of letting go and that, no matter how difficult this part of the process may be, *I am safe.* I must give myself credit for how far I've come because, truthfully, just being able to talk, being able to recognize and acknowledge how I feel, just allowing myself to have feelings and express them, even incrementally, are milestones in themselves. This is about learning to trust the process on a deeper level now, letting it take me, while I learn to let go to it, within my body.

If I consider my body as merely a shell, I am able to accept that my abuser never really touched me, the real me, the energetic spirit of me, because he couldn't—ever—and so he still can't. No one can ever *touch* the real me, the soul that resides in this carapace of a body, the part of me that will one day move on to new life when my body dies. But I fully accept that my abuser's energy affected my energy, and that is what I am ridding myself of, his energetic attachment to my invitingly tasty energy—my innocence.

December 11, 2002

Once again, I awaken early to distant dreams too far gone to recall, but a memory of waking in the middle of the night clenched into a tight ball is crystal clear, especially as I find myself in the same state now. As I search for a sense of self inside this pain-wracked body, I remember that even during the total relaxation of *shavasana* in yoga class yesterday, I couldn't totally relax. I ask my body once again, very gently, to release itself from the ancient ritual of clenching. "It's okay, you don't have to hold anything in anymore. Relax and let it go, just let it go," I say as I flex my limbs, and slowly unfurl from the tight ball I still sleep in every night.

I know I must be vigilant and persistent, that change will only come slowly, as my body memory releases its longstanding rigidity, the shield once so successfully instituted and utilized against the brutalities of life. Once my body understands that those brutalities are no longer present, I expect release will come more quickly.

It's interesting to notice how my body constantly reacts to memories, even to ones so deeply buried that it has taken fifty years for them to surface. I'm aware now that my body's own unique memory system has always been conscious of them, the automatic clenching process so well-established long ago. Deeply rooted, it has been kept in good working order. I'm almost in awe of the ability of the psyche to prevent access, to savor the few moments of peace by keeping me clenched, safely in protective custody. As the intensity and horror of the old memories emerge from their storage containers, from depositories deep in my tissues, I'm thankful for this achingly rigid body. It had done its job well. But I will not settle for the old process now, for I no longer wish to live like this. I turn inward again and find that inner strength at the core of my soul, the strength that once set up this system of clenching and protecting. I ask it to do it's magic to carry me forward now. I ask for a new kind of magic to sweep through me now and free me of everything my abuser once did to me.

I finally get out of bed, a little less stiffly than normal, set the coffee on and go wake the kids for school. My daughter is depressed and nauseous, so I let her stay in bed. I tell her that as long as she doesn't have a fever she'll have to go back to school tomorrow, for I'm sure she'll feel better when she's around her friends, away from the depression of me.

Happy to have successfully averted the usual urge to stay in bed this morning myself, I remain consciously aware of my body as the day goes on. Intent on relaxing my muscles and keeping my shoulders loose, I constantly work at pushing them down out of their normal hunch, though it's really a futile effort as they immediately spring right back up again. I only get in an hour's worth of work at the studio before my son calls to say that school is closing early due to threatening weather. I clean up and, just as I'm about to head out the door, my lawyer calls to tell me that the divorce just came through. I spend the rest of the day at home cleaning and packing, feeling happier than in a long time. The afternoon passes quickly and before I know it, it's snowing heavily and night is upon us once again.

December 12, 2002

I wake to a snowy morning and closed schools. At long last I have an excuse to stay in bed later than normal. I snuggle down under the covers again and my body immediately grabs the opportunity to take me into a memory. Tumbling down into the tunnel of self, I experience my body as completely empty, a mere carcass. I scan it with my awareness, sensing and feeling nothing, neither inside my body nor outside it. Pressing and pinching my skin, I don't feel anything physically either. I'm simply not present in my body—in any sense. I hold onto this feeling of non-existence for as long as possible, this absence of self from body, this state of nothingness, until a dark river of sadness washes over me, plunking me right back into the physical. As I ask my body to relax and let the sadness go through me, I sense hot anger rising from the pit of my stomach, flaming upward. Sensing predatory energy nearby, I kick out, warning it to stay far away.

At the same time that I'm in an old place, recapitulating an old memory, I'm also aware that I must find a way to express the enormity of feelings that are overwhelming my entire being. Somehow I must expel the rising ball of fire inside me, but I just cannot open my mouth and throat to release it. The next thing I know I'm struggling simply to breathe. As if my brain has shut down, no amount of effort or concentration produces a breath. Suddenly something so natural as breathing is impossible. I'm suffocating! In the next second, on the verge of panic, something else takes over and I'm able to suck in a gulp of air. With a loud gasp my lungs expand and then it's easier to take the next breath and the next. I can't believe I forgot how to breathe!

Breathing in deep gulping breaths, I'm surprised to find myself in bed, snow piling up on the windowsills, the room cold, the morning sky gray and overcast, heavy snow falling, my lungs aching. Breathing more fully, giving myself permission to luxuriate in the absence of duty, I contemplate this strange memory. Though it came with no visual memory, no specific time or place, there was something familiar about it. Even though it was a memory solely of dissociation, of being out-of-body, it felt related to something that I've already recapitulated. Perhaps it's the final struggle to fully release an old memory, though it also had the feel of death about it, as if I were not only out-of-body, but also incapable of returning or perhaps was reluctant to do so. Caught for a moment in the struggle to remember how to breathe, it wasn't until something else kicked in that I thought, "Oh yeah, that's how you breathe!" For a few brief moments, however, my body did not have the ability to take a breath, as if my energy was completely absent. I wonder if this experience might relate to the drowning memory I recapitulated last year.

As I scan the many experiences from my past that once held me in their grip, both as they emerged into consciousness and each time I've returned to them, I find that many of them are no longer bothersome. They are beginning to recede, which means that I'm getting somewhere! Whatever this morning's memory refers to, I know that I'll probably have to come back to it, until I'm completely done—desensitized—until it no longer grips me.

Last week, I disappeared into memories quite often. Now I realize I may have used them to escape the tensions at home, to disappear from and avoid the unpleasantness that has arisen, the conflicts and criticisms that seem to come out of nowhere, as I pack and prepare to leave. I'll be moving out in nine days.

December 14, 2002

I sleep bundled up, tightly ensconced in my old position. Though my dreams are about transformation, I am unable to fully bridge them into waking awareness, losing the details immediately upon emergence from sleep. I'm aware, however, that I started out curled up, tightly closed and silent in my dreams, like a hard seed or cocoon. By the end of the night of dreaming and now upon awakening, I'm aware that I've grown and changed. I've unfurled and come alive, having expressed myself vocally and in extroverted fashion all night long, shouting loudly and without restriction. I wake up from this dream experience feeling physically alive and vibratory. Like a butterfly emerging from a cocoon, I feel utterly transformed, a totally new person at last!

Even after my night of transformation, I struggle with the old self all day. As opposed to the person in my dreams, I am restricted and held back. I find myself biting down hard on my teeth, clenching and holding in pain, frustration, disappointments, and rage. I experience the deep sadness of loss as I confront my changing self. After working at my drawing table for an hour, I find that I can barely walk when I stand up, so clenched am I.

In the evening, after feeding the kids and getting them started on homework, I go into my bedroom and punch hard into my pillows. Breathing the recapitulation breath, I exhale the utter stench of my abuser that has been overwhelming me all day and get myself into a calmer place. I do yoga to physically release the steadily mounting tension, aware that a lot of stuff may surface as I face the next few days of packing and preparing to move.

December 15, 2002

I awaken to intense bodily pain, as if surgeons have snuck into my room during the night and inserted a steel bar straight across my pelvis. They've left this bar tightly torqued between my hipbones, pushing them further and further apart, and they are now on the point of breaking. I find that another steel bar has been inserted into my neck, lying heavily against the nerves, keeping it rigid and unmoving. In excruciating pain, all I can think to do is have a freaking tantrum! I punch my pillows as hard as I can, and to a certain extent it feels really good, but I get no relief from the steely tension. I know I must keep my focus on countering it with physical relaxation and incremental release. I'm fully aware that my body is showing me that the current issues will only be resolved in the bones and muscles of my body.

It's Sunday morning after a crazy weekend of everyone in the house getting sick with a stomach virus. I haven't succumbed but now my daughter is sick. In addition, my mother-in-law—always so restricted in her life and now receding into Alzheimer's—has been crying loudly through the nights, releasing with a vengeance. It's a bit like being on a ship in a stormy sea, the passengers moaning and groaning while the ship tosses and turns. The captain, my husband, runs around trying to keep his elderly parents calm, though there is no holding back the churning seas. After a fairly sleepless night I drag myself out of bed, get something to eat, and concentrate on packing, being careful not to breathe too much of the communal air, washing my hands often as I care for my daughter. I've already read four books this weekend, reading to forget, to block out what's churning inside, as well as to gain distance from the rest of the household.

After much procrastination throughout the day, my son finally focused on getting his homework done, but it's late at night now. He's apparently counting on a delay or no school because of a prediction of more snow. Maybe he'll get lucky. My daughter, still not feeling well, will stay home tomorrow anyway. As I tuck them into bed, I tell them they're great kids, doing a wonderful job of holding up, and that I'm proud of them for keeping such a good sense of humor as we go through this dismantling of our lives.

Crawling into my own bed, I lie on my side and note how I immediately clench into a tight and painful knot. I switch onto my back and finally fall asleep. I am conscious, throughout the night, of reminding myself to relax and change positions often.

December 16, 2002

I dream that I'm kicking. I kick out so hard with both legs that I wake myself up. Wow, I kicked! I note that I'm still lying on my back, and I realize I've made a breakthrough of sorts. When I wake my son, the first thing he wants to know is if it snowed during the night.

"Sorry honey," I say. "School today!"

He is utterly disappointed.

The divorce papers arrive in the mail. Now it's done, my transformation papers are in hand; my passport to moving on to new life, dated, stamped and filed.

December 17, 2002

I'm furious when I meet with Chuck, anger bubbling inside. I watch his face brighten as I tell him that I've been sending it into my pillows, hitting them as hard and long as I can.

"You just reminded me that I have an old punching bag in the barn!" he says, and for some reason I already know this.

"I don't know how," I say, a little surprised, "but the other day, as I was hitting my pillows, I had the thought that you had a punching bag in your barn."

He tells me he'll get it out so I can use it another time, but for now he'll go outside to get a stick. While I wait for him to return, I quake with fear at the thought of having to perform, the idea of having to hit a punching bag or anything else abhorrent to me. It goes against the grain of the quiet, peaceful being I am. He comes back into the office and hands me a big stick. Placing a pillow on the back of a chair, he instructs me to hit it. I take a few tentative swings and then, to my surprise, I let the anger come forth. I whack the hell out of the pillow, surprising Chuck as well.

"You aren't just a tiny girl; you could kill a man!" Chuck exclaims.

"Well, that's the point isn't it?" I say, breaking the stick in half as I take another hit.

Chuck goes back outside and gets another, bigger stick.

"This looks sturdy," he says, handing it to me, a big smile on his face. "How about getting some sound out too?"

"I can't."

"Try yelling at him," Chuck suggests, but nothing, not a peep emerges from my lips as I continue to whack the hell out of the pillow.

"Don't worry, it will come," he says, suggesting that calling up a memory of my abuser might help.

"Oh, that's easy!"

Immediately, my abuser is on the ground in front of me, digging a hole in the ground, his back to me. I lift the big stick again and whack him over the head, and then hit him with a steady round until I just can't lift the stick another time. Exhausted, I sink to my knees and hand it back to Chuck.

"I can't do it," I say, my energy depleted.

"What do you mean, you can't? You just creamed him!" Chuck says, clearly delighted with the outcome.

"Yeah, the more I hit the better I felt!" I say, as we sit back down in our chairs to process what just happened.

By the time I leave I feel great, the tension released. I go to a yoga class and then work at the studio finishing up some commissions before the holidays. In the evening, I see Chuck waiting for his daughter in the crowd after the school holiday band concert. I'm waiting for my own kids to gather their things and meet up with me. I am stunned into painful silence at the sight of him. I can't say hi or even look in his direction again. It's almost impossible to take him in outside the intimacy of the office, as if he doesn't really exist outside of those fifty-minute sessions. There's too much intensity, too much personal stuff preventing contact. My inner process must be kept sacred, between two strangers who only coexist for about an hour on Tuesday mornings. At other times, we simply don't exist in the same world.

December 19, 2002

I dream that a guy is trying to force his way in through my door, beating it with a stick. He gets it open, but I'm ready for him. I whack him hard on the arm with my own stick. He howls and goes away. Later he comes back and I'm ready with the stick again. He has three people with him this time, but as soon as they see me with the stick they take off running and yelling. "She's crazy! She's crazy!"

In another dream, I easily carry a huge china cabinet on my back. I feel strong and capable as I walk down the streets of New York City, only slightly bent over by the weight of the china cabinet. I go into a restaurant looking for my father. I find him sitting at a table with two women, drinking wine. "My purse," I say, making a joke about the china cabinet. Then I tell my father that it's time for him to go home. "She means it!" one of the women says. "She's fierce!" says the other. We go outside the restaurant. There's a pathway that winds around the grounds of the restaurant and eventually leads into some nearby mountains. One of the women asks me if I've ever taken this path. "Yes, I have," I say, "but there isn't time now, it's too long and winding. I'm on a different path now." She's reluctant to leave, however, until she's been on 'the path,' and even though I try to dissuade her, she leaves us to take the long route over the mountains.

I wake up in awe, the stick used in my session with Chuck also being put to good use in my dream. Even the women in the restaurant seem aware that I carry a big stick, and that I'm not afraid to use it. I'm strong enough to carry a china cabinet on my back after all, as if it's nothing. This dream seems to reflect the truth of where I am right now, a fearless and fierce traveler taking a more direct route. In fact, I have a specific goal in mind—to finish this recapitulation—and I'm already aware that the old route offers nothing of value. Eager to hurry on, I set out in a new direction, carrying all that I need on my back.

The anxiety of this week of change has everyone in a state of breakdown. The kids are both feeling sick. Anxious and tense, they cry easily. My son feels that no one in the whole world has it as bad as he has it right now. I know he's miserable, but I'm pushing him to go to school and just get through the next two days before the holidays start. My daughter, sick all day yesterday, finally slept quietly through the night, but she needs another day in bed. She's worried about all the schoolwork she's been missing. I calm her down and then almost panic myself as I awaken with a sore throat. I immediately push all thoughts of illness away—I just want to get myself moved over to the new house on Saturday and then I can collapse. I'm trying to hold it all together for the kids, needing to be strong for them, but also for myself, so I can accomplish all that I've set out to do as smoothly as possible. It really does feel as if I'm walking around with a huge china cabinet strapped onto my back!

December 20, 2002

In a dream, I move my futon mattress into the new house. As I drag it across the front porch and in through the door, I notice that it's wider than I thought. I squeeze, shove, and cram it through the doorway, finally getting it into the house where I put it down on the living room floor. I notice a few things have been left behind by the previous owners, but I figure it's still okay for me to move in.

Now my son has the stomach virus and I have the same sore throat I had earlier. I just want to get moved in—then I don't care!

December 21, 2002

Today is moving day! I went to bed early last night, my throat still sore, but I feel much better now. A bit of softening is taking place inside me at the same time that I know I am mentally, emotionally, and even physically stronger than ever. I know I have lots of caring people around me, but right now I just need to get myself moved in and then I can collapse if I need to.

I fend off my parents who call several times, telling them I won't be attending my father's birthday party later in the day. "I'm too tired," I say, "I'm exhausted, I'm moving," and then I have to withstand the harsh comments of my mother's disappointment, old insinuations that I'm just a selfish girl, selfish for taking some time for myself. I don't fall for it, but instead allow myself to take a new stance. I push her stale, long-overused criticisms away and begin to accept the truth: I don't like her. I also see her as a figure in an old world that I'm leaving. She has no role in my new world and I'm not interested in bringing her with me. I stand up to her, wish my father a happy birthday, and hang up the phone. I have no time to dwell on them. I have work to do!

As I begin the move to the new house, an image of a tiny girl materializes. Appearing to be fragile, almost breakable, she's filled with tremendous inner strength. I'm aware that she is truly able to protect herself and she's not afraid to use her inner strength when she needs it. A major factor in her transformational process is the element of surprise, which she uses to her full advantage. I'm aware that I have similar qualities at the core of my being, that I am this little girl. These qualities can never be destroyed. In fact, they support me always, powerfully releasing when needed. I envision a tiny pearl of strength that exerts much power when needed. I tap into it now, even though I feel fragile too, as I carry my belongings out of the old house, pack them into the van, and make endless trips to the new house.

Like the strong woman in my dream, who sent her father home and refused the old pathway, I reject an old sense of duty as I set about moving my things to the new house. As the day goes on my confidence in my ability to handle anything builds, and the sense of that pearl of strength inside me solidifies into a glowing center that never loses its luster, that is calm and eternal, passing from one life to another, seeding itself where it knows it will grow. I sense it has always been present, supporting me, but now I'm more cognizant of it. I'm aware that I must nurture it if I am to reach my full potential. That glowing pearl inside me has saved me, and yet I'm also aware that I must reciprocate by nourishing, tending, and allowing it to grow along with me now, because it too has yet to reach its full maturity and potential.

December 22, 2002

We've spent our first night in the new house! I've only moved a few things in. The rest of our belongings remain in the garage, boxes and furniture piled high. I did the move all on my own, and my futon mattress barely fit through the front door, just as my dream predicted. I had to shove, squeeze, and force it in, but finally, with a great and mighty push, I got it through and laid it on the living room floor where it will stay for the time being. On each trip, I took as much as I could handle, packing the van many times, driving it over, unpacking, and going back for more. I used a hand truck to move the big things. Used to working with furniture on a daily basis in my business, I had no difficulty maneuvering, tipping, and shoving everything into the van, doing the same to get it out. Like the strong woman in my dream, I was not going to be daunted by the prospect of moving everything by myself, even a china cabinet!

I took only the things I wanted, what belonged to me personally, or came from my side of the family. I left the kids' rooms largely intact, still set up for them to go there on their every other weekend visits. Until I finish the painting, and before the new carpeting arrives, everything will stay in the garage, including their beds. The only things I have in the house, besides my futon mattress, are a few Christmas lights, some decorations, and kitchen items.

I had planned on getting a tree tomorrow, but the kids surprised me. They were all excited when they arrived last night. "Look outside!" they said, as they led me to the back door. When I looked outside there was a darling little Christmas tree perched in the snow. We hauled it in and set it up in the living room. The three of us slept on the floor around it, leaving the tree lights on all night. The kids were cute and excited as we cuddled together on the futon under the big new down comforter I'd bought for myself. We opened a few Christmas gifts, had tea and cookies, and just delighted in being in our new house together. We spent a restless night, however, because the new house is somewhat noisy, the sounds unfamiliar. The hot water heater is loud, the furnace louder, the new coffee pot, which I'd set up on a timer so I could wake to the smell of fresh brewed coffee, was *extremely* loud, waking us up with its gurgling and rumbling. But none of it matters. We're just happy to be together in our little house at last.

During the morning we slumber, play games, and have breakfast in bed. Then the kids go back to stay with their dad until Tuesday, Christmas Eve. In the meantime, my plan is to work on the house and get their rooms painted, but after they leave I can't move. I sleep the entire afternoon. Totally exhausted, I can barely lift my head. Slightly achy, coughing, with a stuffy nose and sneezing like crazy, I acquiesce. I am simply worn out. With no phone hooked up yet, I will not be disturbed. And so I allow myself to be exhausted, even as part of me echoes my mother's scolding voice, telling me to just get up and carry on. My body, however, refuses. I lie limp and heavy on the futon on the floor beneath the big down comforter, the lights of the tiny Christmas tree keeping me company. I know I'm doing what's right, letting myself heal by acquiescing to this exhaustion, allowing my body to guide me to rest and recuperation.

I get up around five, have some soup and a cup of peppermint tea, and straighten up a few things. I gather enough energy to paint one of the kitchen walls with a pink wash. I love it immediately, the bright and cheery hue coming from a deep need to be surrounded by joyous color. I'll see how it looks in the morning, I decide, too exhausted from the effort, too weak to do more. Even so, it feels good to be doing something creative, though I know I'm partially using it as an excuse to keep the old stuff from stirring.

At night, I lie on my futon feeling tired, safe, and calm. Now I'm divorced, living in my own home. I have two beautiful, bright, and sensitive children whom I love and care the most about. We will thrive. The three of us will have a great life; this move is only the beginning.

December 23, 2002

My daughter returned late last night. "I hope this is okay," said her dad, as he dropped her off. "She couldn't stop crying." I greeted her with open arms, telling her I was glad she was with me. We went right to bed, but I also told her that she'd have to learn to be away from me, that she'd have to stand it for a few days at a time, that we'd ease into it, and it would get better over time.

"I don't like it there anymore, it doesn't smell right or feel right anymore," she said, and I knew she meant that I wasn't there anymore.

"I know," I told her, as we snuggled together, "it'll just take some time."

I wake feeling much better after no energy, heavy depression, and sadness all day yesterday. I've been so preoccupied and anxious. I even started to panic because I could barely remember anything that had recently transpired. All of a sudden, I couldn't remember half the gifts I'd bought and wrapped up for the kids. I couldn't remember the books I'd just read or where I'd put things. I started to freak out, but finally calmed my nerves, steadied myself, and decided that it will get better as the tension eases and as I settle into my new life.

My daughter and I spend the day together. The phone finally gets turned on and I confirm a previously arranged appointment with Chuck for the morning. In the evening, my daughter goes back over to her dad's for the night, telling me she can do it.

"I'll make it through the night, even though I'll miss you," she says bravely.

I lie exhausted on my futon after she leaves, trying to fall asleep. Tossing and turning in restless unease, I'm suddenly caught in a flashback. A frightening face swoops down over me, grinning wildly in the darkness, as real as if my abuser himself were in the room with me—a face in a nightmare. The sight of him sends me plummeting into old frustration and despair, and before I know it I'm lost, drowning in fright. I can't hold on. My body shakes uncontrollably at this mere glimpse of him, as if aware that something horrible is about to take place. Though I recapitulate nothing beyond this vision of his ugly face, I am overcome with the terror of once again being captured by the predator. And although I desire nothing more than to get up and run away, I know I will not be able to. I can't pretend anymore that nothing happened. I can't pretend *him* away. All I can do is go through the memory, come out the other side of it, and go on—just go on. Just as my dream of riding on the endless train informed me, I must, at all costs, just keep moving.

December 24, 2002

I dream that I'm a child again, living in a house with other children, mostly boys—grubby, fighting and arguing boys. We live on mattresses strewn on the floor with thin blankets to cover us. At night, or at any time during the day, one of us gets called to the man's bed. I see the other children huddling under the blankets in fear and I do the same. I hide under a bed skirt, trying to disappear, shrinking as far out of sight as possible when the man comes looking for me, the new girl. He can't find me. He finally gives up and leaves the room.

Unable to fall asleep after that hauntingly nightmarish flashback came over me last night, I lay in the darkness for hours, until I finally got up and made an herbal decoction. I fell asleep immediately upon drinking it, the soporific effects of the herbs just what I needed. The haunting vision receded, but I fell into restless, anxious dreams of the same haunting caliber. I'm being alerted that I still have more work to do.

I wake up tired, but I have my session with Chuck to get to. By the time I arrive at his office, it's pretty clear that a new memory is emerging. I sit down and hunch over, clenching and shaky, feeling like a bad girl, full of pain and remorse.

"Where are you?" Chuck asks.

I sit for a long time, unable to answer, daring myself to speak. I'm fully aware that as soon as I open my mouth and utter the first words, the memory will take over. And it won't just be present in my body but shared, made real in a new way.

"I'm in the barn," I finally say. "I see my abuser's face, grimacing above me."

At first, I think he's hanging from the rafters, looking down at me, but then I realize he's raping me. As soon as that clarity dawns, I fall more fully into the memory. Pain and anguish sweep into me as if someone has opened a door and a rush of cold air has swept into the room. Vaginal pain, clenching stomach pain, and throbbing pain in my head grip me as I fall to the floor and roll into a ball. I lie curled up in silent blackness, struck by the realization that I can't speak. Try as I might, I cannot feel my throat, tongue, or lips. Like a heavy concrete statue of a fallen woman I lie stiff and unmoving, unable to make a sound for a long time. After what seems like hours, I'm finally able to utter the words: "I'm okay." I struggle to get up and when I do I'm exceedingly, visibly shaky.

"Have you eaten?" Chuck asks.

"No, I haven't eaten anything today, but it's still early and I don't usually eat until later."

"A lot of energy has been expended. Replenish," he advises. "You have great will power, but your body is saying no, enough, feed me now."

He offers me a granola bar, but I thank him and tell him that I'll eat at home, and I really do long for a cup of hot tea and some toast.

I pick up the kids at their dad's house later in the day and we attend a Christmas Eve party at my parent's house. Although I have no interest in going, I will not deny my kids the pleasure of this annual family gathering with their aunts, uncles, and cousins. In the middle of the festivities I feel another sore throat coming on, triggering an awareness that it's time to return to my solitary environment. And so I gather the kids and we head home under a dark and cloudy night sky, predictions of snow in the forecast.

December 25, 2002

We awaken to light snow and threats of a blizzard to follow. The kids open their presents, shyly timid at the dawning of this new life, their first Christmas as children of divorce. My daughter's energy is delightful, lovingly and pleasantly setting the intent of this morning: for the three of us to share a tender and meaningful happy time together. Playing a gentle Santa, my son very sweetly hands out gifts. I make us breakfast and we sit around on the futon. I read their favorite Christmas stories from when they were little, books I get out every year at this time, to be read and appreciated all over again. Basking in the warmth of this tidbit of familial nostalgia, relaxed and calm, we spend a pleasant morning together. I drive them back to their dad's at noon. They'll spend the next few days with him while I continue working on the house. I visit for a few minutes while they open more gifts and then head back home, driving slowly through the rapidly increasing mix of snow and freezing rain.

I have energy today, the same kind of energy raging outside, the blizzard rapidly showing its force. With my tasks set before me, and fully prepared to work, I begin by prepping the last of the walls in the house that still need priming. Late in the afternoon, after several hours of rolling out primer, I start tiling a six-foot square section by the front door. It's hard work. I've never done it before, but I enjoy the concentrated effort of it. Using small decorative terracotta tiles, I figure out what I'm doing as I go along. By the time I'm done, I have blisters on my hands and bruises on my knees and I discover that I can't open the front door! It appears that the rubber sweeper on the bottom of the door is catching. I won't remove it tonight. It's too cold and blustery, with wind and snow blowing against the house, sounding as if a hurricane were raging outside.

At nine o'clock, I turn on the outdoor lights and open the back door with the intention of shoveling a little snow. There's at least two feet of it pressing up against the house and I can barely push the storm door open. I take one look at it and lose what little energy I have left. It's one of those overwhelming situations. I just don't know where to begin, one person with a small shovel against the power and might of nature. I decide to shovel my way to the detached garage to look for a flashlight in case of a power outage, as it's been thundering and lightning too. I dig around in the piles of boxes until I finally find a flashlight. Sticking it into my pocket, I then shovel my way down the driveway and out to the road where I meet a neighbor from across the street. He helps me shovel a bit at the end of the driveway where the town plow has piled the snow to chest height. We stand beside this high barrier and introduce ourselves, yelling into the force of the wind, the blinding snow pelting our faces.

"All of a sudden the driveway is looking *very* long!" I shout, as I thank him for his help and head back inside, exhausted, knowing I'll have to come back out and tackle the rest of it in the morning.

I lie on my futon, tired from all the effort. For most of the day I felt I couldn't stop, that I had to keep going, always two steps ahead of the demon in pursuit. Anxiety creeps in at the mere thought of my abuser and I contemplate getting up again and working all night just to keep ahead of him, just out of reach of memory and too busy for panic. I'm choosing to run on adrenalin and coffee, though I was reminded of Chuck's admonishment to eat. I finally did eat around five, though I had no appetite. I'm planning to eat plenty of protein and stay hydrated as I work, but nothing tastes very good when there is no appetite. I lost track of what day it was too. Once the kids were gone, I made no effort to celebrate the holiday. At one point, I thought that perhaps I should have gotten myself some special foods or a bottle of champagne at the least, but in the end it simply didn't matter. All that mattered were the tasks at hand.

I settle in for the night, hoping the snow will stop in a few hours. More used now to the sounds in the house, I plan on getting up early to shovel. I sense how mentally and emotionally fragile I still am, how pale and thin I look, though I'm physically healthy and very strong. I still have that pearl of strength at my center that got me here in the first place—and I could probably carry a china cabinet on my back if I had to. I set my intent to wake up in the morning with plenty of energy to do the physical work I've got planned, asking it to act as a stiff buffer, as a means of keeping the bad stuff at bay. Committed to keeping that buffer in tiptop shape, I intend to work until I drop tomorrow too.

As I drift off to sleep, I suddenly realize I'm no longer afraid of Chuck, nor am I holding back. The enormity of the truth of my past slowly but surely seeps more deeply into my awareness as I drift off to sleep.

December 26, 2002

I'm snowed in. There's over three feet of fluffy white stuff out there. The carpeting is supposed to be put in today, but I don't know how I'll get rid of all that snow on the driveway by eight-thirty when the installer is supposed to arrive. I'm exhausted already, having worked late and hard yesterday. The blisters on my hands hurt, though the ceramic floor has dried well; the tiles are solidly stuck in place and I like the way it looks.

I call over to the carpet place and after we agree to postpone the carpet installation until tomorrow, I head out with my trusty snow shovel. I am determined to remain undaunted by the amount of shoveling before me. Before long the neighbor, whom I'd met over the pile of snow at the end of the driveway last night, appears with his snow blower.

"Are you going to do that all by yourself?" he asks with a grin.

"Yup!" I shout over the loudness of his machine.

And then, amazed, I watch as he blows the snow away in fifteen minutes, a job that would have taken me hours to shovel on my own. Grateful for new, kind neighbors, I hoist my shovel onto my shoulder and march back into the house, as if I have just done it all on my own. I set to work painting, dealing with calls from the kids throughout the day, as tensions are high on their end too. My daughter tells me she only wants to be with me, my beautiful eleven-year old wanting her mommy. At that age I was being raped, sodomized, and brutalized by a maniac. I was hiding, forced to be secretive, living in terror; such a contrast to this loving and affectionate little girl who only wants and needs me because I make her feel safe and loved.

I work until ten at night when memories begin to emerge. The moment I put down my paintbrushes and rollers, they come. I find myself in a time warp, between then and now, a hard place to be, where nothing seems real. Suddenly the memories intrude, in rapid succession piercing through the thin veils of the time warp, and I can do nothing but acquiesce to them. I let them come. I can't quite capture the details at first, but I see a wooden rocking horse that my abuser brings from his truck into the chamber of horrors. I also realize that I often see his truck parked there in the field on the edge of the woods.

As I recapitulate, I see that my abuser has taken the rockers off the horse, just a little wooden horse; except he's put something on the seat that he forces me to sit on. From my adult perspective I see that it's a phallus, though my child self has no idea what it is. In another memory, I'm lying in his lap like a baby and he's inserting something into my vagina. He walks around carrying me like a baby in his arms, asking me if I can feel it as he jams it in. Now I'm over his shoulders, a baby that he's patting on the back, while one hand still pushes something into me. He paces, walking faster and faster, pushing the thing into me. Finally he lays me on the ground, a baby with my legs wide open, and for what seems like many long and painful hours I lie there while he looks at what he's doing.

I continue to recapitulate. Now I'm on all fours while he's putting things in my rear end. I think how disgusting I am, just a little girl, hating myself for playing his games. Encased in feelings of self-loathing, yet another memory emerges. This time I'm sitting impaled on that rocking horse when he picks me up and carries me around between his legs, as if we are both riding that tiny horse. His penis rubs against me. I feel it on the back of my head, the smell of it in my face as he puts it in my mouth, as he rubs it in my arm pits, between my legs, behind my knees, squeezing me against him. Like a loudly braying donkey, his crazy laughter echoes through my little snowed-in house.

December 27, 2002

I wake out of forgotten dreams and go right into a memory. I am on my hands and knees with my face in the dirt, disgusted and disgusting. Feelings seek escape, but I clench them in as tightly as I can as I roll off my futon bed and out of the memory. Time to get up; I have work to do.

It's Friday morning and the carpet guy arrives early and removes the old stained carpeting and padding, revealing old asbestos tiles on a hard concrete slab beneath. He puts down the new tacking and padding. He'll be back to install the actual carpet on Monday.

I work in the kitchen, unpacking dishes and arranging the pantry while he's here. After he leaves, I work in my daughter's bedroom where I'm painting a mural. It's quiet and calm in the house, no television, no noises except the noises the house makes. I don't even listen to music while I work—I don't need it—the physical movement of painting is enough distraction. Tomorrow I plan on painting my son's room and grouting the tile floor by the front door, which I finally got open by removing the metal sweep. Now it swings nicely, though there's a bit of a cold draft that I've temporarily blocked with a rolled up towel. I'm enjoying the process of creating this new space, determined to get everything painted before moving the furniture in. I'm calm as I work, my energy honed, my imagination allowed free rein. With no one else to please, I paint from my heart. The colors are joyous. It's nesting time at last.

At around nine in the evening I stop and eat some food. My daughter arrives to spend the night with me on my futon in the living room again. She helps stencil some stars on the walls of her bedroom and then we turn in together.

December 28, 2002

I dream. I'm standing on a long line waiting for something, having to be patient, talking to other people waiting on the same line. We're all just waiting, but the waiting is fraught with fear and anxiety. I anticipate that something bad will happen. The line weaves through alleyways and into buildings where I've been many times before in dreams.

I wake in a full body cramp, stiff from neck to feet, unable to move. At a mere hint of the old stuff, even in a dream, I am reduced to a frightened and panicky state. My body fights the fear, my stomach clenches against it as I roll over, off the futon, and onto the floor. I stand up, already exhausted though it's very early, the day not yet begun. I don't want to wake my daughter, so I grab coffee and the coffee maker from the kitchen and tiptoe down the hallway. Once in my bedroom, I close the door and set the coffee to brewing while I sit on the floor and contemplate what I'll do to the walls. At the moment, they're fake paneling, a somber, scruffy feel to them that I can't wait to erase. I want color! I need color! It's part of my therapy, both the color itself and the act of applying it to the walls, allowing my spirit expression. And it's what I want in my new world too.

I sit on the hard floor and mull over the dream I just woke out of. I know it means something is coming, the tension undeniable. Although I'm thoroughly exhausted, I'm also aware that I must keep going and going, like the endless train of my dream, heading into oncoming time. I must keep painting and being creative, staying physically active to counter the memories that creep into my bed each night, seeking to drag me back into an old world. My recapitulation is a constantly shifting process, not only taking me back but also carrying me forward. And so, to keep pace with it, I've been working in big sweeping movements that free my body and nurture my soul. The walls in my new house have become the large abstract paintings I'd envisioned earlier, the new me fully expressing herself, painting the bright future of oncoming time.

My daughter wakes up as I tiptoe back into the kitchen to get a mug and milk, the noise of the fridge turning on waking her. By now the sun is rising and she has plans. She'll spend the day and night with a friend and then go back to her dad's while I continue the painting. I'm thankful that I have this time to spend on preparing the house before the school semester starts up again in January. I give her a big hug when her ride arrives and then set to painting. Of course, as soon as she leaves, the memories return, sneaking in while I'm standing in the open doorway blowing her kisses. As I turn and go back into the house a memory emerges. I am "Piggy" and that's how I feel, like a disgusting piggy, with a disgusting tail.

I'm afraid of toolboxes and what they contain. I'm afraid of tape measures, sticks, and tool handles. I'm even afraid of rocking horses. I'm especially afraid of people. I keep my distance from them. I ponder how the fears implanted in childhood have impacted me, even as an adult. I've elected to live a solitary life. Friendly and personable, always able to make good friends no matter where I've lived, I have preferred my aloneness. When my son was a baby, I know I kept him isolated. Until he was almost three, he spent most of his time with me. I had one good friend who had three small children in the town where we lived in Tennessee and we'd often spend time together, so he was around other children. He had his two favorite babysitters, and a lovely set of surrogate grandparents, but I was reluctant to get too involved or too close. I'd walk for miles and miles, my infant son strapped to my chest while my husband was at work at the university where he taught. I took him to the playground when he was a little older, but only when no one else was there. If I saw people I didn't know, I'd walk right past. More often than not, everyone appeared threatening to me in some way. However, I constantly challenged myself to fight through my fears because I was aware that somehow I had to find a way to be in the world, for my children's sake, if not my own.

December 29, 2002

I dream that I'm hanging upside down like a side of beef until my abuser comes along and cuts me down. I fall to the ground with a thump and lash out at him with my feet, kicking as hard as I can. A boy comes along and tries to grab my legs and I kick at him too. My vigor surprises him as I kick out, striking many solid and painful blows. My tenacity unnerves him and he finally backs off.

In another dream, I'm standing on a long line in a macabre and frightening setting, in a dark and dreary hallway, waiting my turn. I'm inside the same building I dreamed of waiting on line in the other night. Other people are standing on the line, waiting their turns as well, while others are strung up, hanging by ropes and hooks from the walls. There is a sense of hopelessness and dread; everyone is quiet and sad. I'm aware that I've been on this line many times in other dreams, always with the anticipation that something bad is going to happen.

I wake several times in the night, falling out of these depressing dreams. At one point I am so full of pain, my body tense, so tightly paralyzed with fear that I call out.

"HELP! HELP! HELP!"

Startled by the sound of my own voice echoing through the empty house, I am roused from fitful sleep. I know I don't have to be any stronger than I already am, but I can't help myself. I'm so used to clenching down and holding in that it's only in unchecked moments, such as sleep, it seems, that I'm able to truly release, though I try to let go at other times too. I can't say that I'm holding back purposely anymore, my body is just doing what it's always done. I decide I shouldn't exacerbate the tension with too much coffee and so I'll cut back to only one cup in the morning. The rest of the day I'll stick to herbal teas.

I plaster my bedroom walls, covering the brown paneling with a thick coat of joint compound to simulate an old plaster look. I'll paint over that with primer and then layer upon layer of color until I get the exact intensity of orange that I envision. I can't wait to finish it. I'm hoping the carpets will be installed quickly tomorrow because I want to get the kids over here as soon as possible. At the same time, I remind myself that I'm home now, that I can relax, that I don't have to be super woman, and that I can be kind to myself. I have nothing to prove; everything has already been proven. I know I'm a survivor. I've already survived the worst things imaginable. I'll survive this too.

I'll be seeing Chuck tomorrow and I know he'll ask me how I've been doing. Am I sleeping and eating? *Did I eat today?* Yes, I think I ate twice today.

December 30, 2002

In a dream, I'm involved with a crafts show, but reluctantly, and I'm late. I've missed the designated set up time so I have to pay an additional entry fee to get in. The outdoor event is teeming with people. I'm standing and talking to a man and a woman when another woman walks by. As she passes near me, I strike out at her with a small chainsaw I've been holding in my hand, slicing her neck. She immediately cries out, whimpering, but I tell her that the cut is nothing, just a scratch, although in reality she has a huge gash and blood is running down her neck and into her clothing. I am totally devoid of feelings as I watch her walk away. I'm still in the process of getting my booth set up, dragging my feet as if I really don't want to be here, when it begins to rain. This gives me the opportunity to stop what I'm doing and take cover. After the rainstorm passes, I leave the crafts show. I follow a crowd of people onto a narrow sidewalk, but I'm uncomfortable being in the crowd. I don't like being jostled about, so I step off the sidewalk and walk in the middle of the road until I reach an expansive grassy park overlooking a wide river. I stand and look out at the river, over the vast park-like terrain and at the people enjoying the crafts event behind me. As calm as it appears, I am still reluctant to join the show.

I wake during the night several times, in total body tension, anxious all night long. The bloody cut I give the woman in the dream bothers me now, although in the dream I had no feelings whatsoever as I lashed out at her with the chainsaw. When she cries out, I think she's being a wimp and a complainer. I expect her to be strong, taking whatever comes at her, like I've always had to do. I don't get attached to the pain I've caused her. Like a cutter relieving pent up mental pain through a slice to the flesh, I slice *her* skin and leave *her* to deal with it. After all, cutting is something I'd never do to myself.

In the morning I have a cup of coffee, let the carpet guy in, and head out to meet with Chuck. We talk about my dreams and Chuck suggests that I practice some new dreaming techniques, not just reacting and kicking or chasing someone, but by following through to a satisfactory conclusion. He tells me that I'm in control in my dreams, reminding me that I don't have to just take what's served to me. I can stop the action and say, "Hey, wait a minute, what am I doing? I don't have to put up with this!" He reminds me to use my power to act and react in my dreams and actually get back at my abuser.

We also go through the movements of a shamanic form, a magical pass called *Stalking the Self*, which we dub "the sword form" because of the many arm movements that mimic the swings and thrusts of a sword. It's along the same lines as the process of changing and empowering the self through movement that we'd worked on previously, staying always aware of body posture. Chuck explains that the movements offer, as well, a means of attacking and shifting away from predatory energy. The pass involves pulling a sword out of a sheath and using it to fight, building strength and endurance by constantly shifting. Alertness and awareness gradually develop as a flow gets going, along with quick agility, so that you are prepared to fight back no matter what comes at you. We practice it over and over again, attacking with swift and definite strikes, while constantly maintaining a firmly grounded stance.

"Don't try to remember the moves," Chuck says. "Just do them; let them flow. It's the flow that matters, not how you do it, so just get a flow going, first to one side and then the other."

We practice together until I think I have most of it. I am terrible at putting one move after another, one foot in front of the other, my brain not wired to my physical body, and I'm not connected to it either.

By the time I get home the living room is carpeted and the guy is in full swing, moving down the hallway and into the bedrooms. He works quickly and efficiently and by mid-afternoon he's done. As soon as he leaves, I slowly walk through the rooms of my tiny house, taking in the calm emptiness of each room, knowing that it will be many years before I see it this empty again. Intending that only good experiences and happiness envelop us now, I move the kid's bedroom furniture in from the garage and set up their rooms, now painted with cheery murals. I've filled their rooms with the love that poured out of me, from the bottom of my heart, thanking them for taking this journey with me.

Every now and then I stop and practice the moves that Chuck taught me, my feet gripping the nubby carpeting. I let my body remind me of the moves, as I run through them repeatedly until I have a nice flow going. Knife hand strikes, stances stay firm, sword twirls and cuts. "Make the movements matter, make them do something," Chuck told me. So I make them chop and dissect, cutting my abuser in half. I am a fencer with my sword, balletic and graceful, but oh, so deadly. Small, lithe, light on feet, I am dancing to avoid counterattacks, my petite body deceptive because I am oh, so strong. I am swift and graceful with my deadly plunges, quick and able, a darting, daring, dragonfly warrior.

December 31, 2002

In a dream, I'm strung up in a harness in my abuser's chamber in the woods. I determine the best method of reacting to what he's doing to me. I must be definite, effective, and precise. I decide that I must go beyond simply kicking him out of the way. I must beat him at his own game. I must make him want to run from me in fear. I begin swinging in the harness, pumping my arms and legs until I'm swinging like a pendulum. Pumping hard, I build up enough momentum to knock him down each time he approaches. Each time he stands up, I knock him down again, simultaneously working my way out of the harness. I am strong and lithe, able to hoist myself aloft in the swinging harness until I'm standing up. Swinging higher still, I come crashing down upon him and then swiftly jump on top of him, pummeling and beating him into the ground. And then I lift him up and tie him in his own harness, hoisting him like a flag, a beaten man.

In another dream, I'm with two people in a subway tunnel, walking between railroad tracks. The tunnel is open on top, with very high sides, the sky visible high above us. We're trying to find our way out when suddenly the passageway ends. We can't climb up the high walls, so we go back, determined to find another way out.

Then I dream that I'm walking on a college campus. There are rows of men watching all the girls walk by, saying crude things, whistling and staring. They disgust me.

In a final dream, I'm baking a huge blueberry cobbler in an outdoor oven with a friend. While it's cooking, we nibble the crumb topping made with butter, cinnamon, and sugar because it's so good. We just can't help ourselves.

I wake with these dreams rattling through me, the power of my intent to react coursing through my dreams, the intent of the sword form fully realized. At the same time, my intent and my strength are all but used up in the physical world. All I can do now is lie exhausted after days of working in a frenzy, having run on adrenalin in the haziness of life between worlds. I feel the struggle to get out of the tunnel in the second dream, more determined than ever to find a way out now that I can see the sky above me. Apparently I get out of the tunnel, because I dream on, but it's an old scared self who is unable to find an appropriate means of response to the catcalls of the men on the campus. I merely cringe and feel disgusted, as I once did when admired in the same manner as a student. In the final dream, however, something has shifted. I find myself enjoying the sweet taste of blueberry cobbler, an appropriate response to an appropriately innocent activity.

I see the multifaceted process of this recapitulation in this string of dreams, the new me and the old me journeying onward, working our way to some kind of peaceful, happy end. I trust that I will get there, but for the rest of the morning I give in totally to my exhaustion and stay in bed until noon, lying on my futon in the living room. The kids are to arrive in the early afternoon, prepared to stay for good now, until Friday that is, as according to our custody agreement they will spend every other weekend with their dad, beginning this coming weekend.

An old friend visits with her husband and five-year old daughter. Staying with family for the holidays, they live on the West Coast and I rarely see them. I'm able to stay present for most of the visit, talking as if I'm normal, as if nothing has changed, but for brief moments I find myself stepping back, as if going out-of-body. Able to view myself very clearly from a totally different perspective, I experience the realities of both worlds that I currently inhabit—the inner and the outer world—simultaneously. I see myself sitting at the kitchen table, talking, eating the Chinese food we've picked up, acting like I belong in that world, but meanwhile there's a totally different world in which I really reside, the inner world that no one sees. The inner world has been taking precedence for a long time now and, as I sit and converse with my friend and her husband from its distance, I realize that I am no longer a true inhabitant of the world they reside in. After they leave, the kids and I stay up late and greet the New Year together.

As I prepare for sleep, I encounter a strong pull to go back into the past, for I sense that everything I need for this New Year to be different from any other is waiting inside me. The inner world, where I've met the past and discovered the memories, is more enticing than this world, more interesting, more mysterious and enlightening than anything I've ever encountered.

Happy New Year!

About the Author

J. E. Ketchel is a writer, artist, and certified hypnotist, as well as a gifted channel. In 2001 she began a life-changing journey into the lost self, a soul retrieval journey that she documented and now shares in *The Recapitulation Diaries*. In addition, she regularly writes on the mystical and the ordinary in her weekly blog, *A Day in a Life*. Her writings, as well as hundreds of channeled messages from her spiritual guide in infinity, are posted and archived on her website, www.riverwalkerpress.com.

The Man in the Woods
The Recapitulation Diaries: Volume One

The Edge of the Abyss
The Recapitulation Diaries: Volume Two

Into the Vast Nothingness
The Recapitulation Diaries: Volume Three
To be published in 2014

***

The Book of Us
with Chuck Ketchel

www.ingramcontent.com/pod-product-compliance
Lightning Source LLC
Chambersburg PA
CBHW051939090426
42741CB00008B/1201